W1...

AAR
AMERICAN ACADEMY
of RELIGION
Fostering Excellence in the Study of Religion

REFLECTION AND THEORY IN THE STUDY OF RELIGION

Series Editor
Theodore M. Vial, Jr., Iliff School of Theology

A Publication Series of The American Academy of Religion and Oxford University Press

WORKING EMPTINESS
Toward a Third Reading of Emptiness in Buddhism and Postmodern Thought
Newman Robert Glass

WITTGENSTEIN AND THE MYSTICAL
Philosophy as an Ascetic Practice
Frederick Sontag

AN ESSAY ON THEOLOGICAL METHOD
Third Edition
Gordon D. Kaufman

BETTER THAN WINE
Love, Poetry, and Prayer in the Thought of Franz Rosenzweig
Yudit Kornberg Greenberg

HEALING DECONSTRUCTION
Postmodern Thought in Buddhism and Christianity
Edited by David Loy

ROOTS OF RELATIONAL ETHICS
Responsibility in Origin and Maturity in H. Richard Niebuhr
R. Melvin Keiser

HEGEL'S SPECULATIVE GOOD FRIDAY
The Death of God in Philosophical Perspective
Deland S. Anderson

NEWMAN AND GADAMER
Toward a Hermeneutics of Religious Knowledge
Thomas K. Carr

GOD, PHILOSOPHY AND ACADEMIC CULTURE
A Discussion between Scholars in the AAR and APA
Edited by William J. Wainwright

LIVING WORDS
Studies in Dialogues about Religion
Terence J. Martin

LIKE AND UNLIKE GOD
Religious Imaginations in Modern and Contemporary Fiction
John Neary

BEYOND THE NECESSARY GOD
Trinitarian Faith and Philosophy in the Thought of Eberhard Jüngel
Paul DeHart

CONVERGING ON CULTURE
Theologians in Dialogue with Cultural Analysis and Criticism
Edited by Delwin Brown, Sheila Greeve Davaney, and Kathryn Tanner

LESSING'S PHILOSOPHY OF RELIGION AND THE GERMAN ENLIGHTENMENT
Toshimasa Yasukata

AMERICAN PRAGMATISM
A Religious Genealogy
M. Gail Hamner

OPTING FOR THE MARGINS
Postmodernity and Liberation in Christian Theology
Edited by Joerg Rieger

MAKING MAGIC
Religion, Magic, and Science in the Modern World
Randall Styers

THE METAPHYSICS OF DANTE'S *COMEDY*
Christian Moevs

PILGRIMAGE OF LOVE
Moltmann on the Trinity and Christian Life
Joy Ann McDougall

MORAL CREATIVITY
Paul Ricoeur and the Poetics of Possibility
John Wall

MELANCHOLIC FREEDOM
Agency and the Spirit of Politics
David Kyuman Kim

FEMINIST THEOLOGY AND THE CHALLENGE OF DIFFERENCE
Margaret D. Kamitsuka

PLATO'S GHOST
Spiritualism in the American Renaissance
Cathy Gutierrez

TOWARD A GENEROUS ORTHODOXY
Prospects for Hans Frei's Postliberal Theology
Jason A. Springs

CAVELL, COMPANIONSHIP, AND CHRISTIAN THEOLOGY
Peter Dula

COMPARATIVE THEOLOGY AND THE PROBLEM OF RELIGIOUS RIVALRY
Hugh Nicholson

SECULARISM AND RELIGION-MAKING
Markus Dressler and Arvind-Pal S. Mandair

FORTUNATE FALLIBILITY
Kierkegaard and the Power of Sin
Jason A. Mahn

METHOD AND METAPHYSICS IN MAIMONIDES' *GUIDE FOR THE PERPLEXED*
Daniel Davies

THE LANGUAGE OF DISENCHANTMENT
Protestant Literalism and Colonial Discourse in British India
Robert A. Yelle

WRITING RELIGION
The Making of Turkish Alevi Islam
Markus Dressler

THE AESTHETICS AND ETHICS OF FAITH
A Dialogue Between Liberationist and Pragmatic Thought
Christopher D. Tirres

Canlarıma

Contents

Acknowledgments

BEYOND ROUGHLY THE last five years, in which I worked on this project, this book is the product of about fifteen years of engagement with various aspects of the formation of modern Alevism. I was introduced to Alevism as part of a M.A. course on "Religions in Contemporary Turkey" that I took at Marburg University in the winter semester 1994/95. In the final exam I focused on Alevism, earning one of the worst grades ever in my student life. The instructor of that course, Ursula Spuler-Stegeman, was my first academic mentor, and I would like to use this opportunity to acknowledge the encouragement that she provided me at these very beginnings of my academic career.

The research that led to this monograph was made possible by the institutional support I received by first Hofstra University and then Istanbul Technical University, as well as by fellowships I received from the American Research Institute in Turkey/National Endowment for the Humanities, Koç University's Research Center for Anatolian Civilizations, and the Zentrum Moderner Orient (Berlin). I would like to thank these institutions for the different ways of material support they provided and for enabling me to share and discuss my work with other colleagues. In addition, I also greatly benefitted from presenting and discussing work of mine that went into this book at various other academic venues, only a few of which I am able to name here. I benefitted in particular from presentations I gave at several annual meetings of the American Academy of Religion, as well as at a conference on *Alevi-Bektashi Communities in the Ottoman Realm* at Bosphorus University.

I am deeply indebted to all encouragement and criticism that I received in the process of researching and writing this project and would like to thank everyone who helped me in one way or the other to think through the issues discussed in this book. The support from Ted Vial, series editor of *Reflection and Theory in the Study of Religion,* was crucial since my earliest writing stages. He helped me to tune the manuscript more towards a religious studies audience than I had originally intended. For reading and commenting on versions of different sections of this book I am also grateful to Ahmet Karamustafa, Greg Johnson, Adam H. Becker, Ahmet Yaşar Ocak, Hans-Lukas Kieser, Umut Uzer, Marc Baer, Mehmet Ali Doğan, Ruth Mas, Rosemary Hicks, Stefo Benlisoy, and Hans Kippenberg. I also would like to mention the OUP team that guided me very professionally through the final stages of editing and production. Finally I want to acknowledge the generous support of my wife, Hatice Caner, throughout the research and writing of this book. Last but not least, I send my greetings to the Aegean Sea, at the shores of which I really got started writing.

Previously published texts that in modified form went into this book:

Dressler, Markus. 2010 "How to Conceptualize Inner-Islamic Plurality/Difference: 'Heterodoxy' and 'Syncretism' in the Writings of Mehmet F. Köprülü (1890–1966)," *British Journal for Middle Eastern Studies* 37.3:241–260.

Dressler, Markus. 2009 "Irène Mélikoff's Legacy: Some Remarks on Methodology." *Türk Kültürü ve Hacı Bektaş Veli Araştırma Dergisi* 52.3:13–20.

Note on Usage

I have attempted to simplify orthography to a reasonable extent. This means that I as a rule preferred English spelling convention for those terms that have made it into English language. For names and concepts that are within this book situated in primarily Turkish contexts I have used modern Turkish orthography. However, for reading conventions I made exceptions, using throughout *Bektashi* instead of *Bektaşi* and writing the plural of *Kızılbaş* as *Kızılbashes*.

As for the pronunciation of Turkish letters the following rules might be helpful:

c like English j in James
ç like English ch in China
ğ mostly silent, lengthening preceding vowel
ı like English a in mural
ö like French eu in monsieur
ş like English sh in Shakespeare
ü like French u in tu

I have transliterated only general Islamic technical terms in the specialist fashion following *Encyclopeadia of Islam* (Third Edition) standards.

Prologue: Alevism Contested

IN THE LATE 1980s, the Alevis of Turkey (to which 10–15% of the population belong), at that time thought to be widely assimilated, began to assert
their difference in European and Turkish public spaces to an unprecedented extent. They embarked on revitalizing and reforming Alevi institutions and built new networks reflective of contemporary political and
social circumstances that helped them to demand an end to their social
and institutional discrimination, as well as their recognition as a community legitimately different from the Sunni majority population. Both
in Turkey and in countries with a significant Turkish migrant population
such as Germany, the "Alevi question," which comprises matters of representation and relation to the state, as well as questions of cultural and
religious location, has in the last two decades become a subject of intense
public and political contestations.[1] In Turkey, these contestations often
end in lawsuits initiated either (1) by Alevis, suing state institutions for
practices that they regard as discriminatory, often pursuing all stages of
appeal up to the European Court of Human Rights, or, (2) until roughly
ten years ago, by state attorneys suing Alevi associations for their alleged
engagement in some sort of "religious separatism" since violating the
secularist and nationalist principles of the country (see Dressler 2008;
2011a; 2011b).

If we look at general ideas about what *Alevi* as adjective or name and
the abstract *Alevilik* ("Alevism") stand for in contemporary Turkish discourses, we find a wide variety of attributions, mostly of a cultural and

---

1 Consequently, the Alevi issue has also provoked scholarly interest, mainly from social
scientists and anthropologists. For competent studies documenting and analyzing different aspects of the recent developments related to the Alevi revival see Kehl-Bodrogi (1993),
Vorhoff (1995), Dressler (2002), White and Jongerden (2003), Massicard (2005), and
Sökefeld (2008).

religious nature. For most insiders and outsiders, it is today taken for granted that Alevism is part of the Islamic tradition, although located on its margins—margins that are marked with indigenous terms such as Sufi and Shia, or with outside qualifiers such as heterodoxy and syncretism. It is further widely taken for granted that Alevism constitutes an intrinsic part of Anatolian and Turkish culture. Indeed, it is widely believed that Alevi traditions carry an ancient Turkish heritage reaching back beyond Anatolia into the depths of Central Asian Turkish pasts.

The "Alevi Opening"

The question of where to locate the ethnic and religious origins of Alevism continues to be highly contested and comes to the forefront whenever the status of the Alevi community in Turkey is discussed. This has to do with the particular regime of secularism, or laicism (*laiklik*), hegemonic in Turkey, which in practice establishes a state-controlled secular Sunni Islam as quasi-official religion of the country.[2] The following discussion of the "Alevi Opening" aims to clarify this point.

The current Turkish government, formed by the conservative Justice and Development Party (hereafter JDP), which has its roots in the political Islamic movement, has recently made the so far most significant attempts to move toward recognition of the Alevis by the state. In 2007, the JDP announced a new engagement with the "Alevi question," which was quickly labeled the "Alevi Opening." At the center of this initiative were a series of workshops conducted in 2009 and 2010, in which state officials and members of various Alevi organizations, as well as selected academics, journalists, and civil society representatives participated. The workshops discussed possibilities of how to accommodate major Alevi demands, such as state support for Alevi institutions comparable to the support Sunni Islamic institutions receive, or alternatively, as demanded by some Alevi organizations, the state's complete retraction from the organization of religious affairs now vested in the powerful state bureaucracy of the Directorate for Religious Affairs (hereafter DRA); the abolishment of the mandatory school classes on "Religious Culture and Ethics" or, alternatively, adequate and positive representation of Alevism therein; the recognition of the *cemevis* ("Houses of Communion"), where the Alevis

---

2 I have discussed the work of Turkish secularism as it manifests itself in face of the Alevi question from various angles elsewhere. See Dressler (2008; 2010a; 2011a; 2011b).

celebrate their communal rituals, as "houses of worship," a status that is granted to mosques, churches, and synagogues (i.e., to the houses of worship of those religions that are recognized in traditional Islamic discourse as *din* and had already been privileged within the Ottoman state tradition); some form of state recognition and material support for the Alevi ritual leaders, the *dede*s; and finally, conversion of the Madımak Hotel in Sivas, where 37 people of mostly Alevi background died after an agitated mob shouting Islamic slogans had set fire to it during an Alevi festival in 1993,[3] into a museum commemorating the horrific event.

The sociologist of religion Necdet Subaşı, who had been appointed by the government as organizer of the workshops, wrote a final report on the initiative, in which he outlines the "Alevi question" in its various historical and sociological dimensions and offers suggestions for its solution. The report's concluding recommendations are noteworthy since they give voice to a series of Alevi demands that had so far not received much attention by the state. Therein Subaşı urges the state to end regulations and laws that might lead to discrimination against Alevis; to terminate homogenization politics that were established as part of the nation-building process; to have Alevis themselves define what Alevism would stand for, especially with regard to the creed; to provide the Alevis with an opportunity to benefit equally from the DRA (while asserting, however, the DRA's hegemonic position in defining "high Islamic discourse"); to secure a legal status for the *cemevis*, and to confiscate the Madımak Hotel and find a way to remember the Sivas incident in a way that unites rather than divides (Subaşı 2010, 189–194). These are recommendations that many Alevis could be expected to support.

It can be said that the Alevi Opening has contributed to a few concessions made by state institutions on different administrative levels in response to Alevi demands: the Ministry of National Education prepared new textbooks for the mandatory school courses in Religious Culture and Ethics, amended to include more detailed information on the Alevi faith; some municipalities recognized *cemevis* as "houses of worship;" and finally, the state nationalized the Madımak Hotel in Sivas, even if its final destiny is still unclear (European Commission 2011, 29).

---

3 This terrible incident, in its details still not entirely elucidated, contributed in major ways to the reinvigoration of an Alevi identity in the 1990s, paralleling the formation of the Islamic political movement, which the Alevis see as a threat.

While these concessions to Alevi demands are important, from the Alevi perspective they appear as less than satisfactory, falling far short of the general recognition to which Alevis aspire and showing no intention to restructure the current system of state organization and control of religion embodied in the DRA. This system, they argue, amounts in practice to the establishment of Sunni Islam as the state religion and to that extent disadvantages and discriminates against the Alevis in comparison to the Sunni majority population.

It is certainly true that no other government has ever given as much overt attention to the problem of Alevi difference as the JDP. In fact, as has been remarked by the journalist Oral Çalışlar, himself a participant in the workshops, the very fact of these workshops being organized by the government constituted the foremost act of recognition Alevism has ever received by Turkish state institutions. However, he also noted that the dialogue between the state and the Alevis had been severely hampered by the fact that the government and state representatives were not willing to bracket out their Sunni norms of Islam when approaching the Alevi question.[4]

Çalışlar's observation is right on target. The JDP's general approach to the Alevi question clearly displays a Sunni Islamic bias and is thus in continuation with an approach to the Alevi question typical for the Turkish state since the beginning of the republic. In addition, the JDP government has, despite a more liberal rhetoric when it comes to religious rights, displayed the same patronizing approach to Alevism—in fact to religion in general—as earlier governments and does not question the DRA's prerogative to legitimately define and represent Islam in public. The very top-down character of the Alevi workshops, the fact that the Alevis themselves had no participation in the final report, and the report itself testify to an attitude that one could, in positive terms, describe as one of patriarchal benevolence. It has to be acknowledged that the report reflects a will to understand and represent Alevi sensibilities, and aspires to present the Alevi movement itself, as well as the "Alevi question," in an impartial manner. However, the text ultimately remains within the patronizing tradition of Turkish discourses on secularism and nationalism. For example, the report refers approvingly to hegemonic academic wisdom according to which Alevism is best to be understood as "a heterodox current" within Islam, distinguished by its "syncretistic" character (Subaşı 2010, 43).

---

4 Oral Çalışlar, "Alevi Önraporu'ndaki Sorunlar," *Radikal*, February 12, 2010.

Emblematic of the public debate of the "Alevi question" in Turkey at large, the report thus continues a line of argument that takes for granted that the particularity of Alevism, namely its "heterodoxy", needs to be understood and explained in relation to the Sunni Islamic mainstream—the later thus being normalized as "orthodox."

Political analysts have variously pointed out that the Alevi workshops should be seen as a reflection and symbol of a growing democratic maturity of Turkey embodied in JDP governance, which appeared to be dedicated to achieving a breakthrough in the relations between the Alevis and the state (Köse 2010; Soner/Toktaş 2011). Most importantly, the Alevis would for the first time have themselves been directly involved in the discussion of Alevi difference and recognition. In fact, the Alevi Opening had already been preceded by a more tolerant attitude of the state to Alevi claims of difference, reflected for example in the 2003 lifting of a ban that forbade the foundation of associations based on ethnic, racial, and religious differences. This ban had previously often been used to shut down Alevi associations (Soner/Toktaş 2011, 422). The Alevi Opening itself had been initiated in a liberal phase of JDP rule following its reelection triumph of 2007, when Turkey–European Union membership negotiations were still progressing. The democratization process in this period also comprised an even more ambitious "Kurdish opening," which implied an extension of cultural rights, as well as the promise for a political solution to the violent conflict, which has continued to plague the country since 1984, between the Turkish state and the Kurdish nationalist PKK (Kurdish Workers' Party) guerilla organization. Until recently, many liberal observers argued rightly that, with regard to questions of communal difference, the Turkish public sphere had following the JDP's advance to power in 2002 displayed a more tolerant attitude toward claims of communal identities (ethnic and religious), such as those articulated by Kurds and Alevis, respectively. Prime Minister Tayyip Erdoğan and his JDP have received much praise internationally for their dismantling of the Kemalist establishment, in particular their success in reducing the influence of the previously all-powerful military, which has an infamous history of intervening in politics. Most lately, the Arab Spring has provided Erdoğan with a stage to internationally promote Turkey as model for a new democratic-liberal Middle East—in sync with Muslim values and traditions, but still avowedly secular.[5]

---

5 Political pundits sympathetic to the JDP have been doing their best to popularize this interpretation among Western audiences. For example, see Akyol (2011).

Domestically, however, the political atmosphere in Turkey has changed drastically in most recent years. Advocates of a liberalization of the public sphere feel disillusioned and betrayed by the rather authoritarian politics that the JDP has of late embraced. Critics maintain that the dismantling of the old patriarchal, corrupt political elite, which was ideologically committed to the nationalist and secularist politics of Kemalism[6] and institutionally engrained in the military, judiciary, and bureaucracy, has been replaced by a new system of overt and hidden networks of power, organized mainly along religious and economic interests, that is equally if not more oppressive and increasingly less willing to tolerate opposition and dissent. The war between the state and the PKK has picked up once more and a real peace seems far away; the Alevi Opening has—so far at least (December 2012) barely gone beyond the publication of the mentioned report, and accommodation of Alevi demands for equal treatment and recognition as different according to their own terms is not in sight. In 2012, more than thousand oppositional Kurds; over a hundred journalists, publicists and academics; as well as uncounted numbers of members of various leftist groups, rural activists against large state projects (such as hydro-electronic dams), and student activists find themselves arrested on often dubious grounds and not seldom need to wait for more than a year before they get to face their indictments.[7] In short, the last years have seemingly led to a reversal of the democratization process with prospects unclear.[8]

As the cases of the Alevi and Kurdish "openings" demonstrate, the JDP government is eager to retain the power to dictate the speed, content, and limits of any extension of the public sphere. It has continued the top-down, control-obsessive politics of Kemalist nationalism and secularism. The suzerainty over the definition of communal identities, be they of the ethnic/

---

6 Kemalism is the name of the Turkish state ideology, characterized by its state-centric corporatism, a homogenizing nationalism, and an authoritarian secularism. As a political program it was established under the leadership of Mustafa Kemal, since 1934 known by the honorary name Atatürk ("Father of the Turks"), who is recognized as the founding father of Republican Turkey. For a discussion of Kemalism as corporatist ideology see Parla and Davison (2004).

7 See *Amnesty International*, "Amnesty International Report 2012: Turkey." http://www.amnesty.org/en/region/turkey/report-2012.

8 Analysis of the complex national and international factors and motivations which contributed to this development would go beyond the scope of this book. General overviews on political developments in Turkey are provided by the annual reports of the European Commission on Turkey's progress to fulfill EU-membership criteria (for the last report see http://ec.europa.eu/enlargement/pdf/key_documents/2012/package/tr_rapport_2012_En.pdf).

national or the religious kind, remains in the hands of state institutions. This situation is reflected emblematically in a popular theory of layered identities that defines Turkish and Islamic identities as superior/high identities (*üst-kimlik*) of which Kurdishness and Aleviness, respectively, constituted mere subordinate identities (*altkimlik*). The distinction between superior and subordinate identities is embodied in a language that others the Kurds and the Alevis as "our Kurdish" and "our Alevi brothers and sisters," respectively. It is part of a discourse that is interested in keeping Alevis and Kurds within the discursive reach of the nation, explicitly defined as Turkish and implicitly as Muslim, while excluding them at the same time from its normative center.

It would be wrong, however, to understand such hierarchical discourses on communal identities as static. There are indications that the nationalist conviction that Kurds and Alevis could be assimilated in similar ways into the Sunni Muslim and Turkish mainstream is fading. The continuing political resistance of the Kurds, or the Turkish state's failure to assimilate the Kurds, has in recent years led to a new Turkish nationalist discourse that regards the Kurds as outside of the nation, comparable to the non-Muslim minorities (see Yeğen 2007).

When it comes to the Alevis, however, the nationalist discourse has as of yet not shown any comparable inclination to conceive of Alevism as outside the fold of Islam and the Turkish nation—although there certainly are Alevis who clearly prefer non-Islamic systems of reference for their religious traditions, as well as mostly Kurdish Alevis who see the origins of Alevism in Kurdish/Iranian rather than in Turkish traditions. In Turkey, public discussions about Alevism remain for the most part confined to the parameters of a discourse that has historically emerged in conjunction with Turkish nationalism and its secularist, but Muslim, presuppositions. Just why is this the case? Why is there to date hardly any scholarship that takes the claim of Alevism being a "syncretism" seriously in a way that goes beyond branding "non-Islamic" features found in the Alevi traditions as "remnants"? Why is there hardly any serious engagement with Alevi traditions from, for example, the viewpoint of Christianity, or Zoroastrianism, or Manichaeism? Why is it that only Kurdish scholars take seriously an investigation of Alevism from the perspective of Kurdish and Iranian culture? And most importantly, why does it appear to be so difficult for scholars of Alevism and related traditions to move beyond modernist parameters of national and religious origins and essences? The answers to these questions are, I argue, linked to the way nationalist and religious semantics are interwoven in the fundaments of the modern knowledge about Alevism. This book aspires to elucidate why it remains so difficult for not only Turkish popular but also international academic discourses to conceive of Alevi difference outside of the discursive frameworks of Turkish nationalism and Islam.

Writing Religion

INTRODUCTION

Genealogies and Significations

Kızılbaş and Alevi as Historical Terms

The aim of this book is to historicize contemporary hegemonic sets of knowledge about "the Alevis" and "Alevism." As I will show, the modern knowledge about the Alevis, their demarcation as "heterodox" but Muslim and as an intrinsic part of Turkish culture, is of rather recent origins. This knowledge formed in the last years of the Ottoman Empire and the first years of the Turkish Republic, when new discourses of religious and ethnic difference emerged and the foundations of a Turkish nation-state were created.

Modern Genealogies

Reports by Western observers begin to note since the 1880s the vernacular use of the term "Alevi" (or variations thereof), a term that in the language of Islam indicates a close relationship (by descent or chosen affiliation) with Ali Ibn Abu Talib,[1] as a self-designation among Kızılbaş.[2] The designation seems to become more widespread during the Young Turk period.[3] Earlier texts of Western observers in contact with Kızılbaş groups do not mention the term Alevi. But very occasionally the term Alevi as a self-designation, apparently indicating loyalty and/or descent from Ali, also appears in Kızılbaş and Bektashi poems that can be attributed to earlier centuries.[4]

---

1. The cousin of the Prophet Muhammad, who was the fourth caliph in the Sunni narrative and the first Imam in the Shiite tradition; according to the latter he was the only legitimate leader of the Islamic community following Muhammad's death.

2. Luschan (1886, 171; 1889, 212); Bent (1891, 269); Kannenberg (*Die Paphlagonischen Felsengräber*, 1895) as referenced in Grothe (1912, 156); Crowfoot (1900, 305); Grenard (1904, 511).

3. White (1908, 228; 1913); Pears (1911, 265); Luschan (1911, 230); Grothe (1912, 156).

4. For examples see Öztelli (1996, 189–190); Gölpınarlı (1953, 12; 1963, 32).

In Ottoman documents, the term Aleviyye (*'alevîye*) was mostly used as part of the expression *Sadat-ı Aleviyye* (also *Sadat-ı Beni Aleviyye*, "the Alevi Seyyids"), that is, as a referential title for people with an Alid pedigree. We further find the term Alevi used in the sense of Shiite, for example in a text by the bureaucrat and historian Mustafa Ali (1541–1600) from 1589 (Fleischer 1986, 104). An early 19th-century Ottoman example is a text by the chronicler Mehmed Esad Efendi dedicated to the forceful abolition of the Janissary Corps in 1826 and its aftermath, in which he refers to the Bektashis, who were closely linked to the Janissaries, as "this gang of Alevis and [Shiite] heretics" (*bu gürûh-ı 'alevî ve revâfız*) (Es'ad Efendi 1848, 216).

Granted that there are probably more historical examples of that kind to be found in pre-19th-century Ottoman texts, the use of the term Alevi as attribute for Kızılbaş and Bektashi groups remains exceptional. Important is what the term signifies. When, in Ottoman times, the term Alevi was attributed from outside to Kızılbaş and Bektashi groups, it usually was used in a manner that was meant to identify them as Shiites—and for many Sunni Muslims that meant heresy. The term Kızılbaş itself connoted in Ottoman times heresy, political disloyalty, and immorality. This pejorative connotation remained by and large in place when the term Alevi began to appear more frequently in the last decades of the Ottoman Empire. In a document from 1896, in which the killing of a group of Kurds in a fight with army and gendarmerie members is reported, the victims are referred to as belonging to the "mischievous Alevi community" (*alevi cemiyet-i fesadiyesi*).[5] An attachment to the first military report by Zeki Paşa and Şakir Paşa from 1896 on how to bring reform to the eastern Anatolian district of Dersim described the local Kurdish Kızılbaş population as originally of the Shiite faith before having turned to the path of the Ali-Ilahis[6]; it further described them as having entered a "superstitious sect" (*batıl mezhep*) that is caught in innocence (*cehalet*) and would regard it as a religious duty to bring harm to the Muslims (possibly

---

5. BOA, A.MKT.MHM. 658/3, 18/B/1313 (BOA = Başbakanlık Osmanlı Arşivi/ Office of The Prime Minister Ottoman Archives). Accessed through http://www.devletarsivleri.gov.tr/katalog/. The same document further characterizes said Kurds as "a gullible people inclined to Kızılbashism" (as quoted in Akpınar 2012)—an expression that is also used to point to their political unreliability. I am grateful to Alişan Akpınar for sharing his unpublished paper with me.

6. Ali-Ilahi is a nickname given by others in their environment to groups believing in Ali's divine nature, such as the Nusayris, Kızılbaş-Alevis, and Ahl-i Haqq (Bruinessen 2000, 20).

suggesting that the members of this sect are not Muslims themselves)
(Akpınar et al. 2010, 329). In fact Ottoman documents from this period
frequently question whether the Kızılbaş-Alevi are Muslims at all. In a
document from 1891 it is stated that even Kızılbaş-Alevis who claimed to
be Muslims would despise the people of the Sunna.[7] Another document
from the same period explains that "with their superstitious dogmas they
have totally separated themselves from the Islamic religion and with the
exception of their names there has been nothing left that could prove that
they belong to Islam."[8]

In the later period of the rule of Sultan Abdülhamid II, when
the Ottoman state began to turn more explicitly toward a rhetoric of
Islamic unity and endeavored to assimilate groups at the margins
of Islamic discourse, we also encounter the first instances of more
neutral references to the "Alevis." An example is an Ottoman document from 1893, wherein officials are ordered to prevent Muslim
children of the Alevi branch of faith (*Alevi mezhebi*) to visit local
Catholic schools in Malatya.[9] Probably in response to the Dersim
report referred to above, which also mentioned the negative impact
of Protestant missionaries on the local population, in a telegraph
from 1899 the government ordered the governor of the province of
Mamüretülaziz (Elazığ), to which Dersim belonged, to do research
and assess responses with regard to the reported inclination of some
local Alevis (*Aleviler*)—here not further qualified—to Protestantism
(Açıkses 2003, 136–137). Also from this period we have first examples
of the abstract term *Alevilik* (Alevism) being applied to Kızılbaş groups
(see Karaca 1993, 128).

It is important to emphasize that in the late Ottoman period
there was as of yet no necessary connection between the terms Alevi
and Kızılbaş established. In the first Turkish-Turkish dictionary, the
Kāmūs-i Türkī (1901) there is no cross-referencing between the terms
Alevi and Kızılbaş. The term Alevi (*'alewī*) is here attributed the meanings (1) descendant of Ali and Fatima and (2) followers of Ali; the term
Kızılbaş (*qizilbāş*) is given the meanings (a) "a class of soldiers of Shah

---

7. BOA, Y.MTV. 53/108, 27/M/1309 as paraphrased by Akpınar (2012).

8. BOA, Y.PRK.UM. 29/77, 16/L/1311 as quoted by Akpınar (2012).

9. BOA, Y.PRK.UM. 28/70, 29/R/1311. Accessed through http://www.devletarsivleri.gov.tr/katalog/.

Ismail" and (b) "a group of the Shiite gulat"[10] (Şemseddin Sāmi 1901, 949 and 1127).[11] In the 1920s Turkish nationalist authors began to use the term Alevi for the Bektashis as well as groups that used to be labeled Kızılbaş (an early example is Atalay 1924). Very gradually in the first decades of the 20th century, the term also became more prominent in Western Orientalist discourse and began to be mentioned in encyclopedic entries as the self-designation of the Kızılbaş (Cumont 1915, 744; Huart 1927, 1053). Hasluck juxtaposes the term Kızılbaş as a "contemptuous term used to denote the adherents of all sects of the *Shia* religion, including, e.g., the Nosairi and Yezidi, irrespective of race or language" with "the corresponding inoffensive term, by which the Anatolian Kyzylbash designate themselves, [that] is 'Allevi' ('worshippers of Ali')" (Hasluck 1921, 328).

In the following decades the terms Alevi and Kızılbaş would be used interchangeably, with sensitivity about the pejorative character of the latter term gradually increasing both in the general Turkish public and in international scholarship. It took, however, until the second half of the 20th century that in both discourses the term Alevi replaced the term Kızılbaş.

The new signification that accompanied the gradual name change was substantial. While the connotations of the term *Kızılbaş* had been entirely negative, the new term *Alevilik* carried new, more positive meanings. Although the Kızılbaş were in 19th-century Ottoman censuses counted as Muslims,[12] their relation to Islam was seen as rather equivocal. Renamed Alevi, the nationalist discourse integrated the groups under question not only into Turkish nationhood, but decisively affirmed their Islamic character, even if this Islam was declared to be "heterodox." In this way it provided a rhetoric that allowed for the integration of the former Kızılbaş and now Alevi groups into a nation that was conceived of as explicitly Turkish and implicitly (Sunni-)Muslim. Thus I argue that the primary motivation for the reconceptualization of the Kızılbaş as Alevis was political. While it

10. Gulat ("exaggerators"; Arab. *ghulāt*) is an apologetic term that had been established within early Shiism to delegitimize certain practices, such as the exaltation of Ali as divine, the belief in ḥulūl (incarnation of God in human form), and the doctrine of *tanāsukh* (metempsychosis) (see Halm 1982; Hodgson 1955). All of these doctrines we find among Bektashi and Kızılbaş-Alevi groups.

11. The editor of this work, Şemseddin Sāmi, who wrote and compiled various important dictionaries and encyclopedias, was himself an Albanian Bektashi (thanks to Cemal Kafadar for pointing this out to me).

12. See the census records put together by Karpat (1985); cf. Shaw (1978).

can certainly be argued that the renaming of Kızılbaş groups and Bektashis as Alevis already began in the second half of the 19th century and that this renaming was facilitated by the fact that various Kızılbaş groups themselves had begun to use the term in the late Ottoman period, their re-signification as Turkish and Muslim "heterodox" only began in the context of Turkish nationalism since the last decade of the Ottoman Empire. The new thesis, as I will argue, worked well for the nationalists. It (1) provided evidence for the continuity of Turkish national culture by arguing that Alevism would contain remnants of ancient Turkish culture and (2) strengthened the national body by integrating the Kızılbaş as Alevis into the new nationalist construct of Turkish-Muslim unity. The new term gained currency in the critical phase of Kemalist nation-building in the 1920s and 1930s and legitimized the social integration of the "Kızılbaş-Alevis"—a term that I use for those contexts in which both attributes were used parallel to each other and the distinction between meanings associated with the respective designations was not yet clearly established. In short, the reconceptualization of the Kızılbaş as Alevis aimed at reducing—though, crucially, not totally eliminating—their socioreligious and political otherness in order to assimilate them into the nation-in-formation.

Premodern Significations

While the focus of this study is on developments in the late Ottoman and early Turkish Republican periods, it will at the outset be helpful to outline the premodern history of the terms Alevi and Kızılbaş. Within the Muslim world, the name Alevi (Ar. *'alawī*) carries several, sometimes-overlapping meanings. First, it can signify descent from Imam Ali; second, it is a general epithet for "followers" of Ali[13]—this meaning can be restricted to formal Shiites only, or be broadened to include all those Muslims who pay special reference to Ali and the "people of the house" (*ahl al-bayt*);[14] third, the term is used pejoratively to denounce heresy/heretics with Shiite tendencies. In the late Ottoman context, it also appears as name

---

13. For both meanings the anglicized term "Alid" is variously used in the scholarly literature.

14. *Ahl al-bayt* (Turk. *ehl-i beyt*), refers to the family of the Prophet, that is Muhammad, his daughter Fatima, her husband Ali, and the latter two's sons Hasan and Husayn. In a wider sense the term also includes the descendants of Husayn, believed by Shiites to be the legitimate leaders of the Islamic community and bestowed with special qualities.

for specific socioreligious groups, such as the Bektashi Sufi order, as well as endogamous communities, such as the Arab Nusayri, and the Turkish and Kurdish Kızılbaş.

The term Kızılbaş (lit., "Redhead")[15] historically referred to the mostly Turkmen adherents of the Safavi Sufi order, whose charismatic leader Ismail established the Safavid Empire in 1501 and is regarded as the founder of the Safavid dynasty of Iran (1501–1722).[16] The communities in Turkey that are today called Alevis, roughly two-thirds of which are Turkish and the rest are Kurds (Kurmanci and Zazaki speakers), are for the most part descendants of Kızılbaş communities. The latter, associated with the Safavi Sufi order, had rebelled against Ottoman rule in the early 16th century and were ever since regarded by the Ottomans as politically unreliable. The mistrust was furthered by the Kızılbashes' religious deviance from what the Ottomans, who turned more deliberately to Sunni Islam in the course of their competition with the Safavids in the 16th century, understood to be correct religion (Dressler 2005). A major reason why the Ottoman reaction to religious deviance from the mainstream legalist understanding was in this period much more rigid in rhetoric and political practice than what it used to be in the previous two centuries (as well as what it would look like in the following two centuries) is the fact that the Kızılbaş challenge coincided with growing Ottoman centralization efforts since the late 15th century. The political uprising of the Kızılbaş also needs to be seen as a reaction to this centralization politics, which it challenged directly. In this context, religion became a tool for both explaining the Kızılbashes' political deviance as well as justifying their punishment (Winter 2010, 12–17).

After gradual disconnection from the Safavids since the late 16th century, some Kızılbaş tribes over time associated rather closely with the Bektashi tradition. This rapprochement was facilitated by the fact that the sociohistorical genealogies of the two milieus were characterized by certain similarities and overlap. This does not mean, however, that the Bektashi tradition in its various forms and the Kızılbaş groups totally amalgamated. Rather, the Kızılbaş began to associate with the one Bektashi branch that based its authority on lineage (namely descent from the patron saint of the Bektashi order, Hacı Bektaş Veli, d.1270/71). Doing so they integrated

---

15. Reference to the red headgear that the supporters of the Safavi order are said to have worn since the late 15th century.

16. On the Safavi-Kızılbaş connection, see Sohrweide (1965) and Babayan (2002).

the Bektashi lineage into the Kızılbaş network of *ocak* (lit., "hearth") lineages, which are sacred lineages of actual descent (as a rule traced back to Muhammad and mostly also to Anatolian dervish saints in the Babai[17] tradition), on which the authority of the *ocak* members and their representatives, the *dedes* (lit. "elder") depends.[18]

In Ottoman language conventions, the term Kızılbaş became a stigmatizing name for all those groups that were believed to be descendants of the Kızılbaş by blood or in spirit. Associated with the term was religious deviance/heresy and political subversiveness. The *mühimme defterleri* (records of the Ottoman Imperial Assembly) offer numerous accounts of complaints against Kızılbashes such as rejection of sharia law, cursing of the first three caliphs, and immoral behavior (see Ahmet Refik 1932; Imber 1979; also Ocak 1998). Originally a historical term, Kızılbaş became a term by which to denounce as deviant those groups that differed from what was constituted as properly Islamic. The term was therefore not, usually, a self-designation, but a pejorative signification from outside. The ambivalence regarding the relationship of the Kızılbaş to Islam reflected in Ottoman documents is nowhere so evident as in the blame of heresy. The charges brought forward against the Kızılbaş—which until today constitute an important part of the body of knowledge many Sunni Muslims share about them—mark them at the same time as insiders and outsiders: outsiders as transgressors of Islamic law, and insiders due to the fact that they are still charged with committing offenses against Islamic law and conventions.

The Ottomans had no other term available to designate the range of groups comprising those post-Kızılbaş communities organized around *ocak* lineages that were more or less identical with those groups who would later be labeled Alevi. The term Kızılbaş was, however, not exclusively applied to individuals and groups associated with *ocak* networks, but also at times used to defame groups and individuals who belonged, in a broader or narrower sense, to the Shiite tradition. In the early 20th century, when Turkish nationalists developed an interest in assimilating and integrating the *ocak*-centered groups into the new national body, the traditional term Kızılbaş proved, given its negative connotations,

---

17. Name for a group of Turkmen dervishes and their supporters who had launched an uprising against the Rum-Seljuk Empire in 1240; see Ocak (1989).

18. For a competent overview of the intricate historical relationship between the Bektashis and the Kızılbashes see Yıldırım (2010); see also Karakaya-Stump (2008).

In this context, the term Alevi, as shown above, already since at least the mid-19th century used by various Kızılbaş groups as self-designation, appeared a viable alternative. With its various meanings all establishing links to the Imam Ali and his legacy, it did not carry the same negative ballast, but to the contrary firmly located those referred to in this way within an Islamic context.[19]

Objectives

The major aim of this book is to analyze, contextualize, and explain the history of the modern knowledge about the Alevis. When, why, and how did the terms *Alevi* and *Alevilik* acquire the particular sets of meaning that they carry today? Which politics were involved in the renaming and re-signification of the Kızılbaş as Alevi? Starting from these questions, themselves the result of about fifteen years of research on different aspects of Turkish history, culture, religion, and politics, as well as more particularly on academic and popular discourses on Alevism, this book attempts a critical analysis of the making of the modern concept of Alevism.

A major thrust of this book is therefore genealogical, geared toward a contextualized historical analysis of the politics of nation-building in which the writing of modern Alevism was situated. Although a contextualization of Alevism exclusively within Turkish-Islamic culture lacks evidence on historical, cultural, and even linguistic grounds, such contextualization has been paradigmatically established in Turkish discourses (Alevi discourses included). Even most of contemporary scholarship on Alevism still follows a historically rather naïve *longue durée* outline of the Alevi tradition remaining largely within Turkish-Islamic parameters. It assumes a continuity that genealogically and teleologically connects the medieval Babai, Bedreddin, and early modern Kızılbaş and Bektashi movements with the modern Alevis. While I do not deny the existence of historical and sociological connections between these groups, I would caution against making this continuity assumption the dominant or even exclusive framework for the historicization and characterization of Alevism.

The sense of homogeneity that is suggested when the term Alevi is being projected backward in history to a wide variety of different

---

19. A similar case of renaming was experienced by the Nusayris. As with the Anatolian Kızılbaş communities, we find that they began to refer to themselves and began to be referred to by the Ottomans as ‘Alawī since the end of the 19th century (Alkan 2012, 49). For a discussion of what the new name signified see Firro (2005).

contexts and groups needs to be countered with historical contextualizations that provide sufficient space for the specificities of these movements/groups in their various environments. Even today, when the term Alevi is widely accepted by those groups that were referred to by the Ottomans as Kızılbaş and that were historically organized around the networks of sacred *ocak* lineages, the extent to which it is meaningful to subsume, for example, the Turkmen Tahtacı of the western and southern Mediterranean regions, the Aliani of Bulgaria, the Shabak of Northern Iraq, and the Kurdish- and Zazaki-speaking Alevis of eastern Anatolia under one unifying concept could be questioned. To be clear, my aim is not to interrogate vernacular "Alevi" identities and sensitivities with regard to the evidence of the term Alevi as an emblem of historical continuity and communal identity. However, I would hold that homogenizing perspectives obstruct our understanding of how the concept of Alevism has been formulated in the early 20th century within the Turkish nationalist project. The latter played a major role in the normalization of the new name and its significations. In this context, I will also argue for epistemological sensitivity with regard to the work of our concepts and the implicit and explicit knowledges that they are based on.

A comprehensive critical genealogy of Alevism, that is, an analysis of the history of the concept of Alevism within the modernist discourses of religion and Turkish nationalism, remains a desideratum. Such an analysis, as attempted in this book, can be a first step for an emancipation of the scholarly study of Alevism from the shortcomings of nation-centric historiography and the biases of Turkish secularist discourse, both of which crucially influenced Alevi religiography. The term religiography refers—by analogy to the terms historiography and ethnography—to the practice of writing religion, that is, the production of data on religion. The religiography most influential in the formation of the modern concept of Alevism can be characterized as modernist-secular. By that I mean an understanding of religion as a distinct domain of human existence that can be separated from other spheres of life and is universal and ready to be examined in a comparative way by means of analysis of the phenomena and structures of religious practices and beliefs. The application of such a modernist religiographic framework to Kızılbaş-Alevism had enormous implications on the academic and popular discourses established on it since the early 20th century, and also impacted on indigenous knowledge formations of Alevism.

The nationalist authors involved in the historiographic, ethno-graphic, and religiographic practices of re-writing and thus re-signifying Kızılbaş-Alevism were working with the modern concepts of religion and Islam that were available to them in their time. As I will show, their concept of religion was rather essentialist and functionalist, strongly influenced by French positivism and sociology. Parallel to this, they subscribed to an understanding of Islam that accepted legalist Sunnism as its self-evident historical and theological core. Within this framework the place attributed to Alevism was that of the "heterodox" and "syncretistic" other in rela-tion to a proposed Sunni "orthodoxy." While this conceptualization is not surprising within the context of early 20th-century discourses on religion and Islam, what is surprising is that this kind of reading of Alevism is still hardly questioned. Based on the scholarly discussion of Alevism, I aim to offer a comprehensive critique of conceptualizations of inner-Islamic dif-ference undertaken from the viewpoint of implicit normative assumptions about religious and ethno-national essences. This critique is theoretically anchored in recent scholarship on religion from postcolonial and post-secular studies, especially the work of anthropologist Talal Asad and those continuing his critique of the secularist and liberal paradigms of moder-nity and their normative impact on modern concepts and subjectivities.

The nationalist renaming and re-signification of the Kızılbaş as Alevi in the 1920s can not be understood without taking into account an ear-lier phase of writing about the Kızılbaş-Alevis. Since the mid-19th cen-tury, mainly American missionaries, but also other foreign travelers in the Anatolian and eastern provinces had come into contact with Kızılbaş groups and were attracted by what appeared to them as strange practices and beliefs. They pursued various interests (missionary, scholarly, politi-cal, adventurous) and developed a number of interpretive models for explaining the difference of the Kızılbaş as compared to the Sunni Muslim population. Framed in discourses of origins and boundaries typical for 19th-century Euro-American modernity, they tended to see in the Kızılbaş remnants of older layers of Christianity and pre-Muslim Anatolian cul-tures, and engaged in racial speculations about possible Kızılbaş descent from Christian and ancient Anatolian people.

I am particularly interested in the relationship between this first occi-dental "discovery" of the Kızılbaş as crypto-Christians and remnants of ancient Anatolian people, and the later Turkish nationalist conceptualiza-tion of the Kızılbaş-Alevis. Turkish nationalist writers who wrote about the Kızılbaş-Alevis in the 1920s and 1930s sometimes made explicit references to the earlier Orientalist writings about these groups and vehemently rejected the connections these Christian authors drew between Kızılbaş-Alevis and Anatolian Christians (mainly Armenians), and/or to ancient Anatolian populations. I argue that the Turkish nationalist reading and writing about Alevism also has to be understood as an antithesis to these earlier Western interpretations.

Both the initial Western/Orientalist discovery of the Kızılbaş-Alevis and their re-signification by Turkish nationalists are cornerstones of the modern genealogy of the Alevism of Turkey. Clarification of the genealogy of the concept of Alevism will also enable us to situate its more recent transformations since the second half of the 20th century in a broader historical framework. The diverse connotations that have been attributed to Alevi/Alevism during the last century (e.g., Alevis as preservers of pre-Islamic Turkish traditions and culture, Alevism as pre-Marxist class-fight ideology, as Turkish philosophy, as secular Turkish Islam, or as post-Zoroastrian Kurdish religion) are part and parcel of the complicated dynamics of Turkish identity politics in which religious, ethnic, nationalist, and class-based concerns relate and clash. In the context of these politics, Alevis have not only been object of signification but also themselves been engaged in the signification of others. In this context I consider the victimization of the Alevis, to which both Alevis themselves and non-Alevi sympathizers (mostly secularist and leftist Turks and Kurds as well as foreign observers) contribute, as an epistemological hindrance for the clarification of the Alevi genealogy. Such victimization often tends to reduce Alevi history to a history of suffering inflicted upon the righteous by oppressive others, bears the danger of leading to the perception of the Alevis as only passive subjects of history without any real agency, and is ultimately a hindrance to a historicization of the relations between Alevis and their environment. In short, Alevi history needs to be demythologized (cf. Bozarslan 2003).

Conceptual and Theoretical Contestations

To a limited extent the introduction of the terms *Alevi* and *Alevilik* into the public discourse of Turkey helped to suppress the pejorative connotations of the term Kızılbaş. However, as I will argue, the new meanings that would be associated with "Alevi" also carried new ambivalences. When the Kızılbaş of Turkey began to be known as Alevi, the new name signified a very particular, mainly Anatolian-shaped formation, sociologically much more specific than the general meanings the term 'Alawī carries in the Muslim world. This is a point of sometimes more and sometimes less innocent confusion. Such confusion is not surprising when outsiders familiar with the Muslim epithet 'Alawī assume that the Alevis from Turkey are merely another branch of Shiite Islam. When, however, somebody aware of the particularities of Alevi difference tries to explain Turkish Alevism from within the traditional, broader meaning of Alevi as "Shiite" alone then this is often done with the intention to draw the Alevis closer to the Islamic mainstream.

A perspective that takes seriously the work of concepts further needs to pay attention to the methodological problem entailed in the back-reading of "Alevi" history into times in which the modern concept of Alevism did not yet exist. It is rather common both in popular and in academic discourses about Alevism to apply the term "Alevi" not only to the late Ottoman context, in which we find both the first examples of its use by various Kızılbaş groups as a self-designation and the beginning of a discourse about Kızılbaş groups as Alevi, but also to earlier Ottoman and even pre-Ottoman contexts. In these later contexts, however, neither did the term have the modern meanings associated with it, nor were the Kızılbashes—or any other group usually seen as being in genealogical connection with them—called "Alevi".

Another major problem is with the Turkist bias in Alevi religiography. Scholarship in the 20th century has tended to present the Bektashis, Alevis, and groups seen as being related to them within a framework of Turkish culture and tribal networks. Recent research, however, has questioned this story. Historical work on the Kızılbaş shows their multilingual and multicultural character, emphasizing especially—in Turkist perspectives usually neglected—their Persianate roots (Babayan 2002). Challenging traditional wisdom, Ayfer Karakaya-Stump has argued that "the building blocks of the Anatolian Kızılbash milieu were not individual tribes as such, but rather various Sufi circles and itinerant dervish groups who joined together under the spiritual and political leadership of the Safavid shahs" (Karakaya-Stump 2008, 180). As she has shown, many of the Kızılbaş ocak lineage holders or dedes of Anatolia received their formal religious authorization letters from the Wafāʾiyya (Turk. Vefaiye) order (13th–16th century), which blended in the course of the 16th century with the Kızılbaş and submerged between the 16th and 17th centuries into the Bektashi order (Karakaya-Stump 2008, 37). The importance of the Vefaiye order in the early Anatolian history of the ocak-based charismatic communities contradicts the assertion that the latter's history and their religious culture were primarily shaped by Central Asian (Turkish) heritages (Karakaya-Stump 2008, 208–210; see also Ocak 2005). The success of that assertion is very closely connected to the scholarship of Fuad Köprülü, which will play a central role in this book, and to which I will turn below.

Another problem with the *longue durée* perspective on "Alevi" Islam is that it is often not clear what kind of religiosity the attribute Alevi is supposed to refer to. It has to be considered that in the medieval Islam of Anatolia and adjacent areas the boundaries between Shiite and Sunni Islam were not yet that clearly defined and Alid sentiment, or, to use a term coined by Hodgson, "'Alid loyalism" was widely spread beyond the boundaries of explicitly Shiite circles, especially in Sufism (Hodgson 1977; see also Cahen 1970; Nasr 1970; Mélikoff 1998, 47–50). The question as to whether the Babai movement, the first Anatolian formation associated with the modern narrative of the *longue durée* of Alevism, can already be called Shiite has been disputed. Kafadar was probably the first to allude to the politics and teleological assumptions behind modern projections of clear Shiite or Sunni faiths to medieval Anatolian contexts (Kafadar 1995, 75–76).

Karakaya-Stump has shown that until the 16th century Vefai *icazet-names*[20] pay reverence to both "Sunni" and "Shiite" figures. Only in the course of the 16th century did this change and references to, for example, the Sunni caliphs were replaced by the names of Shiite Imams. This transformation corresponded with the coalescence of the Vefai order and Kızılbaş groups (Karakaya-Stump 2008, 80–82). The same period witnessed more conscious efforts by both Ottomans and Safavids to present their respective faiths as the only valid ones. In the context of the political rivalry between the two empires, the boundaries between Sunni and Shiite Islam were defined much more exclusively than used to be the case in previous centuries. In fact, the Safevi order itself began only in the second half of the 15th century to provide Ali with a central role in its religious culture (Babayan 2002, 139–140); the Bektashis—a Sufi order the historical roots as well as the religious practices and doctrines of which overlap to a certain extent with those of the Kızılbaş groups, with some of which they developed close institutional affiliations between the 16th and 17th centuries—did this only in the course of the 16th century in a

20. Letters of authorization in Sufi Islam.

comprehensive manner (Yıldırım 2010, 34). Among the various tribes and dervish groups that eventually merged into the Bektashi order or aligned with the Kızılbaş there were of course groups with deep Alid affinities, ranging from emotional affinity with the closer family of the prophet (the *ahl al-bayt*) to more explicit and central veneration of Ali (see Karamustafa 1994). This does not, however, make self-evident the assumption that Alidism could be regarded as the major principle that connected all of those groups that are today integrated into the *longue durée* of Alevism. While the matter of the extent of the Babais' Shiism is, as mentioned above, contested, it appears even more difficult to qualify the Bedreddin movement—which shows social and structural continuities with both the earlier Babai movement and later Kızılbaş groups—as Alid in any substantial way.[21]

All these messy conceptual issues considered, I caution restrain with regard to the application of the term Alevi as a common denominator for the various historically connected groups from the Babais to the Bektashis, Bedreddin followers, Kızılbashes, and modern Alevis. To argue that the moments of social and religious continuity that connect these groups are adequately expressed by the label Alevi is problematic since what this common Aleviness is supposed to denote remains highly elusive. And even if this commonality would be clearly defined,[22] there still remains the fact that the *longue durée* from the Babais to the modern Alevis contains questionable teleological assumptions. The problem with such teleological operations, embodied in the back-reading of the modern category Alevi into premodern times, is not circumvented when we, as I admittedly have done myself, label said groups at their premodern historical stages "proto-Alevi." This is roughly the same as if one, while writing a history of Christianity, were to label B.C. Jews "(proto)-Christians"—a description that can hardly be accepted from a historical point of view.

The problem is not one of naming itself, but more precisely one of signification. In the emerging field of Alevi studies the practice of projecting modern notions of Alevism back into the past is still extremely widespread. The field is still caught in implicit presumptions of religious and cultural

---

21. The revolutionary Bedreddin movement of the early 15th century was named after Sheikh Bedreddin from Simawna (1358/9–1416), who was an Ottoman military judge in the Balkans before he became the leader of a millenarian movement that challenged Ottoman authority. Between the Bedreddin movement and the milieus of the Bektashi order and the Anatolian Kızılbaş exist clear sociohistorical continuities (Balivet 1995).

22. For typical attempts see Mélikoff (1998), Ocak (2000b), Dressler (2002).

continuity and essence typical of homogenizing modern views on history developed within the semantics of national historiography. In fact, as I will show, the formulation of Alevism as a modern concept by Turkish writers and scholars since the 1920s happened not only parallel to the formation of Turkish nationalism, but was an important part of it. Put differently, the formulation of a *longue durée* of Alevi culture and the assumption of a high degree of homogeneity among different Alevi groups reflects the continuity assumption inherent in the nationalist view on history. Against the continuity thesis, I stress that the modern concept of Alevism is rather new, barely a hundred years old, formed in the context of the Turkish nation-building process and developed within a semantic framework akin to that of the nation itself. This concept portrays the Alevis as a rather homogenous unity of groups that share a cultural heritage that is Turkish and religious peculiarities that mark them as Islamic, though "heterodox." The renaming from Kızılbaş to Alevi was accompanied by a re-signification that turned the Kızılbaş, thus far stigmatized as people of loose morals, professing heresy, and politically untrustworthy, into "heterodox" Muslim Turks. This understanding is still paradigmatic. When the prolific amateur researcher Baki Öz described the Alevis in one of his popular booklets, written in the 1990s as part of the public coming out of Alevism in Turkey, as "an interpretation of Turkism within Islam" he expressed the mainstream sentiment that has not changed since (Öz 1995, 158).

It is truly astonishing that scholarship has so far taken hardly any notice of the conceptual shift from Kızılbashism to Alevism described above. As a matter of fact, I would argue that a considerable part of scholarship on Turkish religion has not yet been able to develop a critical perspective on the modernist obsession with questions of belonging, origins, and vague notions of essence. The same is true for the modern discourse on Alevism. Not only popular, but also much academic writing portrays Alevism as a religious tradition with roots in the Sunna-Shia schism.[23] The story of the Karbala massacre (680 C.E.), in which the third Shiite Imam Husayn was slain by Umayyad forces, serves as a founding myth in this narrative. Other accounts of Alevi origins focus on the 13th century and the cultural and religious mixture following the immigration of Turks into Anatolia as the time period in which Alevism was fermented;[24] and

---

23. For an example see Say (2007).

24. See the work of Ahmet Y. Ocak (see bibliography and chapter 6).

yet another school traces the roots of Alevism back to pre-Islamic, mainly Turkish traditions.[25] What most of such accounts focusing on origins have in common is that they tend to overemphasize continuities and describe the evolution of Alevism as a gradual syncretistic process in which Shiite religiosity mixed with Sufi and pre-Islamic Turkish traditions. The projection of the modern concepts of "Alevi" and "Alevism" into premodern times is fraught with methodological problems congruent to those we encounter in the back-reading of other terms whose meanings changed in the context of the formation of the secular modern nation-state, such as "nation" and "religion". However, I would also hold that a too narrow understanding of the notion "invention"—that is, an extreme constructivist position that remains confined to the claim that the concept under question would be a contingently fabricated knowledge with not much historical anchoring at all—prevents one from grasping the more complex historical dynamics of the discursive shifts through which the concepts under discussion were formed. Inspired by the work of Talal Asad, I argue for a genealogical approach that investigates the changing meanings of concepts and their relation to practices and subjectivities over time. Beyond the constructivist position, it is worthwhile to ask what exactly happened to Kızılbaş practices, identities, and beliefs in the course of their reconfiguration under the new concept of Alevism. This question, admittedly, also points to the limits of the study at hand, which is not dedicated to the formation of modern Alevi subjectivities as such, but focuses on the intellectual and political context of the formation of Alevism as a concept.

There is nothing wrong per se with a search for historical origins and roots of social and religious formations. Such searching requires, however, critical reflection on the work of the categories that we employ in our religiography, that is, in our writing about those aspects of cultural/social history that have been universalized and in the process been typified as religious history. In the study of the religious history of the Turks and Anatolia, terms such as syncretism, heresy, minority, orthodoxy, and heterodoxy are often employed without reflection on their normative underpinnings, which are rooted in and mirror particular religio-political discourses that contribute to the formation and legitimization of religious, political, and historical truths. In other words, these terms take part in the complex dynamics that have created the particular religiopolitical

---

25. See the work of Irène Mélikoff (see bibliography and chapter 6).

hegemonies characteristic of the region. As such they are highly political. In Turkey, practices of religious othering are part of the daily negotiation and confirmation of we-group identities[26] in the public and are shaped by unequal power relations. In this discourse, unbelievers, non-Muslims, Shiites, and Alevis are juxtaposed to the believers, Muslims, and Sunnis, respectively. The practices of othering that these juxtapositions are part of in Turkish religion politics are subtly reinforced by academic discourses. In the case of Alevism, this shows itself when Alevis are evaluated in public debate by means of academic concepts such as heterodoxy and syncretism and are in this way juxtaposed to "orthodox" Sunni Islam. It is important to understand that not only the notion of Alevism is impacted by this process of othering. Rather, the modern othering of the Alevis is dialectically related to the normalization of a Sunni-Muslim identity, just as in the 16th century the Kızılbaş question played an important role in the consolidation of Sunni Ottoman and Shiite Safavid doctrines, respectively.

At this juncture, in order to prevent misunderstandings, it might be helpful to make two clarifications with regard to the theoretical and political intentions of this study. First, my assertion that the concept of Alevism is a modern construct that was formed in the early 20th century implies— although this is not focus of this study—that the formation of a common Alevi identity in accordance with this concept, namely as rather coherent and shared by all those groups who are in some way part of *ocak* networks, is an equally modern phenomenon. This is, however, not meant to delegitimize the political, cultural, and religious aims of continuing activism and community building in the name of Alevi identity—to the contrary, as I will argue. Today, Alevism is a social reality referring to both a distinct social group and a communal identity. When I follow in the subsequent chapters the method of a heuristic constructivism in my approach to the modern concept of Alevism, this is not intended to imply that the groups under question have been lumped together by early 20th-century Turkish nationalist discourse as a creation ex nihilo. The groups that were labeled with the new term can be clearly identified as members of those *ocak*-centered communities that were called Kızılbaş by the Ottomans and who had undoubtedly many things in common. I recognize that these communities share a broad stock of oral traditions (poems, hymns, myths), ritual knowledge, and social structures. Emblematic for this common knowledge, reflecting even consciousness about the internal diversity, is

---

26. The term is borrowed from Elwert (1997).

the widespread saying, "The path is one, the rites are one thousand and one" (*Yol bir, sürek binbir*).

This acknowledged, it can hardly be denied that the modern concept of Alevism created a new knowledge about these groups. This new knowledge became hegemonic in both popular and academic discourses and was also accepted over time by many Kızılbaş-Alevis. Possibly, broader realization of the history of the concept and its manipulation by Turkish national- ist discourse might contribute to an empowerment of the Alevis against hegemonic nationalist and Sunni-Islamic normativities. Challenging the latter, it might even make some Alevis recast their historical narratives and reinterpret their culture and religious traditions. In that sense the genea- logical work on the concept of Alevism bears a not-to-be-underestimated potential for political resistance.

Second, and related to the first point, my focus on the discourse *on* Alevism is not meant to undermine the agency of the Alevis themselves in the formation of modern Alevism. But, as stated before, the Kızılbaş-Alevis' own appropriation of the term Alevi is not the object of this study and also, I would maintain, extremely difficult to reconstruct due to the scarcity of sources on that issue. The subject of this study is ultimately not Alevism as such, but the politics of religion and nationalism that have contributed to the meanings that were associated with Alevism in the 20th century.

The Alevi case provides us with an example of a rather comprehen- sive reinterpretation of a religious tradition within the political project of nation-building. It should, though, be clearly understood that the forces that were unleashed by the project of nation-building, as well as the affil- iated project of top down secularization impacted not only on the Alevis and are part of broader transformations usually discussed under the term modernization. The meanings of religion itself, as well as, more specifi- cally, the meanings of Islam for Sunni Muslims were also affected by the globalizing, that is, Westernizing and homogenizing, dynamics of moder- nity that crystallized in an uprooting and reorientation of the spheres of economy, social life, politics, as well as culture. Obviously, as I argue, the term Alevi in the Turkish vernacular in the early 21st century means something different from what the term meant a century earlier both in Ottoman Turkish as well as in other Islamic languages. But the same can easily also be claimed for the term Sunni-Muslim, as understood by an average Muslim today, as compared to what the term would have evoked in an ordinary Muslim a century or two ago (Ernst 1997, XIV–XV). In other words, my focus on the modern changes of the concept Alevism should not be interpreted as attributing to other traditions of Islam, or other religious traditions in general, a more continuous and authentic character, less influenced by the modern transformations of human life and knowledge.[27] All religious traditions, and the notion of religion itself, have in some way or another experienced the transformative forces of the modern period.[28]

The Köprülü Paradigm: Historiography and Nationalism

This study gives particular attention to the religiography of the historian Mehmed Fuad Köprülü, which serves as a window into the fermentation process of the modern concept of Alevism within the discourses of religion, Islam, and nationalism. While Köprülü's contributions as a scholar are widely recognized, their dependence on the emerging Turkish nationalist paradigm and at the same time their impact on the formation of Turkish nationalism itself, though at times mentioned in passing,[29] with one exception so far has not been subject to systematic examination.[30]

Given the path-defining influence of Köprülü's work on the modern concept of Alevism and its relation to the formation of Turkish nationalist historiography, it is of crucial importance to understand the connections between Köprülü's politics and his scholarship. Köprülü was a convinced nationalist and, although he was not always in line with state-sponsored official history, his work added significantly to the nationalist project by producing important cornerstones for a historical narrative of the Turkish nation that could claim scholarly credentials and helped the nation-state to gain legitimacy at home and—in his time even more important—abroad. I am particularly interested in the role religion played in Köprülü's narrative

---

27. I am thankful to Cemal Kafadar whose insightful query has made me realize the importance of clarifying this point.

28. Exemplary studies illustrating this impact are King (1999), Tayob (2009), van der Veer (2001); for an instructive overview article addressing what this comprehensive remaking of religion(s) in the modern context means for religious studies see King (2011).

29. See, for example, Park (1975, 269–271); Karpat (2001, 401); Leiser and Dankoff (2006, xxxii); Asılsoy (2008); Yıldız (2009, 485 and 487).

30. I refer to the so far most fine-tuned analysis of Köprülü as a nationalist historian, provided by Büşra Ersanlı within her detailed discussions of Turkish nationalism in the early Turkish Republic (Ersanlı 2002 and 2003).

of the historical continuity of Turkish culture. As I will show, in his work "popular" religion is construed as a medium of national consciousness and ideals. This helps him to formulate the thesis of a continuity of the national Turkish sentiment throughout the ages. In this narrative, "heterodox," "popular," and "syncretistic" Islamic movements are reasoned to have functioned as major carriers of Turkish traditions and sentiment, the origins of which are traced back to Central Asia. In other words, I aim to show how Köprülü created the historical framework that made it possible to place certain groups from the periphery of Ottoman-Turkish public and Islamic discourse—groups that we recognize today as "Alevis"—into the center of the narrative of the national and religious evolution of the Turks.

Köprülü's work needs to be situated within the context of the complex politics of modernization that marks the rise of Turkish nationalism in the first two decades of the Turkish Republic. The political context in which Köprülü matured as an intellectual in the later Young Turk period is of crucial importance for an understanding of the link between Köprülü's politics and his historiography—indeed, for the politics of history-writing during Turkish nation-building (that is, in the 1910s through 1930s) in general. In this period he entered a symbiotic intellectual partnership with Ziya Gökalp (1876–1924), one of the most influential ideologues of Turkish nationalism, a collaboration that was driven by both political and scholarly motivations, and in particular the conviction that the study of Turkish history was essential for the creation of a national consciousness. As scholars, both contributed significantly to the translation of Western concepts and methodology into late Ottoman and early republican discourses.

Karakaya-Stump was the first to point out two constants in the study of the Kızılbaş-Alevis from the earliest accounts of American missionaries to subsequent scholarly as well as non-scholarly approaches to Alevism: first, a preoccupation with questions of origin, and second, the framing of the Kızılbaş-Alevi groups as "heterodox" and "syncretistic" (Karakaya-Stump 2004, 331). Köprülü played an eminent—I would argue the most important—role in cementing this perspective by providing it with scholarly legitimacy. His extensive historical studies explained and contextualized the religious character of the Alevis and Bektashis within a narrative of Turkish national continuity and established what can be referred to as the Köprülü paradigm. Through the example of Köprülü's scholarship I will illustrate how the new framing of Alevism as Turkish and "popular"/"heterodox" Islamic was integrated into the nationalist (re-)writing of Turkish history. This entails an interrogation of the underlying values and politics of Köprülü's historiography and religiography, as well as a critique of his methodology, which is still, despite significant flaws, perceived as exemplary—especially, but not exclusively, by many Turkish historians. In particular his research on Turkish Sufism and literature has still a looming presence and even "assumed a kind of immunity from criticism" (Karamustafa 2005, 70).

I hold that what is needed is more attention to the theoretical assumptions, methodology, as well as politics of the work of Turkish nationalist historiography and religiography as exemplified in the scholarship of Köprülü. Beyond nationalism, the two major intellectual contexts within which Köprülü's work needs to be analyzed are, first, contemporary discourses on modernization and religion, and second, Islamic modernism. His oeuvre has been fundamental in the continuing projection of certain Sunni-Islamic and modernist biases on the development of Turkish/ Anatolian Islam. Of course it is not surprising that an early 20th-century scholar such as Köprülü used concepts that were based on modern assumptions about cultural and religious essences, linear historical trajectories, and clear boundaries between cultural entities such as religions. What is remarkable is that his work on Turkish Islam and inner-Islamic difference—despite its must-read status in the study of Turkish Islam—has not yet been subject to critical reevaluation.[31] This negligence points to the relative low level of reception—in Islamic studies in general and the study of Turkish Islam in particular—of recent critical work in religious and postcolonial studies. Engagement with such critical scholarship is necessary, I argue, to transgress the limitations that the biases of nationalism, secularism, and (world) religionism, which we encounter in Köprülü's work, tend to succumb to. This will enable us to embark on a rereading and rewriting of the religious and cultural history of Anatolia and adjacent territories following the Turkish immigration.

Turkish nationalist intellectuals of the first decades of the republic such as Köprülü were engaged in a civilizing project that aimed at providing the new Turkey with an identity that was rooted in ancient history while at the same time thoroughly modern. In light of the conservative religious (Islamic) and ethnic (mainly Kurdish) centrifugal forces from within, which challenged the new state's legitimacy, the state aimed at an integration of the Alevis in the nationalist project qua their subordination under

---

31. The notable though in scope limited exception is Karamustafa (2005); see also Dressler (2010b).

the state's ethno-religious paradigm of a secular Muslim-Turkish nation. This work of integration was extremely complex since roughly 20–30% of the Alevis are Kurdish and therefore the Alevi question represented both an ethnic and a religious challenge for a state with strong centralizing and homogenizing aspirations. The conceptualization of Alevism as "heterodox" Islamic and Turkish within early republican, state-oriented Turkish nationalist academic discourse, which has henceforward been paradigmatic for studies of Alevism as a historical formation, cultural practice, and religious tradition, has to be understood from within this context of nation-building and social engineering. This conceptualization was religionist or religionizing, by which I refer to an essentially secularist framework that conceives of religion within an emerging discourse of world religions as an entity clearly separable from other spheres of life, such as, for example, culture, which in the process is often turned into a conceptual antidote to religion (see Masuzawa 2005).[32]

Scholarship on Alevism has so far failed to examine critically the impact that Turkish nationalism has had on modern conceptions of Alevism. Within the nationalist framework, new readings of Alevism were directed against two polemics: first against the standard Ottoman anti-Kızılbaş rhetoric, which marked the Alevis as heretics and justified their exclusion from the centers of Ottoman life, and at times also their persecution. Second, they militated against Christian authors' emphases on Christian and pagan elements within Alevism, in response to which the Alevis' Turkishness and Islamic orientation was argued. Their Turkish and Islamic character was widely seen as a precondition and strong case for their integration into the newly formed discourse of ethno-national and religious unity.

An important step toward developing a critical historical perspective on the involvement of nationalist politics in the conceptualization of Alevism and Alevi studies was a review essay by the historian of religion Ahmet Yaşar Ocak from 1991. Discussing recent publications on Alevism as shaped by contemporary ideological skirmishes and distinguishing between nationalist, humanist, and Marxist approaches, he was the first to allude to the politics of Alevi representation. In this text he also hints

---

32. The notions (world) religionizing and (world) religionism point to modernism's obsession with origins and evolution, as well as form and essence, through which religions are perceived as clearly definable entities—and as such both distinct from, by definition nonreligious, sociocultural formations and clearly distinguishable from other religions.

to the continuity of this politics since the first publications on "Alevis" in the 1920s and provides a broad overview of publications on the subject throughout the republic. Ocak mentions the role of Turkism and the influence of Ziya Gökalp's sociology on the publications of amateur researchers and historians such as Baha Said and Fuad Köprülü, respectively, who had argued that Alevi and Bektashi currents needed to be studied as representatives of a Turkish religious and cultural tradition (Ocak 1991, 21). Growing recognition of this context in recent years can itself be explained by increased critical awareness of the politics of ethnic and religious engineering in the late Ottoman Empire and the early Turkish Republic.[33] Still missing, however, is a systematic analysis of the genealogy of this association of Alevism with Turkish nationalism. It is a major aim of this study to fill this gap.

Chapter Summaries

From within the context of modernization and nation-building in the late Ottoman and early republican Turkish periods, this book aims to contribute to our understanding of how, in defiance of the prejudices of secular modernism, religious and national identities formed and were formulated in a symbiotic relationship. More specifically, the story that this book tells is about how certain socially and politically marginalized, rural religious communities, since the 16th century labeled with the derogatory term *Kızılbaş*, entered the focus of the late Ottoman and early republican Turkish nationalists and were gradually integrated into the newly formulated identity conceptions of a secular Turkish nationalism. This integration, which meant assimilation into Islam and Turkish nationhood, came along with a renaming of the groups under question as *Alevi*, a term that established their Islamic identity, as well as a reassessment of their history and religious difference from Sunni Islam. Studying the role of religion in the formation of Turkish nationalism with a particular focus on how Kızılbaş-Alevism was re-signified in religious and national terms, I will scrutinize the work of modernist and in particular secularist assumptions in this process and give particular emphasis to methodological questions

---

33. See, for example, Bayrak (1997, 19–20); Livni (2002); Kieser (2002a, 129); M. Küçük (2002, 902); Karakaya-Stump (2004, 331); Massicard (2007, 42–45); Dinçer (2009, 135); Azak (2010, 142–143); Markussen (2012, 138–141).

that are, I would hold, of larger interest to the critical study of Islam, and religious studies more broadly.

The book is divided into two parts. Part I, "Missionaries, Nationalists, and the Kızılbaş-Alevis," traces the roots of the modern concept of Alevism and the various politics through which this concept was fermented. At the center of this investigation is the signification process through which the modern concept of Alevism evolved between the 1850s and the 1930s. It introduces a genealogical approach toward Turkish Alevism distinguishing between two major phases in the making of modern Alevism. The first phase, discussed in chapter 1, is marked by the initial discovery of the Kızılbaş by American missionaries and other Western observers who lived and/or travelled in Anatolia since the second half of the 19th century. The Kızılbaş appeared to these Westerners as a strange people whom they had difficulties categorizing in their religious schemes. Speculations about the origins of their particularities soon led to theories about their close relation to Christianity and pre-Islamic Anatolian civilizations. These theories, controversially discussed among the missionaries and other foreigners familiar with the subject, were driven by decisively modern quests, framed in contemporary civilizationist and religionist language, and focused on questions of religious and racial/ethnic origins and boundaries. The missionaries in particular, carried by a romantic quest to discover and revive the Christian heritage of Anatolia, were looking for clear religious classifications. In this context particular attention is given to the way in which the Kızılbaş were presented within a Western and Christian (and mostly that meant Protestant) concept of (world) religion, which became fashionable in the context of colonialism and increasing globalization as a way to (1) make sense and organize the encounter with religiocultural others in a manner that simultaneously familiarized and rendered exotic; and (2) to justify at home the colonial enterprise and the cultural imperialism that came with it. The chapter situates the Western/Orientalist discovery of the Kızılbaş within post-Tanzimat regional and international political contexts that were marked by heightened competition over sociopolitical and economic capital, and contributed to a remarkable increase of intercommunal violence.

The aim of chapter 2 is to establish the theoretical and historical background that frames the subsequent chapters on the formation of Alevism in the context of Turkish nationalism. Only relatively recently have studies on nationalism begun to question the secular modernization paradigm and to explore the contributions of religions in the formation of nationalisms.

Since secularist approaches to modern history were formulated in a way that tended to ignore or rationalize away the involvement of religion in nationalism and nation-building, they missed seeing the semantic affinities and structural continuities between religion and secular nationalism. Drawing on postcolonial scholarship, in particular the work of Talal Asad and Peter van der Veer, I point to the importance of religion in making nationalism plausible, without, however, claiming that nationalism would simply be a secularized form of religion. In a second step, the chapter turns to late Ottoman thinkers who played important roles in the intellectual formation of Turkish nationalism in order to illustrate the symbiosis of secular nationalist and religious thought in the formation of a Turkish national ideal. The final section of this chapter turns to the more concrete politics of nationalism in the last years of the Ottoman Empire. Of particular importance are the political decisions made by the Young Turkish government during World War I. Strongly influenced by the traumatizing experiences of the Balkan Wars (1912–1913), notions of ethnic and religious difference then became crucial organizing principles of nation-building, reflected in techniques of social and demographic engineering, to which the Young Turks increasingly subscribed. This politics, which focused on the eastern provinces of the Ottoman Empire, where Kurds and Armenians constituted the largest populations, was partially motivated by fear of growing nationalist separatist movements similar to those that had triggered the implosion of Ottoman rule of the Balkans. Politics of social and demographic engineering, which targeted the Christians, the Kurds, and the Kızılbaş-Alevis in that order, would continue during the Turkish War of Independence and early Kemalist Turkey.

The politics of nationalism, as discussed in chapter 2, forms the primary context in which the second phase in the modern making of Alevism needs to be situated, namely the nationalist discovery and re-signification of the Kızılbaş as Muslim Turks under the newly signified label "Alevi" between the 1910s and 1930s. Chapter 3 is concerned with the semantics of this re-signification. It explains the role that the Kızılbaş-Alevis (especially the Kurdish ones) played in the context of late Ottoman and early Kemalist social and demographic engineering and its goal of creating a largely mono-religious and Turkish nation-state in the face of claims of ethnic and religious difference. In this context I argue that the question of the political loyalty of the Kızılbaş-Alevis had an until today vastly underestimated importance in the course of events that led to so much inter-communal violence in the war years between 1914 and 1922. The chapter further makes clear that the question of the signification of the Alevis in both ethnic/national and religious/cultural terms was since its beginnings in the late Young Turk period highly contested. What eventually turned out to become the dominant discourse about Alevi (and Bektashi) difference, namely its embeddedness in Turkish culture and an ambivalence about its position at the margins of Islam, was strongly impacted by the particular politics of ethno-national cum religio-secular homogenization of the new republic that was primarily directed against the Kurds and the religious difference of the Kızılbaş-Alevis, respectively. This dynamic is exemplified in the work of Turkish nationalist writer-activists such as Baha Said Bey (1882–1939). In the context of the Young Turkish politics of nationalization, Baha Said undertook anthropological research among Kızılbaş-Alevis and Bektashis. Based on this research, his publications in nationalist journals in the late Ottoman and early republican years mark the beginning of a public discourse on the Kızılbaş-Alevis and Bektashis as carriers of Turkish culture. The Turkist framework is more pronounced in Baha Said's than in Köprülü's work and shows more overtly the nationalist investment in marking the Kızılbaş-Alevis' difference. For Baha Said, the main characteristic of the Kızılbaş-Alevis and Bektashis was their Turkishness, reflected in their culture as well as in their religion. Therefore he downplayed Islamic as well as other religious influences arguing that the core of their practices was rooted in ancient Turkish Shamanism.

Part II of this book, "Mehmed Fuad Köprülü (1890–1966) and the Conceptualization of Inner-Islamic Difference ," is dedicated to a thorough contextualization and analysis of the methodology employed in the modern scholarship on Alevism with a focus on the work of Fuad Köprülü.

Chapter 4 discusses the formation of Köprülü as a late Ottoman and early republican intellectual whose political and scholarly interests developed largely parallel to each other, overlapping in certain aspects, but never conflating as in the case of his mentor and colleague Ziya Gökalp. Köprülü's early historical work on the literary traditions of the Turks following their Islamization shows how his formation as a scholar concurred with his turn toward Turkish nationalism in the Young Turk period. Köprülü's scholarship and his nationalist and secularist politics was characterized by a complex dynamic of companionship and critique. His ambivalent stance with regard to the Turkish History Thesis, which was formulated in the early 1930s and marked the Kemalist regime's attempt to increase its control over the contested question of Turkish history and identity, illustrates this particularly well. While he was due to methodological reasons, and probably also on a personal level, critical of the revisionism that the new thesis represented and unwilling to entirely discard the Ottoman period or convert its role to that of a negative other of the new nationalist ideal, he was certainly not opposed to the modernizing quest of Kemalism as such. The comparison with Ziya Gökalp shows that in particular his understanding of secularism was akin to the Kemalist version.

Chapter 5 is concerned with matters of methodology and the work of concepts in the description, analysis, and theorization of inner-Islamic difference in general, and the evolution of Turkish religion and Turkish Islam more particularly in Köprülü's writings. As I try to show, Köprülü's nationalist quest was an important stimulus for not only his historiography, which was dedicated to the exploration of the continuity of the "Turkish spirit" over the ages from ancient pre-Islamic Central Asian to Ottoman Anatolian times, but also for his religiography. The Bektashi and Kızılbaş-Alevi traditions played a crucial role in Köprülü's reflections on the origins and evolution of national Turkish culture. They were conceived of as essentially part of the abode of Islam—despite their "heterodox" and "syncretistic" character, qualifiers that retained in his interpretation strong pejorative connotations. The chapter analyzes the work of those taxonomical devices that were most important in Köprülü's religiographic rationalization of Turkish continuity, namely the notion of "popular Islam" as well as the concepts of shamanism, syncretism, and heterodoxy. These concepts are reflective of modern Western discourses on religion of the time period, with all their Orientalist biases, implicit or explicit assumptions of essences, hierarchies, and clear boundaries between religions. This is in itself not surprising, but simply shows that Köprülü was integrated into transnational discussions on religion of his time. It astonishes, however, that so far, despite the overwhelming impact of Köprülü's work on future generations of scholarship on Turkish Islam, no comprehensive theoretical and methodological analysis of his conceptualization of inner-Islamic difference has been undertaken. Such analysis, I argue, is crucial for an exploration of how the modern knowledge about Alevism evolved at the juncture of Turkish nation-building, modern religion discourse, and Islamic apologetics.

Chapter 6 begins with an attempt to trace and systematize the meanings given to the term "Alevi" in the work of Köprülü. This analysis shows that the term Alevi and its derivates were, especially in his earlier work, not yet clearly defined, but carried several overlapping meanings and only gradually moved toward the sociologically more specific meanings that are commonly associated with it today. Still, as I argue, the ambivalences with which the label was signified and its relation to the taxonomic devices discussed in the previous chapter amounted to a conceptualization of Bektashi and Kızılbaş-Alevi difference that would become paradigmatic for generations to come. The second part of the chapter investigates the academic legacy of Köprülü's approach to the study of inner-Islamic difference and the study of Alevism in particular. Similar to Baha Said, Köprülü argued for a *long durée* of Turkish culture epitomized in Kızılbaş-Alevism and the shamanic remnants that it carried. This theory of continuity of Turkish religion, embodied in the Alevi tradition, is discussed and explained with help of overlapping categories of shamanism, Batinism, and Alevism, each of which is associated with particular periods in the development of "popular Turkish" religiosity. Different from Baha Said's, however, Köprülü's evaluation of the Kızılbaş-Alevis' religious pedigree was more attuned to its Islamic roots, highlighting the impact of peripheral Sufi and Shiite currents. Although he never made the Alevis the explicit topic of one of his texts, Köprülü's work was in the long run, not the least due to his academic authority, more influential. His conceptualization of the Kızılbaş-Alevis as both Turkish and "heterodox" Islamic became path-defining for scholarly as well as academic understandings of Alevism until today. Analysis of the work of his direct students, as well as of those later scholars on Anatolian, non-elite Islam who continued to work in his footsteps within the basic paradigm of the continuity of a "heterodox" Turkish Islam, most prominently Irène Mélikoff and Ahmet Yaşar Ocak, shows this clearly.

The conclusion, at last, summarizes the major arguments of the book and provides a final analysis of the remaking of Alevism through nationalist and religio-secularist discourses inherent to the project of modernity. I here give particular emphasis to the role of historiographic and religiographic practices in the process of re-signification that rendered the Kızılbaş "Alevi."

PART ONE

Missionaries, Nationalists, and the Kızılbaş-Alevis

I

The Western Discovery of the Kızılbaş-Alevis

IN THE SECOND half of the 19th century, Western presence in Asia Minor increased considerably due to a combination of economic and political factors. Westerners who lived and travelled in the Anatolian and eastern provinces of the Ottoman Empire (such as missionaries, scientists, diplomats, and bourgeois adventurers), while often primarily interested in the Oriental Christians, inevitably also came in contact with the local Muslim population. The references we find in their writings about encounters with Kızılbaş-Alevis constitute the first modern records of these communities. Irrespective of the biases and apparent misunderstandings they display, these materials (academic and popular publications, letters, and official reports) include rich ethnographic and historical information about the state of the Kızılbaş-Alevi communities in that period, their social and political status, their rites and beliefs, and their forms of social organization.

This chapter will show how in the last decades of the 19th century an international, at first Euro-American, discourse on the Kızılbaş-Alevis began to evolve. The guiding interest of this investigation is, however, not in analyzing this discourse for a reconstruction of the situation of the late Ottoman Kızılbaş-Alevis per se.[1] My primary interest is rather in the mid-term political impact of this discourse, that is, in the role it would play in the context of Turkish nationalism in the late Ottoman period and the early Turkish republic.

American missionaries were the first among Western observers that showed interest in the Kızılbaş-Alevis' ethnic and religious differences from the Sunni Muslim population. The Turkish authors who would in the 1920s begin to write about the Kızılbaş-Alevis, as I will show later,

---

1. For the most comprehensive discussion of the state of the Kızılbaş-Alevi population in the late Ottoman Empire since the 1850s, see Hans-Lukas Kieser's important study, based to a large part on examination of missionary materials (Kieser 2000).

were aware of this earlier discourse established by Western observers and attempted to counter those arguments that they saw as conflicting with national interest. In particular, the nationalist narrative would try to refute speculations and theories about the Kızılbaş-Alevis' non-Muslim and non-Turkish features and origins. In this way the texts that Western observers produced since the mid-19th century about the Kızılbaş-Alevis constitute an important factor in the genealogy of the modern concept of Alevism. I am particularly interested in how Western observers described and theorized the religious and ethnic differences of the Kızılbaş-Alevis in the late Ottoman period. Daniel Dubuisson has argued that "[t]he gaze of European historians or ethnographers can discern religious phenomena only where they perceive facts that recall or evoke, from whatever distance and in however approximate a form, those that the European mind cannot designate otherwise" (Dubuisson 2003, 37). Following Dubuisson, and extending his observation to Western missionaries, my analysis of the portrayal of Kızılbaş-Alevism through Western eyes aims to contribute to our understanding of Orientalist conceptualizations of Turkish and Ottoman Islam/religion in this period. What do the writings of the American missionaries and other Western observers reveal to us about their concepts of religion, race, and culture? What were the religious, scholarly, and political motives behind their interest in the Kızılbaş-Alevi groups? Further, what are the local, regional, and international politics (such as the missionary projects, Ottoman reform and centralization endeavors, and imperialist interests) as they played out especially in the eastern provinces of the Empire,[2] where the question of Kızılbaş-Alevi difference first gained importance? What would be the long-term impact of the encounter between the Western observers and the Kızılbaş-Alevis in terms of the developing vernacular and transnational knowledge about the latter, as well as in terms of the regional political ramifications of that knowledge? Concentrating on these questions, this chapter means to contribute to the genealogy of the earliest stages of the modern concept of Alevism.[3]

---

2. That is, the Ottoman provinces at the eastern boundaries of Asia Minor proper, then dominated by Kurdish and Armenian populations, and today part of the Kurdish-dominated eastern and southeastern parts of the Turkish Republic, namely Bitlis, Mamüretülaziz (Elazığ), Diyarbakır, Erzurum, and Van.

3. My investigation takes as its point of departure the already mentioned pioneering work of Kieser (esp. 2000) with its focus on the encounter between the Kızılbaş-Alevis and especially the American missionaries, as well as a very important article by Karakaya-Stump (2004), in which she discusses 19th-century missionary accounts with a focus on their treatment of Kızılbaş-Alevi religion.

Early Western Encounters with the Kızılbaş

Examples of Western descriptions of the Kızılbaş from prior to the advent of the American missionaries are scarce and usually mirror closely the general stereotypes prevalent in the Sunni Ottoman population. In these texts, Shiism, as well as notions of Iranian and in one example also Turkmen culture figure prominently. Baptistin Poujoulat (1809–1864), a French historian who travelled in Asia Minor from 1836 to 1837, suggested in a letter dated August 1837 about the religion of certain Kurds—to be distinguished from the smaller group of Nestorian (Syriac) Christian Kurds—that they appeared to belong to the "sect of Ali," and that their Islam was tainted with superstitions reminding of the Magi (that is, the Zoroastrians). They would neither care about the mosque, nor about the sacred month of Ramadan, the ritual prayers, or the pilgrimage to Mecca (Poujoulat 1840, 351). It is obvious from his description that Poujoulat must have relied mainly on non-Kurdish, Sunni informants. The allusion to possible remnants of Zoroastrianism is a typical feature of Islamic heresiology, and he seems to not even have been aware of the fact that the majority of Kurds are Sunni rather than belonging to the "sect of Ali." Noteworthy in comparison to the descriptions of the following years by American missionaries is that his account situates these Alid—that is, most likely, Kızılbaş-Alevi—Kurds relatively firmly within an Islamic context.

A similarly vague understanding of the Kızılbaş, possibly also based on hearsay alone, is offered by one of the earliest American missionaries in the region, the Episcopalian Rev. Horatio Southgate, who journeyed through Eastern Anatolia in 1837–38. He reports that between Argaoun and Delikli Taş (in the province of Elazığ) lived "a people who profess to be Mussulmans, while the Turks hold them in great contempt, and called them *Kizzilbash*." As for their origins, Southgate suggests that they might be "descendants of the Persians, brought as prisoners into this region, and that the ancient hatred for them has been handed down, while the cause of it has been forgotten" (Southgate 1840, 297). As a last example, we find in the report of the Anglican missionary George P. Badger on his work in 1842 with the Eastern churches a brief reference to the inhabitants of a certain village, Hassan Teelebi (probably in the Malatya province). He describes them as Turkmen and as "followers of Hussein and Ali, reproachfully called Kuzzal-bash (or Red-heads) by the Turks, and such of the Moslem as consider their own creed more orthodox" (Badger 1850, 94).

The Missionary Project

Protestant American missionaries were the first Westerners to establish contact and write about the Kızılbaş-Alevis in the 19th century. Before delving into these encounters, it will be helpful to first get a general idea about the various, at times conflicting, motives that came together in the missionary movement of the 19th century, especially the relation among missionary, geopious, and colonial interests:

> There can be little doubt that the nineteenth century, like the early stages of the Crusader period, constituted a time in which influences and developments from many different parts of society contributed to an ever-increasing Christian interest in the Middle East. The development of its missions, different from those in other parts of the world, is closely connected not only with the growth of Western political influence in the region, but also with that of "geopiety" as expressed in pilgrimage and eschatological expectations. The blend of these three aspects, missionary, geopious and colonial, proved attractive to a considerable part of Western Christianity. (Murre-van den Berg 2006a, 17)

When analyzing missionary reports, the various motives behind the missionary project need to be considered—even if they are at times difficult to distinguish. Heleen Murre-van den Berg sees proselytizing of Muslims as the initial, though due to lack of practicability soon to be dropped, aim behind the early 19th-century Protestant missionary engagement in the Middle East. She also acknowledges the importance of the narrative of millennialism as shaping a minority of the missionaries' views on the salvational importance of the contemporary age and the particular role of the Middle East therein (Murre-van den Berg 2006b, 463–466). In his latest study, Kieser has put even stronger emphasis on the impact of millennialism. He suggests that the missionaries' quest when entering the "Bible lands" was in a fundamental way shaped by belief in the necessity of the restoration of a Jewish state in Palestine, and the concomitant fall of Islam as well as Catholicism as necessary preconditions for the inception of the millennial "Kingdom of God" (Kieser 2010, 15–16).

The American Board of Commissioners for Foreign Missions (hereafter ABCFM) was founded in 1810 in Boston by members of various Protestant churches. In the spirit of millennialism charted out above, it sent its first two missionaries to Western Anatolia (Smyrna, today Izmir) in 1819 (Kieser 2010, 41); in 1831, it created a base station in Istanbul (White 1940, 8). American missionary engagement in the Ottoman Empire began roughly at the same time when formal economic and political relations between the empire and the United States were established.[4] The first ABCFM missionaries to the eastern provinces of the Ottoman Empire were sent in 1830 to inquire into the conditions of the local Armenian and Syriac Christian communities. Already at that point the idea of "the conversion of Muslims and Jews was more or less abandoned, and the prospect became less apocalyptical. The 'revival' of the Eastern Christians and their empowerment emerged as central issues" (Kieser 2010, 44).

The real establishment of ABCFM missions in the eastern provinces began in the early 1850s, encouraged by an edict from the sultan in 1850, which, in response to Protestant pressure organized by the ABCFM office in Istanbul, allowed Protestants to form their own *millet*, a term that in that time indicated a recognized status of a community based on religion (Kieser 2010, 47; Erhan 2002, 324–325). The primary goal of the American missionary movement had by now definitely shifted to conversion of the various Christian groups of the Ottoman Empire—which they tended to regard as only "nominal" Christian—to the missionaries' understanding of proper Christianity, that is, Protestantism (cf. Murre-van den Berg 1999, 117–118). Unsurprisingly, the recognition of a Protestant *millet*, Protestant proselytizing among Eastern Christians, and the claim of the Protestants to represent the only real Christianity evoked resistance among the Greek Orthodox and Armenian Apostolic Churches (Kieser 2010, 47). At the same time, the idea of proselytizing among Muslims continued to appeal to many of the ABCFM missionaries and was propagated by some of them rather openly in the 1850s—especially after the *Hatt-ı Hümayun* edict from 1856, which was part of the Tanzimat reforms[5] and which they interpreted in a way that suggested a general freedom for everyone to choose her religion (Salt 2002, 155; Kieser 2000, 58). But, as Selim Deringil has shown, there remained a tension between Ottoman

---

4. The Ottoman-American Treaty of Trade and Navigation, which marked the beginning of formal diplomatic relations between the two states, was signed in 1830 (Erhan 2004, 5).

5. The series of Ottoman reform edicts from between 1839 and 1871 known as Tanzimat aimed at modernization (qua centralization and rationalization) of mainly the legal system and the bureaucratic apparatus, introduced basic citizenship rights, and promised equality independent of religion (Zürcher 2004, 56–66; Hanioğlu 2008, 72–108).

declarations of religious freedom in this time period and the state's policies with regard to religious conversion. According to Deringil, an important motive of Ottoman religion politics continued to be the defense of
the Islamic community against proselytizing (Deringil 2000, 556). The
Ottomans were displeased, to say the least, about reports of Muslim
subjects converting to Protestantism and saw this as a threat to public
order. Although the death penalty for apostasy had not been applied in
Ottoman lands since 1844, the missionaries were well aware of the risk
of life and social status for potential converts, and this limited the range
of the missionaries' activities. Overall, the proselytizing success of the
missionaries among Muslims remained negligible (Salt 2002, 155–166).

While proselytizing was the original and immediate aim of the missionary project, it remained not the only one. Kieser argues that "the
power of the Protestant movement resided in the synthesis of discourses
of the European Renaissance and the Enlightenment, and the new scientific discourse of ancient history in the 'Bible Lands'" (Kieser 2002a,
136). More fundamentally, he maintains, it was the millennial expectation of the ABCFM missionaries that made them work toward "a new
social and symbolic order, promoted by their own evangelistic, educative,
and civilizing efforts, and linking their modern belief in progress with
evangelical spirituality" (Kieser 2002a, 120). In other words, the millennialism of the early ABCFM converged with their understanding of
modernity (Kieser 2010, 15). This perspective shines also through in the
ABCFM missionaries' approach to the Kızılbaş-Alevis, whom they had
cast with "the Renaissance's and Enlightenment's concept of the noble
savage…[The Kızılbaş] seemed to be the ideal agent of the change the
missionaries hoped to promote in a Middle East seen as decadent and corrupted" (Kieser 2002a, 123).

Murre-van den Berg summarizes the ABCFM missionaries' goals of
modernization, which were more progressive and liberal than those of
other missionary groups, as including the establishment of good education for everybody (including women), domestic hygiene, efficient private and public households, fair commerce, democratic institutions, free
press, and women's rights (Murre-van den Berg 2006b, 465). From her
perspective, too, the missionary enterprise reflects a peculiar combination
of salvational and civilizational motivations, agendas, and justifications,
which were for the most part rationalized in a way that made them appear
as symbiotic, although they certainly sometimes were in tension with each
other (Murre-van den Berg 2006a, 13–17).

Searching for Origins

Western perspectives on the Kızılbaş-Alevis in the late Ottoman Empire were embedded in the complex web of scholarly knowledge, as well as political, and missionary agendas that informed Orientalist discourses on Anatolia, the Ottomans/Turks, and Islam. For example, European interest in Ottoman provinces displayed a clear Christian bias in that it increased proportionally to the amount of the Christian population living in a particular region. Conversely, the stronger the Muslim population in a particular area, the more one was willing to recognize the legitimacy of Ottoman rule (Boyar 2007, 37).[6]

This does not mean, however, that Western reports on Ottoman lands and its people, as long as properly contextualized, could not provide us with valuable information about Ottoman cultural and political contexts for which we have hardly any other sources. In the context of this study, I am mainly interested in what these texts have to say about the racial and religious origins, essence, and character of Kızılbaş-Alevism. The dominance of discourses that tried to mark the Kızılbaş-Alevis' difference (from Islam and the Turks) qua notions of religious and racial origins, which related them to non-Muslim and particular Christian people and traditions, is typical for 19th-century Western attempts to map foreign territories and thus subordinate and integrate them into Western imaginaries. Notions of race were part of positivist understandings of science, even if not always necessarily connected to racist arguments and politics. It should be remarked that categories of race and religion were at that time not yet that clearly differentiated from each other. It was, for example, not uncommon in evangelical contexts of that time period to speak about the "Christian race." Religions, in other words, were still often perceived as organically linked to a particular people.

The first outsiders we know to have established extensive contacts with Kızılbaş communities were ABCFM missionaries in the 1850s. Rev. George W. Dunmore, at that time stationed in Arapkir, was the first American missionary to write about them in 1854.[7] Dunmore, who had visited the region already in 1852, would establish the ABCFM mission

---

6. For an overview of 19th-century Western anti-Islamic stereotypes and their connection to the Western perception of Ottoman Christians see Salt (1993, 9–29).

7. In the following years, reports by ABCFM missionaries in Anatolia and the eastern provinces in the *Missionary Herald* regularly included information on the Kızılbaş.

in Kharput in 1855 (Merguerian 2006, 245). In his letter to the ABCFM headquarters, Dunmore characterized the Kızılbaş as "a sect of nominal Moslems." He observed their disregard for the Muslim ritual prayer and fasting, praised their openness to the Gospel as well as their belief "in Christ, the Son of God," but also lamented "some absurd notions and idol-atrous practices" (Dunmore 1855, 55–56).[8] Two years later he put forward the idea of the Kızılbaş being "descendants from a Christian stock, made nominal Moslems by the sword" (Dunmore 1857, 220). With regard to the only "nominal" belonging of the Kızılbaş to Islam, Dunmore was quickly seconded by other missionary colleagues. Jasper N. Ball (d. 1870), ABCFM missionary to the Armenians, explained, based on observations he made among Kızılbashes in the vicinity of Yozgat, that they would emphasize the predominance of the Bible as opposed to the Koran in their practice, and know Christ as being identical with Ali and God; further, their reli-gious rite would resemble the Lord's supper.[9] In short, "the Kuzzel-bashes cannot properly be considered Moslems. Their religion seems rather a mixture of Christianity, Moslemism and heathenism" (Ball 1857, 395).

The discourse that ABCFM missionaries established about the "nominal" Islam of the Kızılbaş mirrors closely the way they regarded Catholicism and the Eastern churches as merely "nominal" Christian. It was the Protestant self-understanding that Protestantism was the only true Christian faith, which justified the "true conversion" of non-Protestant Christians (Murre-van den Berg 2006b, 464). Parallel to this in its origins anti-Catholic rhetoric, the nominal Islam argument suggested to Protestant ears that the Kızılbaş were not real Muslims. Since the Ottomans rejected conversion of Muslims, the missionaries' argument was meant to open the door for proselytizing the Kızılbaş to Protestant Christianity.[10]

The ABCFM missionaries early on began to establish a discourse on the Kızılbaş around questions of racial and religious origins and mix-ture. Already in their first writings about the Kızılbaş, the missionaries from the ABCFM established the thesis of the Kızılbaş being proto- or

8. The annual report of the Arapkir mission to the ABCFM from the same year mentions that the "Kuzzel-bash," would "believe in Christ," and be "ready to receive the Gospel" (as quoted by Kieser 2000, 71). See also Anderson (2006 [1872], 179).

9. This is a reference to the most important Kızılbaş-Alevi ritual, the *ayin-i cem* ("Ceremony of Communion").

10. In the case of the Nusayris, too, ABCFM missionary accounts brought forward at times the argument that they would in fact be closer to Christianity than to Islam (Alkan 2012, 39–40).

crypto-Christians, and/or descendants from ancient inhabitants of Anatolia. Questions of the religious and ethnic/racial origins of the Kızılbaş would henceforth remain a major point of interest for Western Orientalists, missionaries, and diplomats. In the case of the Kurdish Kızılbaş it culminated, as I will show, in the theory of their descent from ancient Armenian stock, subsequently, but not totally, Kurdified and Islamized. To a certain extent, such origin speculations played into Western colonial ambitions in the region. They were resented by the Ottomans, who as a consequence themselves became increasingly interested in the Kızılbaş and began to encourage their assimilation into Sunnism. In this way, European discourses of difference (religious, ethnic, and racial) impacted on the perceptions and politics of religious and racial difference and sameness in the late Ottoman Empire.

Ultimately, the quest of establishing origins and defining essences is related to the modern project itself, and to 19th-century discourses on religion, race, and nationalism. Although aspects of these discourses have changed over time, the underlying concerns about boundaries and differences have been surprisingly stable until today. They still play an important role in academic and public debates on Alevism, even when recast in terms of identity, a framework more attuned to contemporary discourses of globalization, pluralism, and human/religious rights.

Kızılbaş-Christian Affinities and the Issue of Conversion

Affinities between Kızılbashism and Christianity, which Dunmore and Ball were the first to emphasize, were not self-evident to all of this early generation of American missionaries in Anatolia. An ABCFM missionary from Arapkir, Sanford Richardson, wrote a report wherein he does not indicate any such affinity. Still, he seems sympathetic to the possibility of conversion of the Kızılbaş and casts them in a manner reminiscent of the noble savage topos: "These Kuzzelbash...are a noble race, true children of nature, yet dark minded and ignorant of the only true way of salvation. Our hearts ache for them, and we long to tell them of that blessed Savior who died that they too might live" (Richardson 1857, 83).

In most cases, however, ABCFM missionaries' arguments for proselytizing among the Kızılbaş were linked to speculations about their Christian origins or affinities, suggesting a re-version to supposedly Christian roots. These efforts were internally debated in light of the pressures from the

Ottomans as well as the local (Oriental) churches resisting proselytism (Kieser 2000, 71–78).[11] Karakaya-Stump rightly suggests that "the particular ways in which the Protestant missionaries construed the Kızılbaş religion helped justify their missionary efforts among the Kızılbaş both legally and morally, as well as sustaining prospects for a possible conversion" (Karakaya-Stump 2004, 332). In other words, we have to assume that the quest for proselytizing impacted on the way in which the missionaries portrayed the Kızılbaş. From this perspective, the differences between Dunmore and Richardson in regard to the Kızılbashes' relationship with Christianity might not be unrelated to their respective positions on the question of Kızılbaş conversion to Christianity, which was judged more positively by the former than by the latter. Dunmore had concluded a report from 1854 by noting that "[t]he Turks seem to regard them [the Kızılbaş] very much as they do the Koords, as worthless heretics, and not worth caring for; and I think that no very serious trouble would come to them from that quarter, if they were to embrace the truth openly" (Dunmore 1855, 56). Richardson, on the other hand, was skeptical of the political feasibility of the conversion of the Kızılbaş to Christianity, although he, too, expressed his belief in the positive effect that such conversion would have on them. In the year of the *Hatt-ı Hümayun* edict (1856), when confronted in Arapkir with a group of Kızılbaş expressing interest in conversion to Protestantism, he responded rather cautiously, arguing that the risk for the converts would be too high and therefore such a step should not be encouraged (Richardson 1856, 296).

Other missionaries, too, recognized that the matter of the Kızılbashes' relation to Islam, or, more precisely, the Ottoman perception of this relation, crucially impacted on the possibility of converting them to Christianity. George B. Nutting was an ABCFM missionary stationed in Urfa. In the summer of 1860 he went to Adıyaman in order to sort out possibilities of establishing a local mission. In this context he first writes about "traces among them [the Kızılbaş] of Christian origin" and establishes the affinity between the local Kurdish Kızılbaş beliefs and ethics with Christianity, even reporting of a tradition among them according to which "in the last times a Christian teacher shall come to instruct them in the true religion." "[D]issatisfied with their own religion," he continues, they would be "waiting for the Gospel" (Nutting 1860, 345 and 346).

---

11. For an overview of missionary accounts from Anatolia in the 1850s and 1860s on the question of Muslim conversion to Christianity see Anderson (2006 [1872], 178–182).

While Nutting develops his case for engaging in active proselytizing of the Kızılbaş, he nevertheless argues that there needed to be caution for the moment due to their unclear status: "Though, according to the present laws of the empire, there is perfect liberty to preach to them, and perfect liberty for them to receive the Gospel, I have thought best to write for a special charter mentioning the Kuzzelbash by name, and as soon as it comes, there will be only the want of strength or of money to prevent our immediately commencing labor among them." Such a charter of course never materialized, and Nutting's optimism in that regard might seem to us, in hindsight, naïve. Still we have to consider that the missionaries, even if they might at times have gotten carried away by their hopes and ambitions, were in general good connoisseurs of Ottoman politics. Viewed from this angle, it is remarkable that Nutting was hopeful for Ottoman protection of the Kızılbashes' formal conversion to Protestantism. As he reasoned, "[t]he Moslems do not consider them [the Kızılbaş] as Moslems, and the only reason why they should oppose their evangelization is that now they have often opportunity to oppress them in various ways…and they fear that when they become Protestants we shall inform the powers above them of their oppressions" (Nutting 1860, 347).[12]

Nutting's report hints to the fact that the Ottomans were—at least prior to the reign of Sultan Abdülhamid II—rather ambivalent in regard to the degree to which the Kızılbaş-Alevis could be considered Muslims. Although the *Hatt-ı Hümayun* edict had promised an expansion of religious freedom, the question remained as to whether the Ottomans were in practice willing to tolerate Muslim or Kızılbaş conversion to Christianity. On the one side, as Dunmore and Nutting maintain, and this position is reiterated in a report that the ABCFM published a few years later, the Sunni Muslims did not regard the Kızılbaş as of their own kind.[13] However, the Ottoman historian İlber Ortaylı maintains that while the ulema and the people regarded the Kızılbaş as outsiders, the state did not consider them as non-Muslims (Ortaylı 1997, 206). The 19th-century Ottoman census practices support this view (see Karpat 1985). Ortaylı observes that Ottoman documents of this period on groups traditionally regarded as

---

12. It is interesting to note that in the editor's short introduction to Nutting's letter in the *Missionary Herald* a certain skepticism in regards to the missionary's elaboration, probably relating to his presentation of the Kızılbashes' affinities with Christianity, shines through (Nutting 1860, 345).

13. "The Kuzzelbashes in Eastern Turkey…are now regarded by the Turks as little better than infidels; nor are the Koords in much higher repute" (Anderson 2006 [1872], 178).

heretical within Sunni-Muslim Ottoman discourse, such as the Nusayri, the Druze, the Yezidi, and the Kızılbaş, are rather silent on the issue of their difference from Sunni Islam (Ortaylı 1997, 210–211). This fits well with the Ottoman position on Kızılbaş-Alevi conversion to Protestantism, which they regarded as apostasy. As the missionaries in contact with Kızılbashes who actually did convert to Protestantism report, such converts in most cases had to suffer discrimination by their social environment and some-times also by the government. And this did not change with the *Hatt-ı Hümayun*, despite the hopes of some missionaries, such as Dunmore. Unlike the Armenians who were, at least from the Ottoman perspective, free to convert to another Christian denomination, the Ottomans refused to accept Kızılbaş conversion to Protestantism. Nevertheless, Dunmore himself was as late as 1858 still hopeful about the prospect of conversion of Kızılbashes to Protestantism, although he, too, remarked that despite the 1856 edict the fear of repercussions was still great among the possible converts (Anderson 2006 [1872], 179). In fact, it proved that Richardson's caution from early on was well justified. Already in the 1860s the connec-tions between the missions and the Kızılbaş loosened and ABCFM reports about the latter tuned down their earlier enthusiasm.

The Ottoman interest in Sunnitizing the Kızılbaş, which became more pronounced under Abdülhamid II, was at least partially a response to the missionary interest in the Kızılbaş-Alevis (Karakaya-Stump 2004, 339–340).[14] The exact same dynamic has been observed by Necati Alkan with regard to the relations between the Ottomans and the Nusayris. While the Ottomans' perspective on the Nusayris prior to the Tanzimat was marked by ambivalence with regard to their religious status, generally referring to them with the same apologetic terms that they used in order to mark the Kızılbashes, with the Tanzimat, and increasingly so during the reign of Abdülhamid II, a remarkable semantic shift occurred, and official rhetoric began to count the Nusayris as belonging to the Muslim faith (Alkan 2012).

The Ottomans wanted to ensure the loyalty of the Kızılbaş-Alevis and other communities at the margins of the Islamic *millet* in a time when especially the eastern provinces with their various non-Muslim and non-Turkish populations became more of a political concern to them.

---

14. It should be noted that the Ottomans closely followed the publications of the *Missionary Herald* as well as other American publications of and about the missionaries (Deringil 1998, 125–127).

From that perspective it is understandable that the Ottoman state was concerned about foreigners' activities, and particularly the proselytizing activities of the ABCFM missionaries, in the area. Since the Ottomans would remain opposed to the conversion of the Kızılbaş, and the latter were when in close contact with Protestants subjected to intimidations and persecution, the missionaries "found themselves compelled to reduce their contacts with the Alevis to a minimum in the 1860s and 1870s...The ABCFM could not help the Alevis gain any improvement in their precarious social position."[15] Still, as Kieser continues, "many Alevis in the eastern provinces of the Empire continued to avow that they were 'Protes' (Protestants)" (Kieser 2002a, 123).[16] An example is the case of two Kurdish Kızılbaş-Alevi villages that in 1881 directed a—in the end unsuccessful—petition to the American mission in Erzurum asking for recognition as Protestants, even if apparently motivated less by religious reasons than by the hope to get exempted from the military draft (Kieser 2000, 167); correspondingly, it has to be noted that, viewed from the perspective of the Hamidian state,[17] its interest in recruiting loyal soldiers from among the Kızılbaş tribes was likewise motivation to Sunnitize the latter (Deringil 1998, 91). In this context, Kieser suggests that the beginning of the substitution of the term Kızılbaş by the term Alevi in the late Ottoman Empire was connected to the gradual opening of lower rank army and administrative positions to the Kızılbaş in this period (Kieser 1998, 283).

Even if he acknowledges that behind the Kızılbaş-Alevis' interest in Protestantism were also more material concerns, Kieser puts emphasis on their genuinely religious motivation. Protestantism, he argues, would have pushed them to introduce "reforms within Alevism to purify it from superstition and to promote the education of men and women" (Kieser 2002a, 123; see also Kieser 2000, 76–78); correspondingly, it "seemed

---

15. Contrary to Kieser, Murre-van den Berg observes a general reinvigorated proselytizing zeal among the American missionaries in the 1870s and 1880s, "facilitated by the growing Western influence in the region, which left less room for the Ottoman and Persian governments to oppose to such activities" (Murre-van den Berg 2006a, 7–8).

16. The existence of "ignorant Muslims" of Dersim who would recognize Protestantism is documented in Ottoman official correspondence from 1893 (Irmak 2010, 255). In an attached document to the earliest official military report on how to reform Dersim from 1896 it is cautioned to take measures against the local population's inclination to the Protestants' inducements (Akpınar et al. 2010, 328–331); Ottoman archival documents from the turn of the century continue to address the possibility of the Christianization of the Kızılbaş of Dersim by local missionaries and priests (Irmak 2010, 267).

17. That is, the Ottoman state under the rule of Sultan Abdülhamid II (r. 1876–1909).

to many Alevis to be the modern way out of discrimination and backwardness" (Kieser 2002a, 136). It certainly appears that at least some of
the Kızılbaş, and more strongly those of the eastern provinces, considered conversion to Protestantism to be a move that promised a brighter
future—provided that they could secure the support of the missionaries
and foreign powers to receive official recognition as part of the Protestant
millet. The material prospects that came along with the missionaries, such
as the establishment of schools and access to the missions' hospitals,
clearly were very attractive to many Kızılbaş. With the Ottomans making
clear their rejection of the Kızılbashes' conversion, the latter's inclination
toward Protestantism—which had been documented so meticulously by
ABCFM missionaries in the second half of the 1850s—appears to have
declined considerably.

Impact of the Missionary Work

In the analysis of ABCFM reports one needs to consider the motivations
and interests of the missionaries. Karakaya-Stump cautions that missionary reports should not be treated as neutral descriptions, but need to be
understood as literary texts that constitute their own genre consciously
written for a very particular North American audience upon whose support the missions depended (Karakaya-Stump 2004, 338–339). Some of
them might have exaggerated the successes of evangelization efforts,
hoping to secure further material support from their parishes back home
(Tejirian/Simon 2002, vi).

The role of the ABCFM missionaries in the region, and their impact on
the Kızılbaş-Alevis more explicitly, is difficult to generalize due to the complexity of the political context in the late Ottoman period. Evaluations of
their work need to reflect this complexity. Kieser, largely remaining within
rationale of modernism, shows much empathy with the missionaries and
credits their work as pursuing enlightened and modern values. He characterizes the ABCFM as "a human rights organization with accentuated
Christian orientation," which demanded equal treatment of Ottoman citizens, especially for Christians, and a liberal federal system (Kieser 2000,
526). For Kieser, the work of the missionaries needs to be evaluated in the
context of the dominant values that motivated their work, namely human-
ism, millennialism, and socioeconomic improvement (Kieser 2010). He
has even argued that a "most important legacy of the missionaries is their
approval of progress and modernization without being subject to the spell

of positivism, nationalism, and Social Darwinism" (Kieser 2002a, 140). A critical reader will note that Kieser's assessment of the missions' intentions mirrors the Protestant missionaries' self-understanding as catalysts of civilization rather closely. It needs to be asked whether he sufficiently takes into account that the missionary reports, on which his interpretations are mainly based, are themselves part of a complex conglomerate of interests ranging from legitimation of their own work to proselytizing and civilizing quests.

This said, it has to be acknowledged that Kieser recognizes the role of missionary activities in the cause of affairs that led to the escalation of intercommunal violence in Anatolia between the 1890s and the early 1920s. He critically remarks on the missionaries' inability to move beyond a discourse that was in its core anti-Islamic. Their support for non-Muslims, and to a certain extent also Kızılbaş-Alevis, created suspicions and misgivings and played into stereotypes of international anti-Muslim alliances, as well as into fears of Christian plans to divide Anatolia. While the educational work of the missionaries contributed to a renaissance of Christian consciousness in Anatolia, by the same token it also reified boundaries between ethnic and religious communities and exacerbated social envy. It would be far-fetched to hold the missionaries directly responsible for the anti-Christian violence during their presence in Anatolia. But the missionaries for the most part missed to see the broader societal responsibility of their work in the context of a time period in which the public enunciation of group identities and rights became more and more politicized. The missionaries simply did not reflect enough on the effect their work had on their environment and displayed a "lack of constructive engagement with the Muslim majority" (Kieser 2000, 535; see also ibid., 501 and 532–535).

Murre-van den Berg gives even more emphasis to the negative political impact that the missions had on local politics, and particularly the escalation of intercommunal violence since the last decade of the 19th century. In addition to the socioeconomic consequences of the missionary work, she also points to the missionary role in the formation of nationalism among the Christian communities, in particular the Armenians.[18] In short, the missionary factor needs to be considered when evaluating the dynamics

---

18. The impact of the missions on the formation of non-Muslim ethnic nationalisms, especially among Armenians and Syriac Christians, has variously been pointed out (Erhan 2004, 5–6; Murre-van den Berg 2006b, 463; Kieser 2010, 35).

that led to the violence that destroyed most of Anatolian Christianity in the last decades of the Ottoman Empire (Murre-van den Berg 2006b, 470).

The Kızılbaş as "Mixture" between Christianity and Islam

The discourse about possible Christian roots or affinities of the Kızılbaş and groups presumably related to them dates back to the earliest writings of the missionaries. It continued to be a theme that provoked the curiosity of foreigners, both missionaries as well as other Western observers. The following examples will show that the evaluations by different Western observers regarding which religious element was supposedly dominant in that mix varied considerably. The main emphases were on Christianity, Shia Islam, and paganism. As I will show in later chapters, the categorization of Kızılbaş-Alevism as a "mixture" or "syncretism" continued throughout the 20th century until today to be a major taxonomical device in the explanation and normalization of their otherness.

The ABCFM missionary Orson P. Allen from Kharput explained in a letter (no date provided) to his colleague Crosby Howard Wheeler that the Kurds in general would be "Mohammedans, at least in name," and have many rites that display a mixture of Islam, Christianity, and heathenism (Wheeler 1868, 47). The "Kûzzlebash", presented as a subgroup of the Kurds, would however be pantheist; while they accepted Christ as divine this would not mean too much since they also accepted other religious figures and living beings, as well as parts of nature, as divine (Wheeler 1868, 47–48). The British archaeologist Theodore Bent (1852–1897) speculated the following about the Tahtacı: "Perhaps in this secret form of religion we may be confronted with the survival of some heathen cult, perhaps it may be a half-formed or decayed form of Christianity" (Bent 1891, 270). His fellow countryman, the Turcophile politician and traveler Earl Henry A. G. Percy (1871–1909) characterized the Kızılbaş as "a mixture of Shiite Mohammedanism, Christianity, and Paganism" (Percy 1901, 90). Almost identically, Ellsworth Huntington (1876–1947), an American geographer and economist who taught between 1897 and 1901 at the ABCFM's Euphrates College in Harput, described the religion of the Kızılbaş as "a mixture of Shiite Mohammedanism and Christianity, with perhaps a trace of primitive paganism" (Huntington 1902, 186). For the Orientalist and explorer Fernand Grenard (b. 1866), the major quality of the Kızılbaş belief was clearly Christian, and he referred to them as a "corrupted Christian sect" that has incorporated Shiite elements (Grenard 1904, 514). An ABCFM missionary stationed at Antep, Stephen v. R. Trowbridge (born there 1881 as son of missionary parents), a few years later wrote about Alevi beliefs and networks in a rather detailed report, which he claimed to be largely based on "conversations with a well-known teacher [of Alevism]," with the objective "to investigate the nature of this faith," and "to consider the relations of the Alevi brotherhood with Islam and Christianity" (Trowbridge 1909, 340). As a result, he situated Alevism squarely between Islam and Christianity, although leaning more to Christianity and definitely "a religion other than Islam," full of "the mysticism and pantheism of the Orient" (Trowbridge 1909, 352).[19]

Evaluations of the mixture theme similar to those by Percy and Huntington related above we find in the various articles of George E. White (b. 1861), who was from 1890 to 1921 stationed at the Merzifon mission in the Amasya Province, where he since 1913 served as Dean of Anatolia College (founded in 1886).[20] White described the Kızılbaş-Alevis—whom he also called "the Shia Turks" and of whom he notes that "they prefer the name 'Alevi' for themselves"—as a mixture of paganism, Islam, and Christianity. Differing from many of his colleagues, he put particular emphasis on the pagan element within this mixture. Trying to figure out "what their religion really is," he suggests that part of it "is pure paganism, some of which in historic origin antedates either Mohammedanism or Christianity" (White 1908, 228). Elsewhere he reasons that "such survivals from primitive culture would be most abundant among the most simple and ignorant. And these are the Alevi folks, whose standard forms shelter much that is a relic of the times of pure paganism" (White 1913, 692). The writings of White, reflect the impact of an evolutionist concept of religion that measures religious maturity by Protestant standards. In White's case this is expressed most strongly in his emphasis on scripture and the importance he attributes to accepting Christ as savior (see White 1907, 163; 1908, 229).

Despite the asserted dominance of pagan elements in the religion of the Kızılbaş-Alevis, White also engages, if carefully, the question of their

---

19. The article is interesting in the way it presents information in a question-and-answer style with the Alevi informant. The latter responds to inquiries about Alevi faith, as well as rather particular ones on theological matters, such as questions regarding Christ, scripture, and the Holy Spirit, and the whole interview has an almost catechistic character.

20. For the history of the Merzifon mission and Anatolia College, see his autobiographic book, which includes valuable information on local Anatolian history and inter-communal relations from the missionary perspective (White 1940).

Christian roots. His observations on that matter are, however, rather formulaic, and he appears to remain ambivalent about it. On the one side we find repeatedly in his writings the assurance that "[t]here is more truth...than is sometimes realised in the claim of Shia Turks, that less than the thickness of an onion skin separates them from Christians" (White 1907, 161; cf. White 1908, 230; 1913, 697). He also repeatedly points out that it would be "very generally affirmed that they [the Shia Turks] secretly observe a debased form of the Lord's Supper" (White 1908, 231; cf. White 1907, 161; 1913, 696; 1918, 245; 1940, 55).[21] In two texts he himself affirms this latter assessment remarking that "our Alevi neighbours have a ceremony resembling the Lord's Super" (White 1913, 697) and that "[i]t is at least possible that this ceremony is a heritage from forefathers of Christian name and faith" (White 1918, 246). In the end, however, White stops short of explicitly endorsing the thesis that the Kızılbaş-Alevis' religion needed to be classified as somewhere in between Christianity and Islam, which had been rather widespread among earlier ABCFM missionaries.

As with the reports by earlier missionaries, White's evaluations are to a certain extent influenced by the question and hope of eventual conversion of the Kızılbaş-Alevis: "For all their efforts to win divine favour, to escape from the burden of sin, to face the future life without fear, they find no real satisfaction, no peace of heart. Some day, in some manner, they will come to understand the meaning of the life and work and teaching of Christ, and then,—would that I might be there to see!" At the same time, he constantly laments the Alevis' ignorance: "their particular ideas of fate, pantheism, and the transmigration of souls make it difficult for them to grasp Christian doctrine" (White 1908, 236).[22]

The idea of religious mixture figures also prominently in a report by the British Captain Louis Molyneux-Seel (d. 1915). Based on observations and conversations relating to the Kızılbaş Kurds from the Dersim province, he

---

21. We find an almost identical phrase in the above-mentioned report by Ball. Elsewhere White reports that "[s]ome believe that in the hour of agony induced by persecution, Christians turned just far enough towards Mahommedanism to escape further alienation, but stopped with the Alevi form of the faith, instead of becoming fully orthodox" (White 1913, 697; cf. White 1918, 244).

22. It is worthwhile to note that White was addressing an audience that went much beyond evangelical circles. White published his main articles on Kızılbaş-Alevism not in the *Missionary Herald*, where most of the earlier ABCFM missionary reports on the subject appeared, but in the *Journal of the Victoria Institute* (Great Britain), a forum for evangelically inclined philosophy, as well as in respected secular scholarly periodicals such as *Muslim World* and *The Contemporary Review*.

suggests that "they must be considered as Mohammedans of the Shiite branch, although their religion contains practices and beliefs borrowed from Christianity." In easy flow he translates terms from Kızılbaş religious institutions into Anglican terminology and vice versa: "[t]heir hierarchy contains the dignitaries Seid [*seyyid*][23] or priest, Murshud [*mürşid*] or bishop, Murshuden Murshudu [*mürşidîn mürşidi*][24] or archbishop" (1914, 64). Molyneux-Seel also writes about their "religious rite resembling the Christian Communion, the identification of Ali with Christ and of the twelve Imams with the twelve Apostles" (1914, 67). Here, as well as in similar earlier accounts by American missionaries, the translation of Kızılbaş-specific terminology into Christian terms creates familiarity for a Western audience, and helps to nourish hopes about their conversion.

Reverend Henry H. Riggs (1875–1943), born in Sivas as the son of missionaries and himself ABCFM missionary in Harput (1903–1910), developed a similar theory about the religious origins of the Dersim Kızılbaş Kurds, whom he considered to be "far nearer to the Christian faith than the Orthodox Moslems" (Riggs 1911, 735). His description of Kızılbaş-Alevi beliefs and practices is based on the explanations of a Dersim *seyyid* whom he calls a friend. Based on this informant he underlines the difference of Kızılbaş beliefs from "orthodox Islam" and their similarity to Christianity. It certainly sounded appealing to Protestant ears to hear about the centrality of "a faith that is for some of them at least, a vital and personal life-relationship," and about the "idea of God's immanence" in the Kızılbaş religion, especially if contrasted against a Sunni Muslim faith that is characterized as formalistic and superficial, epitomized in the "elaborate mummeries and genuflexions of the five daily prayers," which Riggs ridicules as "a travesty on prayer" (Riggs 1911, 737). The pejorative description of mainstream Sunni practice, with prayer formula called "mummaries" (a common Protestant trope to denounce Catholic prayer rituals),[25] functions as negative matrix against which the closeness of

23. The title *seyyid* (Arab. *sayyid*) connotes descent from the prophet Muhammad. The members of the sacred lineages of the Kızılbaş-Alevis, who alone are allowed to lead the main rituals, are said to be *seyyid*. In Turkish language contexts they are mostly called *dede*, while among Kurdish-speaking Kızılbaş-Alevis the title *seyyid* is more common.

24. In Sufism, as well as in Bektashism and Kızılbaş-Alevism, the *mürşid* provides religious guidance to the initiated of lower ranks. The title *mürşidîn mürşidi* ("guide of the guides") is given to somebody who has reached a level on the religious path qualifying him to provide guidance to other *mürşids*.

25. Special thanks to Adam H. Becker for pointing this out to me.

the Kızılbaş to Christianity is established. Also, his explanation that while "[i]n too many cases among Moslems religion is a thing clearly apart from life," the Kızılbaş seyyids, on the other hand, "lay great emphasis in their exhortations on the oneness of religion and life" clearly mirrors conventional distinctions between Protestantism and Catholicism (Riggs 1911, 740). Having given considerable thought to the question of the origins of this "strange and attractive religion" and its people, Riggs concludes that "the Kurds of the Dersim, and some other tribes, while accepting Mohammedanism in name, and losing their Christian religion, yet were only partly transformed, and have gradually developed a religion which keeps, under the name of Islam, much of the spirit and some of the forms of Christianity"—and of the Protestant kind in particular as he seems to suggest (Riggs 1911, 741 and 742).

Riggs was not the first to draw comparisons between the Sunni/Kızılbaş and the Catholic/Protestant religious schisms, respectively. Grenard had pointed out a few years earlier that what mattered in the religion of the Kızılbaş according to their own testament were not their formulas and deeds, but the sincerity of faith and the pureness of the heart. In this way, he argued, they were the "Protestants of Islam" (Grenard 1904, 513).[26]

While the notion of religious mixture was one of the most consistent themes in Western descriptions of the Kızılbaş-Alevis in the late Ottoman Empire, it needs to be emphasized that in some Western travel and academic literature from the mid-19th century onward (mostly European and particularly German) speculation about Christian remnants among the Kızılbaş, be they based on religion or race, is totally absent. In a considerable number of these texts, the Kızılbaş, where mentioned in passing, are portrayed as degenerated Muslims, largely in line with apologetic Sunni prejudices. Variously they are brought into connection with immoral religious practices in their rituals (Lerch 1857, xviii), described often as wild orgies where the "sexes are mingling irrespective of age or family relations" (Gilbert 1997 [1873], 203);[27] referred to as "heretic Mussulmans," probably representing "the dying remnant of an original population... never thoroughly converted to Islam" (Hogarth and Munro [1893], 90) and as

---

26. The parallelism between the Alevi/Sunni antagonism on the one side and the Protestant/Catholic difference on the other is a theme that until today figures prominently in discourses about the religious quality of Alevism.

27. This is the standard Muslim prejudice against the Kızılbaş and other groups at the margins of Islam, which also entered Western discourses. For another example see Driver (1922, 198).

"unorthodox Muslims...loathed by the orthodox Turks" (Ramsay 1897, 105); or characterized as "bad Muslims [*schlechte Muselmänner*]" (Grothe 1903, 67).[28] Less pejoratively, the British traveler and politician Mark Sykes (1879–1919) described the practice of the Dersimlis, who pretended to be Shiites—and whom he interestingly does not call Kızılbaş (a label that he did use for other groups)—as "a mixture of magic and nature worship" (Sykes 1908, 467). The German geographer, Orientalist, and propagandist of German interests in the Ottoman Empire Hugo Grothe gives also little credit to theories of Christian affinities or origins of the Kızılbaş, Tahtacı, and Bektashi. He points instead to commonalities with other ethno-religious groups at the margins of Islam, such as the Nusayri, Yezidi, and Ali-Ilahi (Grothe 1912, 149 and 155 fn 1); he also puts forward the hypothesis that these groups might originate from a common source religion and be connected ethnically (Grothe 1912, 156).

It appears that racial categorizations are more prominent in German-language scholarship, while theories that bring the Kızılbaş in affinity with Christianity tend to be stronger pronounced by Anglophones and especially by American missionaries. This contrast is reflective of differing political and intellectual interests. As discussed above, a major framework for American missionaries was a certain religious romanticism based on the discourse of the "Bible lands" that conceived of Anatolia within the sacred landscape of Christianity and connected this Christian romanticism, which carried within itself a millennial promise, with the hope of discovering remainders of an ancient Christian heritage. This vision enhanced the legitimacy and feasibility of evangelical work. European explanations of the Kızılbaş-Alevis' difference, on the other hand, were often relatively more inclined to racial/ethnic explanatory frames. For many European observers, the religious features of the Kızılbaş-Alevis were, although observed with curiosity, of secondary interest. In European discourses of the late 19th and early 20th centuries, differences between people were debated around notions of race and culture, which were likewise important in the justification of colonialist and imperialist projects of that time. In other words, while the primary interest of the missionaries was evangelical in a way that merged goals of conversion and local development of the "nominal" Christian communities, European incentives in

---

28. A few ABCFM missionaries regarded the Kızılbaş in similarly pejorative ways. George F. Herrick from Merzifon, for example, referred to them as "so called Protestants," who were, however, "though nominally Mohammedans, really *heathens.*" (Herrick 1866, 68).

the Ottoman-Turkish lands tended to be driven by a mixture of scholarly, imperial, and bourgeois interests. Ideal-typically we can therefore distinguish between two Western discourses about Kızılbaş-Alevi difference in the late Ottoman period: (1) an American/Protestant/missionary discourse constructed around notions of religious difference, and (2) a European/positivist/bourgeois discourse based on notions of cultural and racial difference. The following presentation of discussions by Western observers on the relations between Kızılbaş-Alevis and Armenians will help to illustrate how these two discourses converged. The matter of these relations would become highly relevant in the future positioning of Alevism within the context of an emerging Turkish nationalism.

Kızılbaş-Armenian Relations in the Western Imaginary

The first mention of possible Armenian-Kızılbaş racial relations that I could trace is by J. G. Taylor, British consul for Kurdistan, in a report based on explanations, received during a Dersim journey in 1866, from Ali Gakko, a Kızılbaş Seyyid who had converted to Protestantism. Taylor distinguishes between two groups of Dersim Kurds, namely the "Seyd Hassananlees," a Zaza-speaking settled people who had a long time before migrated from Khorasan and, more recently, from Malatia to Dersim, and the "true Deyrsimlees," who spoke Kurdish and lived a pastoral life higher up in the mountains. The latter would be "without doubt the descendants of the original Pagan Armenian stock existing there even before Christianity. The former [the Seyd Hassananlees]...influenced the latter, who in time imperceptibly accepted the tenets professed by the Hassananlees and grafted Karmathic[29] upon their former mixed Christian and Pagan ideas" (Taylor 1868, 318). In short, the older, Kurmanci Kurdish-speaking Kızılbaş of Dersim would be descendants of Armenians only secondarily turned Kızılbaş by immigrating Zaza Kurds.[30]

Variations of this theory also appear in later texts by American and British observers. In an official report of the ABCFM on its missionary activities since the early 19th century we find the general assessment that

---

29. Probably meaning as much as Karmathian, in the sense of an obscure Islamic sect.

30. In contemporary Western literature on the ethnic relations in the eastern provinces one can find occasional references to certain mixing between Kurdish tribes and Armenians. These references are, however, not part of theories of common origins of the two groups. For examples, see Blau (1858, 584), Sykes (1908).

"[t]he Kuzzelbashes in Eastern Turkey have a tradition that their Christian ancestors were compelled to become Mohammedans" (Anderson 2006 [1872], 178). Huntington categorized the Kızılbaş as, next to the Zaza and "Kurman,"[31] one of three subgroups of the Kurds. He considered them, resembling Taylor's account, "a mixed race, the foundation being some tribes of a stock allied to the Persians, who advanced into Turkey along the central highlands. These mountains were inhabited by Armenian Christians, who under stress of persecution became nominal Mohammedans and inter-married with the invaders" (Huntington 1902, 186).

Huntington's description is interesting in that it shows how at this point in time the religious, lingual, and racial boundaries of the groups under question were not yet necessarily distinguished. While the terms Zaza and Kurmanci usually signify language groups, and the term Kızılbaş is a category that is normally used to mark religious difference from Sunni Islam, Huntington differentiates between Kızılbaş, Kurmanci, and Zaza as subordinated to the ethnic/racial category of "Kurd." Such lack of categorical differentiation can not only be reduced to analytical sloppiness. It also reflects a conceptual space in which religion is not yet totally secularized. Religion still makes sense as an aspect of life related to ethnic belonging. There are other examples. The already mentioned Hugo Grothe suggested that the differences between Sunni and Kızılbaş Kurds were not merely of religious nature, but corresponded to a perceivable anthropological difference (Grothe 1912, 148 and 160). Similarly, the British archaeologist and historian David George Hogarth (1862–1927), a companion of T. E. Lawrence, wrote with respect to the Dersim Kurds that they were "more in sympathy with the Armenian Christians than with the Osmanlis. Indeed, they have been said to be actually crypto-Christians of Armenian blood" (1908, 558).[32] Most closely resembling the above-mentioned account by Taylor are the relevant sections of a report by Molyneux-Seel on his journey in Dersim in 1911, published when he was newly appointed British vice consul at Van. Relating information received from Armenian clerics, he describes the Dersim Kurds as racial Armenians only secondarily converted to Shiism by Zaza-speaking Muslims, who would have imposed their language on the new converts. Kızılbashism would therefore be a product of the interaction between Christianity and Shiism (Molyneux-Seel 1914, 67–68).

---

31. The term must refer to the Kurmanci-speaking Kurds.

32. He also reports that the Dersim tribes were "regarded as practically pagan [by the Turks]" and rather belonging to Shiite than to Sunni Islam (Hogarth 1908, 558).

The theory of racial relations between Kızılbashes and Armenians was supported also by German-language Orientalists. The work of the Austrian ethnologist and physical anthropologist Felix von Luschan (1854–1924), a specialist in craniometry who since 1881 regularly participated in scientific expeditions to Anatolia, may be considered the apex of racialist theorizing of Kızılbaş-Alevi origins.[33] Based mainly on the results of comparative cra-niometric work, he argued in his first publication on the subject that the Tahtacı of Lycia,[34] who would "name themselves Allevi," would be descen-dants of the pre-Greek Anatolian population, which would physically be identical with the Armenians (Luschan 1886, 171).[35] In a more comprehen-sive study on the subject a few years later, he reports that the Tahtacı were called "Allevi" and were anatomically identical with the Bektashis.[36] In the same text, he also further elaborated on the theme of strong physical similarities between the Armenians and the "Tahtacı and their relatives," which he explained by theorizing their common descent from the origi-nally supposedly homogenous, ancient population of Anatolia (Luschan 1889, 212). Later he would add further "sectarian" groups to this pedigree.[37] All of these groups as well as the Armenians (and also the Persians) were descendants from the Hittites (Luschan 1911, 241–244).[38]

---

33. On life and work of von Luschan see Ruggendorfer and Szemethy (2009). For a dis-cussion of his ideas about race as embedded in late 19th-century scientific discourses see Laukötter (2007, 91–124). Von Luschan was a racialist, but not a racist, meaning his distinc-tions between the trajectories of different races were not based on ideas of racial purity and hierarchies derived thereof. He believed in monogenesis and explicitly argued against ideas of racial purity, which he attacked, especially in his later work, as naïve and unhistorical (Luschan 1922, 1–13; Laukötter 2007, 107–112).

34. The provinces of Antalya and Muğla in modern Turkey.

35. The same information is provided by Bent a few years later, using the exact same spell-ing ("Allevi"), what might indicate that he is drawing on von Luschan as an unacknowledged source (Bent 1891, 269).

36. This is awkward since the Bektashiye is a Sufi order (into which all Muslims can prin-cipally be initiated). He probably has in mind particular tribes somehow associated with Bektashism.

37. "[T]he Kyzylbash (and the Yezidi) correspond absolutely with the Tahtaji, the Bektash and the Ansariyeh [Nusayri], so that we find a small minority of groups possessing a similar creed and a remarkable uniformity of type, scattered over a vast part of Western Asia. I see no other way to account for this fact than to assume *that the members of all these sects are the remains of an old homogenous population, which have preserved their religion and have therefore refrained from intermarriage with strangers and so preserved their old physical characteristics.*" (Luschan 1911, 232)

38. It is worth mentioning, and points to the fact that these kinds of racial and religious theories of origins were part of broader politics, that von Luschan would in a later work from

With modifications in the details, von Luschan's ethno-racialist speculations would be reiterated by other researchers. The Scottish archeolo-
gist and New Testament scholar William Mitchell Ramsay (1851–1939),
who traveled extensively in Asia Minor between 1880 and 1884, compared the Tahtacı, with explicit reference to von Luschan's work, to early
Christians, Nusayri, and Yezidi. He ignored, however, von Luschan's speculations about the shared racial traits with the Armenians (Ramsay 1897,
286–287). Grothe, on the other side, completely concurred with von
Luschan's theory about the common racial origins of Bektashi, Tahtacı,
Kızılbaş, and Armenians and their possible common descent from the
Hittites (Grothe 1912, 157–159).

The attraction of theories that connect the origins of the Kızılbaş to
ancient Anatolian civilizations found yet a new expression in the work
of the German geographer Richard Leonhard (d. 1916). His ethnographic
observations on the Kızılbaş of Galatia (Central Anatolia) convinced
him that parts of the Kızılbaş were descendants of ancient layers of a
pre-Turkish Anatolian population, only to a small extent mixed with later
immigrants. According to his theory, the physical and somatic particularities of the Kızılbaş could be explained by assuming that they constituted the least mixed vestiges of the Galatian population, which, due to
its energetic character and its seclusion in the mountains, would have

---

1922 slightly but distinctively revise his theory. In this general work, written for a broader
audience with the expressed aim to clarify and complicate the question of race, he integrated
much of the referenced texts from 1889 and 1911 verbatim. More interesting, however, is
what he chose to omit, namely his earlier theory of close racial relations between "sectarian groups" such as the Tahtacı, Bektashi, and the Kızılbaş with the Armenians. He still
held that the mentioned Muslim sects would be racially linked and related to the aboriginal
people of Anatolia, but now totally omits their connection to the Armenians, which he previously had strongly emphasized (Luschan 1922, 105). As in his 1911 article he suggests that
the Armenians would be the racially most homogenous, least mixed group of Anatolia, and
direct descendants from the Hittites; but he does not connect them any more with any other
Anatolian group (Luschan 1922, 142–145). What is further noteworthy—and totally absent in
his earlier articles—is the pejorative tone in which he writes about the Armenians, whom he
characterizes as devious, extremely fertile, unreasonable, politically foolish, and disloyal citizens. He goes even so far as to remark that the most recent tragic events during the war (he
mentions explicitly the "cruel mass murder" in the context of the Armenian deportations)
would be rather understandable given their political disloyalty to the Ottomans (Luschan
1922, 141). It is not possible to deduce from this information the reason that made von
Luschan so drastically change his interpretation of the Armenians. But it seems likely that
this new, negative reading of the Armenians constituted some kind of apologetic reaction to
the Ottoman massacres of the Armenians during World War I, which had been committed
to a certain extent under the eyes of German military advisors. Since Austrians were allies of
Germans and Ottomans during the war a certain sense of indirect complicity and thus a felt
need for such apologetics can probably be inferred.

found the strength to marshal "inner resistance against Islamization by
sticking to the beliefs and cults of Christianity" (Leonhard 1915, 365). The
American Board missionary White was likewise attracted to the idea that
the "Alevi Turks probably come nearest to representing the original inhabitants of Asia Minor," the present culture of which would rest "on earlier
strata, [and] the earliest of which that can be distinguished is the Hittite"
(White 1918, 244; cf. White 1940, 55).[39] Last but not least, Xavier de Planhol
reports with regard to the Tahtacı that some Orientalists even speculated
about their connection to ancient Jewish tribes (Planhol 1958, 368).

At this point, some general observations on the relationship between
missionary literature and the mostly academic writings provided by other
Western observers on the Kızılbaş seem appropriate. It can be remarked
that, with exceptions, both the missionary and the academic discourses
on the Kızılbaş, and groups in their vicinity, seem rather self-contained
with little cross-referencing. On the other hand, two facts that need to be
considered in evaluating the relationship between the missionary and the
scholarly accounts point to a more intrinsic connection between them.
First, the earliest missionary accounts of the Kızılbaş, which focused on
religion and speculations about Christian affinities, were soon to be followed by similar non-missionary Orientalist writings. Second, the major
themes of racial, cultural, and religious character and origins in the two
discourses were similar, sharing largely identical terminological and
semantic frameworks.

In their treatment of the theme of religious and racial origins and mixture, both missionary and non-missionary Westerners' perspectives on
the Kızılbaş-Alevis reflect a worldview that may be marked as modernist, rationalist, and Orientalist and as concerned with categorizing otherness in terms of religious, cultural/civilizational, and racial difference.
From within these discourses the Kızılbaş-Alevis were marked both by
their difference from Sunni Islam as well as by their difference from the
Westerners' own ideals about correct religion. The rationalization of the
Kızılbaş-Alevis as "religious mixture," established already in the earliest
writings about them, continues, recast as religious syncretism, to be a
major theme in discourses about them until today and contributes to the

---

39. Already earlier he had argued, based on personal observation of an artificial hill close to
the shrine of Hacı Bektaş (Kırşehir province), that the pottery fragments to be found there
would bear striking resemblance to Hittite examples, and that therefore "the inference is
inevitable that the Bek Tash shrine goes back in its original foundation to the times when
the Hittite civilisation overspread the country" (White 1913, 695).

rationalization and normalization of their religious difference. Considering the dominance of Turkist interpretations of the Kızılbaş-Alevis since the 1920s (to be discussed in the following chapters), it is remarkable that the notion of Kızılbaş-Alevism being related to Turkish culture is virtually nonexistent in discourses about them until the early 1910s.

(World) Religion Discourse

Based on important earlier philological and historical shifts in the evaluation of religion, the 19th century witnessed the formation of a Western discourse that constructed the content, structure, and historical meaning of religion as a universal (Masuzawa 2005; cf. Mandair/Dressler 2011). The evolution of this world religion discourse, which strongly impacted on the Western perceptions of the Kızılbaş-Alevis in the late 19th century, was part of the secularization and differentiation between spheres of knowledge in Western science. As a result, religion was redefined as a distinct sphere of human experience and practice, and the study of religion evolved gradually as an academic discipline independent of theology, philosophy, and philology. In the 19th century, the sciences played an important role in creating a European self-understanding as a mature civilization based on rational "modern" principles and institutions. The irrational was externalized from Europe by means of two other concomitantly emerging academic disciplines, whose purpose was to create knowledge of non-European cultures and religions, namely anthropology and Oriental studies: "every region of the non-modern non-West was presumed to be thoroughly in the grip of religion, as all aspects of life were supposedly determined and dictated by an archaic metaphysics of the magical and the supernatural ... [T]he supposed predominance ... of religious and supernatural elements was believed to mark tribal society as decisively different from modern European society" (Masuzawa 2005, 16–17). In short, the disenchantment that modernizing Western societies had undergone demanded the existence of an enchanted other that was found in the peoples, cultures, and religions of what was imagined to be "the Orient."

The discourse of (world) religion operates by means of simultaneous strategies of othering and familiarization. On the one side, it others non-Christian religions against the universalized norms created based on Christian/Protestant ideals. On the other side, the universalization of Christian/Protestant standards for religion simultaneously leads to a leveling qua generalization of what so far appeared as particular about the Christian example. Masuzawa argues that "throughout the nineteenth century, endless speculations on the differences and similarities between religions continually provided opportunities for modern Europeans to work out the problem of their own identity and to develop various conceptions of the relation between the legacy of Christianity on the one hand and modernity and rationality on the other" (Masuzawa 2005, 18). Insofar as it proved the rational secularity of Christian Europe in face of the irrational, religious East, the world religion discourse was also "a discourse of secularization" (Masuzawa 2005, 20).

The discourses that Western travelers, scientists, and missionaries developed concerning the religious origins and character of the Kızılbaş-Alevis are part of the modernizing/secularizing dynamics described by Masuzawa, in which complex civilizational, missionary, and political motivations came together. Of course, the Protestant American missionaries were not secularists in the same sense as contemporary European scientists and bourgeois travelers. But while they were men and women of the Gospel, who believed in the salvational quality of the scripture and faith in Christ, their Protestant concept of religion was in itself secular and secularizing in the sense of promoting a rationalist worldview and an understanding of religion that may be described as disenchanted in strong contrast to what they observed as superstitious and irrational practices and beliefs. The following account of American Board missionary White illustrates how this Protestant concept of religion could be applied simultaneously to Christianity and Islam:

> As it is intrinsically clear that the generations that accepted Christianity carried with them into the Church much of what they formerly held as heathen, so Mohammedanism as practiced is mingled with much that was never known to the Prophet. What is neither from the Scripture nor from the Koran must be of Pagan origin; a survival from primitive times which nominally ended nearly twenty centuries ago; and so far as the same superstitions are held, the same ceremonies practiced by people of different races and creeds, thus far there is a common bond among them all. (White 1908, 150)[40]

---

40. The idea of a scripture-based religion polluted over time is modeled on the Protestant critique of heathen elements within Catholic Christianity (see above).

(World) Religionizing the Kızılbaş-Alevis

The main aim of the first part of this chapter was to illustrate how Western observers from the mid-19th century onward initiated with their discussions of the Kızılbaş a discourse of religious and racial difference that played a central role in the evolution of the modern concept of Alevism. Both the race discourse, with a focus on Anatolian origins of various sorts, and the religion discourse, which included speculations about Muslim, Christian, and various heathen influences, were rather speculative and comprised conflicting assessments. This in itself is a reflection of the fact that an authoritative discourse on Kızılbaş-Alevism, at least one that went beyond the language of Sunni Muslim apologetics, was not yet established. The fascination with the theme of origin was part of an Orientalist discourse obsessed with classifications of the foreign by means of categories shaped according to normative standards of Euro-American Christianity. This classification was made possible by means of a universalist approach to religion, which presented itself as egalitarian, but in practice cast Muslims, Orthodox Christians, and Kızılbaş-Alevis as others in relation to perceived standards of modern Christianity.

The Kızılbaş-Alevi case provides us with a window into the consequences of the application of a distinctively Western discourse of religion on non-Western sociocultural formations. I argue that the assessment of the Kızılbaş-Alevis by means of a universalized Christian/Protestant model of (world) religion with a focus on ethics and faith (rather than ritual), as well as on scripture (rather than alternative sources of charisma, such as descent) has to be situated within the broader politics of imperialism and religion in 19th-century discourses on non-European cultures. Creating and organizing knowledge about the Kızılbaş-Alevis by means of the category religion helped to structure and make understandable what at first encounter appeared as foreign and difficult to situate for Western observers. The concept of religion helped to justify proselytizing and civilizing missions since it related them to notions of socio-cultural underdevelopment and religious backwardness or degeneration.

A further accomplishment of the Western discourse on religion was its tendency toward homogenizing differences within what was understood to be distinct religious formations. The focus on Kızılbaş-Alevism's otherness from in particular Sunni Islam enhanced a perception of sameness of the various *ocak*-centered groups traditionally called Kızılbaş and subordinated perspectives that emphasized the ethnic, linguistic, and

religious differences among them. This homogenizing pressure, in addition to the double-bind of universalist orientation and reification of its
Christian rooting, is emblematic for the colonial project itself. A prominent early 20th-century scholar on the Kızılbaş-Alevi and Bektashi traditions whose work exemplifies this is the British anthropologist and
archaeologist Frederick William Hasluck (1878–1920). His posthumously
published article on the "Heterodox Tribes of Asia Minor" was "the first
serious attempt to assess critically the available data on the subject from
the perspective of an historian" (Karakaya-Stump 2004, 330). This article,
which he unfortunately had no chance to finish, marks an important point
in the establishment of Kızılbaş-Alevism as an internationally recognized
subject of scholarly research. Hasluck was the first scholar to undertake a
critical review of earlier literature on the Kızılbaş-Alevis and groups seen
as familiar to them.

Hasluck observes, correctly, that Western observers so far had displayed a strong tendency to conceptualize the "heterodox tribes of Asia
Minor" (among which he counted the Yörük, the Turcoman, the Kızılbaş,
the Tahtacı, and the Bektashis)[41] as "an originally Christian population
half-converted to Islam…[T]he supposed converted Christians are naturally assumed to be a pre-Turkish, and, in default of evidence to the contrary (which is never forthcoming), an aboriginal population" (Hasluck
1921, 310–311). Hasluck criticized this categorization not since he would
have denied any plausibility to the argument of Christian and "aboriginal" traces existing among these groups. As a matter of fact, his entire
work displays a deep interest in disentangling the mutual influences
between the cultures and religions, especially Islam and Christianity, of
the Balkans and Anatolia.[42] Rather he argues that such traces are secondary to two more dominant sets of "influences" on these "heterodox tribes",
namely the "primitive stratum of religion, which survives in superstitious

41. The groups mentioned by Hasluck are not tribes in the literal sense. Yörük and Turcoman
(that is, Turkmen) are broadly used terms—sometimes distinguished from each other and
sometimes used as synonyms—that refer to Turkic nomad tribes of the Oğuz branch. The
Tahtacı, lit. "Woodworker," a name they acquired by way of their specialization in woodwork,
are a purely Turkish-speaking, very exclusive subgroup of Kızılbaş-Alevism with strong ethnic features. They are mainly found in the Aegean and Mediterranean coastal regions of
southwest Turkey (a region stretching over the provinces from Balıkesir to Konya, with a
concentration in Antalya) and they have a series of customs distinguishing them from the
rest of the Kızılbaş-Alevis. See Kehl[-Bodrogi] (1988). For detailed information on ethnic,
tribal, and/or socioreligious groups in Turkey see Andrews (1989).

42. See the edited volume dedicated to Hasluck by Shankland (2004a).

practice among Christians no less than Mohammedans," and Shiite Islam (Hasluck 1921, 311). As for the Kızılbaş-Alevis in particular, he concludes: "It is fairly apparent that the predominating element in the Kyzylbash religion is *Shia* Mahommedanism, and the secondary Christian, the whole having a substratum of pagan animistic elements" (Hasluck 1921, 337).

It needs to be remarked that in Hasluck's text there is no explicit mention at all of the possibility of the impact of pre-Islamic Turkish traditions on the "heterodox tribes" of Anatolia, which would become the dominant matrix for the Turkish nationalist interpretation of these groups in the 1920s. Until the late 1910s, the idea of a connection between "heterodox" Islam and Central Asian pre-Islamic Turkish culture was not yet part of the Western imagination of Kızılbaş-Alevi roots, and (as I will show in chapter 3) had only just begun to enter the discourse on that subject. The morphology of religion that Hasluck employed in his characterization of the Kızılbaş-Alevis is particularly revealing and exemplifies world religion discourse at work. In his already mentioned article ("Heterodox Tribes," 1921) one subchapter is dedicated to "the religion of the Kyzylbash." This subchapter is essentially a survey of mainly academic Western writings on that topic. It is organized by categories that could be taken from any standard course book on world religions: "Theology," "Mythology," "Hierarchy," "Fasts and Feasts and Public Worship," "Private Prayer," "Sacred Books," "Pilgrimage," and lastly "Marriage" are discussed in that order (Hasluck 1921, 332–337). Drawing on and closely following the account by Grenard (1904, 516–518) mentioned above, Hasluck organizes Kızılbaş practices through the generalized language of Christianity:

> The Kyzylbash have neither mosque nor church, but both sexes meet for prayer at the house of the *Seid* [Seyyid] on Fridays. They have a perverted mass: the priest chants prayers in honour of Christ, Moses, and David. Water is consecrated by the priest dipping a stick into it. There is a public confession of sins, which are punished by fines: lights are put out while the congregation mourns its sins. When they are re-lighted, the priest gives absolution, and, having blessed bread and wine, gives a sop to the congregation. Morsels (*loqma*) of the flesh of a sacrificed lamb are given at the same time. Known evil livers are not admitted to the service. (Hasluck 1921, 335)

At first sight, the categorization of not-yet-established religions through the criteria of those historical formations already recognized as religions (primarily Christianity, and to a certain extent also Judaism and Islam), might be regarded as an emancipating act. However, the integration of religiocultural groups by means of the world religions discourse also undermines the specificity of those who are integrated, subjecting them to the discipline and semantics of the new discourse. Categories such as theology, mythology, immanence and transcendence, private prayer, sacred books/scripture, and God are not neutral analytical tools, but reflective of a specific understanding of the contours of "religion" with specific ideas about its structure and texture, distinctions between historical and mythological truth claims, as well as private and public spheres historically rooted and indebted in Western, that is, Christian, and in fact dominantly Protestant, experiences, ideas, and socioeconomic developments.[43] Analogies drawn between the differences among Kızılbaş and Sunni Muslims on the one side, and Protestants and Catholics on the other need to be scrutinized from that angle, too. Such categorization requires the assumption of clear boundaries between religions, which is also a precondition for talk about mixture—in the evolving grammar of the comparative study of religions these assumptions would then eventually be rationalized and reified in the concept of syncretism.

Obviously Hasluck did not share the missionaries' civilizationist and proselytizing ambitions, which naturally made them favor interpretations of the Kızılbaş-Alevis that suited their agendas. Also, his historical training and knowledge of Islamic and Anatolian history made him aware of the parallels between the "heterodox Islam" of Anatolia and other "heterodox" Islamic practices, and in this respect he recognized in particular the prominence of elements of Shiite Islam in Kızılbaş-Alevism. But if we compare the structure of Hasluck's concept of religion with that of the missionaries and other Western observers of the Kızılbaş-Alevis then we also see strong similarities. His criticism of previous Western observers' descriptions of the Kızılbaş-Alevis remained in the end one of historical detail and did not extend to the structure and epistemic assumptions of the formative categories, such as religion and religious mixture, that were until then, and would henceforward continue to be, employed in the study of Kızılbaş-Alevism.

---

43. On the historical and semantic work of the concept of religion see Mandair and Dressler (2011).

What Hasluck shared with the missionaries as well as other Western observers was that they evaluated Kızılbaş-Alevi practices and beliefs in regard to their relation to Islam, Christianity, and various other religious traditions of the broader Middle Eastern context by means of a formulaic set of categories considered constitutive of "religion."

Ottoman Reform and the Institutionalization of Religious Difference

In the second half of the 19th century, when a Western discourse about the Kızılbaş-Alevis began to form, the political interest of the Western powers in the Anatolian and eastern provinces of the Ottoman Empire was growing immensely. Even if the motives behind the Western interest in the early discussions about the origins, as well as the political orientations of the Kızılbaş were complex, some reflection on the broader historical contexts of their arguments is in place. While the Kızılbaş issue was presented by the missionaries as one of religious freedom and salvation, for the Ottomans it was an issue of political loyalty and hegemony. For the various Kızılbaş groups themselves, as far as we can deduce from the relevant sources and as far as it is possible to make general statements about them, a variety of things were at stake ranging from religiocultural and political independence to more material issues, such as economic and social development. The following pages try to elucidate the historical context that formed the political background based on which the Ottoman perspective on the question of ethno-religious difference in general, and the issue of Kızılbaş-Alevi difference in particular need to be evaluated.

The legal reforms that were to introduce equal citizenship rights in the Tanzimat-reform period had unintended consequences. From the perspective of those non-Muslim religious communities that were recognized by the Ottomans as religious communities (*millets*), such as the Greek Orthodox and Armenian churches, the formal acknowledgement and specification of their rights came together with internal shifts in the power relations of the communities. The *millets* were secularized in the sense that their bourgeois lay classes were given a more pronounced role in the organization and representation of their communities. The Tanzimat reforms thus increased ethno-religious consciousness and intensified competition among the religious communities, thus politicizing ethno-religious identities and preparing the ground for nationalist discourses (Yavuz 1993, 184; Zürcher 2004, 61–62). They were an important step in the re-signification of the non-Muslim communities into "minorities" whose rights were protected by the state. The minorities' supposed preferential treatment as a consequence of European interference raised questions with regard to their loyalty to the Ottoman state and prepared the ground for seeing them as outside of the Ottoman and later the Turkish nation.

Ussama Makdisi engaged comprehensively with the question of the impact of the Tanzimat reforms on inter-communal relations. Focusing on 19th-century developments in Lebanon, his important study *Culture of Sectarianism* discusses the role that politics of sectarianism have played in the eruption of intercommunal violence in Ottoman lands since the 1860s. Makdisi explains this violence as a consequence of the Tanzimat reforms, in which increased European pressures (in particular regarding the status of the non-Muslim communities) and Ottoman modernizers' aims to centralize the state's rule and increase control over the peripheries came together (Makdisi 2000, 8–12). For Makdisi, religion now became "the site of a colonial encounter between a self-styled 'Christian' West and what it saw as its perennial adversary, an 'Islamic' Ottoman Empire" (Makdisi 2000, 2). The multiethnic and multireligious empire was perceived by many Westerners as an essentially "Muslim state with large [Christian] 'minorities,'" who were subjugated and in need of liberation both from Islam as well as their own degenerate interpretations of Christianity (Makdisi 2000, 10). In this manner the notion of religious difference became with the Tanzimat reforms a powerful rhetorical instrument in the articulation of political claims and a new civil rights discourse. The new discourse of religious rights would, combined with nationalist rhetoric, play an important role in the formation of sectarian communal consciousness and intercommunal conflicts. It lined up nicely with the religious awakening of the Ottoman Christians, which found support in the missionary work.

The Tanzimat reforms soon became a site of misunderstanding between the Ottomans, who saw the proclamations of equality as part and parcel of Ottoman and Islamic traditions, and the European powers, who made the mistake of interpreting them as an appropriation of contemporary European discourses of religious differences and rights, and viewed them "as a mandate for intervention on behalf of the empire's non-Muslim subjects" (Makdisi 2000, 57). Europeans would take the Ottomans' treatment of its Christian populations as the yardstick of the empire's successful modernization. Pointing to the role of the modernization dynamic in the emergence of sectarianism and intercommunal violence,

Makdisi takes issue with the secularist view of history that has interpreted sectarianism as remainder of a premodern era that needed to be overcome. Against this narrative, which suspects traditional, irrational religion behind the Middle East's purported failure to modernize, Makdisi argues that sectarianism is intrinsically related to the formation process of nation-states and as such itself a modern phenomenon (Makdisi 2000, 2–7 and 166–167). His study is one of the rare and rather recent examples of scholarship on Ottoman history that has problematized secularist assumptions about the relation between religion, nationalism, and modernization.

There is no doubt that 19th-century Ottoman modernization contributed to an increasing consciousness of communal difference. The differentiating, disciplining, and normalizing forces unleashed in the processes of modernization and nationalization naturally impacted the Ottoman peoples' awareness of religious boundaries and difference. An example for the dynamics of colonial encounter and religion-making through which communal identities were shaped in the context of 19th-century Ottoman modernization is the agreement between colonial (British) and imperial (Ottoman) powers to partition Lebanon parallel to religious lines in 1842 (Makdisi 2000, chap. 5). These dynamics also had an impact on the Muslim perception of religious difference within its own tradition, reflecting a "process of religious standardization" that narrowed the space for forms of religious practice different from Sunni "high culture" (Gelvin 2002, 117).

When trying to summarize the most important developments and historical forces that nurtured the religionization of communal politics in the late Ottoman Empire, the following factors need to be considered: (1) the impact of the encounter with colonial Europe, and in particular the reception of Western discourses of religion and political rights; (2) the institutionalization and secularization of religious difference as a criteria for the sociopolitical organization and representation of recognized religious communities during the Tanzimat reforms, which led to the strengthening of the status of the recognized non-Muslim communities, and also (3) the boosting of the centrifugal forces unleashed by spreading ethno-religious nationalism, which then also inspired (4) the formation of an Ottoman nationalism (Ottomanism) in which people aspired to a trans-religious and trans-ethnic national identity based on the Tanzimat's principals of equality. The force of Ottomanism was, however, impeded by (5) reservations of the minorities, who did not want to loose their privileges guaranteed by agreements (so-called capitulations) between their European mentors and the Ottoman state.[44] In addition, (6) the evidence of Ottomanism declined in the last decades of the 19th century under Sultan Abdülhamid II, who mobilized Islamic symbols and institutions to strengthen inner-Islamic solidarity (Yavuz 1993, 187–192; Deringil 1998, 46–50). Ottomanism in this way gradually gained a more and more Islamic orientation, partially in conflict with the ideals of general citizen rights established during the Tanzimat reforms (Gelvin 2002, 121–123). Following the Balkan Wars (1912/13), Ottomanism began to gradually lose its hegemonic position to Muslim Turkish nationalism. In the last decade of the Ottoman state and the early decades of the Turkish Republic, the establishment of a secularist Turkish nationalism based on ethno-religious community boundaries would eradicate the previous privileges of the minorities and establish, discursively as well as physically, the political and economic superiority of the Muslim-Turkish population (Aktar 2003 and 2009).

The Kızılbaş in the Context of Ottoman and International Politics

William F. Ainsworth (1807–1896), geologist, medical practitioner, and traveler, wrote in 1842 the following about the Nestorians (Syriac Christians): "This sudden interest, so explicitly and so actively shown on the part of other Christian nations, towards a tribe of people, who have almost solely prolonged their independent existence on account of their remote seclusion, and comparative insignificance, has called them forth into new importance in the eyes of the Mohammedans, and will undoubtedly be the first step to their overthrow" (Ainsworth 1842, 255). Remarkable about this sentence is less its pessimism with regard to the future of the Syriac Christians than the sensibility it reflects with regard to the dynamics between international interests and local politics, and their impact on marginal groups, who in this way receive in its effects rather ambivalent

---

44. Paraphrasing Fatma Müge Göçek, Shissler writes that "the capitulatory regime in the Ottoman Empire caused the commercial bourgeoisie to emerge unevenly, favouring the Christian millets (non-Muslim religious communities) and encouraging their transformation into separate national communities rather than their dissolution into an Ottoman citizen-state" (Shissler 2003, 15–16). Fikret Adanır has argued (discussing Kieser's *Der verpasste Friede* at an event sponsored by the Human Rights Association of Istanbul, Jan. 29, 2011) that in the late Ottoman context both the minorities and the missionaries tended to be skeptical about secularization measures since they were seen as a threat to the capitulations, which stipulated privileges for the non-Muslim *millets*.

attention. As a matter of fact, the Western interest in the Christians of the Ottoman Empire in general was part of the scenario that would make possible the intercommunal violence in Anatolia in the late Ottoman period with its catastrophic apogee in the Armenian Genocide during World War I. The Western discovery of the Kızılbaş-Alevis and speculations with regard to their origins—in particular theories about their racial and religious affinities with Christianity—, too, had unintended political repercussions for them. In other words, the impact of Western religiocultural and political imperialism needs to be considered when evaluating the Ottoman approach toward the Kızılbaş-Alevis.[45] Religious difference was not the only factor that stimulated Ottoman interest in the Kızılbaş-Alevis. Other political factors, which require a broader perspective, were involved. For that reason it is imperative to get at least a brief overview of the most important actors and their interests as they played out in East Anatolian politics during the late Ottoman Empire. The following section will try to contextualize three main factors of this complexity: (1) the communal relations between Kurds and Armenians in general, and between Kurdish Kızılbaş and Armenians more specifically; (2) Ottoman regional interests; and (3) foreign states' political and religiocultural interests in the region. I will start with the last factor.

The most important foreign nations that had, in the broadest sense of the term, political interests in the eastern provinces of the Ottoman Empire were Russia, the British Empire, the United States, and Germany. The Russians' regional interests were imperial in the classical sense. Already in 1828 Russian forces entered Anatolia, apparently applauded by the local Armenian population. When they withdrew in the following year, many Armenians followed them in fear of reprisals. The consecutive Russian conquests in the Caucasus made them permanent neighbors to the Ottomans, and the Russians' official request in 1853 to be recognized as protector of all of the Ottoman Orthodox population contributed to the Ottomans' suspicions with regard to the political loyalties of the Anatolian Christians (Gaunt 2006, 46–47; Joseph 1983, 80; Zürcher 2004, 53). Following the Ottoman war with Russia (1877–1878) and the Russian conquest, sanctioned by the Berlin Treaty (1878), of the northeastern provinces of Kars, Ardahan, and Batum, which had large

---

45. The religiocultural aspect of imperialism is a particularly under-researched aspect in the historical evaluation of Ottoman politics in the eastern provinces from the mid-19th century onward.

Armenian populations and were adjacent to Kurdish-Armenian provinces in the south, the Russians became an even greater threat to Ottoman sovereignty in the eastern provinces. Russian-Armenian relations began increasingly to be perceived as a political threat to the Ottomans. At the same time, as Michael Reynolds has recently shown, the Russians by 1908 also gave secret support to rebellious Kurdish groups (Reynolds 2011). The German operations, on the other hand—in contrast to Russia Germany was not in direct competition, but acted in cooperation with the Ottomans—were at this stage mostly economic, although their political and military influence in the region increased considerably. It is also important to note that Germany supported the pan-Islamic politics of Abdülhamid II, which had been partly motivated by an urge to sharpen the Ottomans' religious profile against non-Muslim cultural and political claims and reflected hopes for international Muslim solidarity, as well as ambitions of Ottoman mentorship to Muslim communities outside of the empire—Muslim-dominated territories within Russia included (Zürcher 2004, 82; Gaunt 2006, 46–47).

The interests of the United States in the Ottoman Empire remained until World War I restricted to economic and diplomatic relations (Kieser 2010, 37). Tejirian and Simon argue that, considering the nature of U.S. foreign politics prior to World War I, ABCFM missionaries cannot be said to have been a tool of imperialism (Tejirian and Simon 2002, ix). Still, one may argue that, even if not directly sponsored by the U.S. government, the American evangelical movement, and the ABCFM missions in particular, were part of a subtle cultural imperialism that aspired to territorial gains in a metaphorical (evangelical) sense, aiming to reconquer the "Bible lands" by spreading the message of Christ among "nominal" Christians and other "wrong-believers" (mainly Muslims) as well as heathens. This kind of missionary zeal we also find in the Great Britain of that period, here interwoven with rhetorical justifications of colonialism. Salt remarked with regard to European Christian anti-Turkish and anti-Muslim stereotypes that in the 19th century evangelistic fervor in Great Britain rose to a peak: "Other Christians, Muslims and even the heathen were in dire need of the gospel and if proof were needed of the superiority of the Christian message, there it was amid the material triumphs of European civilisation" (Salt 1993, 11–12). It is not surprising then that the British, who had following the Berlin Treaty through their observers (consuls) in the eastern provinces gained a strong political position in the region (see below), were mostly sympathetic to the American missionaries—British diplomats, more influential than their American colleagues, often supported the latter.[46]

The aspirations of both ABCFM missionaries and British Orientalists broadly speaking reflected the general interest in the West in this period to redefine the political landscape of the eastern provinces. In this context they began to favor Armenian independence and were interested in strengthening the Christian position culturally and politically. The formal Ottoman recognition of a Protestant *millet* in 1850, which provided mostly Armenian converts to Protestantism with their own recognized church, had been a first and important success of this politics.

As already mentioned, part of the Ottoman reaction to the close relations between the Christian missionaries and the Kızılbaş-Alevis, as well as to reports about actual and aspired conversions was to show stronger inclination to perceive and present the Kızılbaş-Alevis as nominal Muslims. Given the fragile hegemony of the Ottomans in the eastern provinces, the question of the relation of the Kızılbaş-Alevis to Islam and their loyalty to the Ottoman state carried significant weight. In this context, Ottoman Islamization politics became more focused in the early 1890s. Examples are programs for the training of Kızılbaş imams, the distribution of Sunni Muslim catechisms, the building of schools, as well as the appointment of religious instructors and the construction of mosques in Kızılbaş villages (Deringil 1998, 82; Akpınar 2012).

A side effect of this Islamization politics was that it necessarily brought the religious difference of the Kızılbaş-Alevis into sharper focus (Kieser 2010, 56). Although these measures have not yet been studied in detail, the efforts by the Ottoman state reflect an increasing interest in the Islamic peripheries of the empire and mark the beginning of a more active engagement with Kızılbaş difference—even if limited to assimilative measures. An official exchange from 1898 illustrates this change in politics. Ahmet Şakir Paşa (1838–1899), Ottoman general inspector for Anatolian reform, was informed in 1898 about missionary attempts to convert Kızılbaş-Alevis to Christianity and about very good relations that Alevis entertained with Armenians and Protestants (Karaca 1993, 77). He reacted with orders to focus on the children instead of the adults and to teach them proper Sunni doctrine. The same measures should be taken with regard to "those people

---

46. Ramsay (1897, 223–224); Karakaya-Stump (2004, 339); Erhan (2004, 13–14); Anderson (2006 [1872], 99 and 120). There were, however, exceptions to this general support (Anderson 2006 [1872], 89).

of corrupted dogma (*bozuk akaide*) that are called 'Kızılbaş' and claim Alevism (Alevilik)" (as quoted in Karaca 1993, 128).[47]

An Alevi Renaissance?

It is extremely difficult to establish a coherent picture of the various Kızılbaş-Alevi groups' own perceptions of their social and political relations with their Muslim and non-Muslim environments, the Ottoman state, and the missionaries. It is clear that the Kızılbashes' relations with the state were strained and that they mostly rejected the more outright pressures to assimilate. For example, it is often reported that the Kızılbaş-Alevis tended to ignore the mosques that the state had constructed in their villages under Abdülhamid II (White 1908, 228).

Kieser has gone the furthest in trying to find general answers to the question how the Kızılbaş-Alevis responded to their changing political environment in the late Ottoman Empire. He situates the formation of an Alevi identity in this time, arguing that two periods in particular were significant in that process. The first was the Tanzimat period, during which he finds indicators of an increased Alevi self-awareness. This new awareness would have been sparked both by the possibilities opened up by the reforms and by the contact with American missionaries culminating in the growing desire among some Alevis to be recognized as Protestants, seeking in this way emancipation from Ottoman-Sunni tutelage. Kieser even talks about an "Alevi renaissance" in this context (Kieser 2002a, 136). The second, rather short period that he has likewise termed "Alevi renaissance" comprises the years immediately following the Young Turk revolution from 1908, for which he observes the awakening of a quasi-national consciousness among some Kızılbaş-Alevis in the eastern provinces. He regards 1908 as a watershed that "led the Alevis for the first time since the Kızılbaş uprisings of the 16th century to an open and collective confession of their identity. It allowed for the valorization, possibly also the spread of the suppressed confession" (Kieser 2000, 392). As indicators of this new Alevi consciousness, he provides examples such as a report by ABCFM missionary White, who interpreted the Alevis' engagement in building schools as sign of an "awakening of an Alevi national consciousness" (White 1913, 698; Kieser 2000, 392).

The Alevi renaissance perceived by Kieser needs to be questioned for a number of reasons. First, the amount of empirical evidence that

---

47. For more examples of such concern of provincial Ottoman officials with assimilating the Kızılbaş see Deringil (1998, 82); Kieser (2000, 168–169).

would warrant such a description is rather scarce (the writings of exactly two American missionaries to be precise) and one has to consider that the missionaries had their own, very particular views of the role of the Kızılbaş-Alevis—views that need to be evaluated within the context of the missionaries' own politics. I concur with Fikret Adanır, who has remarked that Kieser approaches the developments in the late Ottoman eastern provinces largely from the perspective of the missionaries, even if he is concerned with maintaining a critical perspective.[48] Second, there is the problem of the diversity of the Kızılbaş-Alevis as a social group, which makes generalizations that suggest a much higher degree of coherence among them problematic; such generalization under one term (Alevi/Alevism), at that time only sporadically used as self-designation by some Kızılbaş groups, bears the danger of a methodologically questionable back-reading of history based on more recent conceptual conventions. Of course, it is entirely possible that some Kızılbaş-Alevis did see the world and themselves in the way the missionaries, and through them Kieser, represented it. There is no reason to doubt, for example, the stories of Kızılbaş-Alevi converts to Protestantism and the reality of some Kızılbaş-Alevi groups seriously aspiring to a social and religious transformation. The degree to which singular accounts of such instances can be generalized is, however, debatable. I would maintain that the evidence is simply too incidental, too locally specific, too sporadic to warrant far-reaching generalizations. Third, and connected to this point, I would be careful with the implicit projection of tropes of decline and revival as done by Kieser when using terms such as "renaissance" and "reaffirmation." Such terms themselves are reminiscent of the language of modern nationalism and religious revivalism, and suggest a long-term continuity of Alevi identity among the Kızılbaş-Alevi groups under question, which is itself (as I argued in the introduction) in need of critical investigation.

Deteriorating Intercommunal Relations in the Eastern Provinces

The close relations between Kurds and Armenians raised particular curiosity among Western observers, and suspicion among the Ottomans. Trying

---

48. Adanır discussed Kieser's *Der verpasste Friede* at an event sponsored by the Human Rights Association of Istanbul, Jan. 29, 2011. At this event, Kieser explained the normative motivation behind the book as humanist, written with the aim to restore the dignity of the people of the eastern provinces.

to analyze and explain these relations, various, often interrelated, theories about the relations between Kurds, Kızılbaş, and Christians (Armenians and Syriac), and the peaceful cohabitation between Kurds (Kızılbaş or not) and Armenians, as for example in the Dersim region, were advanced. Some historical background will be necessary to situate this theorizing and to illustrate the significance of Kurdish-Armenian relations in the second half of the 19th century in the context of regional and international politics.

The eastern provinces had already since the 1820s, when Russia seized the previously Persian-dominated eastern Armenian territories, been under the impact of Ottoman-Russian competition for political influence. In the course of the 19th century, the intercommunal relations between the two largest populations in the eastern provinces, the Kurds and the Armenians, as well as between Kurds and Syriac Christians in the Southeast, deteriorated gradually. As discussed above, the Tanzimat reforms and the positive discrimination they were reasoned to have established for the Christian subjects of the empire played a significant role in this process. An illustration for that is offered by a certain O. Blau, who reports that the governor from Toprakkale, usually a Kurd, would have separated Armenians and Kurds in Alashgird (today Eleşkirt, in the province of Ağrı), who used to live in shared villages, with the result that their villages would now be neatly separated, either Armenian or Kurdish (Blau 1858, 595). Farther south, Kurdish tribes used to live until the early 19th century in close relations with Syriac Christian tribes. With increasing political turmoil in the larger region, these relations deteriorated rapidly since the early 1840s, leading to some local massacres of Syriac Christians.[49] The missions in the region played a role in the dynamics that led to the massacres. Missionary work has been argued to one-sidedly benefit the local Christians and thus exacerbated social envy. Western/ European ambitions in the region and the missionaries' direct contact to the High Porte were regarded by the Kurds as a threat to their regional hegemony. However, as Wadie Jwaideh underlines, the major reason for the regional violent erruptions can be found in the High Porte's desire to advance the Ottoman position in the area, which was achieved by manipulating the relations between the Kurds and the Syriac Christians (Jwaideh 2009, 144–148).

The violent conflicts had important consequences that would influence the further development in the eastern Ottoman provinces. For one, they

---

49. The major victims of increasing intercommunal tensions in this period were, however, the Yezidis (Jwaideh 2009, 119–124).

increased the mistrust between the involved communities in the affected areas. Further, the massacres of Syriac Christians became known internationally, and the European powers began to observe the developments in the region more closely and intensified pressure on the Ottomans regarding the welfare of the empire's Christians. On the other hand, the deterioration of communal relations in the east provided the Ottomans with a pretext to reassert their authority in areas that were so far largely autonomously ruled by Kurdish notables, and often only nominally, or to a rather limited extent, under Ottoman control. Already since the 1830s, the Ottomans had begun to assert their authority in the eastern provinces more forcefully against the local Kurdish leaders (Jwaideh 2009, 114). Ottoman concern with the Kurds further increased in the context of the implementation of the Tanzimat reforms in the 1840s (Soylu 2010).

We can further observe that in various ways, since the middle of the 19th century, the role of religion gained weight in regional politics. For example, since Ottoman centralization efforts cut the influence of tribal leaders, the role of Sufi shaikhs as mediators in political conflicts increased (Gaunt 2006, 29–32; Bruinessen 1989, 302–308). To repeat this important point, the Tanzimat reforms that the Ottomans undertook in the middle decades of the 19th century have to be situated within the context of a felt need to centralize and establish more rational and economic mechanisms of state control. This had consequences for the interaction between the state and its people, as well as between the various communities, the ethnic and religious differences of which were increasingly underlined by state regulation and evolving international rhetoric of minority rights. Matters of religious difference and intercommunal conflict, which used to be resolved on the communal level, became thus drawn into much larger political contexts (Deringil 2000, 566).

It is important to understand that the Tanzimat reforms with their focus on matters of religious freedom and equality were perceived by the Muslims of the empire within the context of sovereignty. Deringil wonders to what extent the Tanzimat reforms might have "caused a panic among Muslims, who felt that their hitherto dominant position was threatened" (Deringil 2000, 567). Due to their ethno-religious composition, the eastern provinces were more vulnerable to intercommunal tensions than the relatively more homogenous western and central Anatolian provinces. In the east, the Turkish-speaking Sunni Muslims—that is, the in-general-most-loyal and less-suspect subjects of the Ottomans—were largely outnumbered by Kurds (Sunni and Kızılbaş), Armenians, Syriac Christians, as well as other ethno-religious groups of smaller size.

The Ottoman-Russian War put the Ottoman position in the east under additional pressure. The following Berlin Peace Treaty (1878) not only legitimized Russian suzerainty over several northeast Anatolian provinces, but also initiated a discussion on how to improve the political situation of the Armenians, among whom national aspirations had begun to develop already since the Tanzimat reforms (Joseph 1983, 81). Russian support for the Armenians had become more explicit during the negotiations leading to the Berlin Peace Treaty (Joseph 1983, 84). Its final version acknowledged the minority status of the Armenians and obliged the Ottomans "to introduce reforms to improve the conditions of the Armenians, and to safeguard them against Circassian and Kurdish aggression" (Gaunt 2006, 38). The European powers interpreted the treaty as granting them the right to oversee the reforms that the Ottomans agreed to carry out in the "Armenian" provinces. To monitor this process, the Americans, British, French, Germans, and Russians established consulates in the East Anatolian and Mesopotamian provinces of the Empire. The consuls reported developments with regard to the state of the Christians of the eastern provinces back home and in this manner in particular "the issue of the 'Armenian Question' became a major theme of foreign policy discussion throughout the world." The international support and recognition of the Armenian case created an important momentum in the formation of an Armenian nationalism. Its militant activism would enhance anti-Armenian and anti-Christian sentiment among Ottoman Muslims and also create a rift between the Ottoman Armenians themselves (Gaunt 2006, 39). In his memoirs, ABCFM missionary White describes the Berlin Peace Treaty as a rather tragic historical event since on the one side it had made promises to the Armenians that would not be fulfilled and thus became one of the roots of Armenian militant nationalism, and on the other side it "angered the Turks by interfering with their authority in the country" (White 1940, 27).[50] At the same time, Muslim Ottoman nationalists such as Namık Kemal (1840–1888) began to target the non-Muslims, who were suspected to be in alliance with foreign interests and due to the capitulations unduly privileged in comparison to the Muslims. The Tanzimat reforms,

---

50. White gives the following haunting account of a young Armenian revolutionary from Amasya, explaining the strategy after nothing had been done following the Berlin Congress: "It seemed necessary for the Armenians themselves to take the lead, to create disturbances by insurrection to show the Europeans that Turks could no longer control or protect the Armenians, or maintain order in the country. They pledged their lives . . . to the sacred cause. They would shed blood if necessary, and they would not spare their own blood. Then the Europeans would remember the Armenians and their promises in behalf of the Armenians and would come to their help" (White 1940, 48).

which had encouraged notions of equal citizenship, enabled non-Muslim communities and Western missions to build modern schools in provincial towns and encouraged non-Muslims to participate more actively in politics. These developments, however, created, together with the special Western interest in the Armenians, considerable social envy among the Muslim population. This envy would trigger a nationalist reaction that soon began to reverse the positive effects of the Tanzimat for the non-Muslim communities (Gaunt 2006, 48–50; Kieser/Schaller 2002, 13–14; Joseph 1983, 87).

Confronted with the possibility of further loss of sovereignty in a period when their power, in particular in the Balkans, was dwindling, the Ottomans tried to increase their hold over the eastern provinces. In particular they began to more actively manipulate the ethno-religious differences and rivalries in the eastern provinces, which they feared could get out of control (Joseph 1983, 86). During the reign of Abdülhamid II, Ottoman control over the eastern provinces was guided by fear of ethnic and religious nationalism and separatism, further Russian advances, and anti-Ottoman political alliances. It is from within this context of contested sovereignty in the eastern provinces that the Ottomans were afraid of the Kızılbaş-Alevis moving toward active opposition against the state. Old prejudices with regard to the supposed inherent tendency among the Kızılbaş toward political subversion are likely to have contributed to that perception. In 1880, there were rumors of concrete attempts, under the leadership of the Dersim Kızılbaş, to form a Kurdish-Armenian alliance (Kieser 2000, 121–122).

Confronted with the possibility of a broad anti-Ottoman coalition between Kurds, Christians, and Kızılbaş-Alevis, the Ottomans, instead of functioning as a neutral broker between these groups, decided to enhance the rivalry between them, usually by aligning themselves with local Sunni (mostly Kurdish) leaders (Kieser 2000, 23–25 and 123–124). In 1891 the Ottomans founded the Hamidiye regiments, which were recruited from Sunni Kurdish tribes. These regiments, the leaders of which were directly subordinated to the sultan, were intended to improve the military presence at the borders with Russia and Iran, quell Armenian sectarianism, and prevent the formation of a Kurdish nationalist movement.[51] This move

---

51. Şapolyo reports that the Hamidiye units also attacked Kızılbaş Kurds, especially in Dersim (Şapolyo 1964, 286). It is generally claimed that Kızılbaş Kurds would not have been admitted to the Hamidiye regiments (Beşikçi 1969, 175; Kieser 2000, 145). However, the story seems to be more complicated. Janet Klein has recently shown evidence that the Ottomans at least played with the idea of including Kızılbaş and Yezidi Kurds (Klein 2011, 50–51). Ottoman official correspondence further documents the request by certain Dersim tribes to be recruited into the Hamidiye (Irmak 2010, 261; cf. Akpınar et al. 2010, 319).

strengthened Kurdish power in the east and helped to enhance the loyalty of the Kurds toward the Ottomans, but was to the detriment of the
Kurdish-Armenian relations (Klein 2011; Kieser 2000, 140–147; Gaunt
2006, 34–36).

During anti-Armenian massacres in 1894–96, in which the Hamidiye
regiments were involved in many locations, as many as 100,000
Armenians are estimated to have been killed in different pogroms across
the country, mostly by Kurds (Kieser 2000, 147–152; Gaunt 2006, 41–44;
see also Bloxham 2005, 49–57).[52] The pogroms can be described as result
of a combination of rigid Ottoman reaction against Armenian nationalist
activities and the general lawlessness of the Kurdish Hamidiye regiments
in the late 19th century within a historical context of increased political
insecurity. They were impacted by politics of Islamic nationalism, demographic changes, as well as fears of economic redistribution (Kieser 2000,
246). It is not incidental that it is just in this time period, the 1890s, that
Ottoman official correspondence shows a heightened concern about alliances between Armenians and Kızılbaş-Alevis, which needed to be prevented. In this context an alleged similarity and closeness between the
two groups and, more specifically, their shared interest in subverting the
Ottoman order were standard tropes of description (Akpınar 2012). All of
the factors that contributed to the pogroms mentioned above would remain
important in Ottoman and Turkish politics in the eastern provinces until
the 1920s. The fact that Syriac Christians were much less affected by the
anti-Christian pogroms of the 1890s can arguably be attributed to the fact
that they were not involved in revolutionary nationalist activities, lacked
international support comparable to that of the Armenians, and thus did
not to the same extent constitute a political threat to the Ottomans (Joseph
1983, 92–93).

The dynamics of the communal relations in the eastern provinces of the
late Ottoman Empire between local, regional, and international factors are
important for two reasons that relate in crucial ways to the main storyline
of this book. First, the political insecurity that these dynamics created,

---

52. However, the Hamidiye were not in all instances responsible for anti-Armenian violence. During the massacres of 1895 in Diyarbakır, for example, the regional Hamidiye chief
İbrahim Paşa protected rather than persecuted Christians while local urban elites were insti-
gating the violence. Based on such local evidence against the grain of generalizing mainstream perceptions, Jongerden argues convincingly for the importance of comprehensive
micro-studies of local power dynamics and their impact on the violence against Christian
communities from the second half of the 19th century through the first decades of the 20th
century (Jongerden 2007, 244–252).

contributed to the Ottoman interest in assimilating the Kızılbaş-Alevis to Sunni Islam and in binding them more closely to Ottoman authority. The state-sponsored Islamization of the Kızılbaş-Alevis began in the 1890s and became more systematic in the early republic. Second, the density of Christian population in these provinces raised Western interest and stakes in the region. These contexts need to be considered in the final analysis of the complex relationship between the Ottoman state, foreign missions and states, and the Kızılbaş-Alevis in general, as well as with regard to Western speculations concerning the Kızılbashes' character and origins in particular—speculations that would later, from the late Young Turk period onward, function as a crucial, if negative, point of reference for the formulation of a Muslim-Turkish Alevism in harmony with the new national paradigm.

It should have become clear that the various motives and aspirations of missionaries, Ottomans, and Kızılbaş-Alevis in the latter's significance cannot be reduced to singular factors and points of view. The largely Protestant rhetoric of the missionaries, the Islamization/Sunnitization efforts of the Ottomans, and the Kızılbaş-Alevis' own interest in improving their socially and economically fragile positions all contributed to the way in which Kızılbaş-Alevism was reframed in terms of culture and religion. The missionaries' emphasis on the Kızılbashes' religious and racial otherness from Ottoman Sunni Muslims and the broader political context triggered in the Hamidian period increased Ottoman interest in bringing the latter closer to the Sunni mainstream. As I will show in the next chapters, this interest would further increase in the Young Turk and early republican periods and would find expression in a new discourse that focused on integrating the Kızılbaş-Alevis into the Turkish-Muslim nation-in-formation. In some of the nationalist literature on the Kızılbaş-Alevis in the 1920s, the earlier Western/Orientalist/missionary claims about the formers' religious and racial origins were explicitly refuted. In this way the Western discovery of the Kızılbaş-Alevis in the second half of the 19th century constituted an important backdrop for their future re-signification within the context of Turkish nationalism.

2

Nationalism, Religion, and Intercommunal Violence

THIS CHAPTER AIMS to provide, first, a theoretical discussion of the role of religion in the formation of nationalism, and second, more specifically, an elaboration of how Islamic sensitivities and semantics contributed to the formation of Turkish nationalism as an intellectual project. Third, it will give an overview on the more concrete politics of nationalism in the Young Turk period. The goal is to show the ideal and practical importance of the factor of religion in the formation of Turkish nationalism. Only from within this context is it possible to understand the dynamics of the emergence of the new concept of Alevism.

The theoretical thrust of this book relates to critical scholarship on the mutual implications of nationalist, secularist, and religionist discourses and practices as they come together in the politics of secular modernity. Originally, this politics was a European project, generally associated with Enlightenment thought. It found its climax in the modernization paradigm formulated most clearly in the mid-20th century, when scholars of sociology and related disciplines (such as history and Middle Eastern/ Oriental studies) systematized what they termed modernizing processes. Doing so they developed macro-sociological arguments according to which modernization not merely originated in the West, but could be expected to expand from there to the rest of the world. This process was conceived of as inevitable, turning "traditional" societies into "modern" ones as a result of closely interlinked and supposedly mutually assertive historical forces such as industrialization, secularization, rationalization, urbanization, mass education, mass political participation, scientific advancement, and last but not least the formation of the nation-state.[1]

---

1. Classical exponents of the modernization theory are, for example, Lerner (1958), Kedourie (1960), and Eisenstadt (1965). For a critical overview of the rise and fall of the modernization paradigm with focus on the role of nationalism see Smith (1998).

If one tries to unwrap the diverse persuasions and theories about progress, evolution, reason, and modernity itself as they came together in the modernization paradigm, one is being confronted with a highly complex web of intellectual and political projects that mark, rationalize, and justify the formation of a European/Western/secular-Christian self, described as rational and modern in opposition to its various (irrational, traditional, and so forth) others. As for the religio-secular aspect of this Eurocentric work of comparison, it required the formulation of religion as a universal (that is, a concept of natural, or, in its later evolution, world religion) that made possible the development of comparative schemes ultimately proving the superiority of European/Western/Christian religion, culture, and civilization: "Because it is born out of a particular religion (Christianity), and in order to justify its claim to be a universal discourse which can maintain its promise of peace, the secular-historicist regime has to be able to *produce* religion in other cultural sites. Yet this could be done only by the assumption of religion as a universal" (Mandair/Dressler 2011, 16).

As postcolonial approaches have argued, and especially Peter van der Veer (1994a and 2001), any analysis of the genealogy of Western modernity as a knowledge regime and political project needs to encompass not only internal European developments such as the Reformation and the Enlightenment and their respective political and intellectual trajectories. It also needs to pay close attention to the European encounter with non-European and non-Christian people as important side of confrontation that made it necessary to develop a framework for how to conceptualize and justify imperialist and colonialist projects. From this perspective, one might argue, the discourse of modernization was not only expansionist, but at the same time also apologetic. Missionaries' rationalizations of their work in Ottoman lands, their concepts of civilization and true religion, as discussed in the previous chapter, provide ample evidence for this kind of dynamics at work—even if, as I argued, their colonialism was of mainly cultural and religious sorts.

In line with the broader narrative of modernization, concepts such as religion, the secular, and the nation were universalized during the colonial encounter in a way that maintained the Euro-Christian claims of cultural and political superiority. At the same time, these notions were clearly demarcated in relation to each other. Following the work of Talal Asad (1993), the study of religion in modernity needs to "be addressed in relation to the historical emergence of the modern idea of the nation and its spread over the world" (van der Veer and Lehmann 1999, 4). In the modernist paradigm, the nation was configured as secular; and religion, which was given the position of the dichotomous other of the secular, was seen as a force inimical to the nation-state as well as modernization in general. However, understanding the universalization of Western concepts of religion (as well as the secular) and nation through colonial encounters, which as such reflect Western domination (scientific/political/economic/cultural), does not mean that non-Western actors had no agency in the translation of these concepts into vernacular sentiments and knowledges (van der Veer 1994a, x).

Secular or Religious Nationalisms?

More than ten years ago, Peter van der Veer and Hartmut Lehmann concluded their introduction to the volume *Nation and Religion* with the observation that their object of study, namely the role of religion(s) in the formation of nationalisms, was a "neglected but highly significant field of inquiry" (van der Veer and Lehmann 1999, 12). This observation still holds today, even if there has been important work done in the last two decades, located in the vaguely defined fields of postcolonial and postsecular studies. Postcolonial and postsecular approaches to nationalism have, however, begun to unmask the modernization paradigm's assumption about secularity's exclusive ownership of modernity and its various embodiments such as the nation and the nation-state.

The discourse of secular modernity is based on a circular argument. As van der Veer has remarked in his important study on religious nationalism in India, "[t]he claim that something like religious nationalism exists will be rejected by many students of nationalism for the simple reason that both nationalism and its theory depend on a Western discourse of modernity... A crucial element of the discourse of modernity is the opposition of the religious to the secular" (van der Veer 1994a, x).

While postsecular approaches have spent much energy on debunking various forms of the secularization paradigm and its implication in imperialist and colonialist politics,[2] and in the process also debased assumptions

---

2. The coming together of a variety of approaches critical of modern(ist) and secularist frameworks in the study of religion may be described as a postsecular turn. Following the pioneering work of scholars such as Edward Said, Jonathan Z. Smith, and Talal Asad, much emphasis is now put on analysis of how religion is practically and discursively constructed. Inspired by this scholarship, current debate is much more interested in the politics of religion, that is, the work of the concept of religion as well as other concepts intimately related to it (such as the secular, which in the modern context has been operating as religion's dialectic other) in concrete historical contexts, than in what religion "is" or how it "functions". See, for example, Asad (1993 and 2003); Dressler and Mandair (2011).

about the secular character of nations, the historical interrelatedness of religion and nation as modern concepts has only to a rather limited extent become the object of detailed historical analysis. Too often, until recently, theoretically ambitious scholarship has lacked in-depth historical analysis, and vice versa. Van der Veer's work has been exemplary in the way it has brought together postcolonial awareness with sociological and historical expertise in the study of religion and nationalism. Integrating theoretical discussions on secularism, religion, and nationalism with the empirical focus on Turkey, this book follows a similar trajectory. The following brief overview of the debate on the relation of nationalism to modernity will help to clarify my argument.

Constructivist Approaches and Their Critics

As late as in 1983 Ernest Gellner argued in his influential book *Nations and Nationalism* that the culture of nationalism-which was a product of industrialization and capitalism-and its demand for rationalization and individualism were by definition secular (van der Veer and Lehmann 1999, 5). Those scholars who marked a constructivist turn in the study of nationalism since the 1970s (such as Eric Hobsbawm, Benedict Anderson, and Gellner) did not show much interest in the role of religion in the formation of nationalism. This lack of attention can to a significant extent be attributed to the fact that much of this scholarship was influenced by Marxism, or at least a vigorous rationalism and methodological materialism, and therefore was strongly indebted to the secularist aspect of the modernization project. Methodologically and theoretically it criticized the conceptual naïveté with regard to the continuities that nations supposedly constituted (Smith 1998, 5–6).

The constructivist turn in the study of nationalism, which established the nowadays dominant view that nationalism is based on the invention of new, "national" identities, needs to be credited for critically interrogating assumptions about national continuities and essences framed in either primordial or perennial terms and for unmasking the political subtext of nationalist claims.[3] However, the assertion of the interrelatedness and contemporaneity of nationalism with secularism and the formation of the modern state remains within the framework of modernism, even if it is

---

3. For a critical overview of primordialist and perennialist approaches to nations and nationalism see Smith (1998, 145–169).

critical of certain politics associated with it (such as capitalism and nationalism itself).

Modernist interpretations of nationalism have been challenged from various positions that share a dissatisfaction with the way the former limit paths of inquiry, such as the possibility that at least some nations might in fact be meaningfully understood as at least partially in continuity with premodern cultural and social knowledges and identities, which are variously described as proto-national, ethnic, ethno-symbolic, cultural, or premodern national (Hastings 1997; Smith 1998, 170–195). One of the most prominent nationalism scholars is the British sociologist Anthony D. Smith, a student of Gellner's. Smith's work provides a modest opposition to the constructivist approach. He has pointed to certain, though often historically fragile and ideologically exaggerated, cultural and symbolic continuities from premodern ethnic to modern national identities (for example, Smith 2008 and 2009). With his "ethno-symbolist" approach, Smith aspires to trace "the role of myths, symbols, values and memories in generating ethnic and national attachments and forging cultural and social networks." His work expresses a "concern with investigating the ways in which nationalists have rediscovered and used the ethno-symbolic repertoire for national ends, in particular the myths and memories of ethnic election, sacred territory, collective destiny and the golden age" (Smith 1998, 224). It is the "ethno-symbolist contention that most nations are formed on the basis of pre-existing ethnic ties and sentiments, even if in time they go well beyond them, and that their nationalisms necessarily use those ethnic symbols, memories, myths and traditions which most resonate with the majority of the designated 'people' whom they wish to mobilise" (Smith 1998, 226). While emphasizing that some nations show historical continuities with previous ethnic social networks and symbolic complexes, Smith does, however, distance himself from "retrospective nationalism." He clearly recognizes the challenge of establishing the historical link between previous ethnic and subsequent national identities without falling in the trap of a naïve back-reading of the modern concept of nation into premodern times (Smith 1998, 196–198; 2004, 258). Similarly looking for a way to go beyond dichotomous construction versus continuity positions, van der Veer has put attention to the processual character of the formation of nationalism, which demands historical contextualization of the details at work in the "invention" of nations: "No doubt, national traditions are invented, as Hobsbawm and Ranger argue, and nations are imagined, as Anderson argues, but that is not all there is to it.

It is not a question of one monolithic imagination or invention, but of several contested versions. Moreover, the cultural material used for invention and imagination is historically produced and thus has to be understood historically. The process of invention and imagination does not start with the rise of nationalist discourse; it is the process of history and culture itself" (van der Veer 1994a, 196–197).

In the discussion of the extent to which the nation is a distinctively modern phenomenon or if it should rather be understood as in continuity with premodern forms of social community and identity, religion is often introduced as evidence for the latter position. Anthony Smith and Adrian Hastings are important authors who support different variations of the continuity thesis while emphasizing the importance of the religion factor.[4] Positioning himself against modernist and constructivist scholarship, Hastings argues that religion, which would constitute "an integral element of many cultures, most ethnicities and some states," was a necessary factor in the formation of nations. He points in particular to the role of biblical concepts and the idea of a Christian people as template for modern national consciousness (Hastings 1997, 4). Unfortunately, Hastings does not provide us with an account of what happened to religion/Christianity following the production of its secular offspring, the nation. He totally ignores the question as to the extent to which religion was affected by its supposed midwifery during the birth of the nation, which would subsequently claim to provide identity and community based on a secular basis.

Smith, too, is interested in the role of religion in the formation of nationalism. He stresses the need to undertake inquiries into the beliefs of world religions with regard to their potential to influence modern secular nationalisms: "We would also need to discover to what extent scriptures, liturgies, clergies and shrines were successful in propagating these beliefs and sentiments in various ethnic cultures and in successive periods of history" (Smith 1998, 227). Smith considers religion to be an important cultural resource that gives "'substance' to the 'political religion' of nationalism by providing it with the . . . sacred elements of ethnic myth, memory, tradition, and symbol, enacted in public rituals and ceremonies" (Smith 2008, 46).

While pointing to the question of the impact of religion on the process through which ethnic groups and identities develop national(ist) features,

---

4. Smith pays tribute to Elie Kedourie (*Nationalism in Asia and Africa*, 1971) for having "brought religion back into the analysis of nationalism," although he retained a modernist perspective, arguing that nationalism was "the secular heir of Christian millennialism" (Smith 2004, 12).

in Smith's work, too, the genealogical interest remains restricted to the concept of the nation, while the category religion is not critically investigated. In his discussion of the formation of nations, religion appears as a phenomenological reality and remains largely unhistoricized (see for example Smith 2004). I would maintain that it is not convincing, within a study of the relationship between religion and nationalism, to critically theorize nationalism and approach it as a historical concept while at the same time presupposing a static concept of religion that lacks such historicization. Smith's essentialist approach to religion shows that he, while criticizing modernist interpretations of nationalism, remains himself caught within a religio-secularist framework. By that I mean that his concept of religion is static and essentialist, bounded against implicit nonreligious/secular others. As Holly Shissler writes about the formation of nationalism, "language and religion, and to some extent folk traditions, are identified as markers of the community and then fitted into an historical framework that gives them a particular meaning as part of a project of modernization that includes a challenge to an existing 'status order'." Functioning as marker of a historical identity, religion is "stripped of history, must be essentialized so as not to compete with the new story...Religion, among the most powerful and widespread varieties of social glue, becomes a set of eternal truths, denied an independent history." Consequently, "religion in history becomes the history of nations in their interaction with religion, not the history of religion" (Shissler 2003, 30).

Shissler's characterization, developed in her study of late Ottoman Turkish nationalism, is helpful in working out the particular role attributed to religion in the secular-national-modernist paradigm. A critical perspective on the work of this paradigm shows that the historicization of the nation is part of a project of secularizing time, that is, the subjugation of heterogeneous concepts of time to a universalizing perception of time with its homogenizing, monolinear, and teleological/evolutionist assumptions, through which local worlds become measurable and assessable according to the logic of modernism. History, which can be interpreted as a product of the secularization of time necessitated by nationalism, provides the "field upon which the meaning of national symbols is defined and the life of the nation validated" (Shissler 2003, 31). Religion, however, is reified in the same process, functioning as an important constant vis-à-vis the flow of history.

A vehement attack against ahistorical approaches to religion has been launched by Asad as part of his critique of modernism and secularism.

Asad's intervention presupposes a going beyond the confines of secular time that makes possible the linear, evolutionist rationalization of the historical transformations that render things religious into things secular and/or national. Fundamentally, Asad argued that religion as a concept needs to be historicized and that the study of nationalism (religious or not) cannot be reduced to making analogies to religion (Asad 1993; 2003, 181–201). Partially parallel to, partially drawing on Asad's genealogical approach to religion, scholarship on nationalism, such as the work of van der Veer on the Indian case, has since the 1990s gradually begun to look for ways beyond the limitations of the secularist modernization paradigm and opened up new ways of inquiry into the role of religion in the formation processes of various nationalisms.[5] Peterson and Walhof, for example, have recently argued that "[r]eligion was never simply the predecessor to nationalism on a linear time scale. Instead, religious reform went hand in hand with the making of national politics" (Peterson and Walhof 2002b, 11).[6]

It is crucial to understand Asad's argument, which in recent years has become very popular and contributed immensely to a gradual shift in how religious studies broadly speaking is conceived. His genealogical approach, that is, his historicizing criticism of concepts such as religion and the secular, and their work in the formation of modern discourses and subjectivities has radically challenged both secularist and religionist approaches to religion (by which I mean approaches that are based on a religion concept that takes religion as an unchanging reality with clearly definable content and boundaries for granted). Consequently, Asad rejects approaches to the genealogy of the modern nation that deduce religion from supposed religious qualities:

> I am not persuaded that because national political life depends on ceremonial and on symbols of the sacred, it should be represented as a kind of religion—that it is enough to point to certain parallels with what we intuitively recognize as religion. One problem with this position is that it takes as unproblematic the entire business of

5. Van der Veer has claimed that "religious nationalism in the nineteenth and twentieth centuries builds on forms of religious identity and modes of religious communication that are themselves in a constant process of transformation during both the colonial and postcolonial periods" (van der Veer 1994a, xiii).

6. For more recent examples of that kind of scholarship see the chapters in part two of Peterson and Walhof (2002a).

defining religion. It does not ask why *particular* elements of "religion" as a concept should be picked out as definitive, and therefore
fails to consider the discursive roles they play in different situations.
(Asad 2003, 189)

Asad's criticism targets functionalist and symbolist approaches, including Carl Schmitt and his ideas about political theology, as well as Clifford
Geertz's definition of religion as a symbol-system. Instead of focusing on
the commonality between certain religious and secular ideas and structures, thereby objectifying them, Asad urges us to focus on the processes
of differentiation between secular and religious discourses and on the historical changes in the various concepts implicated in the processes under
question.[7] In other words, Asad's genealogical perspective redirects our
focus to the historicity of the discourses and practices that are expressed
in the modern context through concepts such as "religion," "secular," and
"nation." From this perspective it is highly problematic to imply structural analogies between premodern and modern contexts and to ignore
the changes that concepts have gone through in the modernizing process. Spearheaded by Asad's studies, recent critical genealogical work on
the concept of religion and its transformation in the context of Western
modernity and its globalization shows this very clearly.[8]

To summarize my criticism of theoretical work on nationalism that
does not reflect on the impact of secularist assumptions in the formation of the concept of nation as both a political and an analytical category: the major point is that the concept and the politics associated
with religion changed in the context of the modern nation-state to an
extent that renders any use of it as an essentialized, objective criterion
for comparison over time impossible. The success story of the secular,
and the way it is configured with concepts of nation and modernity, cannot be divided from how religion is reconstituted at the same time. An
example is the impact of "the emergence of *society* as an organizable
secular space" in providing the state with the possibility to control and
redefine the competence of religion (Asad 2003, 191). Asad has made

---

7. Asad (2003, 189–190). For his critique of Geertz see Asad (1993, 29–54); for his critique
of Schmitt see Asad (1993, 189).

8. Important works that contribute to our understanding of the historicization of the concept of religion in the modern context are, for example, King (1999), Peterson and Walhof
(2002a), Kippenberg (2002), Dubuisson (2003), Masuzawa (2005), Mandair (2009), and
Dressler and Mandair (2011).

clear that "[n]ationalism, with its vision of a universe of national *socie-ties*...in which individual humans live their worldly existence requires the concept of the secular to make sense." And this concept of the secular depends on a concept of religion to which it has been dichotomously connected in the modern context (Asad 2003, 193). In short, if we take Asad's critique seriously we have to tailor our inquiry into the impact of religion on national discourses and practices in a way that, going beyond static and essentialist approaches to religion (such as those by Smith and Hastings), as well as functionalist approaches (such as those by Schmitt and Geertz), systematically pays attention to the historical transformations of the concepts under question.

Religion in the Formation of Turkish Nationalism

As tradition requires continuity and harmony, it becomes necessary to find the connection between the pre-history of the Turk and the metaphysics of religion, and by so doing to develop an Islamic-Turkish philosophy of history. (Gökalp 1959 [1913]b, 96)

Traditional scholarship on Turkish modernization and nationalism has been strongly influenced by the secularist paradigm and often neglected or downplayed the religious dimensions of nationalism. In the traditional narrative, which lines up nicely with the Kemalist project, Turkish nationalism is understood to be a distinctly secular project.[9] As I would like to point out, however, there are many reasons to complicate the story of Turkish nationalism.

According to secularist accounts of the formation of Turkish nationalism, its differentiation from Ottomanism constituted a crucial benchmark in its development. As a set of political principles, Ottomanism focused on shared state and territory, as well as loyalty to the Ottoman dynasty as markers of an ethnically and religiously pluralist polity. From the retrospective of an established secular Turkish nationalism, and in light of the dominance, throughout much of the 20th century, of the idea that the nation-state was a vehicle and expression of modernization, Ottomanism was a stillborn project: imperial, antinational cosmopolitan, based on

---

9. Classic studies that helped to establish that view are Lewis (1961), Shaw and Shaw (1977), and Berkes (1964). For critical commentary on these and other works on modern Turkey see Zürcher (2004, 359–361; 2010, 41–53).

religion—in short, hopelessly outdated, an obstacle to modernity and civilization. According to this narrative, the growing appeal of nationalism to
non-Turkish and non-Muslim peoples on Ottoman territory clearly proved
the inviability of Ottomanism, which had failed to create a social bond and
an identity that delivered more than a vague patriotism and a wish to save
the state within its remaining territory.

There are, however, reasons to question that narrative. In his criticism
of Köprülü on that issue, Karpat has argued that Ottomanism was an absolutely necessary precondition for the formation of Turkish nationalism:

> Ottomanism in the nineteenth century was a wholly new type of
> nation-building process and...the socioeconomic forces restructur-
> ing Ottoman multiethnic society had a power of their own to give
> a new shape to the traditional elements and a new identity to the
> emerging nation. There is no evidence to suggest that the folk cul-
> ture would have produced a modern nation on its own without the
> sophisticated administrative, social, and legal suprastructure devel-
> oped in the nineteenth century, largely as the result of Ottomanism.
> It was Ottomanism, implemented by a central government in a new
> social, economic, and structural framework, that brought together
> the disparate ethnic Turkish urban and tribal nuclei and fused them
> into the new, broad ethnic unit that eventually became political and
> national. The traditional Ottoman elite, who controlled the state for
> centuries, could not have steered society toward a new form of orga-
> nization as long as they lacked the ideology, social structure, and
> motivation necessary for creating a nation. (Karpat 2001, 401)

The motivation for moving toward a nation-state was strongly impacted by
the political developments in the last decade of the Ottoman Empire, when
religion became a—in the secularist narrative strongly underestimated—
driving force in the visualization and rationalization of the national body.
As reflected in the writings of Turkists in the last two decades of the
Ottoman Empire, to be discussed below, as well as in the concrete politics
of nation-building, the influence of religion on Turkish nationalism was
much more profound than the secularist modernism of Kemalist Turkey
would later on try to make itself and the outside world believe.

It is certainly true that the dominant organization of the Young Turk
movement, the "Committee of Union and Progress" (*İttihad ve Terakki
Cemiyeti*, hereafter CUP), which was the major agent of political change

in the last decades of the Ottoman Empire, and the most important social carrier of Turkish nationalism in this period, was strongly positivist (especially if one focuses on its pre-1908 rhetoric; see Hanioğlu 2001). Its antireligious stance was an important factor in the formation of secularist thought in the late Ottoman and early republican periods. But with Turkish nationalism increasing its profile within the Young Turk movement during the course of the Balkan Wars, the role of religion as marker of communitarian solidarity and cultural difference increased immensely. In fact, in this crucial phase of the formation of Turkish nationalism as an ideology that started to move beyond the circles of the Young Turkish elites, discourses on religious and national identity overlapped to a considerable extent. Nevertheless, both in scholarship and in the perception of the Turkish public the role of religion in this period has often been reduced to an opportunistic one, perpetuating the circular argument of secularist nationalism according to which nationalism is part of a larger project of social and structural transformations that is by definition secular. The secularist perspective in this way marginalizes the role of Islam in the formation of Turkish nationalism, or even renders it an anomaly that needs to be rationalized away. Such an approach makes it difficult to understand how religious and secular sentiments and semantics could work hand in hand in the establishment of a nationalist project. Once one is willing to drop the secularist perspective, a much more complex picture emerges.

The Muslim Nation

For some leading members of the Young Turk movement who contributed significantly to the formation of Turkish nationalist thought, the rhetoric of Islamic identity and solidarity was, unlike the secularist narrative likes to suggest, more than mere populism or opportunism. Yusuf Akçura, Ahmet Ağaoğlu, and Ziya Gökalp are important examples of a type of a late Ottoman nationalist intellectual for whom religion played, though in different ways, a crucial role in the formation of the nation. Importantly, for them this was not seen as necessarily in conflict with the political project of a secular state.

Yusuf Akçura(oğlu) (1876–1935) was born in Russian Kazan to a wealthy family of Tatar Turkish merchants. Akçura came to Istanbul as a child, but would remain connected to his land of birth. After studies in Paris (1900–1904), among others with the nationalism expert Albert

Sorel, and completing a master's thesis on the disintegration of the Ottoman Empire, he temporarily returned to Kazan, where he worked for the organization of the Russian Muslims and their civil rights, before finally settling in Istanbul in 1908 (Yavuz 1993, 195–197). Akçura belonged to a number of influential intellectuals of the formative period of Turkism (others were İsmail Gaspıralı, Ahmet Ağaoğlu, and Zeki Velidi Toğan) who were born in tsarist Russia, in the context of which they developed an ethno-religious nationalism originally directed against Russian imperialism and pan-Slavism, and eventually emigrated to the Ottoman Empire (Oba 1995, 141–174). These Russian-Turkish émigrés were less attached than their Ottoman Turkish colleagues to the interrelated Ottomanist ideals of ethno-religious plurality and territorial as well as cultural integrity. Rather, they saw the fate of the Muslims and the Turks in broader transnational contexts. Approaching late Ottoman discussions of nationalism from the Russian-Turkish periphery, where the Muslim Turks had already developed bourgeois cultures, made them understand the importance of the improvement of the political and economic condition of the Ottoman Turkish Muslim population for the formation of a nationalist movement and would make them argue for the nationalization of the economy as a precondition for national development.

Based on their own experiences of political and cultural struggle against Russian assimilationist politics, Russian Muslims had early on realized that religion was a powerful tool in the articulation of ethnic and national distinctiveness. Indeed, for the Russian Turkists the quest for cultural autonomy went hand in hand with the quest for religious revival (Yavuz 1993, 192–194; Karpat 2001, 391–393; cf. Shissler 2003, 14). Among the central ideas of Akçura was the belief in the necessity of a reform of Islam in line with the needs of the modern age; however, he argued that reform needed to be accomplished not against but with Islam (Georgeon 1980, 17). In a way, for Akçura—and the claim could be extended to Ağaoğlu— "Islamic identity, ethnicity, and territoriality became intertwined" (Yavuz 1993, 194). Within the political thought of these men the relationship between Islam and nationalism needs to be understood in terms of symbiosis rather than antagonism (Yavuz 1993, 181).

Akçura and Ağaoğlu were well aware of the centrifugal forces that ethnic and religious differences could arouse when articulated in the new language of nationalism. In his famous essay "Üç Tarz-ı Siyaset" ("Three Kinds of Politics"), which he wrote after his return from Paris to Kazan in 1904, Akçura pointed out the weakness of the idea of Ottomanism, which was not sufficiently attractive to non-Muslims, and put the Turks under danger of assimilation by the Arabs. His assessment of Islamism as an alternative ideological basis of the state was relatively more positive. He recognized the importance of religion as a unifying force in the formation of a national community, arguing that in Islam religion and nation would be one, and thus Islam would eliminate differences based on ethnic and national identities (Akçura 2005 [1904], 56). Nevertheless, he regarded Islamism as a political option that was ultimately not feasible because of the risk of creating dangerous divisions (between Muslims and non-Muslims, as well as between Muslims of various religious persuasions). For Akçura, Turkism was the most viable road in the attempt to transform the Ottoman Empire into a prosperous modern nation-state. He therefore suggested—and this is an argument of his that is usually ignored in the Turkish nationalist reception of his ideas—to let go of the non-Muslims and the territories where they formed the majority and rather work toward the realization of a Turkish Muslim nation, based on language, religion, and race. "Three Kinds of Politics" found little resonance upon first appearance, but became a foundational text for the Turkist movement as it gained strength in subsequent years (Akçura 2005 [1904]; Yavuz 1993, 199–202; Georgeon 1980).

The Azerbaijani Turk Ahmet Ağaoğlu [Agayev] (1869–1939) likewise recognized Islam as an important carrier of Turkish nationhood. Ağaoğlu put particular emphasis on the long tradition of positive contributions of the Turks to Islam. Holly Shissler's study has shown that in Ağaoğlu's work, Islam and nationalism are complementary. He even described religion as "leaven in the formation of nationalities and nationalisms" (as quoted by Shissler 2003, 175). He saw both nationalism and religion, in particular Islamic revivalism, as important agents in the process of modernization. The entering of non-Islamic or superstitious practices and beliefs into Islam would have led to sectarian conflict within the religion and a weakening of its moral unity. Overcoming these sectarian conflicts and establishing rational and authentic religion is therefore an important aspect in the creation of national unity and an eminent task for the national-state (Shissler 2003, 169–181).

Ağaoğlu was born in Shusha, grew up in Tiflis, went to study in Petersburg and Paris, and stayed then for several months in Istanbul before returning to the Caucasus in 1894. There he became politically very active, got involved in the Azerbaijani nationalist movement, and from 1905 onward also—like Akçura, with whom he would become friends and

work closely together—in the Union of Russian Muslims. He worked as
journalist and teacher in Tiflis, Shusha, and later Baku, from where he
went to Istanbul in 1908, fleeing from increasing tsarist pressure, and
soon became active in the Turkist circles of the Ottoman capital (Sakal
1999, 7–26; Shissler 2003, 157–158). Even more so than in the case of
Akçura, for Ağaoğlu national empowerment relied on religious awakening that he cast in the language of modernization. Shissler has emphasized this aspect of his work:

> The whole thrust of his work is modernist, aimed at a "higher syn-
> thesis" of community identity and solidarity, on the one hand, and
> "modern" rational thought and institutions, on the other, in order
> to get the nation back into the main stream of progress. Thus we
> learn that the decline of the Turks is attributable to their lack of
> national consciousness and their overzealous attachment to ossified
> traditions, that the real nature and strength of Islam is in its ability
> to adapt itself to a variety of historical and cultural circumstances
> and that women's lack of personal freedom is a result of the cor-
> ruption of genuine Islamic precept and early historical experience.
> We are told that a strong literary tradition in vernacular Turkish is
> necessary to produce the geniuses that will inspire the nation and
> that Islam is one of three great world religious traditions. (Shissler
> 2003, 32)

A discussion of the role of religion within the formative period of
Turkish nationalism would not be complete without reference to the
thought of Ziya Gökalp, besides Akçura probably the most influential
thinker in the Young Turk period, when Turkish nationalism became a
political force. Gökalp was from the eastern town of Diyarbakır, capital
of the province of the same name, which was predominantly Kurdish
with a considerable non-Muslim population. Following the Young Turk
Revolution he became a major ideologue of the CUP while simultaneously
occupying the first chair in sociology at the Darülfünun.[10] He is generally
credited to have been one of the major architects of Turkist thought. His
reflections on nationalism, corporatism, and secularism were extremely
influential from the Young Turk period through early Kemalist Turkey;

---

10. The *Darülfünun* was the first secular university of the Ottomans. In 1933 it was reorga-
nized as Istanbul University.

though often interpreted in arbitrary and often distorted ways, they have remained significant until today (Parla 1985, 7).

That Gökalp's thought has remained highly contested is partly due to the dominance of secularist-modernist perspectives in the scholarship on the late Ottoman Empire. Scholars of Turkish nationalism in this tradition (such as Uriel Heyd and Niyazi Berkes) tend to reduce Gökalp's emphasis on religion in his conceptualization of Turkish modernization to that of an auxiliary, propagandist means to politically engage the ordinary people. Indeed, Gökalp was certainly aware of the strength of religion as a means to capture the interest of the masses in the context of forming a national consciousness. To deduce from this, however, that he would have been opposed to a continuous role of religion as important dimension of national identity is in my opinion a secularist fallacy. As with the interpretation of Akçura and Ağaoğlu, much of the discussion of Gökalp lacks adequate historical contextualization and has suffered distortion, caught in between rival ideologies (of various combinations of secularist, Islamic, and nationalist sorts; see Davison 1995). The problem that makes some misunderstand Gökalp (and other early Turkish nationalist thinkers) as working toward the kind of secularist nationalism that would be established in the Turkish Republic is based on a retrospective evaluation. Such evaluation is unable to capture the complexity of sentiments and discourses that dominated late Ottoman intellectual life, which cannot be reduced to secularist/Islamist binaries.

Neither Ağaoğlu, nor Akçura, nor Gökalp belonged to the type of diehard antireligious positivists that had dominated early Young Turk thought, even if the latter two had some positivist leanings. In different ways, their respective understandings of modernity and modernization saw religion as positively contributing to the modernizing process. For all of them, religion was a force that needed to be accounted for in the historical exploration and political propagation of the national self. Therefore, Shissler is wrong when she positions Ağaoğlu against Akçura and Gökalp, arguing that the latter two would have "[reduced religion] to an element of culture in the service of nationalism" (Shissler 2003, 181). This assessment might make sense for Akçura, for whom religion was primarily a means in the formation of nationhood, making the latter evident to people who were used to define their communal boundaries with reference to religion. But for Ağaoğlu and Gökalp, who joined the CUP's Central Committee together in 1910 and became friends, religious revival was not only a means but also a consequence of the modernization process at large—and, it should be added, a positive consequence. The difference to Akçura corresponds with their individual stances toward religion, which was in the case of Ağaoğlu and Gökalp much more positive. The young Gökalp had been drawn to Sufism, and this affinity remained visible in his later publications as well as personal letters. I concur therefore with Davison, who argues that the role Gökalp was willing to attribute to religion in the creation of a national consciousness was not merely a preliminary one, as is often argued from a typical secularist point of view (Davison 1995, 195). Gökalp should more appropriately be characterized as a modernist reformer from within the Islamic tradition, convinced of the necessity for disestablishment (between the affairs of religion and those of the state). With qualifications, he can be described as both a secularist and an Islamic revivalist. As an Islamic revivalist and modernist he argued (similar to Ağaoğlu) against superstition and backward-mindedness; as a secularist he argued against clericalism and theocracy. It can be argued that his revivalist and secularist stances converged in his support for the abolishment of the sultanate, which he interpreted as a means to free the caliphate from political tutelage (cf. Davison 1995).

A scholar who has taken issue with the secularist bias of modernist scholarship on nationalism in general and Turkish nationalism in particular is Hakan Yavuz. In a manner that resembles Smith's ethno-symbolism and his assertion that modern nationalism draws on symbolic and textual materials from the realm of religion, Yavuz argues that nationalism can be mediated through religious metaphors and symbols, and that religion in this way creates evidence for new national identities. He also takes issue with the modernist account as exemplified by Gellner, who saw economic and structural changes as causing secularization. For Yavuz, the late Ottoman example displays a different mechanism at work, in which "the construction of an Islamic and finally nationalist identity was embedded in the socio-economic transformation of the Ottoman state. The centralization of power, spread of education, and mass communication in the Ottoman Empire prepared the ground for the politicization of Islam, and this was moulded into a nationalist discourse by the seminal work of Yusuf Akçura" (Yavuz 1993, 207). In other words, Turkish nationalism was historically fermented in an Ottoman identity politics that gradually adopted Islamic religio-nationalist, and then Turkish ethno-nationalist features. Yavuz further points to the impact of Islamism and the way it divided between Islamic and non-Islamic parts of the world in the formation of Turkish national identity, arguing that there is a strong analogy in the processes of communal differentiation through which national and religious communities, respectively, gained self-consciousness (Yavuz 1993, 180). Especially the Sunnification policies in the Hamidian period prepared the ground for the nationalist movement (Yavuz 1993, 187–192). Like Smith, however, Yavuz misses to apply to his discussion of religion the same critical historicizing perspective that he uses in his approach to nationalism.

Methodological Challenges

For a proper understanding of the significance of religion in early Turkish nationalist thought and politics it is crucial to realize that in the first two decades of the 20th century there was as of yet neither a clear conceptual distinction between Turkishness and Ottomanness (Karpat 2001, 394), nor between notions of religious and national community/identity. Naturally, attempts of late Ottoman intellectuals to define Turkishness vis-à-vis Ottomanness necessitated also differentiation between the broader categories of nation and religion. Without understanding this fundamental point, every retrospective interpretation of this periods' discourses on nation and religion must necessarily remain flawed. The discussions then led by nationalist activist-scholars were exactly about how to differentiate between the contours of the national and the various others in relation to which it was imagined and constituted. Without even going into the details of their arguments, already a cursory look at the titles of some publications by nationalist activists of this period (limited here to figures highlighted in this volume) gives an idea about how much this nationalism was about defining the nation and differentiating it from religion: *The Idea of Nationhood and National Struggles* (1913) by Yusuf Akçura; *Turkification, Islamization, Modernization* (1913/14) by Ziya Gökalp; *Turkism, Islam, and Ottomanism* (1913) by Mehmed Fuad Köprülü; *The Question of the Nation in Islam* (1914) by Ahmet Ağaoğlu. The fact that all of these articles were published toward the end or immediately following the Balkan Wars is not incidental, but underlines that this was a crucial phase in the sorting out of the respective plausibilities of political projects organized around notions of constitutional citizenship (Ottomanism), ethno-religious nationalism (Turkism), and religious communalism (Islamism) in relation to each other in a period of rapid social, demographic, and political change. While the major trajectories of Turkish nationalist thought were already laid out in the late Young Turk period, the debate about the contours of the Turkish nation were by no means concluded and continued, with varying intensity, until the early 1930s. The fluidity of the discourse of Turkish nationalism in this period requires methodological carefulness. To the extent that the contours of the national and its relation to the religious were still in the process of being established, it is problematic to discuss positions within this ongoing debate by means of analytical categories that suggest a in reality not-yet-existing definitional clarity.

It can certainly be assumed that the vagueness of the category of the nation had political advantages. It made it possible to launch a process of state- and nation-building in a historical context where a concept of nation as a purely secular construct based on ethnicity, or race, and language was alien to a population that defined its community boundaries through Islam. In such a context only a—implicitly, at least—"religious" concept of nationhood, that is, a concept of nation that, in line with Yavuz's (1993) argument and Anthony Smith's notion of ethno-symbolism, more or less equated the boundaries of the lingual/ethnic community with those of the religious community, could supply the plausibility structures needed for a viable national project.

The formation of Turkish nationalism needs to be understood within the broader historical context of societal differentiation, demographic and socioeconomic transformations, and especially the processes of rationalization, systematization, and delocalization/universalization of religious and ethnic discourses. Within this context, reflective of the grammar of modernization more broadly speaking, the nation tended to be defined in secular (in the narrow political sense), however not necessarily antireligious, terms. For those Young Turkish thinkers who, such as especially Gökalp and Ağaoğlu, did not belong to the extreme positivist wing of the nationalist movement, religion was an important and crucial element of what defined the nation and provided it with a social and moral grid. Almost all Turkish nationalists of the late Ottoman and the subsequent Kemalist periods, even the more aggressive secularist ones, further share an understanding that the members of the Turkish nation are Muslims, even if this argument functions primarily qua exclusion (of non-Muslims). Historically, Turkish nationalism developed against religious (non-Muslim) others in much more direct and explicit ways than against ethnic others.[11]

---

11. In the early republic, inclusion of Muslim non-Turkish speakers into Turkish nationhood was much easier accomplished and welcomed than the possible inclusion of non-Muslim Turkish speakers. See Cagaptay (2006). This pattern continues until today.

In the classical narrative, the Turkish modernization project is told through the binaries constitutive of the modernist project itself, such as modern/traditional, literate/illiterate, central/peripheral, Western/Eastern, secular/religious, and progressive/reactionary. These binaries penetrate not only vernacular Turkish discourses, but are still widespread in use as analytical categories in Ottoman and Turkish historiography. Alternatively, I advocate a postmodernist and postsecularist approach that is able to shed light at those neglected grey areas that are lost if the binary approaches of modernism are applied. I suggest that the dynamics of Turkish modernity can only be understood when taking into consideration more complex historical forces, as well as dynamics of interaction between various and conflicting sentiments, ideas, and hopes that make up the subjective and collective experiences of particular people. Ahmet Ağaoğlu, for example, was moving back and forth between various political contexts (Russian, Azerbaijani, Turkish, Persian), in each of which he drew on different cultural and intellectual resources. Accordingly, he presented himself as Russian Muslim, Azerbaijani, Turk, and Persian (Shissler 2003, 212). This does, however, not mean that he was a culturally or politically indifferent person. Rather, Ağaoğlu's shifting cultural/national self-representation is reflective of a time and space in which the nation-state was not yet established with all its exclusivist and homogenizing force, which would eventually make such shifting or multiple national/cultural/political affiliation appear as inconsistent, if not, politically speaking, as act of treason.[12]

Modernist language is ill-equipped to explain a story such as that of Ağaoğlu and many other protagonists of early Turkish nationalism. Its limitations become obvious for example in accounts that draw on Gökalp's work to reify what are conveniently labeled the "dominant intellectual currents" of that period (i.e., Ottomanism, Turkism, Islamism, and modernism). Representing these currents, about which he wrote rather extensively,

---

12. "There is the appearance of something remarkably unsettled and changeable in the shifts in residence and terms of identity among intellectuals such as Ağaoğlu, but this is largely a misapprehension. Their world was quite cosmopolitan, their political and intellectual consciousness spreading out in ways that did not respect imperial frontiers or narrow communal, cultural, or linguistic boundaries. The borders and ethnic identities, which seem so clear today, were much more open, permeable and fluid then. However, part of what makes this class of men—men who lived in that particular time and place—interesting and worthy of study is that increasingly, precisely in their era, the fluidity I have described was diminishing. By the end of the first quarter of the twentieth century the divisions had become quite defined, quite hard, shaped in the rigid mould of ethno-national identity and nation-states" (Shissler 2003, 4).

as clearly apart and in opposition to each other is a misrepresentation. As many intellectuals of his time, he did not see these currents as oppositional and mutually exclusive. While it is true that his categorizations in a typifying manner pointed out differences between various political projects, his main objective was to show that the substances of these currents (i.e., modernity, Islam, Turkism) could be combined in harmonious fashion. Only from this perspective does the important role that he attributes to Islam as a carrier of Turkish nationalism become visible. Van der Veer has argued drawing on Marcel Mauss's work on "the nation" that in the age of nationalism religion would have become "a defining feature of the nation, and for that purpose it is...nationalized. Thus religion becomes one of the fields of disciplinary practice in which the modern civil subject is produced" (van der Veer 2001, 33). My rereading of early Turkish nationalism with special attention to the role of religion in its formation process supports this view. Discussing the formation of the concept of Alevism at the intersection of discourses of nationalism, religion, and secularism, the goal of this study is to contribute to the liberation of the historical and sociological study of Turkish nationalism and religious history from the secularist straitjacket.

As I will show in the following pages and chapters, secularist/modernist perspectives were instrumental in the formation of both the modern knowledge about the Alevis' affinity with Turkish culture, as well as their ambivalent position in relation to the hegemonic discourse of Islam in Turkey.

Reform and Politics of Nationalism

In the following section I will chart the broader historical and political context within which the beginning Turkish nationalist interest in the Kızılbaş-Alevis needs to be situated. The "discovery" of the Kızılbaş-Alevis as a community of national importance took place within the tumultuous period from the Young Turk Revolution in 1908 to the 1930s in the Turkish Republic, parallel to the formation of Turkish nationalism. The significance of the Kızılbaş-Alevi issue as political, demographic, and cultural factor in the Turkish nation-building process has so far not been systematically examined. Even if the political impact of the Kızılbaş-Alevi factor during this crucial period of nation-building was certainly secondary to other issues more existential for late Ottoman and early Turkish nationalist perspectives, it was still an important issue. In addition, it provides an illuminating window in the cultural-religious, and social-demographic complexities that affected the dynamics of Turkish nation-building.

In the last decade of the 19th century, the Young Turks (*Jöntürkler*), a loosely organized group of reform-oriented Ottoman men, many of whom were still at an early stage of their careers in the army or administration, became the driving force for political change in the Ottoman Empire. Young Turk ideology and politics were never monolithic, and one needs to distinguish between different historical phases in its development. Organized in the CUP, the Young Turks kept until the last decade of the empire a rather pragmatic stance toward matters of ideology. They for the most part remained within the framework of Ottoman nationalism, or Ottomanism, which in principle argued for equality of all Ottoman citizens beyond the ethnic and religious differences that marked the social organization of the society. In the Hamidian period the political raison d'être of the secret CUP organization, most of the members of which were recruited from the new secular military and medical schools, was opposition to Sultan Abdülhamid II, whom they despised.

From its foundation as Society for Ottoman Union (*İttihad-i Osmani Cemiyeti*) in 1889 until the Young Turk Revolution of 1908, the CUP went through a series of transformations and name changes.[13] What remained constant was the aim to reinstitute the constitution, and to expand modernizing reforms following European examples. In its beginnings more a critical observer than itself a political player, the organization gradually took a more proactive stance culminating in the Young Turk Revolution of 1908, when it succeeded in pushing Sultan Abdülhamid II to reinstitute the constitution of 1876, which he had shelved in 1878. Henceforth the CUP, with short interruptions, would dictate Ottoman politics until the end of World War I.

Following the Young Turk Revolution, many had at first placed great hopes in the new regime and expected an increase in political and religious freedom after the authoritarian reign of Abdülhamid II. Erik J. Zürcher described the public reaction to the Young Turks' rise to power as one of "tremendous joy and relief, with people from all walks of life and every community, Muslim, Jewish and Christian, fraternizing and celebrating

---

13. The most important works on the early Young Turk movement are still Hanioğlu (1995 and 2001), and Mardin (1962). For the later Young Turk period see Kayalı (1997). Cf. also Berkes (1964) despite his already mentioned secularist bias. For a concise overview of the Young Turk period with references to further literature see Zürcher (2004, 93–132); see also Zürcher (2010).

in the streets. There was a general, but unarticulated, expectation that somehow life would now change for the better" (Zürcher 2004, 93; see also Joseph 1983, 94–95). The revolution inaugurated a short-term opening of the public sphere expressed in a rapid expansion of print media and assertions of imperial multi-ethnicity, which Michelle Campos has discussed as "civic Ottomanism" (Campos 2010). Unfortunately, all those who had hoped for a sustained liberal politics and an expansion of the public sphere were soon to be disappointed, and the following years would see an increase rather than decrease of tension between ethnic groups along religious lines.[14]

War, Migration, National Threats, and Anti-Christian Sentiments

As a consequence of growing opposition against the CUP clique from both the conservative establishment (lower rank *ulema* and parts of the army) as well as political liberals, the CUP-sponsored government was pushed out of power in 1912 at the beginning of the First Balkan War. However, the bad course of the war provided the Young Turks with the opportunity to return to power rather quickly, and they staged what became known as the Bab-i Ali Coup, which led to the establishment of a Young Turk dictatorship in 1913.[15] Within the CUP, voices advocating ethno-religious, nationalist agendas now became louder and plans for a reshaping of Anatolia in line with a Social Darwinist agenda were advanced.

Niyazi Berkes has remarked that the CUP's return to power in 1913 meant a re-signification of the party's name: "It no longer meant the union of its various ethnic elements, but the unification of the Turks" (Berkes 1964, 335). While the influence of Turkism became certainly more visible in this phase, Berkes's observation is lacking insofar as it ignores

---

14. ABCFM missionary White provides a detailed description of the hopes created by the Young Turk coup and the way it impacted the general atmosphere and intercommunal relations in Merzifon. White also gives account of how the atmosphere began to change during the Balkan Wars, leading to the Armenian tragedy experienced in the province of Amasya during the Great War (White 1940, 65–88).

15. The Young Turks now curtailed the sultan's power significantly and furthered the secularizing reforms of the education and the legal system, which had been brought under way with the Tanzimat reforms. They did this in a manner that foreshadowed the centralist secularism of the Turkish republic. Thus they integrated educational and judicial Islamic institutions into the state apparatus and in this way increased the state's control over them (Zürcher 2004, 121–122).

the religious component that was part of much Turkist rhetoric. As argued in the previous section, the languages of Turkification/nationalization and Islamization did overlap considerably—despite the strong intellectual commitment of especially earlier, more decisively positivist, incarnations of Young Turk thought. This overlap would also impact the way in which the nationalist gaze would view the Kızılbaş-Alevis. From the nationalist perspective, religion was an important aspect of national culture and consequently, as I will show, the integration of the Kızılbaş-Alevis into Turkish nationhood needed to go hand in hand with their religious integration. Since Christians were, within the dynamics of war and violence that marked the period from the Balkan Wars through the early republic, increasingly perceived as a major threat to the Turkish-Muslim national well-being, it would have been unthinkable for the Young Turks to accept the Kızılbaş-Alevis as part of the Turkish nation while conceding that they were non-Muslims and/or Christians as suggested by some Western authors.

Major factors that contributed to Muslim-nationalist chauvinism since the Young Turk period, which would in the subsequent years target particularly the Christian minorities, were (1) the Ottomans' loss of most of its, in the recent past already rather diminished, European territories between 1908 and 1913, especially during the Balkan Wars (1912/13); (2) the human tragedy of hundreds of thousands of Muslim refugees fleeing toward Anatolia as a product of the territorial loss on top of hundreds of thousands of Muslim refugees from the Balkans and the Caucasus, who already in previous decades had sought shelter in Anatolia; (3) fears of Russian advances in the eastern Anatolian provinces, which increased drastically during World War I; and (4) Western presence and pressure, embodied not only in the capitulations, but in a more physical manner also in the various Christian missions, political institutions like the British consuls, as well as in the European reform plans for the eastern provinces, which were biased toward Armenian and Christian interests.[16] The Ottomans often suspected local Christian populations of supporting the enemies of the state—and some parts of them certainly did sympathize with, and smaller portions actively engaged in, nationalist and separatist activities.

---

16. Üngör explains that "[t]he CUP saw Great Power interference in internal politics as a humiliating breach of Ottoman sovereignty, a harbinger of the doomsday scenario in which an independent Armenia would be established in the Ottoman eastern provinces" (Üngör 2008b, 21).

War-induced immigration of Muslim refugees to Anatolia since the mid-19th century was an important factor in the formation of a sense of Muslim solidarity and furthered resentment against non-Muslims. With the migration of possibly more than a million Muslims fleeing the Russians from the Caucasus into Ottoman lands since the 1860s, the Ottomans already then were facing severe economic and demographic challenges (Zürcher 2004, 82). Many of the immigrants, who suffered from malnutrition and disease, died already on their way; the state proved at the beginning to be totally overwhelmed with the situation. Consecutively, these immigrants—almost all of whom were Muslim—were resettled in different parts of the empire with a focus on security and economy (McCarthy 1995, 34–39). The problem with the refugees entering from the Caucasus coincided with rising nationalism especially in the Balkans, where the success of Greek de facto and Serbian quasi-independence earlier in the century had inspired Bulgarian nationalist longings—developments that also inspired the national dreams of the Armenians of Anatolia. As a consequence of the Ottoman defeat in the Ottoman-Russian War (1877–1878), the empire had lost huge parts of the Balkans including Bulgaria, as well as three northeastern provinces to the Russians. This meant that for the first time Ottoman territory with considerable Muslim and Turkish populations was occupied, leading to large-scale massacres of Muslims and forced emigration (Zürcher 2004, 81). Already these developments meant a severe challenge to Ottomanist dreams of a multiethnic national unity. As a consequence of the Balkan Wars, finally, the Ottomans lost a further 80% of their remaining European territory; roughly 800,000 Muslim refugees moved eastward toward Anatolia, but many of them died on the way from disease (Zürcher 2008, 2–6).[17]

When the Young Turks in 1913 established a one-party dictatorship, they did not yet have a clear Turkish nationalist program. The nationalist discourses of the time period comprised at least nominally trans-ethnic and trans-religious Ottomanism, pan-Islamism, as well as Turkish nationalist and (pan-)Turkist ideas. Historians still debate the details of the formation of Turkish nationalism. Questioning the thesis of the Young Turks' gradual adaptation of Turkist politics as a response to the changing political situation, Şükrü Hanioğlu holds that Turkish nationalism was already in the years 1902 to 1907 figuring prominently in

---

17. McCarthy counts more than 400,000 refugees from the Balkans who were resettled in Anatolia between 1913 and 1920 (McCarthy 1995, 161).

CUP publications and that the Young Turks' liberal appearance between the Young Turk Revolution and the Balkan Wars was merely a matter of political opportunism (Hanioğlu 2001, 295–302). As he argues, "the same CUP leaders exploited Panturkist, Panislamist, and Ottomanist policies simultaneously. Scholars have often tried to argue that the CUP adhered to one of these ideologies to the exclusion of the others, but such was never the case" (Hanioğlu 2001, 298). He concludes that—notwithstanding the in-general-pragmatic/opportunistic approach of the CUP to ideological matters—its major political orientation was an inclusive Ottomanism, to which ethno-religious categories were subordinated, even if they became stronger over time. But the Young Turks in these years would more and more have realized that their inclusive Ottomanism was not able to win over ethno-religious communities based on communitarian interests: "Only very small ethno-religious groups such as the Jews..., which could not entertain any notion of a viable separatism and preferred any sort of Ottomanism to becoming a minority in a nation-state, would accept such a version of Ottomanism" (Hanioğlu 2001, 301).

The nature and aim of Young Turk politics is still controversially discussed. Taha Parla, paraphrasing the Turkish sociologist Şerif Mardin, draws an extremely negative and rather monolithic picture of the Young Turk ideology:

> Young Turk thought...was not libertarian but motivated by the "reason of state"; it was not democratic but ambiguously populistic in its simultaneous distrust of the common people and idealization of manipulated mass action; it was bureaucratically conservative and not at all radical, despite a propensity for forceful changes from above...; it was definitely authoritarian and in most cases..."pre-totalitarian"; it was anti-parliamentarian, despite the Young Turks' superficial constitutionalism...; it was definitely elitist in its emphasis on the authority of specialists. (Parla 1985, 20–21)

Michelle Campos has challenged such stark generalizations of the Young Turks. Within the context of her work on Palestine in the Young Turk period, she emphasized the seriousness of Muslims as well as non-Muslims in their support of a civic Ottomanism. Her research also questions the idea, voiced by Hanioğlu, that ethno-nationalism would, due to the communitarian outlook of in particular the non-Muslim groups, have been destined to gain the upper hand in the competition between various approaches to communal identity in the late Ottoman Empire. Campos argues that a perspective that focuses too narrowly on nationalism and implies the incommensurability of national and imperial political formations naturally prevents us from perceiving notions of imperial nationhood and citizenship. Alternatively, she proposes that an imperial multiethnicity played an important role in the formation of new identities (Campos 2010, 5–7). Campos in particular criticizes the notion that the revolutionary ideas of 1908 (freedom, equality, fraternity, and justice) failed due to a lack of commitment to them. Rather, the ideal of Ottomanism lost its persuasiveness as a consequence of contingent political developments, as well as the incommensurability of liberal and communitarian discourses on citizenship. The liberal Ottoman ideal of citizenship undermined ethnic identities, undercut the institution of the *millets*, and especially eroded the role of the *millets'* religious leaders. It thus created fear of loss of privileges and identity based on the old order. The communitarian citizenship ideal, on the other hand, contributed to an increase of ethno-lingual-religious sensitivities and politics after 1908. These two discourses could be found both among Muslims and non-Muslims, and within and outside of the Young Turk organizations (Campos 2010, 245–247). Campos' intervention is important and suggests caution to avoid homogenizing the complex and intricate dynamics articulated in the thoughts and politics conveniently associated with the Young Turk movement. In particular, it points to the danger of taking for granted that Ottomanism necessarily lost political evidence in the face of exclusivist communitarian projects—even if the contingencies of history moved in this direction and the hindsight view might appear to support a more deterministic interpretation.

While Campos makes a strong case for the argument that Ottomanism did not necessarily have to fail, the historical course of events was not working in its favor. In response to war and economic destitution, gradually, more and more Ottomans began to articulate their feelings of existential angst, grief, social and economic envy, betrayal, and revenge in the language of a nationalism that circled around ideas of religious and ethnic difference and renewal. In this context, particularly anti-Christian—that is, anti-Greek and especially anti-Armenian—sentiment became a catalyst for a Turkish nationalism that had from the beginnings Muslim overtones (Köroğlu 2007, 49–50; see also Kayalı 1997, 174–180; Eissenstat 2007, 61). An important aspect to be considered when analyzing this phase of Turkish nationalism is that most of the Young Turk leaders were from Thrace, the Balkans, and the Caucasus (Jongerden 2007, 190–191). They shared the experience of having lost their homeland with little hope of regaining it. The traumatic loss of the Balkans "plunged the Ottoman intellectual elite into a search for what had gone, and drew the Ottomans into a complex of sensations, shame, grief, anger and a questioning about their own identity" (Boyar 2007, 1). In addition, considerable parts of this elite "cut their teeth as military officers in the struggle against Greek, Bulgarian, Serb, and Albanian bands in the area" (Zürcher 2008, 5).

By the end of the Balkan Wars the multi-religious and multiethnic ideals of Ottomanism were largely discredited as a consequence of changed demographic and political realities. The strategic importance of Anatolia had increased considerably. Dreams for a revival of the glory of the empire, or at least its survival, now began to focus on Anatolia as Turkish-Muslim center of the state. Anatolia itself, however, was full of challenges to Ottoman-Turkish political hegemony. In 1914, the Unionist strongman Enver Paşa (1881–1922), known for his pan-Turkist ambitions, led Ottoman troops toward Batum and Kars.[18] He was, however, defeated by the Russians at Sarıkarmış in January of 1915. The fact that the Russians had been supported by Armenians from outside, as well as, to a lesser extent, from within the empire further heightened anti-Christian and anti-Armenian sentiment. During the years of 1915 and 1916 the Ottomans were frequently defeated and suffered serious territorial losses against Russia in the Caucasus and Anatolia.[19] In this context, the Ottoman state's strategic alliance with the Kurds, since the Hamidian era a pillar of Ottoman efforts to stabilize the east, gained additional significance. The Ottomans must have feared the emergence of a strong Kurdish nationalist and separatist movement. Soon, the Turkist homogenization politics would also target

18. Although they never became the primary focus of CUP politics, pan-Turkist ideas were more prominently articulated since the Balkan Wars and through the built-up propaganda prior to entering World War I, pushed by parts of the CUP elite as propagandist tool to shore up support for the war (Köroğlu 2007, 66–71). In the course of the world war, accelerated in its later stages by the retraction of the Russian army as a consequence of the October Revolution and Ottoman advances into Azerbaijan, pan-Turkist dreams of a possible extension of Ottoman influence and rule toward the Turkish-dominated territories of Russia based on ideals of religious and ethnic homogeneity received a further boost, partially overlapping with hopes for pan-Islamic solidarity with the Ottomans.

19. As Üngör remarks, "[i]t was no coincidence that most of the direct killing of non-combatant Ottoman Christians occurred in the eastern provinces, where the threat of a Russian invasion backed by 'Armenian insiders' was most immediate in the paranoid minds of the CUP dictators" (Üngör 2005, 110).

the Kurds. For now, however, the Young Turks continued their integrative approach toward them. They decided to first "solve," with Minister of the Interior Talat Paşa as pacemaker, the "Armenian question."

Demographic and Social Engineering

Recent research discusses the post-1913 population politics of the CUP, which connected an Anatolia-centered and Turkish-Muslim nationalist vision with a positivist pragmatism and Social Darwinist ideas, as a politics of demographic engineering motivated by ethno-religious criteria of differentiation (Şeker 2007; Dündar 2008; Zürcher 2008; Üngör 2008a). Nesim Şeker defines demographic engineering as "state intervention regarding population level, composition, distribution and increase/decrease. In other words, any deliberate state programme or policy originating from religious/ethnic discrimination or initiated for political, strategic or ideological reasons which aim to increase the political and economic power of one ethnic group over others by manipulating population through various methods can be defined as demographic engineering." As he points out, the politics of demographic engineering predate the emergence of the modern nation-state. What was new in the context of nationalism was the goal of achieving a rather clearly defined degree of ethnic or ethno-religious homogeneity (Şeker 2007, 461).[20] Şeker concisely summarizes the aim of the "demographic reconstruction" of the Ottomans' remaining territories, which the CUP decided to implement in 1914, as twofold, namely

> to provide demographic superiority for Turkish ethnicity and to strengthen this ethnicity economically. Demographic superiority was to be achieved through deportation of the non-Muslim population and resettlement of Muslim refugees in evacuated areas. However, ethnicity was the most important criterion in resettlement as the Ministry of Interior repeatedly gave instructions for the dispersal of "unreliable" elements such as the Arabs, the Albanians, the Bosnians and the Kurds...during resettlement. In the resettlement of such ethnic groups the rule that their population should not exceed 5–10 per cent of the Turkish population was to be strictly

---

20. It has to be underlined that "[t]here was nothing taboo about the forcible resettlement of population groups and entire peoples in the first half of the twentieth century. Indeed it was widely practiced...Resettlement programmes were routinely justified by reference to economic and ideological arguments" (Aly and Heim 2003, 285).

observed. The economic nationalism of the CUP consisted of developing Muslim/Turkish enterprises at the expense of the Greeks and the Armenians in commerce and industry, and to form a Muslim/Turkish bourgeoisie which was to form the basis of the state. (Şeker 2007, 465)

The late Ottoman and early republican politics of demographic engineering should be regarded as part of the broader politics of social engineering that accompanied the transformation of the Ottoman Empire toward a nation-state. The social engineering of the CUP was concerned both with "soft" factors, such as social and cultural knowledges, as well as with material factors, such as the economic system, nationalization of which the Unionists would conceive of as requisite for the project of Turkish sovereignty. Its ultimate goal was the creation of a homogenous Muslim population and public.[21] Therefore, analysis of demographic engineering should be integrated into the broader perspective that the social engineering approach offers and not remain limited to those instances when the state uses physical force in order to create new demographic realities, such as resettlement and ethnic cleansing. It is imperative to understand the motivations and rationalities behind both physical violence and the more subtle means of violence that are employed by the state in its endeavor to modernize/civilize/normalize and control in general, and the creation of an ethnically and culturally homogeneous nation-state more specifically.[22]

---

21. See Aktar (2003). For a concise overview on the genealogy of the concept of social engineering, and discussion of its implementation in late Ottoman and early Republican politics see Üngör (2008a and 2008b).

22. For discussions of various aspects of the Young Turks' politics of demographic engineering see the special issue of *European Journal of Turkish Studies* (Thematic Issue No. 7, 2008, "Demographic Engineering"), which contains several noteworthy contributions, some of which open up comparative perspectives to the experiences of other countries, such as the U.S. (Kieser), Greece and Bulgaria (Öktem), or provide helpful theoretical discussions of demographic engineering, and social engineering more generally (Nikos Sigalas and Alexandre Toumarkine, as well as Üngör). The issue is available online at http://ejts. revues.org/index2073.html. For an insightful study of the regional case of Diyarbakır province that shows the interplay between political orders from above, local government, and complex intercommunal relations as factors that played out in the massacres and deportations of Christians within a long-term politics of Turkification see Üngör (2005). See also the instructive article by Kerem Öktem, which points to the "continuum between phases of destruction and construction" in processes of demographic engineering (Öktem 2008, §13). Based on an analysis of name changes in Turkey since the Young Turk period, Öktem introduces the notion of "toponymical engineering" as the politics of renaming following the erasure of mainly non-Turkish names (Öktem 2008, §17).

The deportations and killings of most of Anatolia's Armenian population in 1915 and 1916 arguably constituting the first genocide of the
twentieth century,[23] were the most extreme aspect of the CUP's politics of
demographic engineering. They need to be understood as consequence
and nadir of a tragic dynamic shaped by an extended period of war and
intercommunal violence. According to serious estimates, the "great catastrophe," as it is remembered by Armenians, cost the lives of between
600,000 and according to some estimates even more than 1,000,000
people.[24] The combination of military-strategic, economic, demographic,
and sociocultural considerations as they played out in the planning of the
deportations and killings of Christians (and in particular the Armenians),
as well as in the settlement of Muslim refugees, many from the Russian
front, in the emptied Armenian villages, point to the Social Darwinist convictions of the architects of these events (Kieser 2000, 426–427; Zürcher
2004, 117).[25] In Zürcher's words:

The aim seems to have been to reduce the Armenian presence
to about five percent of the population in any given locality, but
the deportations were used by a radical faction within the ruling

23. Although most independent historians agree broadly with regard to the general description of the historical issues under debate, the question as for how to name it is still controversially discussed, caught in the crossfire of political interests (of the Turkish and
Armenian states, national and international public opinion, and nationalist lobby groups)
as well as fears/hopes of financial compensation. I agree with Öktem, who observes that the
"fixation on the naming of the event," which can be observed since several years ago in international discussions about the Armenian Genocide and which "can be explained with the
prominence given to normative and ethical arguments that sometimes go together uneasily
with analytical and historical approaches," has, due to the polarization of the debate, unfortunately become rather counterproductive to the endeavor of increasing public knowledge
about the historical context and the details of the deportations and massacres (Öktem 2008,
fn 4).

24. An official Ottoman commission itself used the number 800,000 in a report from 1919;
in the following, this number has been used repeatedly by late Ottoman and early republican
political and military figures (Akçam 2006, 183). For a comprehensive discussion of recent
literature on the bitterly contested question of the Armenian Genocide, including an overview of the events as they unfolded, see Kieser (2007); see also Bloxham (2005, 69–111).

25. Talat Paşa and Mehmed Reşid, who played major roles in the implementation of the
genocide, "were Social Darwinists and positivists who believed there was a life-or-death
battle of the fittest between Armenians and Greeks on the one side and Muslims and Turks
on the other" (Baer 2004, 690). For more details on the decisive roles that Talat Paşa, and
on the executive level Mehmed Reşid played in this context see Üngör (2005) and Kieser
(2002b).

Committee of Union and Progress to physically eliminate the
Armenian population...The idea of the perpetrators was to create a
Muslim majority all over Anatolia to prevent what had happened in
the Balkans and the Caucasus from happening again in this land.
(Zürcher 2008, 9)

It has to be stressed that Armenians were the main, but not the only, target
of the CUP's politics of ethno-religious homogenization. Other Christian
communities also suffered heavily. In Thrace and the Aegean coast, intim-
idation drove between 130,000 and 150,000 Greek Orthodox Christians to
leave their homes, businesses, and belongings and seek refuge in Greece
(Şeker 2007, 465; Zürcher 2004, 126); in the southeastern provinces, the
various Syriac Christians were in many cases subject to similar treatment
as the Armenians and mourn themselves more than 100,000 victims
of genocide.[26] Overall, the Anatolian population decreased by one-third
between 1914 and 1922, more than half of which, both Muslims and
non-Muslims, died as victims of war (Kieser 2000, 359).

It is a less known fact, but of great historical significance, that the
CUP's Turkification plans affected also non-Turkish Muslim populations,
mainly the Kurds, the resettlement of considerable parts of whom began
already before the deportation and annihilation of the vast majority of the
Eastern Christians had been finalized:

In April 1916, the CUP ordered the mass deportation of Kurds from
the eastern provinces through a sweeping quadripartite decree. For
the Kurds "not to live their tribal lives and preserve their nationalities where they are sent", the CUP deemed it "absolutely necessary
to separate the tribal chieftains from their people" and to "settle
them separately in Turkish-populated areas in the province". Those
who were unable to travel were to be "distributed individually in
Turkish villages in the province". In the minds of CUP social
engineers all of these measures would prevent the Kurds from
"remaining a useless element by preserving their traditions and
nationalities in regions populated by Arabs and Kurds"...[The]
CUP orchestrated a large-scale attack on Kurdish culture, language,

---

26. See Gaunt (2006) for a general account of the deportations and massacres of Eastern
Christians during World War I with a focus on the Syriac Christians; see also Yonan (1989)
and Tamcke (2007).

and demography, constituencies that could define the Kurds as a
nation in the eastern provinces and therefore supposedly posed a
threat. (Üngör 2008a, §27)

It has been claimed that toward the end of the war an estimated 700,000
Kurds, most of whom probably died on the way due to the lack of food
and shelter, were forced by the Ottomans to move westward (Jwaideh
2009, 257). Still, the relocation of the Kurds was very different in style
from the forced emigration of the Armenians. Annihilation was not its
goal. By means of relocating Kurdish communities in small units among
the Turkish-speaking population, as well as simultaneous relocation of
Turkish-speaking Muslims to the east (many of whom were refugees from
the Balkans), the CUP's policies against the Kurds aimed at Turkification
of their language and culture in order to assimilate them into the Turkish
nation.

The CUP's attempts to resettle and assimilate the Kurds were, at least
temporarily, cut short by the end of the war, which led to an implosion of
the CUP and temporarily interrupted its politics. During the Greek-Turkish
or Turkish Independence War, which was a product of the harsh conditions
dictated to the Ottomans by the victorious Entente following World War I,
the Turkish nationalists' approach toward the Kurds showed in fact a rather
integrative approach that was focused on securing a (Turkish-Kurdish)
Muslim alliance. In terms of actual armed struggle, the war was primarily
fought between Greek and Ottoman Muslim forces (in Anatolia), and secondarily also between Armenian and Ottoman Muslim forces (in the eastern provinces) (Üngör 2008a, §27–35). The Muslim alliance, which was in
the ideological reshuffling that followed the political collapse of the CUP
presented as "Turkish Union" (*Türk Birliği*), gained much of its strength
and legitimacy from othering Greeks and Armenians as internal enemies.[27] Thus, anti-Christian rhetoric and policies of the CUP found their
continuation in the Turkish War of Independence. At the same time, the
propagation of Islam as the uniting banner of this alliance was also meant
to temper the threat of Kurdish nationalism (Şeker 2006, 158–166).

It is the advantage of the concept of demographic engineering that it
provides a perspective that is not limited to anti-Christian or anti-Armenian

---

27. The political opponents of the Turkish Union movement formed under the name "New
Ottomanism" and advocated a return to a more inclusive Ottoman nationalism, but found
little support (Şeker 2006, 166–171).

policies, but puts these within the picture of a broader politics of Turkish-Muslim homogenization that targeted also non-Turkish Muslims, such as Kurds and Arabs, as well as religiously "dubious" groups, such as the Kızılbaş-Alevis (as I will show in the following chapter). This said, it has to be acknowledged that the violence that was applied in the deportation and killings of Christians went, both in scope and structure, beyond anything that Muslims were confronted with. The CUP's politics of demographic engineering was continued by the early Turkish Republic, now targeting mainly the Kurds, as well as non-Turkish Muslim immigrants, who also became subject to resettlement and Turkification (Ülker 2007; Üngör 2008b; Cagaptay 2006).[28]

Attempts to explain late Ottoman and early republican politics of demographic engineering should not remain limited to the ideological worldview of the CUP elites and their reception of Social Darwinist thought. In order to understand why this politics made so much sense to them despite the pluralist vision of Ottomanism that they had previously endorsed, one needs to consider a variety of historical and political developments that shaped the nationalist experiences and political calculations of that time period. The real sense of threat by nationalist separatist movements, the refugee problem, the fact that most of the refuges had been forced out by Christian forces, as well as the peculiar political and military constellation in the eastern provinces during World War I are the most important factors that contributed to the radicalization of the Unionists, and exacerbated anti-Christian sentiments in the Muslim population.

The complexity of the experiences and motivations of the various actors involved and the different local and international contexts that rendered them possible mark the limits of a discussion of late-Ottoman anti-Armenian policies within the framework of demographic engineering alone. Social Darwinist nationalists and envious and/or revenge-lusting Anatolian Muslims were not the only agents involved in the story that made possible the CUP's terror. This is not meant to be a cynical argument by

---

28. The early republican politics of demographic engineering were legalized by the settlement laws from 1926 and especially 1934. In the parliamentary discussion of the latter law, Minister of Interior Şükrü Kaya frankly declared: "This law will create a country speaking with one language, thinking in the same way and sharing the same sentiment" (quoted in Ülker 2008, §8). Kaya embodies the continuity between late-Ottoman and republican politics of ethno-religious homogenization. He has been involved in the CUP's Turkification practices as general inspector (*müfettiş*) of Thrace, and especially as director of the General Directorate for Refugees and Tribes, which was charged among other things with relocation of people in the empire according to ethno-religious criteria (see next chapter).

means of which to turn the blame on the Armenians for the tragedy that they experienced. But a historical perspective, I would maintain, needs to assume that actors make rational decisions, independent of whether we approve of their rationales—even in the case of mass violence and genocide. Therefore, if one wants to understand—not justify—why the CUP elite made the decisions it did, then one also needs to take into account the military and geostrategic threat that Armenian nationalist ambitions in light of their international support, as well as the cooperation of nationalist Armenians with Russian forces, posed to Ottomans during the world war (Erickson 2008).

Independent of how one might evaluate the agency of the Armenians and Syriac Christians in the course of events that cost the lives of hundreds of thousands of them, the question itself brings into clearer focus the complexity of the political dynamics that marked late Ottoman and early Turkish republican politics of nationalism. As the next chapter will try to show, the Kızılbaş-Alevis, too, were decisively impacted by these dynamics. In fact, I argue, that the Ottoman and early Turkish republican treatment of the Kızılbaş-Alevis needs to be reevaluated in the broader context of ethno-religious violence, and the streamlining of legitimate identities in this period.

3

Entering the Gaze of the Nationalists

IN LIGHT OF the late Ottoman obsession of the Muslim elites of the state with the Armenian question (described in the previous chapter), it should be hardly surprising that any speculations about intimate relations between Armenians and Kurdish Kızılbaş-Alevis (as discussed in chapter 1) were a matter of concern for the Muslim elites and strongly rejected by them. In the late Young Turk period, Turkish nationalists began to declare the Kızılbaş-Alevis victims of Armenian propaganda and to underline their Turkishness. Typical is the account of the Unionist and later Kemalist Rıza Nur, who recounts in his autobiography that "[d]uring the reign of Abdülhamit, the Armenians deluded...these Kızılbaş Turks telling them they would be Armenians. And they were successful."[1] Before turning in more detail to the nationalist discourses that emerged in the late Young Turk period on the Kızılbaş-Alevis, I will in the following pages first broadly outline the specific political context in which they have to be understood. Ottoman fears of possible Kurdish-Armenian alliances, as reflected in Rıza Nur's quote, became even more pronounced in February 1914, when the Unionists were forced to sign an internationally guaranteed reform plan for the Armenian territories, which among other things foresaw elections in the eastern provinces. The Unionists feared that Armenians and Kızılbaş-Alevis might form a coalition in such elections and then try to dictate regional politics. World War I prevented implementation of that plan.

While the plight of the Armenians received in the following years considerable international attention, the issue of the Kızılbaş-Alevis, although occasionally addressed by ABCFM missionaries since the 1850s, never became an important topic for the international public (Kieser 2000, 394, 399, and 499). European powers were clearly more

---

1 Rıza Nur (*Hayat ve Hatıratım*, 1968) as quoted in Kieser (2000, 393).

interested in the Christian people of the Oriental churches than in what appeared to most of them as an obscure Muslim sect. By the late 19th century the matter of the Kızılbaş occasionally appeared in the international debate on the Ottoman question, in particular when it came to discussions about demographics, which in the age of positivism played an important role in international debates about the state and fate of the eastern provinces.

The earliest example of population statistics in which the Kızılbaş appear as a subunit to the category Muslim was presented during the Berlin Congress (1878) by the Armenian patriarch.[2] In 1880, the Kızılbaş were also mentioned in population estimates regarding the eastern provinces produced by the British consuls.[3] A critical observer of such statistics has been the Turkish historian Kemal Karpat, who cautions that "[t]he manipulation of population statistics for political purposes by various ethnic and religious groups was widespread and ingenious" (Karpat 1985, 4). He suspects, for example, that the population statistics by the Armenian patriarch from 1912 (within a population statistic for Eastern Anatolia), which put "Kizilbaş, Zaza, Çarikli, and Yezidi" under a rubric "other religions" intended to make the numbers of de facto Muslims appear smaller in relation to the numbers of Christians (Karpat 1985, 5).[4] But there is reason to doubt Karpat's own neutrality on this question. His claim that

---

2 The patriarch submitted the following numbers regarding the population of the eastern provinces of Erzurum, Van, Sivas, Harput, Diyarbakır, and Halep: total number of Christians: 1056,800; Muslims: 770,000 "of whom only 320,000 were Turks, the rest being Kurds, Kizilbaş, and Türkmen" (Karpat 1985, 53 and 192).

3 In 1880 the British ambassador in Istanbul invited several British consuls to discuss the various population figures put forward concerning the eastern provinces (Karpat 2001, 210). Based on estimates by former Consul Taylor, his successor Consul Henry Trotter (named consul of the Kurdish provinces in 1879) presented for the provinces Erzurum, Van, Diyarbakır, and Harput the following numbers: Turks: 442,500; Kurds: 848,000; Kızılbaş Moslems: 200,000; and Christians: 649,000 (Karpat 1985, 52 and 192).

4 Following British inquiry, the patriarch than had to admit inconsistencies in his statistics, which listed only Turks as Muslims (Karpat 1985, 53). Gaunt on the other side has questioned the reason why the Armenian patriarch, or also the Assyro-Chaldeans, who in 1919 submitted a population statistics from 1914 to the Paris Peace Conference with similar detailed differentiation between groups at the Islamic margins, should differentiate that meticulously between such groups and produce detailed numbers. Gaunt suggests that these statistics were most likely be drawn up by Ottoman bureaucrats, who in this time period began to develop an interest in the various ethnic and religious sects and groups in the eastern provinces (Gaunt 2006, 19 and 405–406).

the Kızılbaş would be ethnic Turks reflects his own nationalist bias (see Karpat 1985, 53).[5]

The Kızılbaş Kurds of Dersim and the Unionists

For early Turkish nationalists, the ethnic diversity of the Muslim population and in particular the Kurds were problems. The question of how to assimilate the Kurds into Turkish nationhood was complicated by the fact that a considerable part of them, about 20%, were Kızılbaş-Alevis. One regional example of the CUP's approach to the Kızılbaş-Alevis within the broader context of its social engineering program is the case of Dersim, a remote and mountainous region in eastern Anatolia south of Erzincan at the northern part of the province of Mamuretülaziz (Elazığ), the largest portion of which is today part of the province of Tunceli. The ethnic and religious difference of the Kurdish Kızılbaş-Alevis of Dersim certainly contributed to their determination to resist the state's authority and to the mutual suspicion between them and the Ottomans. The tribes of Dersim had for centuries managed to keep the influence of the Ottoman state on their territory rather limited. As with the other eastern provinces, Dersim, too, was since the second half of the 19th century subject to heightened Ottoman attempts to create closer control over the region. Trying to impose the authority of the central government on the tribes of Dersim, the Istanbul government regularly conducted military expeditions into the region (Akpınar et al. 2010).

One of the major reasons for the Ottomans' uneasiness about the loyalty of the regions adjacent to Russian zones of influence, especially Dersim and provinces such as Van with strong Armenian populations, were the continuing Russian ambitions in the northeastern parts of Anatolia and the threat that the possibility of alliances between the Russians and the Kurds and/or Armenians meant to the state. As for the Dersim region, the Ottomans therefore intensified under the reign of Abdülhamid II their efforts to increase control over and secure the loyalty of the local population, which it regarded with much suspicion. An example for the strategic way in which the Ottomans thought about their engagement in the east is the military report on how to "reform" the Dersim region from 1896, which

---

5 Throughout, Karpat seems to prefer interpretations that favor Turkish ethnic stock in comparison to other ethnicities (in particular to Kurds). It is also rather astonishing that in his discussion of Armenian population figures he does not even mention the massacres of Armenians in 1894–1896 and 1915–1916.

cautioned that a military expedition in the region would bear the danger
of further alienating the relations between the Turks (read: Muslims) and
the Kurdish Kızılbaş-Alevis and therefore only benefit the Armenians
(Akpınar et al. 2010, 319). Following this logic, the state increased its local
presence and built mosques and elementary schools, which marked its
claim of political (and religious) hegemony (Kieser 2000, 167–170; see
also Irmak 2010, 254 and 266–267).

Until the early 20th century, Dersim was inhabited by a majority of mostly Zaza and a smaller number of Kurmanci Kurds, both of
which were Kızılbaş-Alevi, as well as a sizable Armenian minority.[6] It
is often maintained that in contrast to the relations between Kurds and
Armenians in other parts of the eastern provinces, the Kızılbaş-Alevi
Kurds and the Armenians of Dersim were getting along fairly well (Şeker
2007, 468); there were, for example, many villages where Armenians and
Kızılbaş-Alevis lived side by side (Kieser 1998, 281–282). While Dersim
Kurds, too, had participated in the plunder of Armenian property that
accompanied the earlier massacres of 1894–1896, they would not have
participated in the massacres themselves (Kieser 2000, 198–199).[7] One
should, however, be careful with drawing an overtly positive picture of
the relations between Armenians and Kızılbaş-Alevis in Dersim. Ottoman
official sources from the second half of the 19th century provide manifold
examples of Armenians being robbed and harassed, and their property
being destroyed by local Kurds (see Irmak 2010, 255–258).

---

6 The size of the Armenian population in the northeastern regions of the Ottoman Empire
decreased in the course of the 19th century due to Ottoman centralization and Sunnitization
politics, emigration toward Russia, raids of Kurdish tribes, and anti-Armenian massacres
such as those in 1894–1896 (Kieser 2000, 42–43). According to Ottoman general census
figures collected between 1881 and 1893, the counties of Hozat and Mazgırt, which were part
of the Dersim region, counted about 13,000 Armenians of a total population of 54,000 (that
is, 24% of the population) (Karpat 1985, 144–145). In an Ottoman population statistic from
1897, the Armenian population of Dersim is recorded as roughly 15,000 of a total population
of about 114,000 (13%) (Karpat 1985, 196–197). According to 1906/7 census data for Dersim,
13,900 of 69,000 (20%) inhabitants of the province were Armenians (Karpat 1985, 164–165).
The 1914 Ottoman population statistics for Dersim give the number of 13,900 of a total of
79,000 (18%) for the Armenian population (Karpat 1985, 182–183).

7 Here it has to be remarked that "in the years before the Armenian genocide, the question
of Armenian agrarian property, robbed by Kurds, was one of the main issues of Ottoman
interior politics" (Kieser 2008, §11). As Kieser argues convincingly, the agrarian question,
and the Ottomans' inability or unwillingness to solve the property claims of the Armenians
against Kurds as well as new Muslim immigrants, who had also taken their share, has to
be counted among one of the reasons that would make a "final solution" of the "Armenian
problem" appealing to the CUP elites (Kieser 2008).

The relations between the Kızılbaş Kurds and the state underwent tremendous changes in the Young Turk period. In contrast to most Sunni Kurds, the Kızılbaş-Alevis from Dersim are reported to have shown sympathy for the reinstatement of the constitution in 1908 and the new political tone introduced by the Young Turks (Kieser 2003, 179–181; Riggs 1997, 110). Missionary Riggs from the neighboring Harput reports that "[t]eachers and political leaders were sent into the Dersim, and the Kurds were made to understand that they could share in the new liberty." He claims that the Dersim Kurds responded rather enthusiastically to this political change and declared their loyalty to the new rulers: "A new day is dawning for these people as for all the races of Turkey" (Riggs 1911, 736). Missionary White even observed "some awakening of national consciousness among the Alevi Turks since the new Ottoman *régime* came in...The Alevis are engaged in opening village schools as rapidly as their means permit, and are said to have effected an organisation for commercial and political purposes" (White 1913, 698).

The ABCFM missionaries' observations reflect the political optimism created by the Young Turk revolution (see chapter 2). The previous government's military operations in Dersim in 1907 and 1908 had relied on utter force in their aim to discipline and subordinate the Dersimlis. In 1909, the new government, too, would order a military expedition into Dersim. This time around, however, the expedition had an aim and character that was remarkably different from previous ones. The commander of the expedition, İbrahim Pasha, explained this change of politics, reasoning that rather than mere force, building trust to the government and the state would be the only way to reform the Dersim (Tulasoğlu 2005, 28–29).

To be sure, the liberties that the new approach to Dersim would bring were limited. Although this period shows softer means of coercion and assimilation than previous and subsequent ones, it clearly remained within the broader politics of social engineering discussed in the previous chapter. Two reports published by the district governor (*mutasarrıf*) of Erzincan, Şefik, who had been part of the Ottoman military expedition to Dersim in 1909, reflect this new approach.[8] In these reports, Governor Şefik, a CUP member, blames the old (that is, pre-CUP) government for its failed approach to Dersim, which, instead of increasing the loyalty of the Dersim

8 "Dersim Kıtasının Ahval-i Umumiyye ve Esbab-ı Islahiyyesi" and "Dersim Ekrad'ının Ahval-i Mezhebiyyeleri," in *Mülkiyye*, no. 14 and 15 (1326/1910). For a translation into German and contextualized discussion of the two reports see Tulasoğlu (2005).

Kurds to the central government, would have contributed to their alienation. He advocates a change of policy with focus on education (building
schools and spreading knowledge of Islam and the Turkish language), better government, and more integration of the Kurds therein. In short, this
period was marked by a decrease of physical violence, but still remained
within the parameters of increasing state control and sociocultural homogenization as reflected in the emphasis on Turkification and Sunnification.
In these years, some Dersimlis even joined the CUP and made careers
in the state administration (Kieser 2000, 393). In general the relations
between the communities in the whole province of Mamuretülaziz are said
to have improved—despite temporarily increasing tensions following the
anti-Armenian massacres in Adana in April 1909.[9]

Things got worse with the beginning of the world war. The Dersim
Kurds refused to contribute troops to the Ottoman army and tensions
continued throughout the war. At the eve of the expulsion and massacres
of the Armenians, the German pastor Johannes Ehmann, director of an
orphanage in the town of Mamuretülaziz, where he had lived since 1897,
wrote the following in a letter to the German ambassador in Istanbul:

> The Turks say, and probably rightly so, that the Armenians at the
> frontier would have partially defected to the Russians; that the
> Armenian people would be against the Turks; that Armenian irreg-
> ulars would have fought the Turks in the Van region and in Persia;
> that the Armenians would have propagated among the Kızılbaş in
> Dersim for an alignment (Anschluss) of the latter with Russia...;
> and that the Armenians of the interior would, in case of a Russian
> attack, immediately side with the enemy.[10]

The letter provides testament to the CUP's political fears of the time
and illustrates the complexity of the political constellation in the eastern provinces, which was rather daunting—especially if one takes under

---

9 On the other hand, Molyneux-Seel, in his extensive report of his journey through Dersim
in 1911, does not give any indication of an amelioration in the relations between the Dersimlis
and the central government. To the contrary, he points to the immense destruction caused
by the regularly occurring military operations and the violent means by which the government tried to discipline the region (Molyneux-Seel 1914, 51). As a British diplomat he might
have been more critical of Ottoman changes and more inclined to emphasize those aspects
of Ottoman politics that justified foreign intervention in the eastern provinces.

10 "Der Leiter des Waisenhauses in Mamuret ul-Aziz Johannes Ehmann an den Botschafter in
Konstantinopel (Wangenheim)," Letter 18 May 1915. Accessed May 26 2012. http://www.armeno-
cide.de/armenocide/armgende.nsf/$$AllDocs/1915-05-18-DE-003?OpenDocument.

consideration the Ottomans' recent experiences on the Balkans. Outside interests and interference (Russian, European, and American) were seen as undermining (and undermined) Ottoman sovereignty and appeared to many as an existential threat, which by the outbreak of the Great War began to be interpreted in Social Darwinist terms as a struggle for life and death.[11]

The government must have realized that, given the various international interests in the region, and the dense Armenian, Kurdish, and Kızılbaş-Alevi populations in the eastern provinces, their regional authority, which was built on notions of Islamic and Turkish unity, was rather fragile (Kieser 2003, 179–183). In 1915, the CUP failed to convince the Dersimlis to support its military campaign against the Russians (Kieser 2000, 396–397). Following the catastrophic Ottoman defeat against the Russians at the battle of Sarıkamış, "[f]rom 1915 on Armenians and Kurdish Alevis became the main target of political coercion and violence" (Kieser 2002a, 127; see also White 1918, 247; Hasluck 1921, 339; Kieser 2003, 180–184). As Kieser notes, the Armenians generally suffered most in those regions where they constituted together with the Kızılbaş-Alevis the majority of the population (Kieser 2000, 394). Kızılbaş-Alevis from Dersim helped, in parts for money and in parts for free, to rescue thousands of Armenians by escorting them through the Dersim mountains to Russia (Riggs 1997, 112–117).[12]

Following the Armenian deportations, ABCFM missionary White reports of fear that "the next step taken by the governing clique would force the Alevi Turks to abandon their Muslim nonconformity." Allegedly, the CUP now wanted "to create a uniform state, one in Turkish nationality, and one in Moslem orthodoxy" (White 1918, 247). The Kızılbaş-Alevis of Dersim showed the most aggressive opposition against the CUP and subsequent nationalist governments. In 1916, probably in fear of a fate similar to that of the Armenians[13] and with the goal of achieving some form of

---

11 Kieser's biographical study of Mehmed Reşid, one of the architects of the massacres of Armenian and Syriac Christians, shows the gradual formation of a mind that began to see non-Muslims as threat to the national survival and therefore embarked on a terrible crusade justified by the goal of saving the fatherland (Kieser 2002b).

12 According to estimates, roughly four out of five Armenians of the province Mamuretülaziz—which has been labeled the "slaughterhouse province" by American missionaries, who witnessed the tragic events close by—died during the genocide (Kieser 2000, 429–431).

13 This fear is documented in official Ottoman correspondence of that time (Irmak 2010, 258).

independence, several Dersim tribes began to attack state institutions in the region (Kieser 2000, 397). The revolt had been encouraged by Russians and Armenians and broke out at a time when Russia had occupied the neighboring regions between Erzincan and Erzurum. For the Ottomans, the situation was rather precarious. The possibility of a Russian-Kurdish alliance must have appeared as an imminent threat to them. Although the Ottomans were able to subdue the revolt, tensions between the region and the central government continued during the Turkish War of Independence, to the goals of which the Dersim Kurds were unable to relate. Rather, they were inspired by the prospect of self-determination as defined in the Fourteen Points pronounced in 1918 by U.S. President Woodrow Wilson, from which they inferred the idea of Kurdish autonomy within a federal system. Following fruitless negotiations with the Turkish nationalists, in which they even "insisted upon the Sultan as a guarantee for a federal solution" (Kieser 2002a, 132), the Dersim Kurds began in 1920, under the lead of the Koçgiri tribe and with support of some Turkish Kızılbaş-Alevis—but no Sunni Kurds—a guerilla war, which meant attacks on state outposts and occasional clashes with police and military forces. Fighting continued until mid-1921, when the revolt was finally subdued (Kieser 1998, 288–305; Kieser 2000, 398–403).

The case of the Dersim Kızılbaş-Alevis is often referred to as an exception to the generally believed broad support that the nationalists surrounding Mustafa Kemal Pasha are said to have received by the Anatolian Kızılbaş-Alevi and Bektashi groups. As part of his tour through central Anatolia to galvanize support for the nationalist cause Mustafa Kemal visited already in November of 1919 the village of Hacıbektaş, where the mausoleum of Hacı Bektaş and the major lodge of the Bektashi order, seat of the two rivaling branches of the brotherhood, was located. According to a report by the provincial administration of Ankara, the nationalist delegation was not only festively received by Çelebi Cemaleddin[14] and the leaders of the Bektashi order, but also both the Bektashis and the Alevis entered the alliance of the national forces (T. C. Başbakanlık 1982, 77). While there are no detailed historical accounts of this visit, in Alevi and Bektashi

---

14 Çelebi is the title of the head of one of the most prominent Alevi *dede* lineages of Anatolia, namely the lineage (*ocak*) from Hacıbektaş, the authority of which is based on its claimed direct descent from Hacı Bektaş Veli, patron saint of the Bektashi order, venerated also by most Alevis (virtually by all Turkish Alevis—among Kurdish Alevis the veneration of Hacı Bektaş is not that prominent). For a historical evaluation of the role of the Çelebi branch of Bektashism see Yıldırım (2010).

memory it has taken on mythical dimensions culminating in the story of an unanimous support of the Bektashis and Alevis for the nationalist cause (Dressler 2002, 215–220). The historical record, however, shows a much more complex picture as Hülya Küçük's study on the Bektashis during the Independence War has shown. While many Bektashis and Alevis supported the Turkish nationalists, others did not. The activities of the Çelebi in this period illustrate this. While he was in principle supportive of the nationalists' cause, he refused to mediate between them and the Kurdish Kızılbaş-Alevis (H. Küçük 2002, 212–215). During the uprising of the Koçgiri tribe of Dersim the Çelebi did not try to interfere either.[15] Apparently, while he had strong influence on the Turkish-speaking Kızılbaş-Alevis, his influence upon Kurdish Kızılbaş-Alevis was rather limited. This might have been partially due to the Çelebi's closeness to the state, which could have been an alienating factor for the Kurdish Kızılbaş-Alevis, who tended to prefer political autonomy. Although there are conflicting reports, it seems that the Çelebi's interference on behalf of the state and the nationalists has rather discredited his lineage among Kurdish Alevis. The emphasis on the Turkishness of Alevism and Bektashism that Çelebi Cemaleddin, as well as his successor Çelebi Velieddin frequently articulated might additionally have alienated Kurdish Kızılbaş-Alevis (see H. Küçük 2002, 218). While it would be wrong to interpret the antagonism between the Çelebis and the Kurdish Kızılbaş-Alevis in ethno-nationalist terms alone, the fact that the rift between them appeared along ethnic lines might have over time contributed to the formation of Turkish and Kurdish nationalisms among the various Kızılbaş-Alevi groups.

The overall picture of the relations between the state and state-loyal forces on the one side, and the Kızılbaş-Alevis on the other in the decade preceding the formation of the Turkish Republic shows that Turkish Kızılbaş-Alevis tended to be more supportive of both Ottoman state institutions and the Turkish nationalist movement than Kurdish Kızılbaş-Alevis (Kieser 2002a, 136–137). This mirrors their differing experiences with the state. Kurdish experiences were to a stronger extent shaped by violence due to the centralization efforts of the empire. In particular, the eastern Kızılbaş-Alevis were more likely to have been witnesses of the expulsions

---

15 Already at the beginning of World War I, Çelebi Ahmed Cemaleddin had formed an Alevi-Bektashi regiment, the *Mucahidin-i Bektaşiye*, for which he had also tried to recruit Kurdish Kızılbaş-Alevis. But when he presented his case on behalf of the government to the Dersim tribes this was of no avail (see H. Küçük 2002, 125–134; Kieser 2000, 396–397).

and massacres of the Christian populations and therefore more concerned about their own vulnerability.[16]

The Eastern Provinces from the Perspective of the Modernizing State

Since it is important for a proper historical contextualization of the emerging nationalist interest in the Kızılbaş-Alevis and related groups, it will at this point be helpful to summarize the main political issues at stake for the CUP and its subsequent political incarnations with regard to the eastern provinces. In the period 1914–1922, from the world war to the Turkish War of Independence, four interconnected issues threatened the nationalists' claim of comprehensive political and ideological control over Anatolia, namely (1), the national ambitions of the Christian populations, mainly the Greek-Orthodox and the Armenians; (2) the threat of Kurdish nationalism and separatism; (3) the Kızılbaş-Alevis' socioreligious difference, in particular their loyalty to religious and tribal authorities, whose grounds of authority were beyond the spheres of both the nation-state and Sunni Muslim institutions and therefore difficult to discipline; and (4) the fear of alliances between Armenians, Kurds, Kızılbaş-Alevis, and Russians against the Ottomans.

It is apparent that Young Turk thought and policies prepared the seeds for Kemalism and its politics of modernization through secularization and nationalization (see Zürcher 2010). All of the nationalist organizations from the CUP to the Kemalist Republican People's Party (hereafter RPP) were committed to erasing these challenges to the centralist nation-state. In the justification for the discriminatory practices, which this nationalization in practice meant for those that did not or were not willing to fit the profile of the national citizen, sociopolitical mistrust either underwent a powerful symbiosis with economic envy (of the non-Muslims), or was coupled with arguments of civilizational and socioeconomic underdevelopment (in the case of the Kurds). It is easy to see how the political conflicts articulated in the rhetoric of communal interests in the 1910s and 1920s

---

16 The fear of a fate similar to that of the Armenians was allegedly shared also by Turkish Kızılbaş-Alevis of Yozgat and might have been one of the motivations for some of them to participate in a local revolt ("Çapanoğlu Uprising") against the nationalists in the summer of 1920. In this case, too, Çelebi Cemaleddin appears to have ignored Mustafa Kemal Paşa's request to interfere on behalf of the nationalists (H. Küçük 2002, 214–215).

were not only a reflection of nationalism, but themselves also motivation for the creation and institutionalization of an authoritarian nationalism.[17]

From the Hamidian period until the early years of World War I, and then again during the Turkish War of Independence, a major focus of state governance in the eastern provinces was on the strategic alliance with the Kurds. This alliance was drawing on Sunni-Islamic rhetoric, which implied the othering of non-Muslims, and also, to a certain extent, Kızılbaş-Alevis. To this end, the state tried to capitalize on regional competitions, especially between Kurds and Armenians. Following the events of 1915 and 1916, Kurdish fears of Armenian return and retribution, fostered by Turkish nationalist rhetoric, helped to hold the Kurds at bay, as did promises of autonomy. The temporary establishment of an independent Armenian Republic (1918–1920) with Yerevan as it capital and Armenian claims to Ottoman territory provided the nationalists with further arguments to rally Kurdish support (Kieser 2000, 361–362). However, the promise of autonomy given to the Kurds would never materialize and ultimately leave the Kurds with a sense of betrayal that contributed to the tragic dynamics of Turkish-Kurdish relations ever since (Kieser 2000, 363).

In conclusion, following the experience of the Balkan Wars and rationalized by a Social Darwinist worldview, the CUP defined the non-Muslim population of Anatolia as the major obstacle for the establishment of an Ottoman Turkish nation-state and aspired to change the demographic realities in a way that suited their project of ethno-religious homogenization. The Turkish nationalists of the late Ottoman Empire and early Turkish Republic regarded the change of the demographic realties of the remaining Ottoman territories as a prerequisite for the establishment of a modern nation-state. The expulsion and massacres of the Armenians and other Christian minorities in central and eastern Anatolia was the most brutal consequence of that (Kieser 2000, 501). The Turkish Independence War, too, was motivated by the goal of (re-) establishing Muslim-Turkish sovereignty, and "from the very start defined as a struggle against Greek and Armenian claims" (Zürcher 2008, 10–11). After the eradication of the Christian population of Anatolia, the Kurds became the main target of social and demographic engineering. In subsequent instances of state

---

17 Drawing on Miroslav Hroch, Shissler has pointed out that "the presence of an ethnically or nationally relevant social conflict is decisive in a national agitation's catching hold and becoming a mass movement." In the formation of what Hroch calls small-nation nationalism, social struggle and cultural struggle are closely linked (Shissler 2003, 11).

violence, Turkish nationalism and state centralism remained the major sources of legitimation used against the Kurds. The coercive centralization would continue in republican practices of pacifying, disciplining, and further assimilating the southeast in accordance with the vision of a homogeneous Turkish nation-state. In the case of the Dersim region, this sustained coercion, with its peak of brutality in the events of 1937 and 1938, when the state used its comprehensive military means to finally solve what it described as "the Dersim question," was presented to the public as a necessary civilizing measurement meant to eradicate backwardness and ignorance (Kieser 2002a, 134). The still popular argument that the "Kurdish question" would essentially be the product of the socioeconomic underdevelopment, as used until today by the Turkish state to justify its interventions in the Kurdish-dominated parts of the country, is an extension of the rhetoric of Kemalist nationalism and its Unionist roots (Ayata and Yükseker 2005).

The Kızılbaş-Alevis within the Framework of Turkism

A case of a prominent community other than the Kızılbaş that became already in the late 19th century subject to discourses of racial and religious sameness and difference were the Turkish-speaking Orthodox Christians of Anatolia. In the context of Greek nationalism, these populations, which were known as Karamanlı, became subject of ethnographic and lingual studies and theories interested in proving their intimate relation with Hellenistic culture and Indo-European race. As in the case of the Kızılbaş, these initial speculations were soon to be countered by an emerging Turkish nationalist discourse, which since the turn of the 20th century offered a competing interpretation of the Karamanlıs, namely arguing their racial Turkishness. Unsurprisingly, this later interpretation reached its height in the years following World War I, when fears about the dismemberment of the remaining Ottoman territory were at its height, and the population exchange between Greece and Turkey, decided upon with the Lausanne Treaty, not yet in sight (Benlisoy 2003).

However, as discussed above, the emerging discourse of Turkish nationalism in the Unionist period was first of all concerned with the religious homogeneity of the population, and this is one important reason for why Turkish nationalists, even if they were convinced about the racial Turkishness of the Karamanlı, would be willing to let them leave to their religious brethren in Greece (Benlisoy 2003, 931–932). Based on this sense of creating a more homogenous national body, that is, a body that was by definition already widely accepted to be essentially Muslim, the new politics of nationalism focused on ethnic homogenization (Turkification of the non-Turkish Muslims), which itself can be seen as in continuity with Hamidian politics of religious homogenization (Sunnification of the Kızılbaş-Alevis). In this context, vigorous nationalists began to discover parts of the Muslim body whose loyalty to the project of a religiously con-noted nation-state they regarded with skepticism. The emerging debate on the Dönme, descendants of Jewish converts to Islam from the 17th century, who maintained until the early 20th century a distinct identity expressed in largely endogamous social relations, is a case in point. In the context of the evolving nationalism of the Young Turks, who at first were strongly supported by the Dönme, the latter's sense of ethno-religious distinctive-ness raised suspicions (Baer 2010). As explained before, in the Young Turk period the boundaries of what it required to be Turkish and/or Muslim were not yet clearly defined, and tensions between citizenship-based and ethnic, racial, and/or religious modes of defining Turkishness were fer-vently debated. In this context, the case of the othering of the Dönme, simi-lar to that of the Kızılbaş-Alevis, reflects the formation of a Muslim national body that demanded criteria for inclusion/exclusion (Baer 2004, 694).

Both the Kızılbaş-Alevis and Dönme fit uneasily in the new nation-alist imaginations of Muslim unity. Both groups were associated with non-Muslim origins and therefore, in a time of heightened sentiments against non-Muslim subjects, regarded with suspicion. In the mid-1920s both groups became subject of sensationalist yellow press coverage that portrayed them as engaging in morally dubious practices. We find that in this period both groups are being accused of engaging in "extinguish-ing the candles" (*mum söndürmek*). This is a standard defamatory trope insinuating ritual orgies and incest that is known from its use against the Kızılbaş-Alevis, but also used against other nonconformist groups at the margins of the Islamic discourse (Baer 2010, 167–169). Casting doubt on the morality of Kızılbaş-Alevis and Dönme can be interpreted as part of the formation of a new national body, which needed to draw not only its ethno-religious, but parallel to that also its moral boundaries against potentially dangerous elements that could harm it from within.

The discursive differentiation between the Sunni-Muslim and Turkish central body of the nation and groups at its margins such as the Kızılbaş-Alevis, the Karamanlı, and the Dönme converged with the decline of Ottomanism and the concomitant rise of a discourse of national unity around notions of religious and ethnic unity. As Baer puts it, the Ottoman state "was mostly more concerned with recognizing and maintaining difference among its subjects than with producing sameness...The end of empire spelled the end of the tolerance of difference since the founders of Turkey took upon themselves the task of clarifying identities by disallowing mixed identities" (Baer 2004, 686–687). In other words, the twin principles of Turkish nationalism and secularism, as they began to be formed in the Young Turk period and were further boosted in the early Turkish Republic, operated through politics of Sunnification and Turkification that aimed for annihilation of difference, that is, the creation of a unitarian, secular, Turkish-Muslim nation state. The legacy of this homogenizing discourse shows itself in different ways still in contemporary Turkey. Sensationalist books on the Dönme still sell extremely well (Baer 2010, ix). Together with the Masons and the Jews, the Dönme are often mentioned in conspiracy theories related to Turkish politics.

The exact beginning of the CUP's active interest in the Kızılbaş-Alevis and Bektashis is difficult to establish, but needs to be located in the turbulent middle years of the 1910s. According to Şapolyo, Talat Paşa, in his early days as grand vizier (that is, in 1917) declared at a general party meeting that Anatolia would still be a black box, of which one needed to get a deeper understanding in order to better serve the nation. In the same context, Ziya Gökalp declared that "[w]e have made a political revolution...However, the biggest revolution is the social revolution." And in order to accomplish this, one had to learn about the social morphology and physiology of the national community. Following this meeting the party headquarters would have sent out several researchers to investigate particular minority groups; Baha Said was sent to inquire about the Kızılbaş and Bektashi (Şapolyo 1964, 2). We also know that in a telegraph from May 1918, Talat Paşa ordered research in particular provinces on the (Kızılbaş-Alevi) tribes of the Tahtacı and the Çepni, demanding information about "the social situations, numbers, professions, and regional histories of these groups" (Dündar 2008, 128).[18]

This sudden interest in the Kızılbaş-Alevis and related groups can be explained by the political condition in which the Young Turks found themselves toward the end of World War I. Following the Balkan Wars, the

---

18 This is confirmed by Üngör, who argues that "it becomes clear from Ottoman documents that in several instances Talât personally requested detailed information like lists and maps, often covering even the village level. In the end, the CUP research program produced thousands of pages of detailed expertise on the targeted ethnic groups" (Üngör 2005, 20).

Unionists began to inquire into possibilities for establishing a military base in Anatolia, the political and strategic significance of which had increased enormously. The first investigations by Baha Said and other CUP activists in the rural Bektashi and Kızılbaş-Alevi populations intended to learn about the loyalties of these groups toward the Young Turks and to search for new military and political strategies in light of the territorial and demographic shifts caused by the Balkan Wars and World War I (Görkem 2006, xii).

The investigations of the Kızılbaş groups were part of a broader ethnographic research program that needs to be interpreted in the context of the CUP's politics of social engineering. Precondition for successful social engineering was to increase knowledge about the people of Anatolia, and therefore the CUP began to collect data on different tribes, ethnicities, and religious groups in Anatolia. This was done in an increasingly systematic matter within the networks of the Turkist organizations formally independent from but nevertheless in the orbit of the CUP, such as the Turkish Hearth and the Turkish Association, which encouraged sociological and ethnographic work on Anatolia; state organizations such as the General Directorate for the Settlement of Tribes and Refugees (*İskan-ı Aşair ve Muhacirin Müdüriyet-i Umumiye*, İAMM) were particularly active in fostering research on different Anatolian tribes and non-Sunni Muslim religious communities (Dündar 2008, 126–130).[19]

It appears that the Kızılbaş-Alevis and Bektashis became a focus of these investigations only after the annihilation of most of the Anatolian Christians in 1916, when the İAMM, which had also been involved in the planning and organization of the deportation of the Anatolian Christians, was renamed "General Directorate for Tribes and Immigrants" (*Aşair ve Muhacirin Müdüriyet-i Umumiyesi*, AMMU) (Üngör 2008a, §23). Among the men that were commissioned by the directorate to do research on the Kızılbaş-Alevis and related groups were Baha Said and Habil Adem.[20]

---

19 The İAMM was established in 1913 under the oversight of the Ministry of the Interior. It "served two purposes: on the one hand, to advance the sedentarization of the many Turkoman, Kurdish, and Arab tribes, and on the other hand, to provide accommodation for homeless Muslim refugees, expelled from the Balkans and Russia. It would later be expanded to constitute four branches, namely settlement, intelligence, deportation, and tribes" (Üngör 2005, 19).

20 In his autobiography, the nationalist journalist Zekeriya Sertel (1890–1980) reports that at the time when he worked for that directorate he had prepared two separate dossiers on Sufi orders and Alevi tribes; unfortunately, these reports would be lost (Sertel 1977, 82). Regrettably without providing any further detail, Şapolyo mentions that in order to better understand the Alevis many books and handwritten texts were brought from the library of Hacıbektaş to the CUP headquarter for inspection (Şapolyo 1943, 108–109).

Baha Said Bey

With much of state-sponsored Turkish historiography, and to a certain extent also academic work on modern Turkish political history, focusing on Mustafa Kemal Atatürk (1881–1938) as the major point of reference for the narration of the developments that led to the formation of the Turkish Republic, the importance of figures who operated in secondary ranks of the nationalist organizations is often neglected. However, it is obvious that the organization and success of the Turkish War of Independence and the consecutive establishment of a secular national republic was not the result of one man's efforts alone.

One of these second-tier figures, often overlooked, but with an enormous radius in his activities in this important time period of nation-building between the 1910 and 1930s, was Baha Said Bey (1882–1939), born and raised in the small town of Biga in the province of Çanakkale in Western Anatolia. His lifetime was almost identical with that of Atatürk, and this is not the only thing that the two men, who knew each other, had in common. They both went through the secular training of military schools, made careers in the Ottoman army, and devoted their political lives to the national cause. But in contrast to Atatürk, who advanced to the military rank of a pasha, and became the leader of the nationalist movement during the Turkish War of Independence, Baha Said left—due to disciplinary reasons—the army with the rank of lieutenant (Tevetoğlu 1989, 209). Baha Said was an extremely active and dedicated Unionist and Turkist. Making a living first as teacher and then as merchant, he was also a member of the CUP's Central Committee and worked for the "Special Organization" (*Teşkilat-ı Mahsusa*). This secret service established by the CUP in 1913 under the command of Enver Pasha is accused to have been involved in the organization and execution of the deportation and elimination of the Anatolian Christians (Zürcher 2004, 116). As already mentioned, Baha Said worked for the AMMU, in the context of which he is said to have begun his research on the Kızılbaş-Alevis. In 1918 he belonged to the founding members of the secret Karakol organization, which, in continuation of the Special Organization, organized the flow of resources from the capital to the forces of the nationalists around Mustafa Kemal struggling from Anatolia for Ottoman sovereignty (Görkem 2006, 16–28). In the republic he served from 1925 until the end of his life as inspector for the National Air Force (Tevetoğlu 1989, 214).

The style of Baha Said's work can be described as that of investigative journalism, with an at times rather scholarly air, sometimes explicitly political and even polemical. There are conflicting accounts on the question as to when exactly Baha Said started to research the Kızılbaş-Alevi and Bektashi communities. According to the Turkish historian and sociologist of religion Hilmi Ziya Ülken (1901–1974), an acquaintance of Baha Said,[21] the latter conducted his initial field research on the Alevis commissioned by the CUP already in 1914 and 1915 (Ülken 1979, 257 fn 302). More specifically, his research was related to his work for the İAMM/AMMU. It is also possible that it was connected to his work for the Special Organization, for which he traveled to Iran and the Caucasus.[22] Baha Said himself suggests around 1916 as the time when he began to publicly discuss Alevism. He begins his 1926 article on "Alevi Groups in Anatolia" recounting that when ten years ago he would have given a talk on the Tahtacı at the Turkish Hearth, "up to this time Turkish intellectuals had neither talked nor thought about the[se] original children of our country" (Baha Said 2001 [1926]c, 237). In the late Young Turk period, Baha Said regularly presented papers to nationalist organizations. In 1918 he began to publish about the Kızılbaş-Alevis and related groups in nationalist journals and dailies. In the first of an essay series that appeared in 1918 ("Social Groups in Anatolia and the Sociology of Anatolia") he sets out the political context of this research, which can be summarized as the creation of a national subject aware of its roots and distinctiveness, based on Oğuz Turkish culture (Baha Said 2006 [1918], 112–114). In positivist tones he explains the need for a "Sociology of Anatolia": all villages of Anatolia needed to be researched in order to create "an ethnography of the fatherland," which would be as important as the topography of the country (Baha Said 2006 [1918], 112).

In the same article he also for the first time explicitly mentions the Kızılbaş and Bektashi. The context is an extensive discussion of the Turks' religious traditions. He describes Hacı Bektaş Veli as the genius who brought together original Turkish religion with Manichaeism and Islam. Bektashism and Kızılbashism were the two currents who would still follow the old Turkish religion, described as natural religion dedicated to the ideal of "earth is my mother, heaven my father" (Baha Said 2006 [1918],

---

21 Baha Said entrusted Ülken with his unpublished manuscripts before he died. Unfortunately, these documents, apparently now in the hands of Ülken's daughter, are as of yet not published (Görkem 2006, xvii).

22 According to a letter from 1961 by Numanzade Mustafa Tınal (a friend of Baha Said), in these years "upon Ziya Gökalp's advice, Talat Paşa commissioned Baha Said to investigate the Sufi orders of Anatolia, the Alevi groups, as well as the Tahtacı, Çetmi [Çepni], and Hardal Turkmens" (quoted in Tevetoğlu 1989, 209; cf. Şapolyo 1964, 2–3).

121–122). He acknowledges Baba İlyas, one of the leaders of the Turkmen tribes that rose in 1240 against the Seljuk rulers of Anatolia,[23] as "the first Turkist of Anatolia," and he terms Bektashim, historically connected to the Babais, the "national denomination" (*milli mezhep*) of Anatolia (Baha Said 2006 [1918], 122). This national character of Bektashism continued in the rites of the Kızılbaş, Çepni, and Tahtacı (Baha Said 2006 [1918], 126).

The leitmotif that connects this and following publications of Baha Said in the late Ottoman and early republican periods is the alleged connection of certain "sects" of Islam such as the Kızılbashes and the Bektashis with national Turkish culture. In early 1919 he published another article series ("The Inner Face of the Homeland: Secret Sanctuaries in Anatolia") in *Memleket Gazetesi*, a newspaper that had just began to appear and supported the national independence movement that began to form at that time. The first article provides an ideological framework for the series, describing Anatolia as "small Turan"[24] and characterizing groups such as the Druze, Nusayri, Kızılbaş, and Bektashi as "Turanian," in opposition to Semitic sects that retained Jewish superstitions (Baha Said 2006 [1919] a, 127–129). He suggests calling these Turanian sects "Alevi" since they would all join in recognition of Ali Ibn Abu Talib as their highest religious authority. He attributes particular emphasis to the Kızılbaş, whose lifestyle and spirit would be extremely important for the new Turkey: "We will see that this community, which has until now preserved its Turkish essence in its entire being, is from one point of view the strongest pillar, the strongest column among the cornerstones of our national conscience" (Baha Said 2006 [1919]a, 129).

In the final piece of "The Inner Face of the Homeland" Baha Said returns to the topic of Turkish religion. This is the first text of Baha Said wherein he connects references to shamanism with the Kızılbaş-Alevis, namely the Kızılbaş-Alevi subgroup of the Tahtacı—which he, however, at this point had not yet treated as "Alevi" (only in his latter publications from 1926 onward would he include the Tahtacı into the category Alevi). In this text he compares practices of the Tahtacı and the Zazas of the Dersim province with those of the "shaman forefathers" (*şaman atalar*), whom he qualifies as Turkified versions of the Buddha (Baha Said 2006 [1919] d, 150–151). The text reflects an eclectic approach to the question of the

---

23 A reference to the Babai uprising; see p. 7.

24 Turan is the name of the mythical pre-Islamic Central Asian homeland of the Turks.

origins of Turkish religion, mentioning not only shamanistic practices, but also referencing Taoism, totemism, natural religion, and Buddhism as possible sources. In yet another article from the same year, Baha Said again underlines the national character of those "libertarian" groups that he associates with the Kızılbaş-Alevis and Bektashis and whose members would "have lived a national existence and understood religion within a national life and consciousness" (Baha Said 2006 [1919]e, 106).

The writings produced by Baha Said and other nationalist activist-researchers within the CUP network present themselves as mostly ethnographic reports with some sociological and historical elaborations. It is clear that they were not only inspired by Turkish nationalism as an intellectual project, but they were also motivated by more pragmatic political considerations of social engineering, which demanded a better knowledge of the various religious and ethnic communities of the remaining Ottoman lands, and in particular central and eastern Anatolia.

Baha Said's publications from 1918 and 1919 reflect particular aspects of the nationalist quest at the end of World War I, when Ottoman sovereignty was under extreme threat by the Allies' plans to partition Anatolia into influence zones, to extensively strengthen the political status of the minorities, especially the Greeks and Armenians, and even to offer the prospect of a Kurdish independent state. In the third sequel of "The Inner Face of the Homeland," Baha Said alludes to developments during the Paris Peace Conference, where the minorities presented population figures that strengthened their political claims. The heirs of the eastern provinces (i.e., the Armenians) fabricated statistics pretending that "there were so and so many Armenians, so and so many Turks, Sunnis, Shiites, Kızılbaş, Yezidi, Sufis, Kurds, Nasturi/Nestorians!" Unfortunately, the public opinion of Europe would hardly understand the truth and act as "accomplices of the ungrateful children of this soil." The goal of the enemy would clearly be to destroy Turkish unity by presenting the eastern provinces through the kaleidoscope of religion as a patchwork of various nations—a method the purpose of which was to present the Armenians as relative majority. However, neither Nestorianism, or Kızılbashism, nor other religious sects such as the Sufis (*Sufiyan*) and Yezidis could be regarded as distinct nationalities (Baha Said 2006 [1919]b, 139).

These explanations of Baha Said reflect the national concern with being able to argue convincingly that religious sects such as the Kızılbaş were part of the Turkish-Islamic nation. Beyond his reiterated reasoning that the difference of the Kızılbaş-Alevis and Bektashis could be explained with their adherence to ancient Turkish "shaman-istic" practices, he is not, however—and this is, as we will see, in stark contrast to Köprülü—very interested in their religious difference. The major work of the label "Alevi," as suggested by him in the first sequel of "The Inner Face of the Homeland" as an umbrella term for a num-ber of distinct religious communities, is to nominally mark them as Muslim. This allows him to reject what he considers the inimical inter-est of the local non-Muslims and their European allies to present in particular the eastern provinces as totally divided by national and eth-nic sectarianism.

In Baha Said's early writings, the term Alevi and its derivates still carry a variety of meanings. These meanings do already include what would soon become the cornerstones of the republican conceptualiza-tion of Alevism, namely Turkishness (national heritage), Alidism (Shiite mythology), and relation to the *ocak*-centered groups (sociological for-mation). At the same time, in the "The Inner Face of the Homeland" series, Baha Said still used the term Alevi in the traditional, broad sense as an overarching category for various Alid/Shiite currents. But he also employed alternative meanings of the term Alevi without further expla-nation. In another essay from the same year he uses the terms "Alevi," "Aleviyye," and "Alevilik" in the narrower Shiite sense of *ghulāt* ("exag-gerators"), that is, as referents for those "libertarian"—as Baha Said refers to them—Shiite groups that got marginalized by the apologet-ics of mainstream Shiite discourse. He counts the Druze, Nusayri, and Yezidi, and in particular the "Bektaşi-Kızılbaş" groups among those lib-ertarian interpreters of Islam (Baha Said 2006 [1919]e, 105–106). In yet another text he writes, in a discussion of Bektashi and Alevi groups, about the "Turkish Alevi groups of Anatolia," coming already very close to what would become the dominant 20th-century understanding of the term Alevi (Baha Said 2006 [1919]c, 145)—and even more so when he argues that the Sufis, Kızılbaş, and Tahtacı belong together since they were all "nothing but Turks who are 'Shiite' and connected to the 'Ocak of Hacı Bektaş'" (Baha Said 2006 [1919]b, 139). While he does not yet use the term Alevi as an umbrella term for *ocak*-related groups, the refer-ence to the *ocak* system as a common sociological denominator of the mentioned groups already foreshadows the new concept of Alevism as it would soon crystallize more clearly.

In Baha Said's publications after the establishment of the republic—when the Lausanne Treaty had reaffirmed Turkish sovereignty over

Anatolia and plans of establishing Greek, Armenian, and Kurdish political units in Anatolia were dropped—the immediate threat of inner-Anatolian separatism seemed banished and the necessity of emphasizing the similarity of "Alevi" sects in the broader sense of the term (including the Yezidi, Nusayri, and Druze) had lost importance. "Alevi" would now gradually become the technical term more specifically used for the *ocak*-centered groups so far most commonly referred to as Kızılbaş. Still, Baha Said's later texts, too, often remained vague, or, rather, multilayered in the meanings that they associated with the term Alevi. As in his earlier texts, in some instances Baha Said uses the name as an inclusive term for a variety of groups that can be associated with Shiism in the broadest sense (Baha Said 2001 [1926]b, 203); elsewhere, however, *Alevilik* appears as a synonym for the Twelver Shia more narrowly, even juxtaposed to the Kızılbaş (Baha Said 2001 [1927], 161).

The writings by Baha Said and other authors of this time period suggest a number of intertwined motives behind the CUP's interest in the Kızılbaş and Bektashi groups, all within the framework of Turkish nationalism. It is apparent that his research of the Bektashis and Kızılbaş-Alevis coincided with the CUP's interest in these groups in the last years of World War I, an interest that increased following the expulsion and elimination of the Anatolian Christians in 1915–1916. However, although himself part of this research context, he would also point to the limitations of it. In a piece from 1919, he laments that the Turkish Hearth had failed to sufficiently "research the mental suitability of these currents" (Baha Said 2006 [1919]e, 106). It is clear that toward the end of the First World War, when the Ottomans were put under extreme pressure from the Allied forces, who wanted to change the balance of political power in favor of the non-Muslims, the various religious groups at the margins of Islam became a subject of increased interest for the Turkish nationalists, who endeavored to combine forces against non-Muslim aspirations in the region. It is within this political context that one has to situate the CUP's intensified interest in the Kızılbaş-Alevis and related groups.

Habil Adem: The Kızılbaş as Persianate Kurds and To-Be-Civilized Turkmen

Another important nationalist activist-researcher was Habil Adem, who used a variety of pseudonyms for his publications, and whose real name was Naci İsmail Pelister. Upon request of the CUP leaders he began to work in 1912 for the newly established National Security Organization. He then continued his intelligence work with the İAMM and AMMU, in the name of which he did fieldwork on the Anatolian Kurds and Turkmen tribes. Habil Adem's writings reflect—even more openly than those of his colleague Baha Said—the CUP's ambition to collect the data considered necessary for its politics of social and demographic engineering, such as information on basic demographic realities, as well as social and cultural aspects. Results of Habil Adem's research were published in 1918 in two volumes on the Kurds and Turkmen tribes, respectively. The obvious aim of these publications was to create a public knowledge favorable to the nationalization project.

His book on the Kurds, printed in 1918 under the pseudonym of a fictitious German Orientalist ("Dr. Friç"), allegedly only translated by Habil Adem, elaborated on a thesis that would gain leverage in the early Turkish Republic and become very prominent in the 1930s, namely that the Kurds were actually Turks and that Kurdish as an independent language did not exist.[25] In the book's section on the religion of the Kurds, he makes two distinctions that are interesting for our context. First, Habil Adem differentiates between Muslim Kurds and non-Muslim Kurds, arguing that the latter, who lived more primitive lives, resembled the Zoroastrians of Iran. He then differentiates between Sunni and Shiite Muslim Kurds. In Turkey, most Kurds were Sunni even if they adopted Islam in a way "fitting to their own taste" (as quoted in Akpınar 2004). As for the Shiite Kurds, they could be divided in a number of paths (tarikat), such as Yezidism, Kızılbashism, and Mazdaism (Akpınar 2004).

In 1918 the AMMU also published another book of Habil Adem, this one on Turkmen tribes, again using a fictitious pseudonym (Dr. Frayliç and Engineer Ravlig). The voluminous report is poorly edited, contains many reiterations, is not without contradictions, and was only recently published for the first time in Latin script. Nevertheless, it is highly interesting for an understanding of the comprehensive character of Young Turkish ambitions with regard to demographic engineering, which, as the report proves, was not limited to Christians and Kurds, but also included suggestions for a resettlement of Turkmen tribes, both Sunni and Kızılbaş.

---

25 *Kürdler (Tarihi ve İçtimai Tetkikat)* ("The Kurds: Historical and Sociological Enquiries"). An abbreviated transliteration of the text is included in Akpınar (2004).

In this context, Habil Adem's elaborations on the Kızılbaş Turkmen bear a so-far-unrecognized significance for the evaluation of the CUP's point of view on the Kızılbaş-Alevi question.

The picture presented in Habil Adem's report on the relation of the Kızılbaş to Islam is characterized by ambiguity. On the one side he counts them, in contrast to the Yezidi, as among the Islamic sects of the Turkmen tribes (Frayliç and Ravlig 2008 [1918], 313). On the other side, however, he variously remarks that there would be differences between Islam and the religion of the Kızılbaş. While he concedes that it would actually be rather difficult to assert with certainty to which degree the two were related, he also maintains that it is clear that the Kızılbaş faith historically originated from within Islam (Frayliç and Ravlig 2008 [1918], 320). When it comes to the description of the creed of the Kızılbaş, the text presents first an obscure and extremely flawed account of inner-Islamic doctrinal divisions going back to early Islamic theological debates. From within this account the author ascribes to Kızılbaş doctrine in particular the belief in free will (as opposed to determinationism), the divinization of Ali, as well as the divinization of potentially everything (apparently based on a very simplistic rendition of the Sufi doctrine of the *Unity of Being*). This way, the Kızılbaş established a new religion (Frayliç and Ravlig 2008 [1918], 320–322). Turning to the Turkmen Kızılbaş of Anatolia, the author moves away from a discussion of doctrine to matters of religious practice. He describes Kızılbaş religion as entrenched in magic, as for example manifest in the ceremony of extinguishing the candles (*mum söndü*)[26] (Frayliç and Ravlig 2008 [1918], 322–323).

Habil Adem turns again to the Kızılbaş in a section of the book dedicated to the problem of how to bring the Turkmen tribes to adjust to modern life. In this part of the book the social and demographic engineering aspect of Habil Adem's work is most apparent. Here he suggests a need to disconnect the Turkmen from their nomadic, tribal life—seen as the primary obstacle with regard to their modernization—and to bring them into closer contact with the settled Turkish population. In order to increase their relations with the Turks it would be necessary to relocate and civilize the Turkmen and encourage their intermarriage with Turks (Frayliç and Ravlig 2008 [1918], 355–358).

Within the context of resettlement, Habil Adem considered religious differences between the Turkmen and the Turks an important aspect to be

---

26 See p. 125.

considered—in particular since two-thirds of the Turkmen were "Kızılbaş and heretics" (*Kızılbaş ve râfizî*) (Frayliç and Ravlig 2008 [1918], 359). In order to secure the assimilation of heretical groups such as the Kızılbashes, the government needed to recognize them (although it remains unclear what this recognition is supposed to entail). Then it should first resettle them by allotting them to Turkish populations in small groups. The resettlement should be organized and carried through in orderly sequence by military police inspectorates, and economically prosperous neighborhoods should be preferred as primary loci for the relocation. Secondly, the Kızılbaş Turkmens' communal religious ceremonies, which constituted the core of their "heresy" and were irreconcilable with modern morality, should be forbidden. Breaking up the tribes in small groups would prevent them from conducting their major rituals and this, accompanied by their economic and social integration into Turkish life, would gradually lead to the disintegration of their faith (Frayliç and Ravlig 2008 [1918], 360–362). Only following the resettlement could its primary goal, the elevation of the educational and civilizational standards of the Turkmen, be achieved. Focus should be given on the education of the children while education programs for adults should also be initiated. Again, the issue of religion is given importance: "But, in order for the Turkmen to become civilized they have to abandon the empty faith that they are bound to. For that [to happen] doctrinal religion classes should be offered and practical religious education has to be prevented in the school...[T]he children should not be pressured into religious instruction." The text repeats the importance of soft techniques of assimilation in order to prevent backlashes. Only in this way, and gradually, would success be possible and could true religious feelings develop among them. The bonding of the Turkmen with the Turks would require a rapprochement of their faiths, which is presented as a one-sided religious adjustment by the (Kızılbaş) Turkmen (Frayliç and Ravlig 2008 [1918], 364).

To sum up, in the texts of Habil Adem, in stark contrast to Baha Said, Kızılbaş religion is depicted as an obstacle for the civilizing of the Turkmen tribes. Therefore Habil Adem argues for their religious assimilation, to be achieved by the destruction of their social networks and ban on their major religious rituals. His major concern is with how to assimilate the Turkmen tribes into settled and modern Turkish life for the goal of achieving higher civilizational standards for Turkish society at large. For Baha Said, on the other hand, it is precisely certain aspects of the Kızılbaş-Alevis' religious traditions that are given significance as

markers of authentic Turkish culture. Thus, while both authors ultimately work for the same goal, namely the production of knowledge necessary for the formation of an ethnically and religiously homogeneous
nation-state, their evaluation of the Kızılbaş-Alevis and their religious
deviation is starkly different. The tension between the two approaches
to the Kızılbaş-Alevis and the normative ambivalence that is attributed
to them in both accounts will, as we will see, remain typical also in later
evaluations of the Alevis. As I will argue, this tension is also reflected
in the way in which the early Turkish Republic dealt practically with the
question of Alevi difference.

Turkish Alevi Culture

The theory of Kurdish-speaking tribes being of Turkish origins, advanced
by Habil Adem in 1918, became a standard topos in Turkish nationalist discourse and helped to justify Kemalist practices of assimilating the Kurds.[27]
Habil Adem's report was one of the first published texts providing a theoretical justification for the Turkification of the Kurds. The fact that we find
among the Kızılbaş-Alevis both Turkish and Kurdish speakers appeared
to support the Turkist argument. Combining the theory of the secondary
Kurdification of originally Turkish tribes with the theory that Alevism is a
tradition intrinsically linked with Turkish culture makes it seem obvious
that those Alevis who speak Kurdish or claim Kurdish ethnicity have to be
"original" Turks, who got over time Kurdified. If Alevi Kurds were original
Turks then there was no reason why one should not assume that the same
was also true for at least some Sunni Kurds. Following this logic of secondary Kurdification, Besim Atalay would explain that those Turks who were
called "Kızılbaş" were—just as the Tahtacıs and Çepnis—Alevis who were
unwilling to have anything to do with the Turks or Turkism; therefore, it
would be easy for them to come under Kurdish influence (Atalay 1924, 19).
Several years earlier, reflecting on the same problem, Ziya Gökalp made
a very different argument, in which he correlated religion with change of
ethnic culture, which was for him in the first instance a matter of shared
language. He explained that in his native region of Diyarbakır, Sunni
Turkish tribes were assimilated into dominant Kurdish culture while
Turkmen Alevis "continued to be immune to Kurdification" (Gökalp 1959

---

27 See, for example, the series of confidential reports written by N. Sahir Sılan in 1935 and
1946 for various state ministries (Sılan 2010).

[1917], 130).[28] The argument illustrates Gökalp's belief in the importance of religion as a major cohesive force in the formation of a social community. The act of reading Turkishness into other cultures found in particular in the work of Habil Adem foreshadows the biased racialization of aspects of Turkish culture and history that would in the early 1930s become official doctrine with the Turkish History Thesis—even more so when the reverse operation, namely hypothesizing about Turkish-speaking groups being originally descendants of non-Turkish ethnic origins, is denied.

For Baha Said, too, the Turkishness of the Kızılbaş-Alevis was apparent. The constant theme that connects his pre-republican writings with those published in the second half of the 1920s, in which he would provide much more extensive and detailed accounts of various Kızılbaş-Alevi and Bektashi practices, was the emphasis on the importance of the Kızılbaş-Alevi and Bektashi groups for Turkish national culture. The nationalist framework of his writings is the most explicit in his polemical and programmatic introduction to the first of a series of articles published in 1926 and 1927 in *Türk Yurdu*. Reflecting on why these articles, as he claims, were prevented from publication in the last years of the Ottoman Empire, he paints a scenario of both external and internal enemies of the nation, which, following the world war, tried to capitalize on the fact of the Kızılbaş-Alevi difference in their joined effort to dismantle the remainders of the Ottoman state. As part of this effort, some Alevi communities would have been described as "Turkified groups of Orthodox Greeks," in some provinces Alevis would have been registered on Armenian population records, and in some Protestant missionary documents the Alevis would have been referred to as "Christian hybrids." It is in this context, he recalls, that he began to publicize against the idea of the Alevis being "Turkified," and, by implication, Islamized Christians (Baha Said 2001 [1926]a, 105). Interestingly, this article was published in *Türk Yurdu* next to a translation of an excerpt from Felix von Luschan's *Völker, Rassen,*

---

28 Based on linguistic and sociological arguments, Gökalp explained in various places how and why many Turks and Turkmen would over time have been Kurdified (Gökalp 1982 [1922], 230–231; 1992 [1923], 127–130). For a sober treatment of the question of the ethnic origins of the Kızılbaş-Alevi Kurds see van Bruinessen (1997); see also Ağuiçenoğlu (2010); cf. White (2003). The question of the ethnic origins of the Kurds and Alevis is still virulent in rightwing Turkish discourses. A more recent example are the remarks in 2007 by the then-president of the government-sponsored Turkish History Foundation, Yusuf Halaçoğlu, who initiated a heated public debate when he claimed that considerable parts of the Kurds were of ethnic Turkish origin, and many Alevi Kurds actually Armenians. Fuat Dündar, "İttihatçıların bile Dile Getirmediği Tez: Alevi Kürtlerin Ermeniliği." *Radikal,* September 7, 2007.

Sprachen (1922), which questions the relation of the Tahtacı Alevis with Islam and instead points to similarities to Christian customs in their traditions (Hamid Sadi 1926). From the nationalist point of view, publication of this translation may have helped to reaffirm the urgency of understanding the Turkishness of the Alevis. Baha Said in fact himself responded to von Luschan's text in a following issue of the journal wherein he argued that in order to understand the Tahtacı they needed to be situated within Turkish culture. This point, he writes, was missed by von Luschan. Only from this perspective of Turkish national culture could their religious difference be accounted for (Baha Said 2001 [1926]c).

The Christian minorities and their Western allies are not the only ones blamed by Baha Said for separatist aims. The Ottomans, too, were guilty of dividing the nation into Alevis and Sunnis—despite the fact that both were Turkish. Now, however, with the Turkish Republic, "[w]e are finally by ourselves" and the time has come for "Turkish unity" (Baha Said 2001 [1926]a, 105–106). Again, the importance of the Kızılbaş-Alevis for the nationalist project is emphasized. Thus he describes the "Alevi lodges" as a homestead (*ocak*) where the "most traditionalist and purest Turks...and most lately the most enlightened, intelligent, and enthusiastic Turks could taste the pleasure of liberty"; there, "national freedom existed" (Baha Said 2001 [1926]a, 110). Elsewhere he explains that "the Alevi groups that live in Anatolia today are from those pure Turks of us, who have since the 10th century (*hicri*)[29], without submitting to the Ottoman Sultanate, lived an independent religion (*din*), an independent religious interpretation (*mezhep*), and an independent social life while carefully living Turkish customs" (Baha Said 2001 [1927], 154).

The positive evaluation that the Kızılbaş-Alevis receive in Baha Said's writings with regard to their national character is, in his texts from the republican period, to a certain extent interrupted by rather ambiguous evaluations of their religious character. Thus, Baha Said laments that they still wait for the reappearance of the Twelfth Imam, the Mahdi. This expectation he describes as an essentially Jewish and Christian theory, a fact of which the "poor Alevis," however, would not be aware. According to Baha Said, the Alid or Shiite aspects of Alevi and Bektashi beliefs would be secondary additions unknown to the original Turkish culture and traditions of the Kızılbaş-Alevis. Further research, he predicts, would make it obvious

29 The Islamic *hicri* (Arab. *hiğrī*) calender begins with the emigration of Muhammad from Mecca to Medina in a.d. 632.

that "the form and shape of a shaman temple and a Bektashi lodge are the same" (Baha Said 2001 [1926]a, 112). The clearest aim of the "founders" of the Turkish Alevis would have been "to preserve the language, lineage, and blood of the Turks. And they actually succeeded in this. The Kızılbaş remained completely Turkish...The Alevis have conserved their Turkishness, their nationality, their language, and their pre-Islamic traditions in the form of religion [...and this is how] they became atheists and heretics" (in the eyes of the Ottomans, who would have only been interested in their power and did not care about Turkish tradition) (Baha Said 2001 [1926]a, 111). As he concludes, "[w]hen studying the character of the Turkish Alevis—the Bektaşi and Kızılbaş—it is absolutely not correct to reduce them to Ali and the Imamiye [Twelver Shia]...This group is...with regard to its ritual and the rules of its path (erkan-ı tarikat) the same and not different from the Oghuz tradition and the tent of the Shaman Turk." It should not be approached as a philosophical school or as a religious subgroup (mezhep), but studied as an entity by itself: "an institution that has been built on the 'national self' and been extremely successful" (Baha Said 2001 [1926]a, 112).

As these quotations show, for Baha Said the essence of Alevism was to be interpreted in terms of culture and not religion. They further illustrate, to repeat this important point, that for Baha Said the religious significance of Kızılbaş-Alevism and Bektashism was to be explained only with reference to ancient Turkish shamanism. All other religious associations to be found in these traditions, which would make them appear as heretic or Shiite of some sort, would be secondary and should not make one question the Kızılbaş-Alevis' essentially Turkish character.

Secularization, Integration, and Assimilation

As Marc Baer has argued paraphrasing Gauri Viswanathan, in the context of the modern nation-state "[r]eligion was to become less a mark of belief than a social identity since religion was removed as a basis of primordial identity and subordinated to national identity" (Baer 2004, 703). The same dynamic is at work when Baha Said subordinates the religious dimension of the Kızılbaş-Alevis to their function as carriers of national cultural heritage. For Baha Said, aspects of various religions such as Buddhism, shamanism, Mazdaism, Manichaeism, Islam, and Christianity, which the Turks had contact with and appropriated over time, would continue to show themselves in the Anatolian Kızılbaş societies (Baha Said 2001

[1926]b, 208). However, these religious aspects would not be essential, but, rather, lamentable foreign additions to Kızılbaş-Alevi Turkish culture.

The subordination of the religion factor to an aspect of secondary importance reflects Baha Said's secularist stance. In his writings from the late 1920s this secularism corresponded well with the political development of the period, which was marked by an aggressive secularization program. More specifically, it converged with the Kemalist policy of delegitimizing Kızılbaş-Alevi religious practices. In 1925, with the ban on Sufi orders and practices and closures of Sufi lodges and mausoleums, the ritual practices of the Kızılbaş-Alevis, too, were outlawed. This affected in particular the practice of *dedelik*, the office of the *dede*, around which traditional Alevi social and ritual practices were organized (Soileau 2010, 255–262). Habil Adem's suggestions from 1918 with regard to how to assimilate Kızılbaş-Alevi religion were now effectively put in practice. Again, the broader historical context had a strong impact on how the question of Kızılbaş-Alevi difference was approached within nationalist discourses. Only indirectly referred to in Baha Said's main texts on the Alevis,[30] but with a tremendous impact on the national movement, was the Treaty of Sèvres (1920) following World War I, which foresaw and legitimated the partition of the remaining Ottoman lands, reducing Ottoman sovereignty to parts of western and central Anatolia. Although this treaty was superseded just three years later by the Treaty of Lausanne, the traumatizing effect of the Treaty of Sèvres, one aim of which was, as Taner Akçam (2002) has convincingly argued, to punish the Ottomans for their treatment of the Christians during the war, should not be underestimated.[31] In addition, the local uprisings by Kurdish groups in the east, such as the rebellion of the Kurdish Kızılbaş-Alevi tribes of Dersim in 1920–1921 and the Sheikh Said uprising in 1925—which was motivated by a mixture of Kurdish nationalism, as well as resistance to the new regime's aggressive secularization (the caliphate had been abolished in 1924) and centralization policies—contributed to heightened sensitivities with regard to the articulation of claims of communal difference. Consequently, Ankara toughened its stand against the two groups it viewed with particular suspicion: the Kurds and the Sufi brotherhoods. Thus, following a period

---

30 For example, in Baha Said (2001 [1926]a, 105).

31 In the collective memory of Turkish nationalism, Sèvres is routinely evoked to point to the danger posed by enemies as well as potential "traitors" from within (especially non-Muslim minorities) and at times to legitimize discriminatory practices against them.

marked by a more inclusive approach to the Kurds, Ankara continued Young Turk practices of control and coercion in the east with the goal of a total assimilation of the Kurds (Üngör 2008a, §37–47). In 1924, the public use and teaching of Kurdish had been restricted, and Kurdish elites were resettled to western provinces (Zürcher 2004, 170–171). All of these developments contributed to the government's use of the Sheikh Said uprising, presented as mainly being motivated by a fanatic and backward religiosity that was now equated with the Islam of the Sufi orders, as a pretext for the ban of Sufi practices in 1925.

It is probably not incidental that writings on the Bektashis, Kızılbaş-Alevis, and other non-Sunni "Muslim" groups in *Türk Yurdu* in the early republic, such as those by Baha Said, appeared exclusively in the years between 1925 and 1928. The felt need for justification of the radically restrictive intervention with regard to the Sufi orders and the Kızılbaş-Alevis is obvious. Kemalist nation-building had entered its Jacobean phase (see Cagaptay 2006). What said texts in *Türk Yurdu* have in common is that they emphasize the Turkish character of the Bektashis and Kızılbaş-Alevis, constructing their cultural and religious traditions as mixture. But only in the first article, by Fuad Köprülü ("Origins of Bektashim"),[32] which was published in May 1925 and thus preceded the ban of the Sufi orders and their practices in September of that year, was the dominant religious framework for the Bektashis clearly Islam. What most of the following articles, published after the ban on the Sufi orders, share is that they seem to support a perspective that (1) subordinates the religious dimension of the Kızılbaş-Alevis and Bektashis to their national significance, (2) criticizes aspects of their religious beliefs and institutions as backward and superstitious, and in that way appears to (3) implicitly support the ban of the Sufi orders (including the Bektashi lodges) and the impact this had on the Kızılbaş-Alevis.

In the political context of that period, it was rather opportune to underline the national character of Alevism while delegitimizing Kızılbaş-Alevi religion. This was expressed, for example, in the presentation of the *dede*s as ignorant charlatans: "These religious guides (*mürşidler*) have left this essentially Turkish community in deepest ignorance" (Baha Said 2001 [1926]b, 205). We find a similar argument in a piece from the following year by Süleyman Fikri [Erten], another amateur anthropologist, who endorses, based on observations on the Tahtacı of Teke (province of

---

32 This was a translated conference talk he had given two years earlier in Paris.

Antalya), doubts by European Orientalists with regard to the Islamic character of the Tahtacı, while at the same time reaffirming their Turkishness (Süleyman Fikri 2001 [1927]). The last essay in the series of articles on the Bektashis and Kızılbaş-Alevis in *Türk Yurdu* in these years is the harshest in its evaluation of the Bektashi institutions, and, furthermore, even totally ignores the in the journal's up-to-this-point-customary laudations of the Bektashis' national character. The observations of the author, Mimar Hikmet [Onat], were based on his stay at the Bektashi lodge in Hacıbektaş, which he had visited in 1924 in his function as an architect commissioned to construct a guest house that, as another contemporary source tells us, was built by the government in recognition of the Bektashis' support for the nationalists during the War of Independence (Hamid Zübeyr [Koşay] 1926, 365). Mimar Hikmet describes his Bektashi hosts as very hospitable, friendly, and humorous, but also as uneducated and simple-minded. He concludes his report with a paragraph that wholeheartedly justifies the dissolution of the Bektashi order, which he characterizes as an organization that administered ignorance and dragged the nation into disaster. Since they did not contribute to the welfare and the independence of the nation, these "breeding grounds of laziness" needed to be destroyed (Mimar Hikmet 2001 [1928], 318).

In conclusion we can say that the texts published in *Türk Yurdu* in the years immediately following the ban of 1925 had a double effect. On the one side, they worked, with one exception, toward a recognition of the Bektashis and Kızılbaş-Alevis as an important part of Turkish culture. This culturalist approach served to integrate said groups into the Turkish nation, and made it at the same time possible to delegitimize their religious "ignorance" and in this way justify the ban. The texts published in *Türk Yurdu* in this period were accompanied by a series of journalistic essays on the Bektashis and Kızılbaş-Alevis in newspapers and popular magazines, which, in a much more sensationalist style, equally appear to have worked toward a legitimization of the secularist agenda of Kemalism. These latter texts, however, put—compared to *Türk Yurdu*—much less emphasis on the Kızılbaş-Alevis' and Bektashis' alleged Turkish character. Exemplary is a series of essays by Habil Adem on Bektashism in 1926–1927 in the weekly magazine *Büyük Gazete*. The author produces a sensationalist narrative that draws on traditional anti-Kızılbaş prejudices of scandalous moral behavior and political unreliability, marking the Bektashis as ignorant enemies of the civilizing national project: "Dear Reader…Please read these texts line by line with contempt and disgust, and remember these nests, which have for centuries kept us behind civilization, with curses. Remember with respect the name of our Great Gazi [Mustafa Kemal], who, after having achieved national independence, freed all Turks from these sockets of shame and scandal; advance fast toward the goals of civilization, welfare, and prosperity that he has delineated[!]" (Habil Adem 1926, 4).

Baha Said Bey's and Habil Adem's pre-republican and republican texts converge in their nationalist orientation. At the same time they bear witness to the fluidity of Turkish nationalist discourse in its formative period, when neither its religio-secular nor its ethno-cultural content and boundaries were as of yet finally determined. As Turkists, Baha Said emphasized that the Kızılbaş-Alevis are pure Turks and Habil Adem that the Kurds are secondarily Kurdified racial Turks. However, comparison also shows differences. Habil Adem's interpretation of the Kızılbaş within Kurdish-Persian culture is in tension with that of Baha Said, who discussed Kızılbaş-Alevi culture as an entirely Turkish phenomenon. As shown above, Baha Said's goal was to prove that the Kızılbaş-Alevis could be integrated into the new Turkish nation. From this point of view he argued, in a manner as we will see similar to the more scholarly approach of Fuad Köprülü, that the Kızılbaş-Alevis were carriers of Turkish national culture as evidenced in their shamanistic features dating back to ancient Turkish traditions. Thus, Baha Said recognized the importance of the religious difference of the Kızılbaş-Alevis even if he subordinated the factor of religion to that of national culture. For Habil Adem, on the other side, religion was an outright obstacle to the successful integration of the Kızılbaş-Alevis into modern Turkish life and therefore they needed to be assimilated. He regarded the culture of the Kızılbaş-Alevis as being of various Persianate origins. Correspondingly, the Turkishness of the Kurds would be hidden behind the Persianate culture that they had adopted.

Following Habil Adem's series on Bektashism, *Büyük Gazete* published in the spring of 1927 another related series of sensationalist articles, this time directly dedicated to the Kızılbaş. Its author was the young nationalist Enver Behnan [Şapolyo], who had been a junior Young Turk and an admirer and follower of Ziya Gökalp. He begins the first of a series of essays by asking "What is Kızılbashism, I wonder. Is it a religion (*din*)? Is it a religious subgroup (*mezhep*), or even a Sufi order (*tarikat*)?" ([Şapolyo] 1927a, 8). This is the very same question that the Alevis of today, 85 years later, are still confronted with in the public contestation about the nature

of their difference from Sunni Islam. It exemplifies the astonishing continuity in the way in which inner-Islamic difference has been organized by
the nationalist discourse in relation to basic Islamic categories. However,
Şapolyo's assessment differs considerably from earlier discussions in *Türk
Yurdu* with regard to the question as to whether the Kızılbaş were part of
Islam. Reminiscent of Habil Adem's argument, Şapolyo rather argues that
they belong to Mazdaism, and that Bektashism contradicts Islamic dogma
and rather was a religion in its own right ([Şapolyo] 1927a, 9).

The differences in the evaluations of the Kızılbaş-Alevis in the
early republic in the popular magazine *Büyük Gazete* as compared to
the nationalist journal *Türk Yurdu* reflect, on the one hand, competing visions about how and on which grounds of inclusion to define
and develop the national community, and, on the other, the simple
fact that an authoritative national discourse on the Kızılbaş-Alevis
and Bektashis was not yet established. In Şapolyo's account, the
Kızılbaş-Alevis are portrayed as utterly ambiguous both with regard
to their loyalty to the nation, and even more so with regard to their
religion. On the one side, the possible value of an integration of
these groups under the cloak of Turkish nationhood is emphasized.
Şapolyo, too, reports that many Kızılbaş feel enthusiastic about
Turkishness ([Şapolyo] 1927a, 8). On the other side, however, the
nationalists also had their concerns with regard to the Kızılbaş-Alevis'
ethno-national loyalties. The fact that parts of the Kızılbaş-Alevis were
Kurdish raised suspicions in a time when Kurdish resistance to the
Kemalist state had become the major interior problem.

The doubts about the Kızılbaş-Alevis' loyalties to the nation were
mostly not extended to the Bektashis, who were generally considered to
be Turkish. However, as members of a Sufi order the latter also received
their share of negative press following the Sheikh Said uprising and the
subsequent closure of the Sufi lodges. It is from within this context that
Şapolyo has to be understood when he reports that the Kızılbaş-Alevi *dedes*
or religious leaders worked as missionaries among Sunni villagers, who
would begin to realize only after entering the community that they had
been taken hostage by a group that had suspended all morals and religious
doctrine ([Şapolyo] 1927b, 12).

The overall impression that one gains perusing late-1920s texts on the
Kızılbaş-Alevis and Bektashis is that of ethno-national and religious ambiguity. In the context of a new secularist fervor that targeted forms of Islam
that it regarded as incompatible with the emerging ideal of a Kemalist

modernity and therefore marked as fanatic/militant, backward/tradition-alist, irrational/superstitious and so forth, the nationalist discourse pro-vided new space for old apologetic stereotypes against the Kızılbaş-Alevis, centered around accusations of immorality (in particular sexual debauch-ery) and political disloyalty. Such accusations overlapped with secularist arguments that implicitly differentiated between modern/rational forms of Islam (that is, Sunni Islam) and deviated forms of Islam in need of reform (that is, Kızılbaş-Alevism). While the texts of Baha Said, too, were ambivalent with regard to the religious aspect of Alevism, his texts exemplify how the secularist/modernist reading could also work toward integration of the Alevis. His texts contributed significantly to a still pow-erful discourse that presents Alevism as a positive example of a modern, national religion juxtaposed to the stereotype of an antimodern, fanati-cal Islam: "They did not take two wives. They did not divorce their mar-ried wives. They truly lived solidarity... They did not spoil their language. They stayed true to their traditions. They honored their sacred homestead (*ocak*)... The women did not veil. Since the Kızılbaş woman did not veil she has been accused of harlotry" (Baha Said 2001 [1926]a, 111).

In Turkish public discourse, and to a lesser extent also in academic dis-course, both assessments of Alevism—negative as immoral, superstitious, and politically unreliable and positive as secular-modern, and national—continue to resonate even today. Within these two ideal-typical poles of interpreting Kızılbaş-Alevism (and Bektashism), the work of renaming in which the benevolent interpreters of Kızılbaş-Alevism engaged when they began to call the Kızılbaş "Alevi" can be described as a work of re-signification that underlined the cultural importance of their religious difference and made it possible to connote them positively within a nation-alist discourse. Baha Said's texts on the Kızılbaş-Alevis are an example of this reading. He also claims that both Alevis and Bektashis benefitted from the republic since it liberated them from the "Sultanate of Yezid"[33] (Baha Said 2001 [1926]a, 111).

From the viewpoint of the Kızılbaş-Alevis, Baha Said's work legitimated their culture by proving its essential relevance for the establishment of a Turkish nation. This reading of Kızılbaş-Alevism still finds appreciation

---

33 Yezid is the name of the Omayyad Caliph held in the Shia tradition to be responsible for the Kerbala massacre. The name has therefore a very bad standing among Shiites, and also Alevis, and is sometimes used as a pejorative stereotyping of Sunni Muslims in general.

today.[34] The integration into the Turkist narrative, however, simultaneously delegitimized alternative Kızılbaş-Alevi claims based on Kurdish ethnicity and culture. In comparison to the term Alevi, the term Kızılbaş continued to be used especially to point to the Kurdish part of the Kızılbaş-Alevi tradition and remained more closely connected with the negative prejudices historically associated with it.

The texts produced by nationalist activist such as Baha Said and Habil Adem on the Kızılbaş-Alevis and Bektashis can be interpreted as responses to the conundrum posed by the religious and ethnic difference within the Muslim population, which alone was considered as eligible for Turkish nationhood. This conundrum itself was a product of the political developments since the Balkan Wars, in the course of which non-Muslims— with the exception of the Jews—were perceived as disloyal to the national cause. But the nationalist goal of a largest possible degree of homogeneity of the population did also target Muslims—namely those who differed either ethnically or religiously from the Turkish Sunni majority population. Nationalist discourses with regard to the origins of both the Kurds as well the Kızılbaş-Alevis were therefore implicated in practices of homogenization and assimilation. In his autobiography, Rıza Nur (1879–1942), who had been one of the leaders of the Turkish delegation at the Lausanne Peace Treaty negotiations, makes clear that not just the Kurds and the non-Muslim communities were a matter of nationalist concern: "The Europeans recognize three types of what we call minorities: racial minorities, language-based minorities, religious minorities. For us this is a pretty serious matter, a great danger … Based on the category religion they would make even the two million Kızılbaş, who are pure Turks, a minority" (Nur 1968: 1044).

With the restriction of minority rights to non-Muslim communities by the Lausanne Treaty, the Turkish delegation managed to prevent internationally recognized guarantees for the Kurds and the Kızılbaş-Alevis (Oran 2004, 61–63). Rıza Nur's account exemplifies that the possible extension of minority rights was perceived as a threat to the fragile unity of the new country. The nationalist memory of the disintegration of the Ottoman Empire and the intercommunal rivalries and violence that accompanied it was unambiguous about whom to blame for all of that (in particular the

---

34 Despite the derogatory language of Baha Said in his assessment of Alevi religion, Bedri Noyan (1912–1997), as *dedebaba* head of the Turkish branch of the Bektashi order, fully endorsed Baha Said's nationalist interpretation of the Alevis and Bektashis (Noyan 2006, 163 and 291).

local Christians in collaboration with European imperialism) and consequently fostered an at-times-chauvinist Turkish nationalism with strong
Muslim undertones. The emerging state ideology of Kemalism presented
the Turkish nation as overwhelmingly Turkish and Muslim and made
sure that claims of difference based on ethnicity, language, or religion
remained suppressed. Against the demand of ethno-religious homogeneity, the Kızılbaş-Alevis appeared in the nationalist view as a Muslim sect
of dubious character. The dominant state approach toward them was to
play down their difference and/or to encourage their assimilation into
the Sunni-Turkish mainstream. As I have argued, since the early stages
of Turkish nation-building religious and national identities evolved from
strongly overlapping sentiments. While the public gaze continued to
cast Greek and Armenian citizens as religious-cum-national others, the
Turkish nation was implicitly identified as Muslim. The Muslims, including the Kızılbaş-Alevis and the Kurds, were expected to integrate into
Turkish nationhood, which was an ethno-religious formation. Though not
always made explicit, this ethno-religionist tendency of Turkish nationalism would continue throughout the republic. There is a powerful understanding in the Turkish public that a real Turk is a Muslim. This comes
through in discriminatory discourses against non-Muslims, whose belonging to the Turkish nation is regularly questioned, as well in the debate
on Alevism, in which Alevis are keen to not be categorized as "minority"
(azınlık) since in Turkey the term is used only for non-Muslims—who can
be citizens, but are in nationalist discourse not regarded as part of the
nation (see Oran 2004).

With regard to the religious difference of the Alevis, the Ottoman-Turkish
state tradition pursued since the 1890s a Janus-faced strategy of at times
ignoring this difference and at times encouraging Alevi assimilation into
Sunni Islam.[35] With the secularization of state and public, and the parallel nationalization of religious belonging, the question of Alevi difference became even more pressing. In the pre-Tanzimat Ottoman context,
the people had been conceived as subjects of the sultan principally independent of religious affiliation, although in practice religious-community
rights were recognized, at least those of the major faiths of the empire.
With the Tanzimat these rights were formalized in what became known as

---

35 The same basic mechanism can be observed in the recent advances by the current government toward solving the "Alevi issue" as exemplified in the "Alevi Opening" discussed in
the prologue. Here, too, recognition of Alevi difference has been made dependent on integration in an Islamic framework as defined by the norms of Sunnism.

the *millet* system. Under the regime of Turkish nationalism, which aspired to mono-religious unity as part of national unity, religion then acquired, in a process that had already begun during the reign of Abdülhamid II, a new role in the formation of the citizenry, namely that of enhancing social cohesion—much in the manner as Ziya Gökalp had theorized in his political sociology. While Ottomanism had been based on the idea of a community of different people and faiths, Turkish nationalism idealized homogeneity of the people and unity in religion. The work of Turkish nationalist writers from the last years of the Ottoman Empire through the first decade of the Turkish Republic on the Kızılbaş-Alevis reflects this homogenizing tendency. To the extent that the latter could be portrayed as Muslim and Turkish this work of homogenization had an integrative manner. In both Baha Said's as well as—as I will show—Köprülü's work this homogenization is achieved by attributing to the Kızılbaş-Alevis a largely positively connoted and important role in the reconstruction of Turkish and Muslim national culture. While Baha Said's work on the Alevis is emblematic for their Turkist reevaluation, Köprülü's approach is in addition also concerned with integrating them into an Islamic framework. However, in the latter's work, too, the religious dimension of Alevism would continue to be cast as ambivalent. As I will show in my discussion of Köprülü, the integrative, national reading of the Kızılbaş-Alevis could always be challenged by pointing to their religious "heterodoxy" or their "syncretism," which created suspicion in the eyes of those who saw Sunni Islam as the norm of religion and were wary of the potential of social disarray that religious deviation as a social phenomenon could bring along.

PART TWO

Mehmed Fuad Köprülü (1890–1966) and the Conceptualization of Inner-Islamic Difference

4

Nationalism, Historiography, and Politics

The Formation of a Late Ottoman Intellectual

Mehmed Fuad Köprülü embarked on the academic writing of history during the early Young Turk rule, which allowed for a degree of intellectual and academic freedom unknown before. Already in his first historical writings, Köprülü would prepare the basis for his future fame as a Turkologist and expert on Turkish literature and history, and as the first Turkish scholar to gain international recognition.[1] In fact, as Gary Leiser and Robert Dankoff put it, already his early work "caused a sensation among knowledgeable European scholars." It was for the first time that a Middle Eastern scholar showed not only proficiency in Western scholarly methodology, but produced original work dedicated to the evolution of central aspects of Middle Eastern, Islamic, and especially Turkish culture (Leiser/Dankoff 2006, xxxi). Leiser, who has translated several of Köprülü's works into English, praises him as "the most outstanding Turkish scholar and intellectual in the twentieth century" and "the father of modern, scientific Turkish research on the culture and the history of the Turks" (Leiser 1992, xi).

Köprülü's work is still today widely read by students of Turkish history. Several of his most important articles and monographs have been translated into primarily English, but also other European languages such as French and German.[2] His scholarship and his engagement in academic institution building contributed enormously to the establishment

---

1 Since the early 1920s a regular invitee to European conferences, Köprülü received honorary doctorates from several prestigious European universities and was honorary member of Western academic societies (Akün 2002, 477; Leiser/Dankoff 2006, xxx-xxxi).

2 Recently a Turkish publisher (Akçağ) republished Köprülü's monographs as well as collections of important articles of his; some of these new editions contain work for the first time made available in Latin transcription.

of history, literary studies, folklore studies, archaeology, and Turkology as academic disciplines in Turkey. Given the tremendous impact Köprülü had not only as a scholar who left an impressive legacy both in his work in itself and through his students, who would become major figures in the development of different scholarly disciplines of cultural and historical studies, he and his work have been the subject of a number of scholarly publications.[3] Still missing is an in-depth, systematically historicizing analysis of Köprülü's work that would enable us to recognize, analyze, and ultimately go beyond the conceptual and political biases in the work of his, as well as of those who followed in his footsteps. One of the aims of this book is to start filling this gap.

Born in 1890 into a side branch of the Köprülü family, one of the most influential Ottoman families, from which several grand viziers in the late 17th and early 18th century had emerged, the young Köprülüzade Mehmed Fuad visited secular Istanbul schools before he enrolled in 1907 at the Darülfünun to study law. Unhappy with the instruction he received, he left after only three years without degree. From then on Köprülü continued his academic career as an autodidact, immersing himself in the study of the French language, and classical as well as contemporary European, mostly French, works of literature, history, philosophy, and sociology.

---

3 For an encyclopedic overview on Köprülü's life and work see Akün (2002, 481). The most comprehensive discussion of Köprülü as an intellectual and activist is the dissertation by George T. Park (1975). This widely neglected work includes ample information on Köprülü's biography and his academic and political networks, useful summaries of his scholarly and political writings, as well as the most comprehensive reconstruction of his intellectual development both as a historian and a politician interpreted in the context of Turkish modernization. Next to be mentioned is the dissertation by Abdülkerim Asılsoy (2008), which in terms of the general evaluation and the description of his academic and political careers overlaps in scope and content with Park's work, but offers the most comprehensive and detailed contextualization of Köprülü's contributions as a historian. While Park focuses more on the political dimension of Köprülü's work, Asılsoy's primary interest is in Köprülü's historiography and in questions of methodology. Asılsoy also offers the most comprehensive bibliography of Köprülü's publications (2008, 246–291). Another attempt to critically situate Köprülü's work within the evolution of modern Turkish historiography has been the booklet by Halil Berktay (1983). Comparing Köprülü to other nationalist historians of his time, Berktay specifically emphasized Köprülü's high methodological standards. Other monographs on Köprülü remain in regard of their analytical value rather shallow, such as the various publications by his son Orhan F. Köprülü (d. 2006), himself also an Ottomanist (for example, *Fuad Köprülü*. Ankara 1987); a small booklet by Ali G. Erdican, a member of the youth organization of the Democratic Party, which is mostly concerned with Köprülü's political views and not very original (Erdican 1974); as well as several unpublished Turkish master's theses focusing on selected aspects of his life and work, such as for example the thesis by Doğan Kaplan, which aims at bringing together what Köprülü wrote on Anatolian Alevism. This thesis does not, however, go beyond a rather uncritical reproduction of Köprülü's views without sufficient contextualization (Kaplan 2002).

Early Intellectual Activities

Köprülü published his first poems and literary essays in 1908 and 1909. Gradually being drawn into the politics of his time, he was initially critical of nationalist approaches to language and literature (Park 1975, 279–283). In 1909 he was among the founders of the literary group *Fecr-i Âtî* ("Dawn of the New Age"), which defended the use of Persian and Arabic elements in Ottoman Turkish literature; together with the journal *Servet-i Fünun*, it represented the literary avant-garde of the late Ottoman period, inspired by European, mainly French, literary trends (Park 1975, 16–17). In 1911 and 1912 he published several essays against the *Genç Kalemler* ("Young Pens"),[4] who supported the nationalization of Turkish language and literature. In response to this movement, Köprülü argued, as paraphrased by Park, that "in a century of increasing contacts and relations between nations and civilizations, a totally 'national' literature is impossible" (Park 1975, 281).

Though still critical of the nationalization of language and literature, Köprülü had already as a young adult a curiosity about Turkish nationalism, as his early membership in the *Türk Derneği* ("Turkish Society"), one of the first organizations that promoted a cultural nationalism, indicates. He joined the *Türk Derneği* already in 1909, within one year of its foundation (Park 1975, 14–15). In hindsight he would describe the time period after the Young Turk revolution of 1908 as a time of national awaking, when the Ottoman ideal of a multiethnic nation lost appeal among both non-Muslims and Muslims: "The Turkish element, which was dominant in the empire, thus needed a new ideal; this was the national ideal" (Köprülü 1987 [1934], 957). As with many contemporary Ottoman intellectuals, the Balkan Wars propelled and radicalized his political persuasions.

Köprülü's early writings mirror his gradually increasing interest in nationalist ideas. In the foreword to his first monograph, "Intellectual Life—Scientific Research," he argued that Turkish society would, in addition to the political revolution under way, also be in need of a mental and social revolution.[5] His gradual turn to Turkish nationalism made him reevaluate his positions on language and literature. Previously, he had evaluated questions of language and culture mainly from aesthetic

---

4 The group, among which we also find Ziya Gökalp, published a journal of the same name, which was an important organ of the early Turkish nationalist movement.

5 *Hayat-ı Fikriyye—Tetebbuat-ı İlmiyye. Garp Ediplerinden Bazıları Hakkında bir İnceleme* ("Intellectual Life—Scientific Research. A Study on Some Western Literary Men"), Istanbul 1910. For an English translation of its forward see Park (1975, 355–357).

viewpoints. Now, he adopted, possibly under the influence of his reading of Durkheim and enhanced by his acquaintance with Ziya Gökalp,
a more positivist position and began to inquire into the potential role of
language and literature for the national awakening.[6] Köprülü became a
protégé, comrade, and friend of Ziya Gökalp after the latter had moved to
Istanbul in 1912.[7] It is said that Gökalp was influential in drawing Köprülü
closer to the Turkist movement and also in facilitating his academic career.
In the same period Köprülü developed close relations with the circles of
the Turkist nationalists organized around the pan-Turkist Turkish Hearth
(*Türk Ocağı*) association, which had been founded in 1912 (Akün 2002,
473–474). In 1913 he not only stopped writing for *Servet-i Fünun* and
instead began to publish in nationalist periodicals, but even changed his
own writing style, reducing the quantity of Persian and Arabic words and
grammatical constructions in favor of Turkish ones (Park 1975, 286–292;
cf. Leiser/Dankoff 2006, xxviii–xxix).

Turn toward Turkism

Glimpses of nationalism were already visible in Köprülü's first publications in *Türk Yurdu* in 1913, the year when he began to teach Turkish literary history at the Darülfünun. In face of the Turkish military disaster in
the Balkan Wars and the political depression ensuing from that, Köprülü
published here his first outwardly nationalist piece with the title "Hope and
Determination: To the Turkish Youth."[8] This was an emotionally expres-
sive polemic, pledging revenge in the name of the Turkish nation and
formulating the hope that the desolate political situation would inspire a
national awakening:

> You, Turkish youth, if you want to save your sacred, noble nation,
> which the enemy wants to destroy, and if you utterly want to one
> day take revenge on him, then close your eyes in moments of
> exhaustion and hopelessness and listen to the iron and sacred cry

---

6 On the impact of positivism on late Ottoman intellectual life and Ziya Gökalp, see Ülken
(2006 [1942], vii–xiv).

7 For a testimony of his close relationship with Gökalp, see the short commemorative essay
Köprülü wrote in honor of the latter; the essay includes a letter by Gökalp to Köprülü that
illustrates their intimate connection (Köprülü 1989 [1965]).

8 "Ümit ve Azim: Türk Gençlerine." *Türk Yurdu* 2.1913, no.8, 240–247.

coming from the desserts of Asia and the Altai, where your forefathers died...: "For the Turkish nation I did not sleep at night, did
not rest at day, and struggled until death!" (Köprülü as quoted in
Kuran 1997, 244)

The emotional and solemn texts Köprülü published in 1912 and 1913 are
emblematic for the deep impact that the catastrophe of the Balkan War
had on patriotic Turkish-Ottoman intellectuals of the time, and indeed
on the formation of a national consciousness (Oba 1995, 107–120). These
poems and essays bore titles such as "The Song of War," "Prayer of the
Turk," "Flight Mourning," "The Ballad of Maritsa," "National Defense,"
"Under the Bayonet," "From Narrations of the Flight,"[9] and "The National
Sentiment in Our Literature." Some of these texts, for example "Prayer
of the Turk" and "National Sentiment," already show a basic theory of
Turkishness and Turanism.[10] In the latter text he laments that as a result of
foreign cultural influences (he explicitly mentions Arab, Persian, Greek,
and Armenian influences) the Turks have lost their national spirit; due to
a lack of national consciousness, until recently even among the intellectuals and the upper classes, Turks were still be bound to these non-Turkish
influences (Köprülü 1913).

Köprülü regarded a moral and spiritual crisis as the underlying reason
for the defeat in the Balkans. In this context, the idea of a nationalist awakening was expressed in terms of a moral and religious renewal.[11] Köprülü's
writings of that phase reflect the intricate relationship between religious
and ethnic semantics in the nationalist discourse, which, as argued before,
was not yet secularized in the sense of a clear distinction between religious
and ethno-national sentiments and ideas.

As with most of his intellectual peers, Köprülü did in 1913 still display political loyalty to the Ottoman Empire, articulated for example in his

---

9 "Harb Şarkısı," *Donanma Mecmuası* 4.1912, no. 31–7 (September); "Türk'ün Duası," *Türk
Yurdu* 2.1913, no. 10, 289–296, and no. 11, 324–330; "Hicret Matemleri," *Türk Yurdu* 2.1913,
no. 14, 437–442; "Meriç Türküsü," *Türk Yurdu* 2.1913, no. 15, 475–477; "Müdafaa-i Milliye,"
Tasvir-i Efkâr, Feb. 11, 1913; "Süngü Altında," *Halka Doğru Mecmuası* no. 13, July 4, 1913;
"Hicret Hikayelerinden," *Halka Doğru Mecmuası* no. 16, July 16, 1913.

10 *Prayer of the Turk* consists of a large series of poems reflecting on the war; it was even set
to music and put on stage at the headquarter of the CUP (Tansel 1966b, 644).

11 This theme is developed in "İntibah Yolları," *Tasvir-i Efkâr*, Feb.22, 1913 (see Park 1975, 369).

essay "Turkism, Islam, and Ottomanism" (*Türklük, İslâmlık, Osmanlılık*).[12] The piece defends Turkism against its Ottomanist and pan-Islamist critics: "We regard the continuous protection of Ottomanism and Islam as possible only through the awakening and advancement of Turkism" (Köprülü 1999 [1913]a, 372). Against those advocating religion as the exclusive base for an Ottoman national identity, he argued that "[o]ne of the most influential factors in the formation of a nation is religion. To a certain extent, national history means religious history. However, the importance of religion does never prove that it takes on the form of a separate nationality" (Köprülü 1999 [1913]a, 374). In other words, religion is an important element in the formation of a national consciousness, but it is not itself a nationality. Nationalist consciousness is based on, but also transgresses religious identity. Consequently, Köprülü attributes the political misery of Turks and Arabs to the fact that they had not yet been able to develop a national consciousness. He asserts, however, that they surely would do so in the future, since "[w]here ever one finds a group that possesses a distinct geographic location, a distinct language and literature, and distinct customs and traditions, it will definitely form a distinct spiritual unity" (Köprülü 1999 [1913]a, 375). This spiritual unity is provided by the national consciousness, which is based on territory, and cultural achievements such as language, literature, and customs. While indirectly criticizing purely-religion-based models for national unity, he assures the reader that the advancement of Turkism will necessarily also lead to an awakening of Islam and should not be seen as the latter's enemy; neither should Turkism be seen as inimical to the Ottoman Empire, since the goal of Turkism was not to establish a separate state. To the contrary, the awakening of national consciousness among the Turks would strengthen the Ottoman state (Köprülü 1999 [1913]a, 375–376).

Such a diplomatic approach, which tried to strengthen the Turkist position while maintaining its loyalty to Islam and Ottomanism, was very much typical for the Turkist movement until the later years of World War I. In the late Ottoman Empire, ideological positions of (pan-)Islamism, (pan-)Turkism, Ottomanism, and Westernism—although differentiating more clearly in the course of the Balkan Wars and the world war—were not as bounded as they would appear to many later observers, and rather

---

12 The title reminds of Akçura's *Three Kinds of Politics* (1904), which had also distinguished between the ideologies of Ottoman Nationalism, Pan-Islamism, and Turkism, and favored the latter as basis for a national state (see pp. 90–91).

should be understood as rivaling, but not necessarily in every aspect contradicting, programmatic emphases within an overarching nationalist and state-centered paradigm. Pan-Turkism, Pan-Islamism, and Ottomanism were "coexisting ideologies and political options of the CUP, which were put to the forefront according to the political agenda" (Kieser/Schaller 2002, 19). All of them were nationalist and aimed at modernization—even if they conceptualized modernity differently. It was the strength of the CUP to be able to accommodate all of these different ideas and the social circles associated with them under the shared concern for saving the empire (Köroğlu 2007, 24–37). As discussed before, Turkish nationalism became more aggressive and gradually began to dominate political discourse only following the Balkan Wars.

In Köprülü's early intellectual formation, which would have a lasting impact on his understanding of science and his methodological convictions, he was influenced by Hippolyte Taine, Gustave Le Bon, Gabriel Tarde, Auguste Comte, Henri Bergson, Gabriel Monod, and Alfred Fouillée—to name just a few authors that he studied and commented on intensively (Park 1975, 10–13). His early writings comprise lengthy discussions of Western philosophical, historical, and sociological debates on questions of contemporary methodological and theoretical issues and concepts, such as evolutionism, positivism, the subjectivity-objectivity binary, and historical truth. While positivism certainly had an important influence on his early thought, he did not embrace it completely. Thus he was critical of the idea that the methodologies of the historical and social sciences should be modeled on those of the natural sciences. In his first work of an academic nature within the field of history, "Method in the History of Turkish Literature" (1913) he argued that "[i]n order for independent sciences to form, every branch of science needs to have its own methods fitting to its character" (Köprülü 1999 [1913]b, 4).[13]

In the same article, he critically evaluates contemporary European approaches to science, history, and particularly the history of literature, arguing for a tempered positivism committed to the objectivity of empirically rooted science, and the task of history to reconstruct and make alive the past. In this context he also praises the important role of history in the nation-building process (Köprülü 1999 [1913]b; cf. Boyar 2007, 16–17). At the age of 23, shaken by the political developments of the time, Köprülü had embarked on what would be one of his major intellectual

---

13 For an English translation of this article see Leiser (2008).

contributions to late Ottoman and early republican thought, namely the project of providing a scientifically sound narrative of the evolution of the Turkish nation.

Köprülü's intellectual engagement with the French philosopher Alfred Fouillée (1838–1912) illustrates well the influence of contemporary French philosophy on his intellectual development.[14] In the introduction to *Intellectual Life*, wherein he discussed selected examples of Western litera-ture, Köprülü cites him as a thinker who, next to Stuart Mill and Auguste Comte, asserted that "advances in philosophy cause societal progress" (quoted in Park 1975, 356). This is an allusion to Fouillée's best-known philosophical contribution, namely his concept of the *idées-forces*.[15] Fouillée defined ideas as "all mental states more or less conscious of themselves and their object."[16] Elsewhere he explicates that "every idea . . . is *inclined to realize itself*" (Fouillée 1907, 530). Ideas were thus not passive, such as in Descartes' *cogito ergo sum*, but rather active forces in the world, leading to the realization of their objects (Fouillée 1911, 37). In implicit opposition to the materialist philosophy of his time and in explicit rejection of Spencer's mechanistic evolutionism, Fouillée argued that "the forces of the ideas consist in that the mental, instead of being just a secondary *reflection* of the universal evolution, is one of its essential *factors*" (Fouillée 1907, 530).[17]

As the following chapters will illustrate, the concept of the *idées-forces* resonates well with the way Köprülü understood the relationship between ideas and action as an immediate and causal one. In a newspaper article from 1913 on "Popular Literature," Köprülü links, clearly echoing Fouillée's *idées-forces*, the fate of a nation with the degree of the development of its spirit: "The spirit of the nation and the strength of the nation are the life force of the nation, the spirit of the people and the strength of the people are the life force of the people."[18] Köprülü's interest in Fouillée was one of

---

14 Among the volumes that belonged to Köprülü's library (see fn 22 below) we find several monographs by Fouillée: *Descartes* (1906), *Histoire de la philosophie* (1907), *La morale l'art et la religion: d'après Guyau* (1909), and *La pense et les nouvelles écoles anti-intellectualistes* (1911).

15 See *L'evolutionisme des idées-forces* (1890); *La psychologie des idées-forces* (1893); *La morale des idées-forces* (1907).

16 According to the "law" of the *idées-forces*, affective and intellectual life cannot be sepa-rated, but follow the "principle of monistic psychology" (Fouillée 1911, 32–33).

17 For a text in which he comprehensively refuted materialist approaches to biological and sociological life, see Fouillée (1904).

18 "Halk Edebiyatı I," *Tasvir-i Efkar*, 20 May 1913. As quoted in Asılsoy (2008, 182).

the intellectual threads that connected him with Ziya Gökalp, whose early idealism was also strongly influenced by the concept of *idées-forces*. For both of them this concept embodied a belief in the productive potential that ideas carry—a belief that guided them in their academic and political activities, which were in this way organically connected. Both having read and independently of each other been impacted by Fouillée and Durkheim, Köprülü shared with Gökalp the vision and the vigor to change the cultural identity of the country. The conviction of a causal relation between idea and action, expressed by Gökalp in the concept of *mefkure* ("ideal"), which he coined, helped them to develop a philosophy of scholarly activism in the service of the nationalist project, or the national ideal.

Büşra Ersanlı defines both Gökalp and Köprülü as *politician-historians*, a term with which she points to the emergence of a new kind of social actor in this time period, namely historians who played key roles in nation-building processes—be it by becoming professional politicians themselves or by forming and leading nationalist and nationalist-scientific or educative organizations and journals (Ersanlı 2003, 108–109). Indeed, one has to recognize the crucial role that intellectuals played in the period from the Young Turk revolution throughout the first decades of the Turkish Republic, especially as (social) engineers and advocates of Turkish nationalism, but also in politics more generally (see Park 1975, 310–311 and 321–327).

Historiography, Sociology, and Nation-Building

From 1913 onward we see an increasing interest in history, particularly Turkish history, in Köprülü's publications. In line with Gökalp, he identified a lack of historical consciousness among the Turks and began to write about the importance of such consciousness for the evolution of a national identity. At the same time, he began to himself trace the history of the national Turkish feeling back into pre-Islamic times (see Park 1975, 370–371).

Köprülü's first scientific publication on Turkish literature was his widely acclaimed "Method in the History of Turkish Literature." In this early piece already, "he was laying the groundwork for a shift away from literary history which concentrated on the literature of the Ottoman elite, towards a history which would search for the national genius in Turkish folk literature" (Park 1975, 215). The focus on popular literature as the locus of the national spirit meant a rather sharp and fast turn from his previous positions on that matter. In an essay entitled "The People and Literature" (*Halk ve Edebiyat*, 1911) he had argued, as paraphrased by Park, that "true literature can not be an explanation of the simple ideas and common pleasures of the masses" (Park 1975, 364). While Köprülü as late as in mid-1912 continued to argue that the nationalist language movement would neglect aesthetics in its turn to the needs of the masses, he seems to have changed his opinion by early 1913, when he began to take a more critical stance toward elitist positions and began to focus on the people as the locus of the national soul (Asılsoy 2008, 181–182; also Park 1975, 367–368).[19] It is clearly his changing view on Turkish nationalism that made Köprülü alter so thoroughly his positions on literature, language, and the place he ascribed to popular culture in the project of national recovery (Park 1975, 286–292).

Köprülü would continue to periodically write on that subject until the mid-1920s. The basic theme remained the same: in order to accomplish a national awakening, a national literature needs to be created based on the cultural knowledge of the ordinary people; this cultural knowledge needs to be discovered and made available by the elite and then brought back to the people in order to create a national consciousness (Asılsoy 2008, 183).[20]

While his academic interests were strongly influenced by his politics, his scholarly writings would be much more sober in style than his political essays, or his poetry. Köprülü's main significance is in the very scope of the ambitious task he was taking on, namely to trace the historical evolution, extension, and continuity of Turkish culture through an examination of Islamic mystical literature from Central Asian Turkish origins in ancient times to its arrival and flourishing in Anatolia in the Seljuk and Ottoman periods. This project was as much a genuinely historical project as it was informed by the politics of Turkish nationalism, which was at that time in desperate need of

---

19 Durkheimian ideas lurk through in Köprülü's justification for a nationalization of literature. In a series of essays from 1917 he would argue that a "literary personality" was a writer capable of correctly representing a given society in a literary way; since immersed in national sentiment and culture, this personality constituted a social rather than an individual phenomenon. Literature was a social product, ideally reflecting the norms and values of a society. Accordingly, literature that failed to represent the national culture was abnormal (as paraphrased in Park 1975, 288–289 and 373).

20 Similarly, Gökalp had emphasized the importance of the literary traditions of the ordinary people, of which a nation needed to be aware if it aimed at developing its national literature (Okay 1996, 128; Davison 1995, 206).

a historical anchoring of its national ideal. This is exactly what Köprülü set out to do, and this is also the context within which his conceptualization of Turkish Alevism needs to be situated. As I will show, already in his very first historical essays we find ample references to this nationalist quest.

The Köprülü-Gökalp Symbiosis

I have already alluded to the strong Durkheimian influence on the young Köprülü. It has been variously argued that it was Gökalp who had inspired Köprülü "to take [Durkheim's sociology] as point of departure for an extension of Turkism to the depths of Central Asia" (Akün 2002, 474). Indeed, from the beginning of his project of a (re-)construction of Turkish history we find that Durkheimian terminology and theoretical assumptions take a prominent place in Köprülü's work. The library of Köprülü[21] shows that he owned a considerable amount of Durkheim's publications in original copies, translations of his work into Turkish, as well as the influential review journal *L'Année Sociologique*.[22]

We know from Köprülü's early publications that he already read, translated, and published on sociological questions before he met with

---

21 A larges part of Köprülü's library is today incorporated into the Yapı Kredi Sermet Çifter Research Library in Istanbul, allegedly roughly 10,000 volumes. While, unfortunately, the collection was incorporated into the library system without an inventory of it first being made, the books that stem from the Köprülü library are marked.

22 Unfortunately, Köprülü was an extremely meticulous reader who refrained from marking his books. The extent to which he worked with a particular book can only be judged by its physical state. While it is obviously not possible to draw definite conclusions from the outer condition of these books, some observations still deserve to be mentioned. Of all of Durkheim's publications that are found in Köprülü's library, the original 1912 print of *Les formes elémentaires* is the copy that is in the worst shape, with the front page having come off and other pages also about to fall apart, seemingly as a consequence of heavy usage. The book of Durkheim in the second worst condition is a 1910 print of *Les règles de la méthode sociologique* (1895). Köprülü's library further included an original copy of *Sociologie et Philosophie* (1924), Turkish translations of *Formes elémentaires* in two volumes (1924), *L'Éducation morale* (1927—the pages of this book still un-cut), and a book by Georges Davy on Durkheim including selected texts of the latter (*Emile Durkheim*, Paris 1911). Remaining from Köprülü's library are further volumes IX (1904–1905), XI (1906–1909), and XII (1909–1912) of *L'Année Sociologique*, the journal that was founded and edited by Durkheim, who used it for publication of his own work, as well as that of his students (such as, most prominently, Marcel Mauss). The journal did comprise extensive reviewing of books in the fields of sociology, anthropology/ethnology, religious history, psychology, history, and Oriental studies providing readers with a comprehensive overview on contemporary research in these areas. The copies date from those years in which Köprülü began to familiarize himself with sociological questions and methodology and look as if they were read.

Gökalp in 1912. In a series of essays that he wrote for *Servet-i Fünun* in 1910, Köprülü discussed major sociological topics and deplored the lack of attention paid to this academic discipline in Turkey (Park 1975, 362). The question of influences of ideas, and in this case primarily the extent to which Köprülü was directed by Gökalp in his sociological thought and whether the latter in fact initiated him into the sociology of Durkheim, as often claimed, is difficult to answer in a final way. As Park points out, "many of their ideas and theories came from identical sources. Both read the works of Gabriel Tarde, Gustave Le Bon, and Alfred Fouillée, for example. Accordingly, Köprülü would have had much to offer in any exchange of ideas. Indeed, he may have influenced Gökalp in certain fields, such as sociology" (Park 1975, 31). It seems clear that Durkheimian thought became much more pronounced in Köprülü with the beginning of his collaboration with Gökalp. Gökalp, on the other side, had found a congenial partner who was able to realize his historical ambitions. In sum, it is clear that their collaboration can best be described as a symbiotic one.

An early product of the collaboration between Gökalp and Köprülü was the series of articles that they published in 1915 in *Milli Tetebbular Mecmuası* ("Journal for National Research"), which they edited jointly. The most important pieces of this series were two articles by Köprülü on the Turkish minstrel tradition and the origins of Turkish literature (first and fourth issue),[23] as well as, chronologically placed in between, two articles by Gökalp (both in the second issue): the first one a largely methodological outline that develops principles for how to properly study the history of Turkish culture ("The Method To Be Followed in the Research of a People"); the second one, of more empirical sort, discussing "The Symmetry between the Social Formations and the Logical Classifications among the Old Turks."[24] These four seldom-cited articles in combination had a programmatic character, setting out an agenda for the sociohistorical research and nationalist re-appropriation of Turkish history and culture through a reconstruction of its historical evolution. Gökalp's "Method To Be Followed" set the tone of this enterprise. Drawing closely and explicitly on Durkheim's ideas on

23 "Türk Edebiyatında Aşık Tarzının Menşe ve Tekâmülü hakkında bir Tecrübe," *Milli Tetebbular Mecmuası* 1.1915, no.1, pp. 5–46, and "The Origins of Turkish Literature" (Köprülü 1999 [1915]). Already in 1914 Köprülü had begun to publish newspaper essays on methodology, and the importance of the study of folklore and pre-Islamic Turkish literary traditions for the reconstruction of the Turkish spirit; for annotated references see Park (1975, 372).

24 "Eski Türkler'de İçtimaî Teşkilât ile Mantıkî Tasnifler Arasında Tenâzur," *Milli Tetebbular Mecmuası* 1.1915, no.2, pp. 385–456.

the evolution of culture from primitive to organic—that is to say modern—
societies and states, he charts out parameters for the study of this cultural
evolution in the case of the Turks (Gökalp 1915, 204–205). And this, as he
makes apparent in plain instrumental language, would not be an end in
itself, but has direct political implications: "Only after Turkish culture has
been researched scientifically from the early beginning until today will we
be able to understand in which direction it has to be directed, and with
which means it has to be lifted to its heights" (Gökalp 1915, 205). It is only
from within this context of discovering the Turkish past as a contribution
to the contemporary nationalist awakening that the political dimension of
the Gökalp-Köprülü symbiosis can be properly evaluated.

Although he obviously lacked the historical distance that might have
enabled him to appreciate the entire scope and especially the political
thrust of Gökalp and Köprülü's cooperation, the German Orientalist
Martin Hartmann realized early on the scientific importance of their publications in *Milli Tetebbular Mecmuası*, which he praised in a review essay
published in one of the leading Orientalist journals of the time. He was
especially impressed by the sociological method that Köprülü applied to
historical materials and lauded Köprülü's first article on the origins of
the Turkish minstrel (*aşık*) tradition as "a testimony of an unusual energy
of scientific thought in combination with the secure method acquired
in Europe" (Hartmann 1918, 310); he found very convincing in particular Köprülü's way of explaining the emergence and evolution of the
aşık-literature as a reflection and product of social conditions (Hartmann
1918, 305).[25] Hartmann recognized in Köprülü already at this early stage
of his career "the leading man in Turkey on this area [of Turkish litera-
ture]" (Hartmann 1918, 311)—a huge compliment for the young professor,
who had no formal academic degree and had only rather recently begun
to publish in this field.

Köprülü's nationalism was, at least in his academic writings, much more
subtle than that of Gökalp. Still, the main thrust of his research was exactly
what Gökalp had constructed as prerequisite for the takeoff of Turkish
nationalism, namely a firm historicization of its evolution. Köprülü's

---

25 *Aşık*, lit. "lover," a term from the Islamic mystical tradition, is one of the names by which
the religious bards of Anatolia were called. The *aşık* tradition of bards, whose songs cover
all spheres of life from mystical to profane love, and from ritual to mundane topics, is particularly strong among the Kızılbaş and Bektashi groups, but is also regionally found among
Sunni Muslims; it was also spread among Armenians. See Reinhard and de Oliveira Pinto
(1989); Köprülü (1966 [1962]).

conviction regarding the necessity of that kind of historical-cum-national program was already visibly in "Method in the History of Turkish Literature," which he concluded after 49 (in the original publication) erudite and rather dry pages on methodology with a paragraph the tone of which constitutes a total stylistic break with the previous pages:

> Every young Turk enthusiastic about the history of literature has...to try to contribute at least one stone to this great national and scientific monument none of the building blocks of which are as of yet available. This amazing monument, which will take shape, will, by showing the unity of the Turkish national genius—that displays the mental and emotional aspects which the great and honorable Turkish nation has gone through over centuries in different environments, and [which are] the aspects through which it shows itself—induce the same goal of unity in future generations. How could one imagine a nobler and more sacred aim for the historian of Turkish literature than this! (Köprülü 1999 [1913]b, 47)

In the same spirit he exclaimed in a newspaper article from the following year that "[o]nce the history of Turkish literature is brought to life by the magic touch of a strong hand, all Turks will better understand the spiritual unity and move closer to each other in spirit."[26]

Politics and Scholarship

Köprülü's scholarship has established a paradigm of interpreting the Kızılbaş-Alevis and other groups closely associated with them, such as the Bektashis, within the parameters of Islam and a Turko-centric history. One aim of this narrative was to refute theories that located these groups in Christian and ancient Anatolian contexts:

> As wrong as the judgments of some anthropologists and ethnographers are, who claim that there would exist among the Bektashi and Kızılbaş a number of old local cults, that is, beliefs that stem from the pre-Christian area of Anatolia, in the same way err those who claim—seeing the existence of some Christian Bektashis and of some rituals and beliefs that resemble similar ones found in Christianity—that this order [the Bektashiye] would have been

under strong Christian influence. The [fact of the] continuity of a number of local beliefs and practices among the local people, who lived there for many centuries, although they have entered different religions and thus changed their outer forms, the existence of similar dogmas and ceremonies among people with a similar degree of religious evolution, and the commonality of some religious places and the customs associated with them among people of different religion living in their vicinity is a commonplace knowledge within the anthropology as well as the history of religion.

It is for that reason necessary not to draw wrong and general conclusions by falling for some external similarities and proclaiming the sameness of things that have totally different origins and are often also of totally different character. The real identity of Bektashism manifests itself when these general principles from the sociology of religion are borne in mind, and when it [Bektashism] is investigated within the general history of the religious-Sufi currents of the Islamic and Turkish world. (Köprülü, 1979 [1949], 463)

The apologetic tone of Köprülü's refutations of interpretations that could question the essentially Turkish and Muslim character of the Bektashis (and by implication also the Kızılbaş-Alevis) reflects the importance that he attributed to issues of ethnic and religious belonging in the context of Turkish nation-building. Köprülü's criticism of those scholars who had interpreted the Bektashis and Kızılbaş-Alevis in ways that did not recognize their Islamic and Turkish origins is therefore unambiguous. His narrative acknowledges syncretism at work in the formation of Bektashism, but based on an essentialist distinction between its "outer forms" and its "real identity" he maintains that the major framework for understanding it needs to be Turkish culture and Islam. The rigidness with which Köprülü asserts his argument does not allow much space for alternative viewpoints. Here and elsewhere, for example when he employs a grave tone of voice when pointing out the ancient roots of national Turkish sentiment, Köprülü cannot hide his nationalist bias underneath a—undeniably genuine—scholarly agenda.

Perceived from the distance, it is rather astonishing to see with how much certainty Köprülü was able to produce a narrative of the continuity of Turkish culture based on certain historical assumptions that he was himself only partially equipped to verify. Examples are the thesis of the ancient Turks' shamanism, and may be even more fundamentally, the assumption of the continuity of elements of ancient Turkish culture throughout times full of geographic, religious, socioeconomic, and cultural disruptions. Of course, Köprülü has to be approached as a child of his time, influenced by a number of contemporary intellectual currents. In Köprülü's nationalism we can detect a Platonic romanticism, in which the continuity of Turkishness becomes palpable in atemporal notions of national "spirit" and "taste." His concept of religion bears similar marks of romantic idealism. This is most apparent in his theory of religious evolution, which follows a Durkheimian trajectory in its explanation of the differentiation of cultural spheres, one of them being religion (see Köprülü 1999 [1915]; 2005 [1925]). Then, however, somewhat departing from Durkheim's concept of religion and more reminiscent of Fouillée's *idées-forces*, religion appears in Köprülü's account at times almost like an ideal waiting for its objectification qua differentiation from other spheres of life. As Dubuisson has pointedly argued in his critical analysis of the Western concept of religion, "once religion is the issue, a Western mind, however agnostic, easily reaches the Platonic paradise of eternal ideas" (Dubuisson 2003, 164). In the case of Köprülü and other romantic nationalists of the 19th and early 20th centuries, such Platonic visualizations are of course primarily directed toward the idea of the nation.

Köprülü's historiography is culturally essentialist, idealist, and romantic, as is the case with many other scientific projects conducted within a nationalist frame in this time period, and as he in later years partly admitted (Köprülü 1940). At a time when the contours of Turkish nationalism were still a matter of fierce debate, and a national master narrative not yet established, he put forward important historical evidence for the formulation of a national Turkish subject that could remain recognizable in a long-term historical perspective. Köprülü's historiography provided the Turkish nation with consciousness about its own past and traditions. In a foreword to a translation of a selection of articles by F. W. Hasluck he maintained that research on the religious history of Anatolia was an almost existential matter for the Turks: "We can say explicitly that for our country this inquiry constitutes not only a 'scientific,' but a 'national' necessity." In order to improve the Turkish situation in the present, to achieve national unity, it was essential and indeed an existential task to understand the reason why the Anatolian Turks had over centuries been living as rather divided segments (Köprülü 1928a, vi).[27]

27 The selection was published by the Institute for Turkology (*Türkiyat Enstitüsü*), which had been created in 1924 upon Mustafa Kemal's directive, and to which Köprülü was appointed as director during his tenure as under-secretary at the Ministry of Education. The creation of a Turkological institute had been brought under way soon after the declaration of the republic with Mustafa Kemal ordering Köprülü to prepare a dossier in that direction, and was motivated by the need for further scientific research on the origins and history of

While Ziya Gökalp approached his scholarship and his politics as two faces of one continuum, Köprülü seems to have more consciously tried to separate his scholarly work from his political convictions. Although he wrote nationalist essays in the Young Turk period, Köprülü was not to the same degree committed to political activism as some of his nationalist friends and colleagues. He also never became himself a member of the CUP—although he was close to many of its organizations (Park 1975, 29 fn 7). This might have not been entirely a matter of personal choice. The journalist Cihad Baban claims that during World War I Köprülü would, through Gökalp and Ömer Seyfeddin, have applied with the CUP for a seat in parliament, but was rejected by Talat Paşa as being too young and overly ambitious (Baban 1970, 343). Possibly such a rejection might have contributed to a certain distance he kept from the party even while he supported the nationalist project. In August of 1919 he argued in an article in *Türk Dünyası* that Turkish nationalism could not be blamed for the—at this point publicly discredited—politics of the CUP. On the other hand, there is evidence that he had as late as in early 1919 been involved in illegal financial transactions in connection with the *Teşkilat-ı Mahsusa*, which at this point was one of the major Unionist organizations in support of the national resistance in Anatolia (Asılsoy 2008, 54–55). But after being temporarily jailed for participation in subversive activities in early 1920, Köprülü seems to have taken a step backward from active political involvement.[28] There is no indication that he showed any decisive political stance during the Turkish-Greek War following his imprisonment.

the Turks within national parameters (Dölen 2010, 257–259). The primary purpose of the institute was, in Köprülü's own words, to contribute to the "study of the religious ethnography of Turkish groups" of Anatolia and its adjacent territories (Köprülü 1928a, vi). Its publications aimed at making available to Turkish researchers selected works of Western Orientalists in translation. In this regard Köprülü praises the work of Hasluck as, despite its lack in regard of Turkish and Islamic sources, solid scholarship that made extensive use of Christian sources and reflected deep knowledge of the Christian heritage of the country. Therefore it would be valuable for comparative purposes and a more comprehensive and systematic account of the religious history of Anatolia (Köprülü 1928a, vii).

28 In his autobiography, Zekeriya Sertel provides an interesting account of a small organization he was about to found together with friends against the Allied forces following the British occupation of Istanbul in March 1920; among the group were Köprülü, Hasan Ali Yücel, Ahmet Ferit [Tek] (the latter two would later take on cabinet positions under Atatürk); the organization was, however, busted by the police at its very first meeting. Sertel recounts that in the one week that he and Köprülü had to spend in jail, Köprülü was very depressed, apparently regretting to have participated in this political adventure; consecutively, he separated himself from the others, withdrew to a certain degree from their social circles, and refrained from further political activism (Sertel 1977, 85–90).

This can probably be attributed to a number of further reasons, including the difficult situation for nationalist intellectuals in Istanbul under British occupation and a certain political disillusionment with the CUP networks following the World War I disaster. In his writings in the popular press he now focused on matters of national language, literature, history, and education (see Park 1975, 376–381).

Despite keeping a low political profile between 1920 and 1923, Köprülü would from the early republic onward entertain good relations with Kemal Atatürk and belonged to his wider intellectual circle.[29] He was a critical supporter of the secularist modernization project in principle and contributed to it in manifold ways, even if he disagreed sometimes in the details. In 1924, Köprülü served for a while as under-secretary to the Ministry of Education; between 1923 and 1926 he was a member of three scientific commissions that planned reform of the education system; in 1928, he headed a committee of Darülfünun professors from the Faculty of Divinity, which had been asked to develop a plan on how to reform Islam;[30] in 1929, Köprülü chaired a working group of Darülfünun professors who were ordered to reflect on how to facilitate the adaptation of the Latin alphabet (Azak 2007, 140); in 1933, he headed a task force that organized a newspaper campaign for the collection of locally used Turkish equivalents of foreign words which ought to be replaced in the context of the language reform (Park 1975, 301); in 1934, he led a language commission asked to reflect on how to adjust literature education in schools to the requirements of the new language (Azak 2007, 238). Despite previous criticism regarding the adaptation of the Latin alphabet, Köprülü did adjust to the new realities, and as a member of the Turkish Language Society created by Atatürk contributed now actively to the Turkification process. In 1935 he became, upon the request of Atatürk, who had a policy of appointing a certain amount of intellectuals to parliament, parliamentary representative of Kars. Later on he was one of the founding members of the Democratic Party, and served between 1950 and 1956 as minister for foreign affairs.[31] Although he continued publishing sporadically and never

---

29 In the years between 1932 and 1938 alone Köprülü made more than hundred official visits to Atatürk, unofficial visits not being recorded (Park 1975, 61).

30 Discussed in more detail below.

31 Many of his writings and speeches as politician in this period were dedicated to the goal of increasing democracy. In this way he since the mid-1940s tailored his criticism against the totalitarian one-party regime of the RPP. In a newspaper article from 1949 this criticism even extended to the last decade of Atatürk's life and presidency, claiming that Turkey

totally lost contact to academia, his political activities from the mid-1930s to the late 1950s, especially the phase between the mid-1940s and mid-1950s, impacted on the breath of his scholarly output.

The critical question is how to evaluate the impact of Köprülü's politics—his political convictions more broadly speaking as well as his involvement in concrete political activities—on his scholarship. Köprülü's student and friend Fevziye Tansel remarked that "Köprülü always had a national objective in his research" (Tansel 2006 [1966], xlvi). Undeniably, Köprülü's politics and his historical work were closely interrelated and have to be understood, maybe not as a continuum such as in the case of Gökalp, but at least as being in a continued dialogue.

But one has to be careful with where to take this criticism of Köprülü's political biases. Recognition of the political thrust inherent in modern interpretations of nationhood and national narratives should not make us categorically discard scholarship that has been inspired by nationalist ideas. My criticism of Köprülü's nationalist bias does not imply an ideal of scholarly objectivity. Nationalist perspectives on history are not necessarily more distorting than other ideological convictions (be they of the materialist or of the metaphysical kind). Knowledge of these convictions in the background can even help us to better understand the motivations behind particular nationalist narratives.

Scholarship is always historically situated. In order to do justice to the influence of Köprülü's nationalism on his scholarship it is necessary to make apparent this situatedness. Doing so, one will have to take into account that during the years of his major academic contributions there was "no clear dividing line between the spheres of culture and politics. This was particularly true during the formative period of Turkish nationalism and the days of single party rule when cultural issues such as the language and history reforms were everyday matters of state" (Park 1975, 323).

The Turkish History Thesis

Köprülü's loyalty to the nationalist project as defined from above was not without limits. This became starkly apparent in the early 1930s, when he took a critical position toward the new Turkish History Thesis. After

---

had from 1927 onward turned into a dictatorship ("Neler Yaptık? Neler Yapmadık?," *Vatan*, October 29, quoted in Asılsoy 2008, 217). The return to non-democratic practices would later on also be the main reason that made him resign from the Democratic Party in 1957. For an overview of Köprülü's political career see Park (1975, 72–121).

the experiment with a second political party in 1930 was cut short when
its immediate popularity threatened the elite of the reigning RPP, the
Kemalist modernizers embarked on an unprecedented effort to consolidate the control of the state/party over the public sphere.[32] Besides centralization of political power, one of the focal points of this streamlining
politics was the creation of a new knowledge with regard to national identity and history.

According to the Turkish History Thesis, which became official doctrine at the beginning of the 1930s, the Turks belonged to the Aryan race
and had begun to migrate in prehistoric times from Central Asia to other
parts of the world, in the course of which they contributed to the formation of various civilizations in Europe, North Africa, and Asia. Focusing
on prehistoric and ancient times, the Turkish History Thesis brought
together the Turanian idea of an original homeland of the Turks in Central
Asia with claims to Anatolian land and culture as basis of a national identity. This it achieved by arguing that the civilizational reach of the ancient
Turks had extended to Anatolia. The ancient civilizations of the Sumerians
and the Hittites, which ruled over Asia Minor in prehistoric times—and
consequently would have preceded the Greeks and Armenians, who also
claimed Anatolia as their fatherland—were allegedly Turkish.[33] This move
allowed for the assimilation of the non-Turkish Muslim elements of the
republic based on claims of their original (racial) Turkishness and enabled
the Turkish History Thesis to establish a national Turkish identity with
references to two fatherlands, namely Turan and Anatolia (Tachau 1963;
Copeaux 1997, 50–51; Adanır 1994, 374–375).

"Outlines of Turkish History,"[34] the manifesto of the Turkish History
Thesis, marked the preliminary end of a phase of ambiguity about how to

---

32 In 1931 even the Turkish Hearth associations were closed down, replaced one year later
by the People's Houses (*Halk Evleri*), which served principally a similar function of spreading nationalist ideas, but were controlled by the RPP; in 1935 the Turkish Women's Union
and the Turkish Freemason Lodges were also shut down (Zürcher 2004, 180–181).

33 The emphasis on Anatolia as a fatherland had already been propagated in the short-lived
and politically not very influential *Anadoluculuk* ("Anatolianism") movement, a circle of
university students, which, centered around the journal *Anadolu Mecmuası* (1924–25), had
envisaged the identity of the new nation to be connected with Anatolian territory and its
people. The movement rejected, contrary to the Turkish History Thesis, racist and ethnic
conceptions of Turkishness as a valid basis for national identity (Tachau 1963).

34 *Türk Tarihinin Ana Hatları*, ed. Mehmet Tevfik et al., Istanbul 1930. The book was considered a draft, of which less than 200 copies were printed and which was not made publicly
available. In 1931, a much shorter, revised version was printed with 30,000 copies for broad
distribution (*Türk Tarihinin Ana Hatları. Methal Kısmı*, Istanbul) (Ersanlı 2002, 124–125).

integrate Ottoman and Turkish republican history. Ottoman history had until the late 1920s been considered an important part of Turkish history. But by the early 1930s, the "'official line' proclaimed that the Ottoman Empire should not be regarded as a legitimate predecessor of the newly founded Republic" (Ersanlı 2002, 121). The authors of "Outlines of Turkish History" "agreed that what made the Empire great was its 'Turkishness', while the Ottomans came to carry the blame for the disintegration of the Empire" (Ersanlı 2002, 130).

Marginalizing the role of Ottoman history, the Kemalists also targeted the role of Islam, now believed to have been, besides the negatively connoted cosmopolitanism and racial mixing in the Ottoman period, a major reason for the perceived decay of the empire (Ersanlı 2002, 137–138 and 144–146). This had consequences for researchers interested in Ottoman and Islamic history. Köprülü was among those scholars who defended the legacy of the Ottoman Empire as part of a broader Islamic civilization with a strong Turkish element against those Kemalist revisionists who saw the Ottoman period as merely an aberration in the historical evolution of the Turks or even as outside of Turkish history altogether. These aspects of Köprülü's theory of Turkish continuity made him difficult to digest for the supporters of the state's new history doctrine (Karpat 2001, 401).

As the offspring of a prestigious family closely connected with brighter periods of Ottoman history, Köprülü might have had a certain nostalgic attachment to the Ottoman past. His primary reasons were, however, certainly of scholarly nature. His work as Turkologist and Ottomanist was invested in a historically grounded narrative that made Turkish culture visible throughout its subsequent affiliations with various civilizations from ancient Central Asian to modern times and clearly understood Ottoman civilization as a legitimate and important part of this narrative. In a fourth-grade elementary-school textbook of his from 1928 on "National History," Ottoman history is clearly integrated in a broader Turkish-Islamic history. Furthermore, the part of the book that is dedicated to the Ottomans exceeds by far those parts dedicated to the "ancient Turks," the Seljuks, as well as the general overview provided over Islamic history (Köprülü 1928b).[35]

---

35 Köprülü was not the only textbook author who in the early years of the republic still gave the Ottoman past a prominent place in the treatment of Turkish history. The major historian colleague of Köprülü who also saw Ottoman history as part of Turkish history was Ahmet Refik (1881–1937) (Boyar 2007, 18); the "History of Turkey" (*Türkiye Tarihi*) by Hamid and Muhsin, published originally in 1924, reprinted in Latin script in 1930, was also still centered on Ottoman history (Ersanlı 2002, 124).

Two main sets of reasons made the establishment of a sense of a Turkish self that was independent from the Ottoman past desirable from the perspective of the Kemalist state. The first set of reasons is built into the rationale of secular Turkish nationalism, which aimed at establishing its identity against the constitutionally Islamic and ethnically and religiously pluralist Ottoman past. The second set of reasons had to do with the need to increase its political authority and legitimacy. Since the CUP had been discredited due to its war politics, the nationalists around Mustafa Kemal were throughout the Independence War, the following peace negotiations, and the early years of the republic extremely cautious to distance themselves from the Unionists. The nationalist movement aimed at international recognition and political sovereignty and therefore needed to make credible to the international public that they neither had anything to do with the Unionist policies against the Ottoman Christians, nor any inclinations to pursue the CUP's irredentist agendas (Akçam 2002). Distancing itself from irredentist claims, the new Kemalist regime also rejected pan-Turkism, which had become a rhetorical factor in late Young Turk nationalism, as a practical politics (Shissler 2003, 26).

Mustafa Kemal and his entourage mistrusted the old CUP cadres whom they wanted to keep away from the center of power. The political purges in 1925 and 1926, legalized by means of the creation of "Independence Tribunals," led to hundreds of executions and thousands of arrests. Pursuing an authoritarian politics against political opposition, the new regime tried to annihilate the threat that the CUP and its claim to be the legitimate leader of the Turkish nationalist movement still posed, and made it indefinitely clear that it would not tolerate challenges to its political hegemony (Zürcher 2004, 171–175). Both their aim of distancing themselves from the CUP and their aim of creating a new national identity made it desirable for Mustafa Kemal and the Turkish nationalists to erase or at least minimize the connections between Ottoman and Turkish Republican times. The Turkish History Thesis therefore emphasized that the new republic constituted a total break with the Ottoman past (Shissler 2003, 24–25). To a certain extent it might seem as if Köprülü supported the idea of a radical break between Ottoman and republican times. A closer look reveals that for him the decisive historical break occurred with the Young Turkish revolution, which effectively ended the Hamidian era. But as critical as he was of the Hamidian era, he did not reject the Ottoman past entirely.[36]

---

36 Already in his "National History" (*Milli Tarih*) from 1922, Köprülü had painted a picture of the years under Abdülhamid's rule as a period of injustice, in which books were banned

Köprülü used his academic work as a means of subtle resistance against the new paradigm, and he continued to research the economic, religious, cultural, and legal dimensions of Ottoman history within broader historical frameworks, always taking into account aspects of continuity with elements of pre-Ottoman Turkish history. Köprülü's major resistance was directed against the idea that the Ottomans were not Turkish. Even during the high time of the Turkish History Thesis, Köprülü continued to write about the Ottoman Empire within the framework of Turkish-Islamic culture. *Origins of the Ottoman Empire*, published originally in French in 1935, was his major contribution to this debate. Therein he argued that the historical elements—civil, military, and legal—that were needed for the creation of the Ottoman Empire were with minor exceptions already found among the Turks. He concluded this study with the following sentence: "This state [the Ottoman Empire] was not a new *organism*, or a new *ethnic and political formation*...; contrariwise...it was a new *synthesis*, a new *historical composition* born from the political and social maturation of Anatolian Turkism between the 13th and 14th century" (Köprülü 1991 [1935], 110).

It would be wrong to claim that Köprülü was at all times and in all respects rejecting the propositions and the general aim of the Turkish History Thesis. Some sequences of texts of his from the early 1920s show that beyond his methodological provisos Köprülü must have, at least at an earlier stage, also had sympathies with some aspects of its basic historico-political agenda. In *History of Turkish Literature* he had

---

and European influences and ideas condemned. Against the darkness of this period, the years after 1908 are described as a period of hope initiated by the re-installment of the constitution, which liberated the people and the press—a freedom, however, which unfortunately would have led to political fragmentation (Köprülü 1922, 63). Six years later, in a history coursebook for fourth graders, the basic story line has hardly changed. Again he depicts the Hamidian period as a time of despotism followed by a first independent Turkish parliament, which, unfortunately, was negatively impacted by non-Turkish elements from within as well as European interference from outside in pursuit of interests detrimental to the country: "The Greeks, Armenians, Bulgarians, and even the Albanians, and Arabs wanted to separate our country. All, but the Turks had closely embraced their nations" (Köprülü 1928b, 146). These remarks point to the lateness of Turkish nationalism and to its necessity as a means of survival in light of the centrifugal forces that the various non-Turkish national movements had unleashed in the late Ottoman Empire; they further served Köprülü as a neat transition to the War of Independence and the secularist achievements of the early republic (Köprülü 1928b, 158). Not only did his praise of early republican accomplishments have the effect of making the late Ottoman state appear as an anachronism that deserved to be overcome, but he also blames late Ottoman institutions for having failed to provide the Turks with a national identity, thus casting the late Ottomans as an obstacle on the Turkish way to national self-awareness and fulfillment.

emphasized the Turkish contribution to the formation of the Islamic civilization, which would exceed even Persian and Arabic influences (Köprülü 1980 [1920/21], 97–98). And in his booklet *History of Turkey*, which sketched the history of the Turks from ancient times until their arrival in Anatolia in the wake of the Seljuk conquest, written for a broad, nonacademic audience, we find a line of argumentation that even appears to foreshadow the Turkish History Thesis:

> In conclusion, from China and Siberia to India, inner Europe, North Africa, Yemen and Basra there is hardly any place where the Turkish flag has not been raised, where Turkish blood has not flowed. The histories of the Slavs, Germans, Latins, Iranians, Chinese, Indians, and Arabs are more or less from their beginnings full of Turkish heroism. From this perspective we can say that unless the examination of Turkish history moves forward many points of world history will remain in darkness. (Köprülü 1923, 4–5)

Still, Köprülü's subtle criticism of the Turkish History Thesis would not be without consequences for him. In 1931 he lost his position as dean of the Darülfünun's School of Literature and was demoted to a fifth rank within the salary system—formally because he lacked an academic degree, but it is rather obvious that the major reasons were political. Soon, however, he adopted a more opportunistic stance that would save his career. While some of the more vocal critics of the History Thesis were forced into exile, Köprülü was already in 1933 reinstituted in his former rank of professor and position of dean (Akün 2002, 478; Tansel 1966a, 625).[37] The fact that Köprülü was able to save his career without totally embracing the new ideology can probably be attributed to a number of reasons, ranging from good personal relations with Kemalist elites and his principal support for their political project, to his accomplishments for the creation of a national Turkish narrative, his international scholarly reputation, and undeniably also a certain opportunism. In this context it is interesting to note, and speaks to the political ambivalences of the time period, that in the same

---

37 Others were less lucky. A prominent example is Ahmet Refik, who, due to his Ottoman sympathies was gradually demoted between 1927, when he was made to resign from chairing the Society for Turkish Historical Research, and 1933, when his teaching position at the Darülfünun was terminated. He lost his academic appointment in the course of the streamlining of the university, which was part of the state's endeavor, accelerated in the early 1930s, to consolidate its hegemony over the public sphere (Ersanlı 2002, 128).

year (1931) in which Köprülü was demoted as a consequence of his criticism of the Turkish History Thesis, he was still commissioned to write
sections of Turkish high school books (Berktay 1983, 59).

While the more mature Köprülü did certainly not abandon his grand
narrative of the continuity of Turkish culture, the nationalist allusions
in his work became more subtle over time. In a foreword to a Turkish
translation of Wilhelm Barthold's *Mussulman Culture*,[38] Köprülü would
reflect over several pages on the relationship between romantic nationalism and objective scholarship, discussing first historiography in general,
then Turkish historiography, and finally his own work. The arguments
that he presents oscillate between self-criticism and self-righteousness,
and reflect the beginning of an, if still limited, historicization of the historiographic tradition of which he himself was a major part. He embarks
on this reflection proclaiming that his own critical comments—in the
introduction and as an appendix—to Barthold's text would be "entirely
objective," and independent of any "romantic viewpoint of national history." While romanticism would be, with all its exaggerations, typical for
early phases of nationalism and in fact be beneficial for its initial take
off, it would eventually be overcome by the "calm rationality of science"
(Köprülü 1940, xxxvi). The following section of this text is very revealing about his understanding of the dialectics of national historiography
and a good example for his passionate trust in the ultimate objectivity
of science:

> It is a very *painful* and *useless* enterprise to employ *history*, in the
> name of scientific and human dignity, as a false witness for *political*
> ends, or even with the aim to defend *pathological* ideologies. But we
> can say with contentment that such movements are *transient* and
> that…everywhere in the world men of science, who are *searching*
> historical *reality* in a totally objective manner, are *becoming more*.
>
> Naturally, *Turkish nationalism* has also experienced a *romantic*
> period in its understanding of *national history*; against the very
> unjust *negative evaluations of the Turks* by European historiography,
> which were bare of any scientific basis, the *reaction* of our romantic
> historiography had to necessarily be very *extreme* and *exaggerated*—
> and this is in fact how it was. (Köprülü 1940, xxxvi–xxxvii)

---

38 Published originally in Russian as *Kultura Musulmanstva* (1918).

The Turkish History Thesis and the Kızılbaş-Alevis

The reevaluation of the Ottoman past through the prism of Turkism in the 1920s and 1930s also impacted the interpretation of Kızılbaş-Alevism. As argued earlier, the conceptualization of Alevism as Turkish and "heterodox" Islam has to be understood as part of the formation of Turkish nationalism and its efforts to assimilate—in stark contrast to the ethnically and religiously pluralist concept of Ottomanism—religious and ethnic difference into the national body. Within this framework, some nationalist writers attributed the blame for the division and violence associated with the Sunni-Alevi divide to the Ottomans, who are in this rhetoric depicted as traitors of Turkish unity.[39] The reinterpretation of the Ottomans as a force inimical to Turkish culture and the simultaneous reevaluation of the Kızılbaş-Alevis as Turkish elements struggling against the Ottomans are clearly connected. Previously routinely depicted as subversive forces in alliance with the Persian Safavids, the ideological change allowed for the Kızılbaş-Alevis to be positively reevaluated, now associated with pure Turkishness. I have argued that his continuing loyalty to the Ottoman heritage as part of Turkish history and culture distinguished Köprülü from many of his co-nationalists. This also reflected on his reading of Alevism. Köprülü did not, and this distinguishes him starkly from other early nationalist authors who wrote about Alevism, such as Baha Said, engage in a rhetoric that othered the Ottomans from the perspective of a triumphant Turkish nationalism, declaring them incapable of satisfying the quest for national Turkish unity and therefore discriminating against the Kızılbaş-Alevis, now being hailed in nationalist rhetoric as "pure Turks." I would argue that his knowledge of Ottoman sources, his broad historical perspective, and his attention to methodological accuracy prevented him from resorting to such simplification. On the other hand, even if he did not approve of and follow the most exaggerated expressions of the thesis of continuity, such as expressed in the Turkish History Thesis, the narrative of Turkish continuity was with no doubt a major political-cum-historical focus of his work as a whole and was intrinsically linked to the role that he attributed to the "popular heterodox" Islam of the Alevi tradition within the narrative of the Turkish nation (see next chapter).

---

39 See, for example, Gökalp (1959 [1923]a, 107); Baha Said (2001 [1926]a, 105–106).

Formations of Secularism

The historiography of Mehmed Fuad Köprülü reflects the ambiguities and the dramatic political changes of the time period in which he lived. As an academic, Köprülü was deeply influenced by Western intellectual traditions. This is apparent in his terminology and methodology that combined a modernist worldview with a romantic nationalism. An example is the connection he establishes between socioeconomic arguments and hierarchies of doxa (such as more and less Sunni or "orthodox" forms of Islam, see chap. 5). To the extent that it subordinates religion to socioeconomic factors, and thus implies that religion can analytically be neatly separated from the sphere of the socioeconomic, such hierarchization reflects a secularist framework and is part of a decisively Western understanding of religion. This acknowledged, however, the work of Köprülü shows that attempts to classify him along stereotypes of "Western" versus "Oriental" scholarship are futile since the intellectual traditions he drew on, and the projects he was involved in, cannot be reduced to such either-or-style localization. Köprülü was a late Ottoman intellectual, well read in Islamic historical scholarship as well as in contemporary European scholarship. The way he combined knowledges from different cultural traditions was complementary rather than put forward in an antagonistic manner. Therefore, the assumption of an antagonism between Occidental and Oriental scholarship is not helpful to understand the complex intellectual formation of a scholar such as Köprülü. The work of Köprülü is a good example of the extension of the originally European discourses of nationalism and (world) religion into new territories, in this case the territory of Turkish Islam. But, as the case of Köprülü shows, the triumph of the language of nationalism and a secular religion discourse should not only be seen as a quasi-imperialist subjugation of yet another territory to Western intellectual hegemony. Rather, Köprülü's secular nationalism should be perceived within a "multiple modernities" perspective as a creative appropriation of these discourses for a distinctively Turkish modernization project (see Eisenstadt 1999).

From within a broader perspective on intellectual discourse in the early 20th century, the argument of Davison that the work of Ziya Gökalp needs to be understood in the context of the "secularization problematic of modern political thought" can also be extended to Fuad Köprülü (Davison 1995, 190). Park (1975) has discussed the work of Köprülü within the context of Turkish modernization, and his analysis leaves no doubt that the latter, too, operated firmly within a secular framework. However, as I will argue in the following pages, Gökalp and Köprülü were secularists in not quite the same way. Their differing attitudes toward religion reflect a principle tension that has been with Turkish secularism since its formative period. It can be described as a tension between an integrative secularism, which conceives of religion/Islam and nationalism as symbiotic forces that work together in the modernizing quest, and a liberal secularism, by which I mean a secularism that conceives of religion as a force that hinders rather than works toward modernization. When I compare the respective stances of Gökalp and Köprülü to religion/secularism, the aim of this comparison is not to ascribe static positions to these scholars. The enormous political changes that accompanied their lives must obviously have impacted on their ideas, especially with regard to such an important matter as the role of religion in society and politics. Of course, had Gökalp not died already in 1924 he might well have changed his positions on that matter, and therefore the comparison with Köprülü, who continued to be politically active until the late 1950s, is lopsided. But it still helps, I claim, to work out the particular kind of secularism that informed Köprülü's thought and impacted his studies.

Karpat has remarked emphatically that "[Gökalp's] nationalism was all-embracing, had a mystic touch, offered emotional nourishment, and could easily serve as a substitute for religion, as in fact it did" (Karpat 1970, 559). However, I would argue that Gökalp was less interested in merely substituting religion, than in redefining it within the context of a secular political arrangement, which meant (1) a freeing of religion from both its curtailment by the state (though within a political framework that was anticlerical and demanded disestablishment) and superstitions, making thus possible (2) for religion to unfold its force as both a source of inspiration and strength for the individual and as a source of morals and bond for society at large.

Gökalp's secularism was not without contradictions, and his demand for a separation of religion and state was not total, as is shown by the far-reaching secularizing reforms that he proposed in the Young Turk period. In a newspaper article from 1909 on the state of Sufi orders, their contributions to Islamic civilization, and the need for a reform of their organization within a reconfigured state organization of religious affairs in general, Gökalp stated that "it has to be admitted that all the religious communities such as the Kızılbaş, Yezidi, Nusayri, and Druze, which have deviated and withdrawn from the saved people of the Sunna, have spread from hashish-soiled cells of the dervish lodges that have branched out from the Sufi orders." But, as he continues, the danger that would emerge from such "heretical" (*fırak-ı dâlle*) movements could be contained if the Sufi lodges would be regulated and reformed by the office of the Şeyhülislam[40] (Gökalp 1976 [1909], 86). A few years later he demanded "the disestablishment of the office of the Şeyhülislam, the transfer of the administration of the religious courts to the Ministry of Justice, and of the supervision of religious schools to the Ministry of Education, as well as the abolition of the Ministry of Pious Foundations (*evkaf*)"; partially, these reforms were implemented (Parla 1985, 40). But in the same period he also vigorously defended the separation between state and religion:

> The separation between religion and state is a goal sought by all civilized nations. Not only politics, but even ethics, law, and philosophy have freed themselves from their previous dependence on religion and have gradually won their autonomy. In spite of the separation of these areas of social life, religion has not lost its appeal to the heart. On the contrary, religion has begun to fulfill its function more excessively as it has demarcated its private domain. (Gökalp 1959 [1913]a, 102–103)

In other words, while he recognized that "[t]he primary meanings for human beings in their cultural-national and civilizational-international groupings would no longer be 'religious'," at the same time, and this point has been missed by many, for Gökalp this was not meant to lead to a decline of religiosity in general (Davison 1995, 209). In his thought, religion does remain an important element of national culture, namely as a "cultural phenomenon that fulfills several functions in the collective soul of the nation" (Davison 1995, 217). To the contrary, for Gökalp secularization as differentiation, especially between the spheres of religion and the state, meant liberation of religion:

> [T]he attachment of religion to the state in our country has not been to its advantage, but rather to the extreme detriment of religion. The reason for this can be seen easily. The state is a legal machinery; it tends to legalize and formalize any social force upon which it touches. It is because of this fact that Islam started to loose its

---

40 Highest office of Sunni authority integrated into Ottoman state administration.

vitality from the moment it began to be fused with the political organization and began to be formalized as a system of law. (Gökalp 1959 [1913]a, 103)[41]

Beyond the obvious contradictions in the details of his secularist demands, it can certainly be argued that for Gökalp secularism was supposed to be to the benefit of religion. Although we find an echo of this idea in many texts apologetic of the secularist reforms in the early republic, such as in the famous "Speech" (*Nutuk*) of Mustafa Kemal from 1927,[42] the idea of a revival of Islam was for most Kemalists hardly more than a propagandist plot. At least this is the impression one must get from the actual politics of Turkish secularization, which went far beyond Gökalpian ideas, which had remained within a paradigm that saw religion/Islam as working in a symbiotic relationship with nationalism toward modernization of the country.[43]

Gökalp is often given credit for the secularist orientation of the Turkish Republic (Berkes 1959, 13–14; Azak 2010, 7). As I tried to show, such a view is based on a simplification of Gökalp's ideas, which were different from Kemalist secularism. Gökalp was rather serious about the idea that the separation of religious institutions from the state and the privatization of religion would be beneficial for a revival of the Islamic faith. It is therefore a misrepresentation to simply reduce Gökalp's secularism to that of a precursor to Kemalist laicism. Gökalp was a secularist in terms of separation between political and religious institutions, and he might be characterized as a laicist in the original French meaning of the term (i.e., anti-clericalism). But I am not convinced that Gökalp, be it as a private citizen who felt strongly about religion or be it as a political thinker, would have supported those practices

---

41 Gökalp would elaborate his thought on the reorganization of religion in his writings in *İslam Mecmuası*, a journal that he had launched in 1914 together with nationalist comrades and with support from the CUP for the purpose of propagating ideas about Islamic reform (Azak 2010, 7).

42 Therein Kemal addressed the nation explaining and justifying the course of Turkish politics since the War of Independence. In the section addressing the rationale for abolishing the caliphate he justifies his case to the National Assembly with the argument (among others) "that it is indispensable in order to secure the revival of the Islamic faith, to disengage [the caliphate] from the condition of being a political instrument, which it has been for centuries" (Mustafa Kemal as quoted in Landen 2007, 234).

43 The secularist reforms in the early Turkish Republic targeted not only Islamic institutions and networks (such as the caliphate and the Sufi orders) as potential loci of political opposition, but also tried to secularize the public sphere according to Western models and to reeducate the population in terms of secular tastes, habits, and sentiments. See, for example, Çınar (2005).

of Turkish laicism that displayed a general mistrust against public forms of Islam and not only aimed at regulating, but also at annihilating traditional Islamic institutions such as the Sufi orders. Religion for him was a source of morals and social coherence indispensable for the formation of Turkish nationhood. His worldview had strong mystical leanings and in this sense was presecular, that is, it did not understand religious and secular spheres as clearly differentiated spheres of life in the sense of Western liberal secularism. He was therefore a secularist mainly with regard to organizational structures and politics, arguing for the separation of religion and state, and the subordination of religious institutions to political ones.

Compared to Gökalp, Köprülü displayed in his writings throughout a more distanced position to religion/Islam, and he only very rarely engaged publicly with the question of secularism directly. But when he did, he seems to have been in harmony with the Turkish form of secularism. In the rhetoric of modernism, pointing to infrastructural achievements (railroad lines, streets, industry, schools) on the one side, and the advances of secularism on the other (secular legal system, abolition of the caliphate, closing of the religious schools and Sufi orders), Köprülü praised in a history book for fourth graders the achievements of the new republic, in particular the total separation of worldly and religious affairs (Köprülü 1928b, 158). Kemalist laicism was not content with subordinating religion to politics, but demanded that public spaces should be cleared of religion, now reconceived as not a symbiotic partner of nationalism, but as subordinate to nationalism, if not a rival to the hegemony of Kemalism. An illustration is a report on how to modernize Islamic practice from 1928 by a commission of Darülfünun professors chaired by Köprülü. The report made recommendations on how to adjust the public practices of the Islamic religion to the necessities of changing social life. It recommended among other things pews and cloak-rooms for the mosques, use of Turkish translations of the Koran, Turkish instead of Arabic as a ritual language, as well as the introduction of instrumental music into Islamic worship (Park 1975, 63–64; Azak 2010, 52–53).[44] Although this report, which created a public

---

44 These recommendations remind of the first strophe of Ziya Gökalp's famous poem *Vatan* ("Fatherland"), in which he expresses his vision of Turkish national independence: "A country in which the call to prayer at the mosque is read in Turkish / Where the peasant understands the meaning of the prayer during the ritual / A country in the schools of which the Koran is read in Turkish / Where young and old everybody understands God's commands / Oh Son of the Turks, this is your fatherland!" (Gökalp in Tansel 1989, 100). The poem must be from 1918 or earlier (Tansel 1989, 340).

outcry among conservative segments, was only very partially adopted,[45] the language employed is a good illustration of the new understanding of secularism, which began to conceive of religion as a rival of nationalism. It argued that "the great Turkish revolution [represented] the nationalization of the social institutions... according to the precepts of Science and reason... Religion also is a social institution. Like all other social institutions, it ought to satisfy the exigencies of life and pursue the process of development" (quoted in Levonian 1932, 123–124).[46] In other words, religion is subordinated to the Turkish modernization process and to nationalism, to which it is, however, still expected to contribute.

In Köprülü's political activism the question of secularism did not figure very prominently. Exceptions are a speech in parliament in 1949, in which he cautioned against the threat of reactionary religious propaganda, and a newspaper piece from 1958, wherein he called on secularism to defend against the danger posed by the revivalist Nurcu movement (see Park 1975, 415 and 413).

In conclusion, I suggest that the differences between Ziya Gökalp and Mehmed Fuad Köprülü with regard to their approaches to religion can be perceived as representative of the differences between on the one hand an integrative secularism, appreciative of religion as a force and domain that can in principal be helpful in the process of national revival and modernization, and on the other hand a secularism that carries the biases of liberalism, which was skeptical about the possible contribution of religion to modernization and rather preferred to see the role of religion restricted to the realm of the private. The latter position, to which Köprülü was undoubtedly leaning, also implied a religionist perspective on the Islamic tradition. This religionist perspective, as I have argued, is in a dialectic relationship with a secularist worldview in the sense of categorical distinctions between things religious and things secular and clearly marks Köprülü's religiography. Accordingly, Köprülü differentiated in his work much more clearly than Gökalp between religion and other domains of life. For example, he separated religion explicitly from culture, which in

---

45 From 1932 to 1950 the call to prayer (*ezan*) was recited in Turkish instead of the traditional Arabic version (see Azak 2010, chapter 2). In 1932, Atatürk also launched a campaign to use Turkish translations during worship in the mosques, but protests caused the experiment to be abandoned (Wilson 2009, 431).

46 It should be noted that the authorship of the final report is disputed (see Asılsoy 2008, 81).

Gökalp's work appeared as closely interrelated with religion, but which for Köprülü belonged to the realm of the secular.[47]

Within the first two decades of the republic, religion ceased to function, as it had still done at the beginning of the republic, as a cornerstone of Turkish national identity. The role of religion was gradually demoted to that of merely one among other social institutions of Turkish society that ought to work for and represent new Turkish modernity. This does not mean that religious semantics would not still have been strongly implicated in some aspects of national identity. Especially when it came to the demarcation of the boundaries of the national Turkish subject, religion continued to figure prominently in Kemalist nationalism. The best example is the mistrust and the at times chauvinist attitudes developed from within Turkish nationalism against non-Muslim minorities, as well as the patronizing attitude of the state against the Kızılbaş-Alevi population. The implicit and explicit politics of discrimination these groups had to experience clearly prove that there was—and to a certain extent continued to be—an implicit understanding, widely spread within mainstream Turkish nationalism, that the Turkish nation was, or ought to be, a Sunni Muslim nation (Cagaptay 2006; Azak 2010, 148–162). It appears that the function of religion as a social bond, which Gökalp had underlined, continued to make itself felt in the othering of minorities, and despite the fact that a laicist and national republicanism was hailed to have replaced the public functions of religion.

---

47 See Köprülü's discussion of the differentiation of religion from culture in the history of the Turks (see pp. 203–204).

5

Religiography

TAXONOMIES OF ESSENCES AND DIFFERENCES

I UNDERSTAND THE writing of religion(s) just as the building of nations as a modern practice that relies on modern concepts and semantics. Analyzing the conceptual framework and the taxonomies that Mehmed Fuad Köprülü used in his conceptualization of inner-Islamic difference, this chapter will try to work out the micro-mechanics of his religiography. It will in this way address what I consider the basic problems with Köprülü's conceptualization of inner-Islamic difference.

Popular Religion and the Continuity of Turkish Culture

To make visible the ancient roots of Turkish nationhood was an essential task for Turkish historians in the formative period of the Turkish nation-state. At stake were both the formation of a historically grounded national identity and international recognition as a legitimate nation. Both political (territory and state), and historical (continuity) preconditions needed to be met in the formation of the nation-state. Köprülü and his scholarship played a major role in this process of legitimation. He employed contemporary social scientific theories on the evolution of cultures, nations, and religions in a manner that made plausible historical claims of a continuity of Turkish culture.

Religion played an important role in Köprülü's legitimization of national continuity. The intellectual and political parameters that shaped his approach to religion and in particular Turkish religion therefore deserve closer investigation. As I will argue, his scholarship on Turkish religion reflects the range and limitations of contemporary secular knowledge on religion and Islam, and shows also familiarity with traditional Islamic scholarship. Köprülü's work in general reflects a bias toward a secularist and nationalist path of modernization. He created, based on assumptions about the longevity of certain religious practices and beliefs, a complex narrative that intended to prove the continuity of the "national spirit" as transmitted over time through religious institutions that were themselves depicted as being within a productive historical tension of continuity and change. This approach has been accepted by future researchers as a master narrative and continues to impact scholarly and public discourses on Turkish history and religion. By analyzing key concepts employed by Köprülü in his narration of the religious history of the Turks, this and the following chapter aim at creating space for fresh inquiries into this history, and into Kızılbaş-Alevism and Bektashism in particular.

Origins of Turkish Literature

Köprülü developed the conceptual framework for the narrative of Turkish continuity, which could be perceived in "popular" and mystical religious traditions, already in *Türk Edebiyatı'nın Menşe'i* ("The Origins of Turkish Literature," 1915; henceforth: *Origins*). The text constituted a first attempt to systematize his thoughts on religious evolution. This extensive article shows probably most clearly how strongly Köprülü was impacted in this formative time of his maturation as a historian by European discourses on religion and particularly by the works of Durkheim and Gökalp, which provided him, among other things, with a theory of religious evolution.[1] In a 1915 article on "The Social Functions of Religion," Gökalp had further elaborated on the evolution of religion as a reflection of the development of society from primitive to organic stages. According to this theory, which seems to have been directly inspired by Durkheim's *De la division du travail social* (1893), primitive societies, in which distinctly political or cultural customs do not yet exist, are based on customs of an essentially religious nature. In organic societies, by contrast, political and cultural customs are fully developed and represented by political, cultural, and religious authorities, which are independent from each other. In short, organic societies are characterized by functional differentiation unknown to primitive societies (Gökalp 1959 [1915], 184–185).[2]

---

1 In this text, he makes explicit references to Durkheim's *Les formes élémentaires*, as well as Gökalp's above-mentioned "Symmetry between the Social Formations."

2 Gökalp's theory of differentiation, in the course of which nations are fermented through realization of their cultural identity, lines up nicely with his distinction between culture, religion, and civilization. See Berkes (1959, 24).

In *Origins*, Köprülü applied the same evolutionist framework. He argues that in order to learn about the beginnings of a specific national literature one needed to inquire into the social life of its earliest, "primitive," societal forms. Explicitly following Durkheim's theory that human intellectual activities had in its origins been religious and only gradually transformed into nonreligious forms, he reasons that, as a consequence of foreign civilizational influences and societal differentiation, old rites had lost their religious significance and became profane plays; the arts in general, including literature, had evolved and emancipated themselves from religious forms (Köprülü 1999 [1915], 49–65). As for religion, the earliest Turkish societies could be described as a form of shamanism, which he relates to totemism.[3] The ancient Turkish poets were called by different names among different Turkish people: the Tonguz Turks called them *Şaman*, the Altay Turks *Kam*, the Kırgız Turks *Baksı* (also *Bahşı* or *Bakşı*),[4] and the Oghuz Turks *Ozan*.[5] In the not-yet-differentiated, primitive Turkish societies these individuals were highly respected among the ordinary people and acted as magicians, musicians, and healers: "In these ceremonies, the shaman or *baksı* would reach a stage of ecstasy and sing a number of songs while playing on his own musical instrument. These lyrics, which were accompanied by melodies and possessed a magic character, represent the oldest form of Turkish poetry" (Köprülü 1999 [1915], 58).

With the Turks coming under the influence of expanding civilizations (such as the Indian, Chinese, Iranian, and Islamic ones) they also accepted new religions and this impacted the social and religious roles of the *ozan* and *baksı*. The historical evolution from primitive to organic societies, as manifested in the social division of labor, led to a division of the multiple functions of the old Turkish *kam-baksı*, which were now taken over by specialized experts in healing, poetry, religion, astrology, fortune-telling, et cetera (Köprülü 1999 [1915], 58–65). In the course of this process, poetry got separated from its religious roots. However, remnants of the old *kam-baksı* tradition could still be found in the Anatolian *aşık*,

---

3 Again, we see the similarity to Durkheim, who had equally conceived of totemism as the most elementary religion (Durkheim 2008 [1912]).

4 According to Köprülü the word *baksı* has the meaning of "priest." Later, he dedicated a whole article to its etymology, in which he concluded that "the *baksı* are magicians who, under a superficial Islamic varnish, continue to live the remainders of the old paganism" (Köprülü 1966 [1942], 155).

5 In the rest of the article, and in most parts of his later work, Köprülü seems to use these names interchangeably without any noticeable preference.

whom he describes as "the Islamized form of the old Turkish priest-poet," as well as in the popular Turkish Sufi tradition epitomized in the texts ascribed to Ahmed Yesevi and Yunus Emre (Köprülü 1999 [1915], 67).

Origins marks a decisive moment in the development of Köprülü's thought. His search for the roots of Turkish literature leads him to the ancient "shamanistic" and "totemistic" Turkish societies of Central Asia. He regards particularly poetry as the preferred form for the expression of national sentiment and ideals; hence, it would be in the poet that "the national taste has found itself a representative, a translator" (Köprülü 1999 [1915], 120). It deserves to be remarked that Köprülü was the first, already four years before the publication of his early masterpiece "Early Mystics in Turkish Literature" (hereafter: *Early Mystics*),[6] to connect the thesis that the ancestors of the Turks professed shamanism with the idea of a continuity of aspects of this ancient shamanism in the Turkish traditions of Anatolia, and particularly in popular Sufi currents.

Early Mystics in Turkish Literature

We have seen that a Ṣūfī literature whose major elements derived from popular literature and the national taste began with Aḥmad Yasawī and continued to Yūnus Emre, and beyond him to the present day in the form of a long chain connecting one poet to another. (Köprülü 2006 [1919], 369)

The theme of continuity, expressed by Köprülü metaphorically in the notion of "the national taste," was part of a rhetoric of nationalism that was in need of historical legitimation. *Early Mystics*, at its core dedicated to an investigation of the "literary evolution of the Turkish nation," embodies this nationalist quest in an emblematic manner (Köprülü 1966[1919], 3). While Köprülü's main focus was on temporal continuity, he also pointed to the geographic continuity/extension of Turkish culture. In the introduction to *Early Mystics* he defined the themes of temporal and geographic continuity, which would remain characteristic for his investigation into the evolution of Turkish culture, in the following way:

---

6 *Türk Edebiyatı'nda İlk Mutasavvıflar*, first published in 1919; for an English translation see Köprülü (2006 [1919]).

[N]obody has as of yet been able to understand that the literary evolution of the Turkish nation as a whole, from inner-Asia to the shores of the Mediterranean, which has a history of at least thirteen to fourteen centuries, has to be studied as a whole. In the hands of researchers who regard the different Turkish branches as distinct nations unrelated to each other, who do not understand the various connections between them, and who do not understand the necessity of studying the general Turkish history as a whole this important part of world history will forever remain an enigma. (Köprülü 1966 [1919], 2)

This new narrative of continuity would, as I will show, impact decisively on the new significations that Kızılbaş-Alevism and Bektashism received in the context of early Turkish nationalism. The shamanism thesis, which began to acquire a central role in the narrative that presented the Kızılbaş-Alevis and the Bektashis as carriers of ancient Turkish culture, is emblematic for this Turkist framing. In Köprülü's work shamanism became a metaphor for the continuity of Turkish culture from ancient to modern times. Within the same framework of national continuity, other contemporary authors, such as, most prominently, Baha Said and Yusuf Ziya Yörükan, would soon further expand the theory of the Kızılbaş-Alevis having been carriers of Turkish culture as apparent in shamanist remnants.

It is important to note that in his early work Köprülü did not yet postulate a direct and unbroken link between ancient Altai Turkish traditions and the religious milieus associated with the Kızılbaş-Alevis and Bektashis. He did at this point regard Batinism (Arab. *Bāṭiniyya*),[7] Shiism, as well as the "heresies," which he detected in the Babai and in later movements in their footsteps (such as the Bedreddin movement, the Kızılbaş, and the Bektashis), as being the result of a development that took place after the Turkish invasion of Anatolia (Köprülü 2006[1919], 200). For the young Köprülü, the Turks of Central Asia were Sunni Muslims, and the Yeseviye—to which *Early Mystics* attributes a decisive role in the historical

---

7 In Köprülü's work the term Batinism (Turk. *batıniye*) is used as a general category for Islamic currents that cherish a dualist worldview and distinguish between outer (*zahir*) and inner (*batın*) meanings of Islam. Historically, the term emerged within Islamic apologetical discourse. It was used to question the Islamic legitimacy of groups such as the Ismailis, philosophers, and various Sufi currents, who were accused of subverting the actual massage of Islam by claims to hidden meanings, which were thought to relativize the Koranic message and the law derived from it (Walker 2012).

transfer of pre-Islamic Turkish cultural and religious traditions to the Islamic period— was a popular, though ascetic, Sunni Sufi order. However, their Sunnism was challenged by the open spirit of Anatolia and a number of factors contributed to a gradual change of the religious atmosphere: Greco-Roman and Christian traditions of Anatolia, the *waḥdāt ul-wujūd* ("Unity of Being") philosophy of Ibn al-Arabi, Batinism, and varieties of a law-defying Sufism.

In *Early Mystics* Köprülü argued that historical comparison would reveal a stark contrast between Central Asian and Anatolian Turkish Sufism, epitomized in the texts of the 12th-century Central Asian Sufi Ahmed Yesevi and the Anatolian Sufi poet Yunus Emre (mid-13th to early 14th cent.), respectively. These texts would show a drastic change in style—namely, from the sober mystical lyrics characteristic of the former toward the more exuberant, pantheistic poetry of the latter (see Köprülü 1966 [1919], 185 and 288). While recognizing this difference in style, Köprülü reconstructs the lives of Ahmed Yesevi and Yunus Emre and evaluates texts ascribed to them with the intention of showing the continuity of Turkish literary tradition from Central Asia to Anatolia. According to *Early Mystics*, the substance of the continuity that connected Central Asian and Anatolian Turkish culture manifested itself in the literary tradition of popular Islamic mysticism epitomized in the poetry of Yunus Emre.

Köprülü began his introduction to *Early Mystics* with the following sentence: "In order to understand the national spirit and national taste (*millî rûhu ve millî zevki*) in Turkish literature after the advent of Islam, a period most worthy of study is that of the great Islamic mystics, who, by using the language and meter of the people, addressed a very broad audience, and whose works have lived on for centuries" (Köprülü 1966 [1919], 1). Köprülü found traces of ancient, pre-Islamic forms of national Turkish culture and sentiment in the literature of "popular Turkish Islam" such as that of the Yesevis, Bektashis, and related currents. He "believed that by studying all the literary products that revealed the intellectual evolution of a nation over centuries one could shed light on its spiritual life" (Leiser/Dankoff 2006, xxxi–xxxii). The importance of this project for an emerging Turkish nationalism in search of a historical anchoring of the national narrative is apparent. In line with Fouillée's concept of the *idées-forces*, both Köprülü and Ziya Gökalp were convinced that access to the popular Turkish literature could function as a catalyst in the formation of a national Turkish identity. Their project thus entailed a valorization of the culture of the ordinary rural Turks as being necessary for the recovery of the Turkish spirit.

In the introduction to *Early Mystics* he explains: "Since our own national personality (*millî şahsiyetimiz*) has been lost due to the impact of formerly Iran, and, since the Tanzimat, Europe, this popular literature has been, just as everything that belongs [to] or emerged from the common people, regarded in a negligent, disregarding way" (Köprülü 1966 [1919], 1).

The key issue here is the recovery of "national personality." As Gökalp had asserted in "Turkification, Islamization, Modernization," the individual (*fert*) would mature into a personality (*şahsiyet*) once he lived in accordance with the ideals of the common society; *şahsiyet* would thus refer to "the totality of the thoughts and feelings existing in the consciousness of society and reflected in the consciousness of the individual" (Heyd 1950, 53).[8] The personality or personal character of the nation can thus be understood as the state of a people aware of its historical identity. Since this identity was lost, it needed to be reestablished. Köprülü saw Turkish identity as being epitomized in the poetry of Yunus Emre: "In particular the artistic genius of Yunus has created a Turkish Literature, which, unparalleled by other Islamic literatures, has such a strongly national and original character style—a style that has, throughout the centuries, been able to represent the national taste in the best manner—that it possesses an unmatched value within the history of literature" (Köprülü 1966 [1919], 307).

Again, Köprülü regarded consciousness of the historical continuity of "national" identity as an important brick in the (re-)formation of the Turkish nation. In his narrative it is a vague notion of "national Turkish spirit and taste" that manifests this continuity in the long journey of the Turkish people from Central Asia to 20th-century Turkish Anatolia, a journey in the course of which the national culture accustomed itself to different civilizations and different religions. This spirit appears to have found its most fitting embodiment in popular Sufi literature and culture. He describes the Turkish bards (*ozan*) as transmitters of the national heritage, keeping the old Turkish customs alive in Anatolia (Köprülü 1966 [1919], 207). In the same vein he argues that the Turkish-speaking members of the Bektashi order—whom he sees, just like the *ozan*, as following in

---

8 Durkheimian influence is apparent. Heyd also points to the influence of Sufism in Gökalp's notion of individuality as a quality that ultimately needed to be overcome for the sake of the greater good of society (Heyd 1950, 56–58). Parla, on the other side, emphasizes the corporatist and solidaristic morality in the thought of Gökalp, who "saw the potential harmony of the moral and social communalism of Turkish culture and Islamic Sufism with comparable elements in European solidaristic corporatism. In all these systems the individual loses his individualism as he assimilates into the community" (Parla 1985, 26–27).

the footsteps of Yunus Emre—"valued national language and literature" (Köprülü 1966 [1919], 300).

Köprülü's argument in *Early Mystics* that early popular Turkish Islam as epitomized in the Yeseviye Sufi order was Sunni, and that only in Anatolia, where it came under Persian influence, it was drawn to "heretical and schismatic" directions appears to be in some tension with his theory of the continuity of Turkish "national spirit and taste" in popular religious literature. In order to resolve this tension one needs to assume a somewhat clear distinction between national, literary, and religious culture. Such a distinction makes it possible to argue that while said literature shows continuity with a pre-Islamic Turkish heritage, the elements of this continuity needed to be located not in the realm of religion but in the realm of national and literary culture. Already a few years later, however, he would adjust this argument and reason that Turkish national continuity showed itself most clearly in the religious culture of popular Islam. In the 1920s Köprülü would revise his earlier work and begin to stress the non-Sunni character of Ahmed Yesevi and the Yesevi Sufi order, and the influence of Batinism already on pre-Anatolian Turkish culture.[9] He now also began to address the vestiges of shamanism in "popular" Anatolian Islam more systematically. While Köprülü included most of *Origins* into *Early Mystics*, he had therein reduced his reflections on shamanism and the continuity from the "shaman" *kam* and *baksı* to the Anatolian *ozan* bards to a footnote (Köprülü 1966 [1919], 207 fn 88).

At this point it should not be left unmentioned that recent scholarship on the early Yesevi tradition is closer to Köprülü's initial interpretation in *Early Mystics*, according to which Ahmed Yesevi was a relatively orthodox Islamic mystic. As Karamustafa argues, contrary to Köprülü's assertions "there is no trace of Shī'ism or Bāṭinism in Yasawī." In addition, there is no "firm evidence that even a small number of Yasawī dervishes came from Anatolia to Central Asia" (Karamustafa 2005, 78–79; cf. Ocak 2010, 53–54). The latter point is of great importance for all those who argue, in the footsteps of Köprülü, that the continuity of Turkish culture from Central Asia to Anatolia can be traced in the religious tradition that connected the Yeseviye directly with the Bektashi Sufi order as epitomized in the hagiographic knowledge that Hacı Bektaş Veli (d. 1270/71), patron saint of the Bektashi order, was a disciple of Ahmed Yesevi (d. early 13th cent.). Karamustafa shows that even if one assumes that there was indeed a

---

9 See Köprülü (1993 [1922]; 2002 [1925]; 1929).

personal connection between these two Sufis—although it seems unlikely given that their lives overlapped only minimally, if at all—the claim of a Yesevi-Bektashi connection, or of a Yesevi identity among 13th century Anatolian Sufis, is implausible since both the Yesevi and the Bektashi traditions developed as historically distinguishable Sufi formations only centuries after the death of their respective eponymous patron saints (Karamustafa 2005, 83–84). He therefore argues that "it is high time to abandon the view of Köprülü that the Yasawī path played a crucial role in the development of Anatolian Sufism and, consequently, in the formation of Turkish popular Islam" (Karamustafa 2005, 93). Since the theory of continuity of Turkish culture is based on Köprülü's argument of a continuity of "popular" religious culture in general, and the Yesevi-Bektashi connection in particular, Karamustafa's criticism of Köprülü's interpretation of the Yeseviye dismantles one of the major pieces of evidence of continuity of Sufi-Muslim culture from Central Asia to Anatolia.[10]

Praise

One of the aims of Köprülü's investigation in Turkish literature was to challenge hegemonic Orientalist scholarship that denied the Turks a major role in the broader history of Islamic civilization. In contrast to the assertions of Orientalist scholarship, he argued that Anatolian Islam was more influenced by Turkish traditions than by Persian culture. Popular Turkish literature would reveal the Turks' "national genius" (*millî dehâ*) and match even grand Persian literature. The mistake of Orientalist scholarship was—a criticism he would repeat and further develop in future publications—to focus too narrowly on very limited historical time frames, geographic territories, and event history.[11] This limited perspective obscured the longevity and transregional character of the Turkish literary tradition and prevented Western Orientalists from grasping the continuities of Turkish Anatolian Islam and culture with pre-Islamic Turkish traditions (Köprülü 1966 [1919], 1–3).[12]

---

10 In his critique Karamustafa draws largely on a forthcoming book by DeWeese (*The Yasawī Sufi Tradition*); see also DeWeese (2006).

11 In the introduction to *Early Mystics*, he in this context specifically mentions Joseph von Hammer-Purgstall and E. J. W. Gibb (Köprülü 1966 [1919], 2).

12 He formulated this criticism most systematically in *Islam in Anatolia* (Köprülü 1993 [1922]) and *Bektaşiliğin Menşeleri* ("The Origins of Bektashism," 2002 [1925]). In *Islam in Anatolia* he directly tackled recent publications by the German Orientalist Franz Babinger. The latter had argued that the Islam of Anatolia was primarily under Persian influence

Early Mystics contributed greatly to the historical essentialization of features of "Turkish" culture, in other words, the historicization of a Turkish subject. Although it did not receive much attention in war-ridden Ottoman Turkey after its first publication in 1919,[13] the book gained Köprülü international recognition as an eminent scholar of Turkish and Anatolian history. In their reviews of the work, European Orientalists respectfully acknowledged his mastery of both Occidental and Oriental scholarship and especially his application of Western methodological standards.[14] More importantly, the major theses of *Early Mystics* were widely accepted by Western Orientalists and led to a new appreciation for the role of the Turks as not merely passive imitators, but an active force that greatly shaped Islamic and world history. The German Orientalist Theodore Menzel, in an article largely based on *Early Mystics* and published in a leading German Orientalist journal, even argued that it was only due to the Turks that Islam became a great historical force (Menzel 1925, 273). Menzel followed the nationalist reasoning of *Early Mystics* to a considerable extent,

---

(Babinger 1922). In his response, Köprülü acknowledged Persian influence, but asserted that Turkish influence on Islam in Anatolia was much greater, particularly on popular Islam (this debate is discussed in more detail below). Parts of Köprülü's *Islam in Anatolia* were immediately translated into German and contributed to his growing stature among European Orientalists ("Bemerkungen zur Religionsgeschichte Kleinasiens," *Mitteilungen zur Osmanischen Geschichte* 2.1922, 203–222). In *Origins of Bektashism* Köprülü continues his critical engagement with European Orientalist scholarship, taking on in particular Ignaz Goldziher, Theodor Nöldeke, and Louis Massignon for overemphasizing Persian influence on Anatolian Islam (Köprülü 2002 [1925], esp. 68–69, 72). A few years later he was willing to concede gradual, though still insufficient, advancements in the Western study of the (religious) history of Anatolia (Köprülü 1928a, v).

13 There have been several new editions in later years: 1966, 1976, and an English translation in 2006.

14 J. H. Mordtmann went so far as to praise Köprülü emphatically and in rather Orientalist fashion as "müdschtehid," (*mujtahid*), a title given to Islamic jurists authorized to make judgments based on their independent reasoning (Mordtmann 1923a, 122); for an equally laudatory review of Köprülü's originally-two-volume *Türk Edebiyatı Tarihi* by the same author see Mordtmann (1923b). From the same year and no less praiseful was Clément Huart's review of *Early Mystics*. The French Orientalist expresses his astonishment with Köprülü's— recognized as a patriotic author—mastery of Western methodology and terminology and refers to *Early Mystics* as an epoch-making work (Huart 1923, 147). In 1925, W. Barthold, S. Oldenburg, and I. Krachkovsky wrote a report in preparation for Köprülü's election to the Academy of Sciences of the USSR, which held similarly high praise for *Early Mystics* and which included supportive remarks by Martin Hartmann. As paraphrased by Tansel, "[i]n Hartmann's view, Köprülü's works were in complete conformity with the European scientific method and contained profound scholarly thought. Other characteristics of his works were his success in showing everywhere in excellent fashion the relationships between the history of literature and social life, and in providing new theories to shed light on historical events" (Tansel 2006 [1966], xlv). See also Leiser and Dankoff (2006, xxxi–xxxii).

even back-reading Turkish nationalism into pre-modern times. For example, in several instances he refers to Bektashi poetry as well as the poetry of Yunus Emre as "nationalist" (Menzel 1925, 286–288).

The significance of a Turkish scholar being credited with not only making a benchmark contribution to Orientalist scholarship, but beyond that with having developed an authoritative historical narrative demonstrating the continuity of an autonomous Turkish subject cannot be stressed enough. Menzel's remarks were made just two years after the international recognition of a sovereign Turkish state by the Lausanne Treaty. From the perspective of Turkish nationalism, the international recognition of *Early Mystics* must have been of considerable symbolic significance. It can be interpreted as both contributing to the international recognition of the validity of an autonomously formulated Turkish history and as reflecting the political success of the Turkish nationalist movement.

Criticism

Early Mystics is still regarded as a classic in the study of Turkish Islam in Anatolia. More than 90 years after its initial publication, many specialists still consider it "the starting point for research on the cultural genesis of the Turks" (Leiser/Dankoff 2006, xxxiv). Karpat even claims that *Early Mystics* has "survived the test of time" (Karpat 2001, 398). This is, however, a rather questionable assessment. Devin DeWeese, a specialist on Central Asian Islam, has recently pointed to a number of serious methodological problems in *Early Mystics*. Its very status as a classic prevented its critical reexamination, especially among Turkish scholars unaware of more recent developments in the historical study of Central Asian cultures (DeWeese 2006, viii–ix). DeWeese argues that *Early Mystics* shows only a very rudimentary knowledge of Central Asian culture and religion. This made it possible for Köprülü to attribute to Central Asian origins those elements in the popular Sufi tradition of Anatolia that he was unable to trace back to Islamic origins.[15]

The back-reading of elements of Anatolian Islam into Central Asian Turkish traditions points to the heart of the methodological problems in Köprülü's narrative of the continuity of a national Turkish consciousness (DeWeese 2006, xvi). *Early Mystics* created an Anatolia- and Turco-centric

---

15 DeWeese points to a certain naïveté with which Köprülü took the possibility of a clear distinction between "legendary" and "historical" sources for granted. Therefore he was in general rather uncritical in the assessment of the quality of information that he had categorized as "historical" and treated even polemical treatises as trustworthy historical sources (DeWeese 2006, xv–xvi).

knowledge of pre-Islamic Turkish religion. Narrating the story of Turkish religious culture from the viewpoint of its particular Anatolian forma-tion, it turns this formation into a matrix from which to understand pre-Anatolian and pre-Islamic Turkish culture. Throughout *Early Mystics* the terms nation (*millet*), national (*millî*), and nationality (*milliyet*) appear as signposts of this continuity. What Köprülü positively accomplishes by this is the establishment of a "historical identity...[that was] not lost or obscured in Ottoman or traditional Islamic history" (Leiser/Dankoff 2006, xxxii). However, the reader is not offered clear definitions of what the term nation and its derivatives are supposed to positively convey. The concept of the Turkish nation remains therefore rather obscure. The focus on Turkish national spirit and on Islamic influences naturally blends out the contributions of non-Turkish and non-Muslim elements in this story line. The outcome is a rather structuralist narrative that connects ancient pre-Islamic Turkish religion and culture with Turkish Islam (particularly the Yeseviye) and more recent nonelite forms of Islam. The basic structure of this narrative would remain rather constant in Köprülü's future work.

Another criticism against Köprülü has been raised by Karamustafa. Against the former's argument for an examination of the Islamization of Anatolia within a larger geographic and historical framework, extend-ing in particular to Central Asian Turkish pasts, Karamustafa suggests readjusting the focus in the study of Anatolian history on developments in Anatolia itself (Karamustafa 2005, 94). Such focus on Anatolia will obviously need to address more systematically encounters between the Turkish immigrants and their cultures with other immigrants, as well as the predominantly Christian local populations and thus venture beyond Turkish and Islamic contexts.

In order to do justice to the nationalist subtext of Köprülü's early histor-ical work, it has to be evaluated against the background of its time. *Origins* appeared in September 1915, in the midst of the horrific Battle of Gallipoli (1915–1916); *Early Mystics* was completed in 1918, when the Ottoman Empire was rapidly disintegrating, and published in 1919, just prior to the begin-ning of the Turkish War of Independence. We know that the events of World War I deeply troubled him, as his popular writings and nationalist poems of this period make very clear.[16] It is hardly surprising to find him impressed

---

16 Examples are four poems which appeared in *İkdam* in 1915 and 1916 with the titles "Dream of the Martyr," "The Martyr and the Crescent," "The Last Raid," and "Grave of the Martyr"—all referenced in Tansel (1966b, 645–646); further, at the end of the world war,

with the tragic incidents that marked the last years of the Ottoman Empire and to see him develop a yearning for national awakening.

Another criticism that can be raised against Köprülü is with regard to his elitist and hierarchical, as well as modernist, approach to Islam. Köprülü widely followed the classical approach of Islamic cultural elites as well as Western Orientalists, who tended to look down on forms of popular religious culture, measuring the latter against the standards of what they considered to be properly Islamic. For Köprülü these standards were since his earliest work defined by Sunnism. We can see that when he uses apologetic Islamic terms in his description of inner-Islamic difference: for example, when, in a discussion of the Bektashis, he refers to them as *ghulāt*, that is, "exaggerating/extreme (*ifratçı*) Shiite-*bâtinî* currents"; when he argues that the flexibility of the Bektashis in matters of dogma and practice made them attractive and successful "among the ignorant Muslim and Christian masses"; and when he asserts that through the continuing adaptation of elements originally not part of it, the Bektashiye became more and more syncretistic (Köprülü 1979 [1949], 462); when he claims that "the Babai incident has to be seen as an important starting point for the heretical and schismatic (*rafz ve i'tizal*) movements in opposition to the Sunni doctrine…leading to the formation of sects (*tâife*) such as Kızılbashism and Bektashism" (Köprülü 1966 [1919], 178); or when he qualifies belief in metempsychosis (*tenasüh*) and the circle of reincarnations (*devir*), which could be found among certain Alevi groups, as "corrupted dogmas" (*bozuk akiyde*) (Köprülü 1935b, 31). Cloaked in the mantle of secular scholarly authority, such discourse normalizes certain religious formations, while denying originality and authenticity to those socioreligious movements that do not comply with its theological norms. In short, in Köprülü's case "properly Islamic" meant mainstream Sunni Islam.

From the introduction to *Early Mystics* onward, Köprülü argued that the character and sentiment of the Turkish people found its medium of expression in the "literature of popular Sufism" (*halk tasavvuf edebiyatı*) (Köprülü 1966 [1919], 1). This was the case when the orientation of this Sufism was an ascetic Sunnism, such as was reflected in the Yeseviye[17] and continued in those currents that he would describe as "heretical and

---

"National Duty" (*Tanin*, 1918), and "To Our Martyrs" (*Büyük Mecmua*, 1919) (see Özerdim 1951, 172–178).

17 As discussed above, this evaluation of the religious character of the Yeseviye would change in his later work.

schismatic." The Bektashi, for example, who were close to the people, "valued national language and literature" and managed to apply the style of their poetry to the "Turkish taste" (*Türk zevkı*) (Köprülü 1966 [1919], 300; see also Köprülü 1980 [1920/21], 250). The common ground and problem with all these descriptions of varieties of "popular Islam" is, as Karamustafa has pointed out, that the latter is interpreted as something static, largely immune to change—and often, I would like to add, devoid of agency; consequently, the notion becomes rather "impervious to historical explanation" (Karamustafa 1994, 5).

Structural Accounts of Socioeconomic and Religious Dichotomies

With his search and discovery of the national sentiment and culture in the literature of "popular" Islam, Köprülü followed the lead of Gökalp, who had suggested that it is the common people who are the carriers of culture. The roots of the Turkish spirit were to be found not in elite Islamic institutions, but in mysticism, myth, and folklore; those were the areas that needed to be researched and revealed in order for the Turks to be able to affirm their national identity, a precondition for their participation in Western civilization (Gökalp 1959 [1923]c, 290; Berkes 1959, 30; Heyd 1950, 69–70). Such populism was a strong element in early romantic Turkish nationalism. Supported by the leaders of the nationalist movement it even led to a short-lived journal: *Halka Doğru* ("Toward the People," 1913–1914). In this context Gökalp also argued that the appearance of the Kızılbaş, cast as Turkish rebels against Ottoman rule who cherished sectarian and Sufi beliefs, would have been a consequence of the unresolved tension between center and periphery (Gökalp 1959 [1923]a, 107). Köprülü followed this line of thought and provided ample historical evidence for the antagonism between an elite urban culture that he would associate with "orthodox" religion on the one side, and rural culture associated with "heterodoxy" on the other. His language in the description of the "popular" Islamic culture of the Turks thereby contains a certain romanticism reminiscent of *noble savage* literature.[18] This romanticism did, however, as the examples already provided show, not overwrite strong pejorative

---

18 This romanticism was even stronger in the writings of Gökalp, who had argued that only through contact with the national folk culture the élite of the Turkish nation would be able to nationalize itself (Gökalp 1959 [1923]b, 260).

undertones in his description of the religious differences of this "popular Turkish" culture.

In his first footnote in *Early Mystics*, Köprülü explained that he would use the Turkish term *halk* ("[ordinary] people") as equivalent to the French "populaire." The term would, as he underlines, not imply depreciation of any sort and should not be seen as referring to a particular social class (Köprülü 1966 [1919], 1). As I will show, however, he was not always applying the term in such allegedly objective, value-free ways—especially not when he correlates matters of religious orientation, social location, and political interests.

In his work, Köprülü provides ample historical evidence for the antagonism between elite urban culture and "orthodox" religion on the one side, and rural culture, "heterodoxy" and "syncretism" on the other. In a late article of his on the Anatolian *aşık* tradition he discusses the role of the Sufi orders in its formation and development. The Sufi orders over time adjusted to the social environments in which they lived. Some of these orders, fitting to the religion policies of the government, displayed an "orthodox" character in urban contexts, "appropriate to Sunni dogma," while at the same time, when in a tribal environment, they appeared "totally heterodox, that is, removed from Islamic doctrine" (Köprülü 1966 [1962], 184). Köprülü also points to the political dimension that the antagonism between urban centers of Islamic "orthodoxy" and the "heterodoxy" of the mostly nomadic Turkmen periphery entailed (Köprülü 2002 [1925], 72). I would like to illustrate the multiple levels of binary antagonisms that characterizes Köprülü's scenario of the Ottoman Anatolian periphery with a lengthy quote from *Origins of the Ottoman Empire* (1935), which discusses the influence of the Babai dervishes of the 13th and 14th century on the Islam of the Anatolian Turks—an Islam that is, not in the quote itself but in the surrounding text, qualified as "heterodox."

> The Islam of these Turkmen is not like the totally orthodox Islam of the urbanized Turks, but a syncretism resulting from the blending of the ancient heathen customs of the old Turks and a simple and popular form of an extremist (*müfrit*) Shiism, outwardly cloaked in the mantle of Sufism, and some local remnants. Since it was the only force they were able to hold on against the central administration, religio-political propaganda was never missing among these Turkmen tribes, who were strongly inclined to 'Mehdi expectations.' These Turkmen sheikhs, called Baba, who drew, with their

weird clothing, their unlawful (*şeriate muğayir*) customs, and their exuberant lifestyles the severe criticism of the orthodox Sufis, were the main governors and judges of the moral lives of the villagers and nomads. Since they were unable to relate to the mentalities of these currents, neither the religious scholars, nor the sheikhs of the bourgeois Sufi orders were able to compete with those Babas. (Köprülü 2009 [1935], 117)

In short, in Köprülü's oeuvre's distinctions between "orthodoxy" and "heterodoxy" are correlated to economic, geographic, cultural, and political factors.

The structural connection that Köprülü posits between socioeconomic context and religious preference can be compared to Ibn Khaldun's *Muqaddima* from the 14th century, which Köprülü praised as a "philosophy of history" and "blueprint of sociology."[19] The *Muqaddima* is concerned with the forces that drive history and necessitate the rise and decline of dynasties, and it tries to establish the sociological laws governing this dynamic process (Nagel 1981, 58). Central to its narrative is a distinction between urban, sedentary life and *badāwa*, that is, the rural, tribal life of the Bedouins (Rosenthal 1932, 6–8). While the sedentary life of the city is organized by law, the rural life is regulated by *'asabiyya*, a term that denotes tribal solidarity and egalitarianism, and is located at the center of Bedouin and Arab culture (Nagel 1981, 58–71). Alike in Ibn Khaldun and Köprülü's respective juxtapositions of urban and rural culture is a certain romanticism with regard to the latter. For Ibn Khaldun, *'asabiyya* is a force of strength and renewal, and—though not altogether absent in the town—at its most powerful among the Bedouins. Also, he considers the Bedouins as in general more virtuous than the city dwellers, who followed the law instead of their instinct and got spoiled as a result of their luxurious lifestyle (Nagel 1981, 58–59; Ibn Khaldun 1967, 120). Similarly, for Köprülü, who followed in this point closely Ziya Gökalp, Turkish culture was found in its finest, undiluted ways among the peripheral Turkmen tribes of Anatolia.

In other aspects, however, Köprülü's description of the relationship between urban and rural life departed significantly from that of Ibn

---

19 Köprülü reverently described Ibn Khaldun as one of the greatest philosophers of the history of the classic and medieval periods, representing the apex of Islamic historiography (Köprülü 1980 [1920/21], 93).

Khaldun. For one, in Ibn Khaldun's text the dichotomous nature of urban and rural culture was part of a larger, cyclical conception of Islamic civilization, where forces from the countryside would periodically enter the urban center and rejuvenate the urban culture. In Köprülü's work we find a more static juxtaposition of center and periphery. Also different is the way they each evaluated the relationship between center and periphery with regard to religiosity. While there is no essential value difference between urban and rural forms (and everything in between) of socioeconomic organization and culture in Ibn Khaldun's text, he did assert that rural people tended to be more religious due to the hardships of life (Baali 1988, 98). Ibn Khaldun leads extensive discussions about different forms of Islam and points out the social role of religion in a way that seems to foreshadow Durkheim. What he does not do, however, is correlate inner-Islamic differences—for example between jurists and muftis, on the one side, and the Sufis, on the other—with the distinction according to lifestyle (urban/rural) (Ibn Khaldun 1967, 360). In Köprülü's work, on the other hand, we can see the impact of Orientalist and Islamic revivalist thought, which made him depict the cultural periphery with regard to religion as impure and inferior (expressed through notions of "popular" and "heterodox" Islam) in comparison to the scripture- and law-based Islamic culture associated with urban contexts. In other words, Köprülü can be seen as an early representative of a tradition of thought that connects the (Khaldunian) idea of the opposed but complementary character of urban and rural Islamic cultures, respectively, with the Orientalist distinction between "orthodox"/"high" and "heterodox"/"popular" Islam. Talal Asad has written about this move and criticized in particular Ernest Gellner for presenting Islamic culture in a way that reifies essentialist notions of Islam in contrast to a (in the process equally essentialized) Christianity. Fundamentally, Asad argued that "[i]t is wrong to represent types of Islam as being correlated with types of social structure" and proposed instead a discursive approach to the Islamic tradition (Asad 1986, 7). The linking of notions of political geography (center/periphery model), and normative theology (orthodoxy/heterodoxy) as a way to organize hierarchically different forms of Islam is akin to functionalist models of social organicity.[20] It is exactly the easy flow of such models that should make one suspicious.

---

20 Sociological functionalism evaluates the meaning of religion in accordance with its social functions and is undergirded by an understanding of society as forming an organic whole, the parts of which are assumed to be symbiotically related.

The example of Ibn Khaldun shows that the use of structural and functionalist categories to describe the dynamics of Islamic civilization is not a
prerogative of Western Orientalists, but has roots in the Islamic scholarly
tradition itself.[21] Neither is a concept of Islam that organizes religious practices in normative hierarchies distinctively Western.[22] Such hierarchies have
been part of Islamic apologetics and discursive practices from early on.

Agendas and Concepts

Köprülü's work displays both religionist and secularist biases. This shows
itself in the way he conceives of religion as a historical reality and as an
analytical concept clearly distinguishable from other spheres of life. His
distinction between culture and religion is the best example. It is only their
confusion that leads to "heterodoxy" and creates a religio-political as well as
an analytical problem. The religio-political problem is one of ambivalence.
While aspects of Turkish culture within Islamic religion are interpreted as a
pollution of Islam by non-Islamic elements, this "polluted" (in other words,
"syncretistic" or "heterodox") religion at the same time carries remnants of
ancient Turkish religion and culture and therefore constitutes an essential source for the (re-)construction of the national consciousness.[23] For
Köprülü the analytical problem is about how to dissect secondary cultural,
and foreign (non-Islamic), religious elements from the essentially Islamic.
To this end Köprülü began, from the mid-1920s onwards, to use the term
"heterodox" (*hétérodoxe*, or *heterodoks*) to characterize forms of Islam that
he had previously labeled, in line with the scholarly Islamic tradition, as
"heretical and schismatic" (*rafz ve itizal*).[24] While he had previously used

---

21 Thanks to Rosemary Hicks for directing my attention to this point.

22 "Western" here understood not in a geographic sense but in the sense of a commitment to the project of secular Western modernity—and therefore not excluding Muslim
scholars.

23 The remnants argument has been an early theoretical tool in the modern study of cultures and religions. Already E. B. Tylor, one of the founding fathers of the modern comparative study of religion, reasoned in *Primitive Culture* (1871) that savage and barbarian aspects
within civilized cultures could be explained as remnants from primitive pasts (Kippenberg
2002, 55).

24 *Early Mystics* does not yet contain the words heterodox or orthodox, or derivates of them.
Köprülü begins to use the term heterodoxy selectively in "History of Turkish Literature"
(Köprülü 1980 [1920/21], 337) and "History of Turkey" (Köprülü 2005 [1923], 121). The ortho-
doxy/heterodoxy binary becomes much more prominent in later works, such as *Origins of
the Ottoman Empire* (Köprülü 1992 [1935]).

traditional terms such as "People of the Sunna" (*ehl-i sünnet*), or legalistic terms such as *müteşerri* (meaning as much as "in line with the sharia")[25] to mark the normative center of Islam, he now began to refer to Sunni Islam as "orthodoxy" against which deviation could be measured. The shift in interpretation is presented without explanation. I argue that to the extent that Köprülü's heterodox/orthodox distinction is simply a secularized version of Sunni-Islamic apologetics, it is unable to explain inner-Islamic difference.

To the degree that Köprülü conceives of notions of (Turkish) culture and (Islamic) religion in an essentialist manner, more dynamic factors (economy and geography) and the issues of power that speak through them are from the outset reduced to a status of secondary relevance. In other words, the focus of the narrative is throughout on continuities (mainly, if not exclusively, within the realm of religion and culture) more than changes (and dynamic factors such as economic relations and geographic location). Implicit in this narrative is further an argument about the dominance of culture over religion, which becomes visible, for example in the claim that the Turkmens "can never support but a form of religion that allows for the continuation of their old national customs" (Köprülü 2002 [1925], 71).[26]

Many of the central categories and concepts that Köprülü employed as markers of the Turkish cultural tradition are rather static, such as his concepts of primitive society, popular religion, and heterodoxy, or lack specificity, such as his concept of shamanism. His reliance on notions of origins, influences, and continuity, as well as the hierarchies that he inscribes qua differentiation between levels of religion reflect an essentialism typical for contemporary approaches to culture and religion. His writings are full of taxonomic arrangements where essences (the original/authentic) are juxtaposed to additions (the contingent/inauthentic), "orthodox" beliefs and practices to "heterodox" ones, or old to new "characters."

Köprülü's treatment of Turkish shamanism illustrates particularly well the analytical weakness of his concepts. An exemplary piece in this regard is the "Religious History of the Turks" (*Türk Târîh-i Dînîsi*, 1925), an unfortunately-never-revised collection of notes for a course with the same title that he gave in 1924 at Darülfünun's School of Divinity. Reflecting

---

25 Köprülü (1966 [1919], 306 and 280 fn 50, respectively).

26 The argument of the dominance of national culture over religion in the continuity of Turkishness is akin to the Kemalist nationalist view.

on contemporary European sociological and anthropological discourses on "primitive religion" and religious evolution, notions of shamanism, totemism, animism, and paganism appear here as markers of pre-Islamic Turkish religiosity. But their exact meanings and relation to each other remain opaque. Thus he writes that in old times, when the Turks lived in not-yet-united, separate clans, their religion, manifest in nature and in their social structures, was totemism. When the Turks later entered into other religions, these old totemist religious practices would have become part of their "national custom" (*millî bir âdet*) (Köprülü 2005 [1925], 39).[27] In the same work he asserts that the Tatar Turks used to follow shamanism, which he classifies as part of animism (Köprülü 2005 [1925], 55–58). Clear traces of old Turkish paganism he finds in the Yeseviye, which he counts as the first Turkish Sufi order (Köprülü 2005 [1925], 147; see also Köprülü 1980 [1920/21], 194). In a later work he identifies the pagan period (*paganizm*) of the old Turks as that of the *kam* or shamans (*şaman*) (Köprülü 1966[1942], 153). These examples show, beyond the unsystematic manner in which he categorized ancient religious practices among the Turks, that shamanism was his preferred qualification for pre-Islamic Turkish religion.

One goal of this study is to contribute to a critical review of the conceptual toolbox of the scholarship on Islam, particularly with regard to the description and analysis of inner-Islamic plurality/difference. I argue that this scholarship needs to take more seriously the work of its concepts—especially where it takes recourse to problematic binary pairs such as the orthodoxy/heterodoxy distinction, which is charged with a functionalism and essentialism that confuses dogmatic (normative in a theological and a political sense) and analytical perspectives. I find it very unsatisfactory to simply put ambivalent conceptual terms such as heterodox, popular, and so forth into quotation marks, as often done. Acknowledging awareness about a potential problem of such terms while continuing to use them is not enough. In order to conceive of inner-Islamic difference and plurality in a more fruitful way I will (1) side with discursive approaches as outlined by Talal Asad against nominal and substantive approaches and (2) draw

---

27 In his slightly earlier *Türkiye Tarihi I* ("History of Turkey"), which targeted a broader audience, he had subsumed ancient Turkish religious practices under the categories of, primarily, totemism, and, secondarily, shamanism (Köprülü 1923, 37 and 50). In addition, he also mentions manaism as having been spread among the Turks. His description of *mana* as worship of the souls of the forefathers is somewhat odd and seems to fit more with animism (Köprülü 1923, 38). This suggests that his knowledge of the literature and concepts of late 19th- and early 20th-century anthropological debates on primitive religions was, despite his familiarity with Durkheim's work, in the end rather superficial.

in addition on insights from the late antiquity scholar Daniel Boyarin, who has argued for a wave-theory model instead of static and functionalist models in the discussion of the relation between religious traditions.

Shamanism

The thesis that the ancient Turks of Central Asia were shamans was originally developed by Russian Turkologists such as Friedrich Wilhelm Radloff (*Das Schamanenthum und sein Kultus*, 1885) in the late 19th century (Kafesoğlu 1980, 22; cf. Ocak 2000a, 56–57). Since his earliest publications on the roots of Turkish Islam and the migration of Turkish culture from Central Asia to Anatolia, references to shamanism are multiple in Köprülü's work. In *Islam in Anatolia*, Köprülü describes the Turkmen *babas*, an epithet that frequently appears from the 12th through the 15th century for venerated religious men in the Turkish-speaking countryside of Anatolia and the Balkans, as "popular saints, as Islamized versions of the old Turkish *kām/ozān*" (Köprülü 1993 [1922], 5). They "inspired the Oghuz clans, in a language they could understand, with mystical but simple and popular versions of Islam that conformed to their old ethnic traditions" (Köprülü 1993 [1922], 11). He presents Baraq Baba, a 13th-century figure associated in hagiographic literature with the Babai movement, as a typical example for this form of Islam. This man, "who denied the next world and affirmed the transmigration of souls, who said that God first united spiritually with 'Alī and then with Sultan Öljeitü Khudā-Banda [a Mongol ruler, d. 1316], and who considered everything forbidden by canon law to be permissible, outwardly reminds us of the Turkish shamans of the Altay" (Köprülü 1993 [1922], 23).

Köprülü had already in *Early Mystics* written about Baraq Baba as an example of a nonconformist Turkish Sufi of the 13th century. However, here he did not yet connect him directly with vestiges of ancient Turkish tradition or shamanism (Köprülü 1966 [1919], 179–180 fn 37). Developing an idea he had in a rudimentary way first articulated in *Origins* and repeated in *Early Mystics*, he argued in *Islam in Anatolia* that there are "definite similarities between the roles, attire, and rapturous dances of these old Turkish *bakhshı/kām*…and the roles, attire, and litanies and songfests of the Turkmen *bābās*…" (Köprülü 1993 [1922], 68 fn 32). He continued this line of argument in "Origins of Bektashim": the Oghuz tribes began already within the first Islamic century to convert to Islam, "[b]ut under the outer coat of Islam, they remained under the influence of their old national customs and primitive religions" (Köprülü 2002 [1925], 70). In other words, elements of the ancient shaman religion of the Turks would continue under an Islamic varnish.

Köprülü's reflections on Turkish shamanism reach its height of systematization in a small booklet published in 1929 as *Influence du Chamanisme Turco-Mongol sur les ordres mystiques Musulmans.* This tiny study has been the only piece in which he put the question of shamanism into the center of his investigation. As in his other work, he is relying less on pre-Islamic Central Asian materials than on certain practices of Anatolian Sufism, which he regards as a window into pre-Islamic Turkish religion. Köprülü's main focus is again on the Yesevi Sufi order. Since the Yeseviye was the oldest Turkish Sufi order, it constituted the logical starting point for an investigation into the "influences of shamanism" on the Turkish Sufi traditions (Köprülü 1929, 5–6). After some reflections on terms used among different Turkish people for "shaman," recycled from *Origins*,[28] Köprülü lays out his empirical evidences for shaman traces in Turkish mysticism. These evidences are, however, rather meager. His starting point is the observation that, according to certain sources, unveiled women participated in Ahmed Yesevi's *dhikr* ritual. He hypothesizes that the Turks regarded the first Sufis as *kam* (i.e., shamans), and therefore would not have cared about separation of the sexes; in fact, the Yesevi *dhikr* included multiple traces of ecstatic dances characteristic of the shaman nomad tribes of Northern Asia (Köprülü 1929, 7–8). He further compares certain miracles attributed to Yesevi Sufis and also found in Bektashi hagiographies, for example the metamorphosis of a saint into a bird and the capability to fly, with those found among Buddhist saints and concludes from this the possibility of Buddhist and Indian influences on ancient Turkish shamanism (Köprülü 1929, 9–10; see also Köprülü 1966 [1942], 153). The final focus of the booklet is on Baraq Baba, who is again—but with more detail than in previous publications—portrayed as the prototype of a "heterodox" Turkish dervish influenced by Mongolian shamanism (Köprülü 1929, 14–19). In conclusion, the Yeseviye and its Anatolian heirs such as the Bektashiye are depicted as carriers of shaman traits and as having a highly syncretistic character.[29]

---

28 Cf. Köprülü (1999 [1915], 57–58).

29 He subsequently reiterated this or similar accounts; see, for example, Köprülü (1979 [1949], 462).

Recently, Köprülü has been criticized for his approach to Turkish shamanism, especially for overemphasizing pre-Islamic Turkish traditions,
underestimating the integrative power of Islamic Sufism, and assuming
too-rigid boundaries between pre-Islamic and Islamic practices in his
account of the formation of popular Turkish Islam:

> Köprülü, who was generally right in his insistence that Sufism
> lay at the core of Turkish popular Islam, was mistaken in view-
> ing Turkoman babas as but superficially Islamized shamans.
> This is not to deny the significance of pre-Islamic Turkish beliefs
> and practices in the Islamization of Turks. Continuity between
> pre-Islamic and Islamic belief and practice among the masses of
> Turkish speakers, however, does not mean that no recruits could
> have been made to Sufism from amongst them or that any such
> recruits could only have come from among the necessarily small
> numbers of shamanic figures active in such communities. On
> the contrary, it seems much more reasonable to think that such
> shamanic figures would have been the group most resistant to
> Islamization. In any case, it is beyond doubt that, whatever their
> social origins—urban, peasant, or nomadic[—], a certain number
> of Turkish speakers "entered" Sufism, absorbed and digested at
> least a good portion of contemporary Sufi teachings and prac-
> tices, and successfully adapted these to their own linguistic and
> social contexts. Turkoman babas should be seen in this light.
> (Karamustafa 2005, 95)

DeWeese has critically remarked that Köprülü never seriously pushed
his study of Turkish shamanism beyond what remains in the end a
rather superficial and speculative deduction of shamanism from practices of medieval hagiographic texts about Anatolian and Balkan saints,
which he then projected back onto Turkish practices in Central Asia.
He never undertook a systematic study of ancient Turkish shamanism
itself, to which he was so willingly attributing features of Turkish religious practice that he was unable to attribute to other sources (DeWeese
2006). Elsewhere, DeWeese has convincingly formulated a more principal criticism, questioning whether pre-Islamic Turkish religion could be
sufficiently described as shamanism and arguing instead that shamanist
practices were performed only by a limited group of religious specialists
who would have been called upon for very particular occasions (DeWeese

1994, 32–50). Despite this criticism, the shamanism thesis is still prominent, especially among Turkish historians.[30]

Attention to the intimate relationship between the rise to prominence of the shamanism thesis in early Turkish nationalism and the comprehensive reconceptualization of the Kızılbaş-Alevis and Bektashis within early Turkish nationalist scholarship has so far been very limited. An exception is the Turkish Muslim theologian Süleyman Uludağ, who correctly recognized that the claim that the Alevis continued old Turkish beliefs and were connected to shamanism emerged not earlier than at the beginning of the 20th century in the context of Turkish nationalism (Uludağ 1999, 159). In the 1990s this claim received a new boost as part of the Alevi coming-out. Within the context of the invigorated secularist nationalism of this period, which needed to refurbish its arguments in the face of a newly empowered movement of political Islam, the shamanism thesis became widely accepted knowledge among many Alevis (with the major exception of Kurdish nationalist Alevis) and widespread also among non-Alevi publics (Vorhoff 1995, 97–98; Bahadır 2005, 25).

I argue that the introduction of the term "shamanism" into the discourse of Turkish nationalism fulfilled two purposes. First, shamanism became a token for the asserted unbroken continuity of elements of Turkish culture from Central Asia to contemporary Anatolian life and played thus a vital role in providing evidence for the narrative of the Turkish nation. As the texts of both Baha Said and Köprülü show, the Bektashi and the Kızılbaş groups, which in this time period began to be labeled "Alevi," were depicted as Anatolian carriers of remnants of this shamanistic past. This move, second, helped to integrate the Kızılbaş-Alevi into the national domain against claims of their political subversiveness, as well as their alleged relation to non-Turkish elements. However, from an Islamic point of view the connection with shamanism also pointed to the Alevis' alleged "syncretistic" and "heterodox" character, further cementing their religious otherness relative to Sunni Islam. In short, the shamanism thesis in its application to the Alevis sought to prove, first, that the later were Turks and not Kurds, or ancestors of ancient Anatolian people, and, second, that they were not crypto-Christians but Muslims—although it was argued that their Islam was tainted. The shamanism thesis thus marked Alevism as highly ambivalent from a perspective of national, implicitly Turkish-Muslim, unity.

---

30 This does not mean that there would not also have been prominent Turkish historians, such as Ülken (1969), and Kafesoğlu (1980), voicing strong criticism against it.

Syncretism

Rather than being a bounded "thing," religion is constantly being discursively identified and reified. While syncretism is often seen as a gradual process of melting and mixture, of "growing together," it should be understood that the "process of selection and reconciliation" is simultaneously one of rejection and contestation. What is frequently striking in the use of the term *syncretism* is that it hides the relation of syncretism to processes of religious expansion and conversion. Syncretism as a historical phenomenon is often not a "natural" process of growth, a random combination of heterogeneous elements, but rather an appropriation of religious symbols in the construction of religious regimes (van der Veer 1994a, 199).

Although he privileged Turkish elements in his investigation of the religious history of the Turks, Köprülü did not understand the connection that he drew between Turkish shamanism and the "popular"/"heterodox" Muslim practices of the Turks as an exclusive one. His description of the religion of the Turkmen tribes was broader, delineating "a syncretism, which was the result of the amalgamation of the old Turks' pagan customs, with a simple and popular form of extreme Shiism, painted at the outside in the color of Sufism, and some local remainders" (Köprülü 1991 [1935], 99). Thus, Köprülü described the rural Islam of Anatolia as a "heterodox" and "eclectic and syncretistic system" (Köprülü 2002 [1925], 72).

To the extent that, as I have shown above, elements of ancient religious practices and beliefs could be used to prove the cultural continuity of the Turks, religion played a crucial role in the reconstruction of the history of the Turks. Within this narrative of continuity, Köprülü emphasized diverse "'influences" of pre-Islamic Turkish traditions, on the one hand, and more or less marginal Islamic currents and ideas, on the other.[31] It is not that Köprülü would have denied influences from non-Muslim and non-Turkish cultures. He did consider non-Muslim and non-Turkish influences on Anatolian Islam. But he did not show much interest in researching them in greater detail, usually referring to them only in passing.[32] In

---

31 In *Early Mystics*, the major Islamic elements he mentioned as components of this "syncretism" were, besides Yesevi Sufism, Ismailism and Batinism (Köprülü 1966 [1919], 176).

32 These possible influences would stretch from local faiths of Anatolia and Iran, Christian sects, diverse philosophical and mystical ideas such as neo-Platonism and Buddhism, to old Indian and Chinese traditions (see Köprülü 2002 [1925], 72; 1929, 9; 1980 [1920/21], 23–24 and 249; cf. 1923, 43–44).

Early Mystics, for example, Köprülü argues that in the Seljuk period there certainly would have been some exchange of traditions between local Christians and settling Turks. The nomadic Turks, however, remained untainted by such influences (Köprülü 1966 [1919], 163).

It is worth reflecting on the work of the notion of influence in Köprülü's grand narrative. I argue that it functions as a device that ascribes historical essence to Turkishness and Islam, both of which are in this process objectified as in their kernel unchanging entities and in this way set apart from those traditions which are said to be "influencing" them. To the degree that it operates as a demarcation line between presumably clearly isolatable cultural units, the notion of "influence" is based on questionable assumptions of religious/cultural boundaries. Instead of approaching cultural and religious traditions as being in an open-ended and dynamic conversation, the notion of influence is "unidirectional" as Galit Hasan-Rokem has critically remarked (as cited in Boyarin 1999, 10). Similarly, Cemal Kafadar has likened the notion of influence to a sexual act in an unequal relationship: "The influencer is like the one who penetrates and is proud, and the influenced is like the one who is penetrated and thus put to shame" (Kafadar 1995, 25). I think that the allegory to the sexual act as imagined in homophobic discourses shows well how the notion of influence can itself become a heuristic tool for the tacit justification of the power imbalances inherent in religio-political discourses.[33]

What did the concept of syncretism accomplish in Köprülü's writings? Gauri Viswanathan has critically raised the question as to whether syncretism would offer "possibilities for a merging of religious difference" or whether it would rather be "a code word for the incorporation and assimilation of 'minority' cultures into the culture of the dominant group." She further asks about the role of historiography in the representation of rivaling religious groups (Viswanathan 1995, 21). What can we say about Köprülü's concept of syncretism in light of these questions? At a first glance, his approach might appear as rather dynamic. In his article "The Influence of Byzantine Institutions on Ottoman Institutions" (1931), Köprülü argued that "quite many remainders of the pre-Islamic period continued to live fairly naturally among the Turks; sometimes they would *hide* their *old character* underneath an Islamic varnish; sometimes they would, while *protecting old forms,* begin to take on a *new character*"

---

33 For a critique of Köprülü's use of "influences" see also DeWeese (2006, xv-xvi).

[my emphasis].³⁴ This description carries not only plenty of functional-ist metaphors, it also shows strong religionist biases. In addition, one ought to question the notion of agency reflected in this kind of syncretis-tic process, articulated through the notions "hiding" and "protecting." To what extent can we, when we talk about syncretistic processes, attribute agency—in terms of consciously committing "syncretistic" actions—to historical individuals and groups who might not have considered their practices or beliefs as a break with an old tradition or adaptation of a new one? We may indeed assume that what we describe as syncretism are in most cases gradual processes of change, which might stretch over genera-tions and are thus not necessarily perceivable as change from within the historical situation wherein they occur. In other words, what constitutes an act of syncretism for outside observers of future times might often have been experienced as continuity in its own time. Additionally, what Islam meant in one historical context, and how boundaries of Islam were con-stituted accordingly, depended on the social and cultural location of the Muslim environment in question. It would be short-sighted to assume, for example, that the urban Islam centered on *madrasa* learning and the traditions of rural Islam, the authority of which was based on charisma and lineage rather than book knowledge, drew the same boundaries of Islam even when living in the same historical context (Karamustafa 2010, 45). In short, when the syncretism concept is employed as an a posteriori historicizing operation that projects backward contemporary concepts of religion based on clearly identifiable boundaries and continuity, this is bound to produce anachronistic arguments.

Some regard it as a merit of the syncretism perspective that it sheds light on the wandering and exchange of ideas and practices between religious traditions. However, when highlighting movement between religions, the notion of syncretism remains within the assumption that religions can and have to be treated as from each other clearly distin-guishable entities.³⁵ Köprülü's notion of syncretism remained within the

---

34 As quoted in Berktay (1983, 69). Köprülü argued in this text that the similarities between Byzantine and Ottoman institutions could largely be explained not by direct influence but as a continuity of Islamic institutions, which had been inspired by Byzantium at an earlier historical stage (Ersanlı 2002, 149).

35 This inherent essentialism of the concept of syncretism—implying the existence of clear boundaries between religious traditions qua a focus on processes of merger and differentiation—is one of the reasons why it has as an analytical concept, after a prolific period of debate in the 1960s and 1970s, been widely abandoned in the field of religious studies. Now terms such as hybridization and creolization are preferred for the description of cultural mixtures (Kraft 2002, 142–145).

framework of such a static and ultimately essentialist concept of religion, presupposing clear boundaries between religious traditions in a manner typical of early 20th-century Orientalist discourses. In this way he characterized Bektashism as "like all Sufi orders a *syncretism* of a *mix of different elements*... which contains the remnants of all kinds of different religious sects and paths such as traces of the *Kalenderiye, Yeseviye, Hayderiye* [Sufi groups], that is, [traces stretching] from *Shamanism* to *neo-Platonism*" (Köprülü 1980 [1920/21], 249).

Critical attention also needs to be directed to the theologico-political work of syncretism language. The remnants thesis, which is part of this language, is a point in case. It can function as an apologetic device for the justification of particular religious hegemonies, and all the implicit and explicit hierarchies that these hegemonies are interested in establishing. Syncretism theory of the remnants kind carries a quasi-theological bias. It makes an implicit distinction between two kinds of religious traditions. The first kind we might label primary or core traditions, such as Islam, Christianity, and within Köprülü's narrative also shamanism. Implicitly, primary religions are understood as authentic, meaning their essence is time-resistant. The second kind of religious formations is historically and ontologically secondary to and dependent on these primary traditions. By pointing to processes of incorporation of elements of primary religions into secondary ones, such a syncretism theory presupposes clearly definable and time-resistant boundaries between the primary religious traditions involved. Correspondingly, the secondary syncretistic formations are marked by their lack of such originality and authenticity (see Figure 5.1). Between the eclecticism of the latter and the historical continuity of the primary religions opens up a gap of essence and authenticity.

In order not to give a wrong impression it has to be emphasized that not all approaches to syncretism are essentialist and endorsing hierarchies between religions.[36] Already the sociologist of religion Joachim Wach has argued that from the viewpoint of its prehistory, every religion would be syncretistic (Wach 1924, 86). Beyond such rigid historicizing of religions, I would concede that in particular discursive approaches to syncretism can be heuristically useful for analysis of the power dynamics at work during processes of differentiation and othering between religious formations. An example of a noteworthy attempt to rescue the syncretism concept

---

36 For a good overview of classical and contemporary perspectives on syncretism see Leopold and Jensen (2004). For critical discussion of the work of syncretism see also van der Veer (1994b).

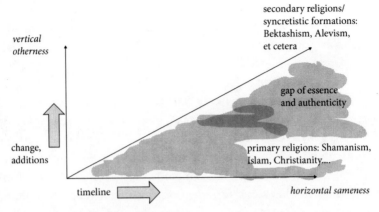

vertical
otherness

secondary religions/
syncretistic formations:
Bektashism, Alevism,
et cetera

gap of essence
and authenticity

change,
additions

primary religions: Shamanism,
Islam, Christianity....

timeline

horizontal sameness

FIGURE 5.1: The Work of Syncretism

is the work of anthropologists Rosalind Shaw and Charles Stewart, who
attempted to circumvent the danger of essentialism by casting syncretism
as the "politics of religious synthesis," by which they refer to the dynamic
process in which syncretism as well as "anti-syncretism" (i.e., "the antagonism to religious synthesis shown by agents concerned with the defence
of religious boundaries") evolve within specific relations of power (Shaw/
Stewart 1994, 7).

To do justice to Köprülü's approach to syncretism, it has to be evaluated
in light of the theoretical apparatus that was available to him. He was an
intellectual who operated within what I would term a secularist-religionist
paradigm, strongly influenced by contemporary European discourses on
religion, most notably by the work of Durkheim. Within these discourses,
terms for religio-political distinction and classification that appear problematic to us, such as sect, heresy, as well as the binary pairs high Islam/
popular Islam, and orthodoxy/heterodoxy match up nicely with the concept of syncretism. What marks these concepts as secularist-religionist
is their implication in the creation of boundaries between historical religious subjects with clearly identifiable origins, as well as a history marked
by continuity and more-or-less systematized content. The way in which
Köprülü reified essences and his tendency to dissect religions into their
morphological elements further remind of the phenomenological school
of religious studies (outstanding examples and contemporaries of Köprülü
being Rudolf Otto and Gerardus van der Leeuw). Such phenomenological
disposition shines also through when he concludes a discussion of Shiite
inclinations among Sunni Muslims and Sufis stating that "[i]n the study
of the history of religion, one must try to understand the true nature of

real beliefs, their origin and significance, more than external labels and outward forms. These are always below the surface" (Köprülü 1993 [1922], 6). On the other hand, he certainly was too much of a positivist to accept the methodology of the phenomenologists, who argued that the religious would reveal itself in subjective experience.

Analytical concepts are of heuristic nature and can at best be claimed to be ideal-typical representations of sociohistorical realities. The concept of syncretism, if configured discursively, may be helpful to describe religious phenomena subject to a modern religion discourse with its preferences for categorical notions of essence and difference. However, the usefulness of analytical perspectives that project syncretism onto premodern contexts, where such certainties with regard to the boundaries of religions did not necessarily exist to the same extent, seems less evident to me. Historical data make clear that in 11th- to 15th-century Asia Minor—and to a certain extent also later—religious practices often were shared among adherents of different traditions, and religious boundaries, especially in regions dominated by oral culture, remained diffuse (Kafadar 1995). Projecting the concept of syncretism on contexts where the boundaries between religious traditions—at least among ordinary practitioners—are fluid, and where self-aware religions (in the sense of their adherents consciously understanding themselves as different from more-or-less clearly defined religious others) did not yet necessarily exist does not seem to be a self-evident operation.

The syncretism perspective as it has until today remained paradigmatic in the academic study of the religious history of Anatolia,[37] and of Alevism more specifically, is based on a modern concept of religion. Köprülü's mode of describing the Alevis is in that regard not essentially different from Hasluck's description (discussed in chapter 1), with the major difference being in the elements they saw at work in the Alevi syncretism, the former privileging Turkish, and the later Christian elements, in addition to the Islamic components on which they agreed. While Köprülü was also influenced by Western and Orientalist discourses on religion and Islam, it is clear that his normative matrix of religion was in addition strongly shaped by Sunni Islam, whereas Hasluck's concept of religion

37 A recent example is Veinstein (2005); for a critical review of this volume see Dressler (2009). For a methodologically and theoretically more astute edited volume dedicated to a comparative discussion of various Middle Eastern socio-religious communities at the margins of Islamic discourse see Kehl-Bodrogi, Kellner-Heinkele and Otter-Beaujean (1997).

was naturally shaped more profoundly by Christianity/Protestantism. Hasluck needs to be credited for having been an early critic of the survival/remnants thesis. While he did not reject the possibility of continuity of sacredness between different cultures, he was highly skeptical of an approach that regarded such continuity as the norm: "He [Hasluck] shows scant regard...for any presumption that one culture may 'survive' into another over time in any straightforward way, and at the same time insists that the causal basis for any cultural continuity must be set in the way present factors selectively shape the past" (Shankland 2004b, 18). In other words, Hasluck already at an early stage arrived at a remarkably "dynamic theory of culture which implies that the past is continuously reinterpreted by the present" (Shankland 2004b, 20). More recently, similar criticism against the remnants model of syncretism, which conceives of religious formations as bounded and relatively time-resistant, has been launched by Bruce Privratsky. Within a discussion of Kazak religion, he argued that once certain elements from one religious tradition had been appropriated by another tradition they should be understood as constitutive parts of this new tradition (Privratsky 2001, 15–19). The remnants theory, however, whether employed by scholarly observers or by members of a specific "source religion," connects the fact of this appropriation process with an implicit hierarchization between different kinds of religion.

Going beyond the remnants approach, I argue in favor of a historicizing perspective critically investigating any claims that imply clear essences, boundaries, and one-directional historical trajectories. One should be highly suspicious of all approaches that (1) assume the possibility and historical meaningfulness of a clear distinction between "original," "authentic" source religions, on the one hand, and secondary religious traditions imagined as assemblages of remnants of such "original religions," on the other hand, and (2) perceive the secondary religious traditions as being impacted by source religions in the form of "influences" or "remnants." I find much more plausible dynamic approaches such as the one offered by Boyarin, who in his discussion of the relationship between Judaism and Christianity in late antiquity has suggested a wave theory (derived from models in historical linguistics) to conceptualize the relations between "religious" traditions in a way that does not privilege essentialist/functionalist/linear models, but instead puts emphasis on the overlapping and undetermined character of much of the practices and views that we conveniently subsume under the category of religion (Boyarin 1999, 7–19; Boyarin 2007). Drawing on Homi Bhabha's insights on cultural hybridity, arguing especially against organicist metaphors of kinship in the description of the relations between cultures, he proposes "a model of shared and crisscrossing lines of history and religious development" (Boyarin 1999, 8). Boyarin suggests that we regard religions as "conversations" around traditions that are sometimes more intertwined than clearly separated, and thereby uproot discourses of divergence and syncretism. This approach changes our perspective on what happens at the boundaries between cultures. Rather than perceiving them as clearly demarcated points of entry/exit we should conceptualize boundaries as, to borrow from Mary Louise Pratt, "contact zones" or spaces of "transculturation," where "disparate cultures meet, clash, grapple with each other, often in highly asymmetrical relations of domination and subordination."[38]

Finally, one needs to address the question as to what the concept of syncretism does within the political context of nationalism. Van der Veer has argued that "such terms as *tolerance* and *syncretism* belong to discursive strategies that try to determine the national culture" (van der Veer 1994a, 201). Viewed from that angle, the work of syncretism as a taxonomy to determine the characteristics of Alevism reveals normative ambivalence. The "Alevi syncretism" helps to explain the combination of pre-Islamic Turkish ("shamanistic") and Islamic aspects. It is their syncretism that renders the Alevis both "heterodox" and "Turkish." In other words, their alleged syncretism makes the Alevis on the one side attractive for the nationalist cause, while their religious difference at the same time creates tensions with regard to nationalist claims of ethno-religious homogeneity, reflected since the Hamidian period in state efforts to assimilate the Alevis into (Sunni) Islam.

Concluding my criticism of the syncretism concept, and more specifically of the concept of religion that it is based on, I would hold against it that the inquiry (historical and anthropological) into the social structures of Muslim societies in general, and its cultural and religious practices in particular, should question modernist assumptions of clear boundaries, as well as one-dimensional notions of sameness and difference. It should rather put the focus on divergence, fuzziness, as well as sociocultural dynamics where religious practices are shared and/or travel between social groups.

---

38 Pratt (*Imperial Eyes: Travel Writing and Transculturation*, 1992), as quoted in Boyarin (2007, 74).

Secular Modernism and Islamic Revivalism

DeWeese remarks that in *Early Mystics* "Köprülü was paving the way for projecting a 'tainted' Islam, either rife with 'Shamanic' holdovers from pre-Islamic Turkic religion or colored by excessive compromises with presumed 'popular' religious tastes, as the wellspring of the Yasawī tradition" and by extension also Bektashism. Although Köprülü's view could not be substantiated historically, it remained dominant "no doubt because it harmonized well with certain approaches to Islam in twentieth-century Turkey" (DeWeese 2006, xvi). Indeed, the scenario of an Anatolian Islam as drawn by Köprülü, in which popular and high culture forms of religiosity stand in stark contrast to each other, resonates well with modern discourses on religion and Islam. Influential currents within Islam have since the late 19th century been shaped by revivalist utopias pervaded with notions of purity and origins, which are themselves akin to the language of modernism.[39]

İsmail Kara has argued that Islamism, historically and semantically a product of modernism, has internalized Orientalist stereotypes about Islam and developed a homogenizing and centralizing character that shows itself in ideals of unity and legalist thought against the historical plurality of Islamic culture (Kara 2004, 38–43). This would become particularly obvious in the distinction between "real" and "living" Islam, a distinction historically introduced by Islamic modernizers to delegitimize aspects of ("living") Islam that they considered ill-suited for the modern project. In this way, Islamic revivalism is intrinsically connected to secular modernism (Kara 2004, 43–44). Within Islamic revivalist discourse the accusation of practicing—according to legalist approaches illegitimate— "innovations" (*bid'a*) is dialectically related to the construction of Islamic "orthodoxy." This is why the scholarly definition of Muslim groups and currents as syncretistic renders them heretical in the eyes of revivalist interpretations of Islam, which have in the modern period been able to assume powerful positions in many Muslim societies.[40]

Not only the semantics of Islamic revivalism, but also other religionist constructs such as the shamanism thesis, the syncretism thesis, and

---

39 Köprülü's longing for pure origins shines through, for example, when he asserts that pre-Islamic Turkish poetry, and by implication pre-Islamic Turkish culture, was hardly influenced at all by other civilizations (Köprülü 1966 [1919], 7).

40 Especially interpretations of Islam close to Sufism, traditionally at the center of many Muslim cultures, were marginalized in this context (Ernst 1997, 199–202).

binary conceptions of Islam are part of the discourse of modernism. As the work of Köprülü exemplifies, they can be interpreted to serve, besides a scholarly and nationalist quest, also, though less overtly, a theological agenda. This agenda shines through when Köprülü chooses mainstream Sunni Islam as point of comparison for the various sorts of deviation that he describes. It is part of a set of claims around notions of purity, authenticity, essence, and continuity that perceives diversions from its own standards as a challenge in need of externalization. Both Muslim revivalists and historians of Islam such as Köprülü interpret inner-Islamic plurality, since it is perceived in relation to an implicit standard of Sunni Islam, through notions of difference—if not deviance—from this standard.

The political dimension of the resemblance between modernist and revivalist Islamic and secularist Orientalist discourses on Islam becomes most apparent when the historical and theological arguments conflate in a rhetoric of normalizing Sunnism. Part of what Köprülü and those following in his footsteps did when they conceptualized groups such as the Bektashis and the Kızılbaş-Alevis as syncretistic was—consciously or not—to provide secular scholarly evidence for delegitimizing those groups' Islamic authenticity.[41] The translation of analytic academic concepts such as syncretism into normative (for example religious or nationalist) discourses rendered these concepts powerful tools for the establishment and normalization of particular theologico-political programs. Modern Turkish secularism, or laicism (*laiklik*), is the best example. Its interest in controlling the content and boundaries of religion, and its authority to define what kinds of religious practices are legitimate in public spaces reflect the merger of Islamic modernism and political secularism, which has been part of the Turkish modernization experience, and impacted Turkish religion politics since the late Ottoman period.

The work of Köprülü bears witness to this merger. In a review of a book by Şemsettin Günaltay with the programmatic title "From Darkness to Light," Köprülü supports the author's claims with regard to the reasons for the fall of the Islamic civilization in typical modernist and revivalist fashion. Lamenting the impact of superstitious leanings from non-Islamic traditions of Jewish, Indian, and Iranian origin, which he describes as

---

41 It is from this perspective that historians of Islam were able to argue, quoting Karamustafa, that "[t]he halfhearted and in most cases merely nominal Islamization of these masses barely in touch with high literate traditions…led to the introduction of non-Islamic, especially shamanistic and animistic, beliefs and practices into Islam" (Karamustafa 1994, 11).

"parasitical, ignorant, asocial," and detrimental for Islam, Köprülü paints an ideal of Islam based on the Koran and the Sunna alone. In the continuation of his argument he develops his critique by reference to a concept of religion that he relates to Kant. According to the latter, real religion would be based on reason and law and not on myths and superstition. The real Islam would be a religion of reason and wisdom and therefore not in conflict with progress.[42] This rationalist bias is clearly visible in his scholarship. In *Early Mystics*, for example, he qualifies Bektashi beliefs as "obscure," "childish," and "far from a coherent system" (Köprülü 2006 [1919], 367). True religion is understood to be rational and coherent.

Köprülü's normative understanding of Islam is the major reason, I would argue, for the ambivalence in the way he describes the Bektashis and Alevis, especially in the early and middle phases of his work. Their "heterodoxy" and "syncretism" integrated them into the Turkish nation, while it at the same time othered them from the perspective of an Islamic mainstream influenced by modernist and revivalist notions of purity and essence. The following section from *Early Mystics*, which comes after an explanation for why the Bektashis preferred "national language and literature" over "Persian language and literature," illuminates this ambivalence:

> It is for this reason that the poets who grow up among them—most of whom have not seen any formal religious education (*medrese tahsili*) but are aware of the national taste (*millî zevk*)—have a primitive mentality bowing to superstitious beliefs (*ibtidâî ve âdeta hurâfelere tapan bir zihniyete mâlik*)..., and that they further, although they mostly use the meter and poetic forms of the *aruz* [classical Ottoman poetic meter] very badly and with mistakes, are able to use the national meter and national [poetic] forms in total harmony with the Turkish taste. (Köprülü 1966 [1919], 300)[43]

The Problem with Binary Constructs

In the work of Fuad Köprülü, the particularities of Turkish Islam are developed by means of a number of interrelated and mutually enforcing

---

42 "Tenkit ve Tahlil: Zulmetten Nura," *Tasvir-i Efkar*, June 1, 1913, as quoted and paraphrased in Asılsoy (2008, 186–187).

43 One has to concede that in his later academic work Köprülü would for the most part refrain from such strong normative language.

binaries such as center/periphery, high Islam/popular Islam, and ortho-doxy/heterodoxy. These binaries mutually reassert each other, and amount—in the way they are situated within a concept of religion that is organized around vague notions of (religious) essence and (syncretistic) change—to a circular argument of authenticity and deviance. This nor-mative conceptualization undermines the analytical value of Köprülü's interpretation of the role of inner-Islamic dynamics following the appro-priation of Islam by the Turks. The distinctions he draws between "popu-lar" or "heterodox" Islam on the one side and Sunni Islam on the other are a case in point. As with the orthodoxy/heterodoxy dichotomy, and comparable devices for the categorization of inner-Islamic difference such as Sunna/Shia, Shia/*ghulūw*, or Sunna/*rāfiḍī*, the popular/high religion dichotomy is a binary that, while clearly rooted in theological and apologetic discourses, has also been appropriated by historians of religion as a descriptive category. In the case of Islam, "[t]he operative assumption...has been that there was a watertight separation in premod-ern Islamic history between high, normative, and official religion of the cultural elite on the one hand and low, antinomian, and popular religion of the illiterate masses on the other hand" (Karamustafa 1994, 5). A criti-cal discussion of Islamicist contributions to the debate on the orthodoxy/heterodoxy binary in its application to Islam shall help to explicate my skepticism with regard to the usefulness of binaries as a heuristic tool for the categorization of inner-Islamic plurality.

"Orthodoxy" and "Heterodoxy"

Why are we heterodox? (question by a student in a class on Alevism at an Alevi center in Istanbul; Markussen 2012, 147)

Robert Langer and Udo Simon have shown that the usage of the terms orthodoxy and heterodoxy by scholars of Islam reflects a broad range of conceptualizations ranging from rigid rejection, to attempts which sup-port applying the term based on discursive definitions, to substantive posi-tions (Langer/Simon 2008, 276–280). The authors themselves seem to imply that the terms orthodoxy and heterodoxy can in principle, as long as conceived dynamically, be appropriate terms for the description of Islamic difference. In response, I would first of all argue that the broad variety in which the two terms are used in Islamicist literature points in itself to a certain conceptual ambiguity and confusion in the field of Islamic studies.[44]

Discursive definitions of "orthodoxy" and "heterodoxy" are based on the assumption of clearly definable structures of authority and power in a given historical context. It is, however, questionable whether such structures can always be clearly determined. In his critical discussion of the historiography on the early Ottomans, Kafadar has rightly argued that "it is in fact extremely difficult, if not impossible, to distinguish orthodoxy and heterodoxy in those regions or among those segments of the population that were not dominated by such structures of authority as could define and enforce a 'correct' set of beliefs and practices in the mode of learned Islam" (Kafadar 1995, 73).[45] Until the 16th century, clear boundaries between "orthodoxy" and "heterodoxy" were not yet established in Anatolia, and Kafadar therefore suggests to rather "[conceptualize] the religious history of Anatolian and Balkan Muslims living in the frontier areas of the period from the eleventh to the fifteenth centuries…in terms of a 'meta-doxy,' a state of being beyond doxies, a combination of being doxy-naive and not being doxy-minded, as well as the absence of a state that was interested in rigorously defining and strictly enforcing an orthodoxy" (Kafadar 1995, 76). Similarly, Karamustafa has argued in his discussion of early Sufi movements in Anatolia that they defy any clear boundaries between different traditions and outside influences since the kind of institutionalization that such a perspective presupposes did not yet exist. This period has to be studied in its complexity and fluidity rather than projecting later, more clearly differentiated situations on it (Karamustafa 2005, 94–95).

Using the orthodox/heterodox dichotomy for pre-16th-century Anatolian Islam, scholars such as Köprülü and those following in his footsteps are effectively back-reading concepts that are based on later historical realities into earlier contexts, thus implying a questionable structural connection between them. Kafadar observes the same problem of back-reading with regard to the Sunna/Shia distinction, which has become

---

44 Brett Wilson likewise has recently argued against the heuristic usefulness of "orthodoxy," which as analytical concept has become a burden due to the multitude of meanings attached to it: "Based on uneven criteria, theological, legal, political, and factional definitions of orthodox(y) result in a conceptual morass with no clear referent" (Wilson 2007, 172).

45 Similarly, Daniel Boyarin has observed for the relationship between Jews and Christians in late antiquity that "without the power of the orthodox Church and the Rabbis to declare people heretics and outside the system it remained impossible to declare phenomenologically who was a Jew and who was a Christian" (Boyarin 1999, 15).

a standard rhetorical device for the postulation of a continuity of "heterodox" Islam from the Babai, through Hacı Bektaş Veli and the Bektashiye, to Bedreddin, the Kızılbaş—and, as one might continue, the modern Alevis. While the Kızılbaş display clear Shiite traits, Shiism is in fact difficult to attribute to its forerunners: "The religious picture of Anatolia in the thirteenth and fourteenth centuries appears much more complex than the neat categorizations of a simple Sunni / Shi'i dichotomy would allow" (Kafadar 1995, 75–76).[46]

Kafadar's observations point to the problem of the static structure and the functionalism inherent in many applications of the orthodoxy/heterodoxy binary pair. This binary is often employed as explanatory device for the ordering of empirical data with little questioning of the historical and theoretical premises on which it is built. It is more than time for scholarship on Islam in general and on Ottoman/Turkish religious history in particular to question the normative underpinnings and heuristic value of the conceptual apparatus which it employs in the attempt to make sense of historical data. One should especially be critical of simplistic binary constructions. Scholarship on Turkish religious history is urgently in need of conceptually more critical and self-conscious perspectives that not only take seriously the complex realities and specific power relations within particular historical contexts, but also create awareness of the particular histories of these binaries themselves. Rather than getting wound up in a seemingly never-ending debate about the heuristic usefulness of certain binary pairs it might be more interesting to follow a genealogical approach and ask about the work of such concepts and the power dynamics in which this work unfolds.[47]

For a critical investigation of the scholarly debate on matters of inner-Islamic plurality/difference, it is useful to make explicit two kinds of distinctions. First, we need to distinguish clearly between substantive and discursive approaches, or, as Paula Schrode refers to them, between dogmatic and interactional approaches (Schrode 2008, 395–396). Second, we need to differentiate between emic (i.e., culturally specific) and etic (i.e.,

---

46 As for pre-16th century Anatolia, the question of the spread of Shiism has received more critical academic attention than the more fundamental question of the extent to which it makes sense at all to postulate for that historical context the existence of clearly distinguishable Sunni and Shiite "orthodoxies." For references to the first question see Kafadar (1995, 171–172 fn 40–43); for the second see Dressler (2005).

47 Talal Asad's work on the genealogies of "religion" and the "secular" are path-breaking examples in that regard; see Asad (1993 and 2003).

culturally neutral), perspectives. It is self-evident that emic perspectives on those matters that scholars of Islam discuss with concepts such as orthodoxy and heterodoxy are of the substantive variety. A first methodological problem is with regard to the extent to which we can claim that analytical (etic) concepts of the Western scholarly discourse on religion, such as orthodoxy and heterodoxy, are adequate representations of culturally specific (emic) but by no means homogeneous realities of non-Western societies and cultures. It is rather difficult to find an Islamic equivalent to what the term orthodoxy connotes in Christian discourses, wherein it was coined. Translated into the discourse of Islam the term loses descriptive and analytical clarity. The various terms offered by Islamicists as Islamic equivalents "refer to characteristics that cross legal, theological, and religio-political divides and depend upon interpretation to be applied to particular groups, beliefs, and practices" (Wilson 2007, 172).

Since the terms suggested in Islamicist literature as indigenous equivalents of "heterodoxy" carry the same problems (see Langer/Simon 2008, 282–288), one ought to ask what can be gained from discussing matters of inner-Islamic difference by means of concepts foreign to Islamic discourses instead of, paraphrasing Asad, trying to translate and represent the historically situated discourses of culturally distinctive actors (Asad 1986, 7). This also points to the question of agency and the problem of who, within the encounter between scholarly discourses and historical life-worlds, is in a position to ascribe hierarchies and norms of Islamic dogma in an authoritative way—and, one might further ask, authoritative for whom and on which grounds. Whereas secular as well as Islamic religionist positions hold on to the claim of adequate representation and justify substantive definitions of Islamic "orthodoxy" and "heterodoxy," discursive/interactional approaches are more tuned into the politics and dynamics that create "orthodoxy" and "heterodoxy" as positions of relative strength or lack thereof within a particular religio-political discourse.

While I do not want to deny that such discursive approaches to "orthodoxy"/"heterodoxy" can have heuristic value, there still remain some critical methodological questions to be addressed. To be precise, I do not mean to contest the existence of binaries as discursive reality within certain religio-political contexts. What I do want to put into critical perspective, however, is the work that is done when binaries—especially those with roots in particular theological discourses—are objectified as analytical categories. In the case of inner-Islamic plurality, its description through binary oppositions virtually renders this plurality into difference, the contours of which tend to become sharper and less pervious the more a (modernist) religion discourse based on notions of essences and clear boundaries takes hold.

Approaching religious difference qua binary oppositions reflects the legitimate aim to structure complex social and historical realities. The orthodoxy/heterodoxy binary was initially introduced by outside observers as a classification tool with the objective of reducing complexity in an attempt to make sense of intricate theological and political realities of Islam by creating an analogy with Christian conventions of dogmatic differentiation.[48] Vernacular Islamic discourses, however, have their own concepts with their own specific significations,[49] and this again brings us to the question of what is happening in the process of the translation of emic into etic concepts and discourses. To the degree that apologetics are a constitutive element of inner-Islamic discourses on the legitimacy of religious difference, one could say that these autochthonous, apologetic discourses are more honest than the terminology of Western Islamicists cloaked in the mantle of scientific objectivity. Muslim vernaculars are also more complex and nuanced, as a brief overview of those terms that were historically used by Muslim apologetics to mark forms of religious deviance, and secondarily associated by Islamicists with "heterodoxy" and/or "heresy," shows.

The Koranic *kāfir* (Turk. *kafir*), "unbeliever" is the most general term used for those considered outside of the realm of acceptable religion; also Koranic is the term *mulḥid* (Turk. *mülhid*), which signifies disbelief, blasphemy, and/or apostasy. Non-Koranic are the terms *zindīq* (Turk. *zındık*), used for both non-Muslims and Muslim heretics, usually translated as heresy, atheism, or unbelief;[50] the term *ghālī* (pl. *ghulāt*), used in Shiite heresiography for "exaggerators"—especially with regard to the role and status of Ali, whom those labeled by the term were accused of considering

---

48 The overview of such Islamicist conceptualizations provided by Langer and Simon shows this clearly. See Langer and Simon (2008); for the term orthodoxy see also Wilson (2007).

49 For a historical overview of the concepts used by Islamic heresiographers in their attempt to classify inner-Islamic difference and establish normative standards of Islam see Ocak (1998, 1–68).

50 "This term became prevalent during the consolidation of Sunni orthodoxy beginning in the tenth century, when classical Sunni heresiographies identified a broad spectrum of non-conformist groups and individuals. This development cleared the ground for an identification of 'orthodox Muslims,' designated from then on as the 'people of the Sunna and the community' (*ahl as-sunna wa-'l-ǧamāʿa*) or the 'people of the consensus' (*ahl al-iǧmāʿ*), i. e. 'the Sunnīs'" (Langer/Simon 2008, 284).

divine; and *rāfiḍī* (Turk. *rafizī*), another term designating a heretic or schismatic, originally formed within an inner-Shiite apologetic context, used to indicate the nonrecognition of the Sunni tradition as expressed in the cursing of the first three Sunni caliphs, who according to the Shiite narrative of early Islamic history were usurpers of an office that had been reserved for Ali (Winter 2010, 17; Langer/Simon 2008, 284–285).

These pejorative signifiers are discursive tools by means of which the legalist and scripturalist tradition of Islam historically delineated its boundaries. One should reflect on the context and scope of such othering practices. Where apologetic discourses are established, a need is expressed to mark socioreligious difference in a definite and dogmatic manner. The Kızılbaş-Alevis have been subject to all of these terms. In Ottoman documents they were referred to in derogatory and apologetic language, variously being labeled *rafizī*, *mülhid*, and *zındık* and at times punished on grounds of their heresy (see Ahmet Refik 1932; Imber 1979; Ocak 1998).

Beyond their obvious theological biases there is another caveat that should be considered when dealing with apologetic discourses. Independent of the non-dogmatic and potentially very material claims that such discourses may aim to justify, they tend to be the discourses of religious elites, which do not necessarily tell us much about the reality of the implied differences in the social interactions between various individuals, groups, and institutions. In other words, apologetic discourses should first of all be taken as just that—discourses. The question of their relation with social practices is important and should always be considered, but for analytical reasons be treated separately. Apologetic discourses are not necessarily descriptive representations of social facts/practices, but often rather propagandist tools of socioreligious defamation (and justification thereof).

The case of the Kızılbaş is a good example that illustrates how apologetics are related to politics. It was precisely the political confrontation between the Ottomans and the Safavids that helped—by denouncing the religious orientation of the respective other—to establish Sunni and Shiite standards of faith, respectively. In the process, the Kızılbaş, squeezed in between Ottoman and Safavid political interests, were marginalized as heretics not only by Sunni Ottomans, but gradually also by the Shiite Safavids with whom they previously had been aligned.[51] It is for

---

51 See Dressler (2005). Similarly, Boyarin has suggested that "Christian orthodoxy produced itself via the making of heresy and heretics" (Boyarin 1999, 16).

this reason that I am skeptical of approaches to "orthodoxy" and "hetero-doxy" that fail to specify the causal connection between the establishment of religio-political authority and the delegitimization/marginalization of competing others.[52]

Caveats of Cross-Cultural Translation

Apparently not concerned about the work of signification done by apologetic terms, Köprülü employed them as if they were but descriptive categories. While continuing to use apologetic language from within the Islamic tradition, his writings from the mid-1920s onward also introduced language from outside of the Islamic tradition, as discussed above. In the following, "heterodoxy" in particular became charged with reducing the variety of marginalizing terms from within Islamic apologetics to one single concept. Consequently, the specifics of Islamic apologetic language were reduced to their otherness from what was posited as "orthodox," that is, Sunni, Islam.

The problem of translation is not confined to the arguably dated original writings of Köprülü himself, but is still very much with us. Instances of this can be seen in the translation of *Early Mystics* by Gary Leiser and Robert Dankoff. Thus they translate, for example, the expression "Ehl-i Sünnet akîdelerine aykırı," literally "against the dogmatic principles of the people of the Sunna," which is an expression that refers to those who follow the tradition of Islam in line with the recognized schools of Sunni law, as "unorthodox" (Köprülü 1966 [1919], 280 fn 50 and Köprülü 2006 [1919], 355 fn 57). In the same book they render the expression "müteşerriâne ve zâhidâne bir ahlâk umdeleri," the literal translation of which would be something like "sharia-conform and ascetic ethical principles" into "principles of an orthodox pietistic asceticism" (Köprülü 1966 [1919], 260–261

---

52 Langer and Simon, for example, define orthodoxy as "a dominant position in a dynamic interacting system which balances change and stability, and it is something to be gained and to be lost. There is no religious orientation that is *per se* destined to represent orthodoxy in Islam. Orthodoxy begins with a claim and must meet certain requirements, such as a body of texts, a genealogy, flexibility, comprehensibility, the ability to integrate deviation, to manage boundaries, and produce consent" (Langer/Simon 2008, 281). The emphasis on "integration of deviation" and "production of consent" might fit well with the self-representation of particular religious groups in dominance. What this definition fails to specify is the role of power and politics in the relationship between "orthodoxy" and "deviation." It thus gives the in my opinion questionable impression that "dominant positions" within particular contexts tended to be established in rather conciliatory ways.

and Köprülü 2006 [1919], 309). Especially the last example reflects a terminological de-Islamization and Christianization of Köprülü's original text,
written at a time when he himself still used primarily Islamic concepts in
his description of inner-Islamic difference.

In the study of Anatolian Islam there has as of yet not been enough
sensibility regarding the impact of the use of apologetic qualifiers as conceptual tools, be they of the Christian (such as heresy, sectarianism, heterodoxy), or the Muslim kind (*kufr, ghulūw, ifrāṭ, rafḍ, ilḥād*). It is apparent
that with the translation of concepts from religious into academic discourses and vice versa these concepts obtain new meanings. This needs to
be considered. Such translation is a rather serious matter for those labeled
by these terms. It is one thing to be called a heretic on religious grounds,
where the rules of argumentation are marked by religious semantics and
the possibility of coercion and punishment limited by religious law and
custom; it is a different matter being declared religiously deviant by secular authorities and their often more immediate ways of coercion within
the context of the nation-state. One needs to understand that the offense
of heresy is always more than merely a transgression of dogma. To the
extent that religious formations are social formations, religious deviations
are social deviations and their repercussions cannot be reduced to a religious sphere imagined to be totally separate from other spheres of life—
contrary to what the modern religion discourse with its secularist bias
would make us believe.

Another issue is the translation of concepts between cultural contexts. It
can be argued that over the past two centuries, within the historical dynamics shaped by colonial encounters and the globalization of Western-style
models and modes of secular modernity, the conceptual spaces of the
Western discourse on religion and discourses of Islam got intertwined
to an unprecedented extent. Post-Enlightenment conceptions of (world-)
religion were appropriated to Islam by both Muslim and non-Muslim
scholars and activists (see Tayob 2009). As Karamustafa argues, this inter-
twining is intricate and complex, and scholars have barely started to pay
attention to the theoretical questions and the methodological challenges
that it raises. The pitfalls of viewing Islam through the spectacles of a universalized, but in its basic structure and semantics Protestant/Christian,
understanding of religion have been noted, and attempts have been made
to explore the ways in which the category of religion informs modern
Muslim understandings of *din*. I agree with Karamustafa that the politics
involved in the modern reconfiguration of Islam as a "world religion," as

well as the casting of Islam as the mirror opposite of a privatized religion in line with the demands of liberal secularity, all require further in-depth analysis (Karamustafa 2015).

I argue that the parallel use of concepts from within the Islamic apologetic tradition and concepts from outside the Islamic discourse (such as syncretism, heresy, and heterodoxy) without distinguishing between emic and etic concepts and the translation processes in between obscures their normative work and contributes to analytical fuzziness. The introduction of concepts such as orthodoxy, heterodoxy, and syncretism into historical rationalizations of inner-Islamic plurality contributes to a leveling of the particularities of inner-Islamic plurality and in that sense constitutes a secularizing act.

The translation of Christian assumptions of religious difference and their relation to theological authority structures onto Islam leads to questionable results. When those formerly referred to as *rafizī, mülhid, zındık,* or *kızılbaş* are reconceptualized as heterodox, then the specific meanings that had traditionally marked those who were labeled in this way get lost.[53] Subsuming and uniting the more complex apologetic concepts of Islamic discourse under the term heterodoxy is a reductionist procedure based on the problematic epistemological assumption of the translatability of the Christian/Western concept of religion onto realities outside of its discursive universe.[54] From the opposite perspective, the translation of apologetic significations from within the Islamic tradition into Western discourses on religion is equally problematic. To the extent that the pejorative connotations of terms such as *rafizī, mülhid,* and *zındık* are being retained in the term heterodoxy, the implicit promise of emancipation that the latter term carries, namely to have as an Islamically neutral term the potential to free the thusly signified from the normative confines of Islamic discourse, and ground their otherness on a less biased basis, is rendered pointless. We need to pay more attention to the implications of the translation of concepts from the universalist (world-)religion discourse into other "religious" contexts and in particular Islam. We should on the one side ask

---

53 *Zindīq* (pl. *zanādiqa*), originally a Persian designation for Manichaeans, has in the Muslim context secondarily been associated with religion outside the Islamic law and apostasy, often used synonymously to the term *mulḥid* (De Blois 2002). *Mulḥid* is of Koranic origin and was since earliest Islamic times used to designate religious deviators from within the Islamic tradition (Madelung 2012).

54 Derrida has referred to this process as *globalatinization* (Derrida 1998). For a sharp methodological criticism of this translation process see Dubuisson (2003).

what happens when concepts formed outside the Islamic discourse (such as religion, ethics, morality, ritual, mysticism, law, orthodoxy/heterodoxy, heresy, syncretism, secularism/secularity) are applied to and get integrated into the languages of Islam. Equally important is the question as to how Islamic concepts such as for example *din, sharia, tasawwuf,* and *madhhab,* to name just a few prominent ones, are impacted by sub-integration under a generalized concept of religion and the translation processes that this sub-integration asks for. Translation should thereby not be seen as a necessarily mono-directional practice. The concepts of the modern (world-) religion discourse do not remain untouched by those things that they name and signify. Contrariwise, we have to assume that they themselves are being modified during the process of their own expansion to various "religious" traditions outside of the contexts from which they have historically emerged. In short, I argue that we need more critical awareness with regard to the various practices of translation and their normative work that scholarly work on religion/Islam is based on and part of.

Power Imbalances and Agency

The relationship between Orientalist scholarship and its objects of study is marked, as we know at least since Edward Said, by power imbalances. Such imbalance is also strongly felt in the complex politics of translation of "religion" beyond the Christian West. While acknowledging this fact, it should at the same time not lead us to underestimate the agency of "non-Western" locals in the discursive practices through which "religion" and its associates are locally appropriated (in whatever form). Charles Hallisey has discussed "the cultural interchange that occurs between the native and the Orientalist in the construction of Western knowledge about 'the Orient'" as "intercultural mimesis" (King 1999, 148). In other words, we need to think about the appropriation of the Western discourse of religion in a manner that does not reduce local actors to the role of passive objects, but instead focuses on "local productions of meaning"—that is, takes seriously the agency of locals in the encounter with Orientalist knowledge and practices (King 1999, 149–150; see also van der Veer 2001). This perspective leads us to a so-far-not-discussed aspect of the translation of Western concepts of religion into non-Western contexts, namely the subsequent sedimentation of these concepts within different layers of non-Western vernacular languages, in particular their appropriation by those to whom they are applied.

It is not surprising that, as has been observed, contemporary Alevis are appropriating certain language from the scholarly discourse, such as the terms heterodoxy and syncretism (Langer/Simon 2008, 285; Karolewski 2008, 437 and 456); nor that they adopt some of the narratives that 20th-century discourses about them have produced, such as, for example, Köprülü's idea of their shamanist heritage or his assertion that Alevism has roots in the Yesevi tradition—which is, as Ocak has pointed out, not part of the traditional knowledge of the groups in the broader Alevi tradition (Ocak 2005, 244). It is, however, not enough to assert, as Privratsky did within a different research context, that "Kazaks believe they are shamanists because their ethnographers have told them they are" (Privratsky 2001, 10). The questions that need to be addressed as a consequence of this observation are: What do terms such as heterodoxy and syncretism signify once translated into the Alevi vernacular and thus becoming a means of Alevi self-representation? What are the claims that are put forward through them, and who is the audience they are directed to? And finally, what are the broader politics (of secularism and nationalism) into which such intercultural mimesis is integrated?

These questions ought to balance modes of inquiry that tend to represent local actors and discourses as subordinated if not victimized in relation to the academic and political power of authoritative discourses. Instead, attention needs to be given to the dynamics of the interaction between various actors in the inscription, adjustment, and appropriation of concepts and discourses of "religion." Hege Irene Markussen's study of classes on Alevi faith at an Alevi center in Istanbul provides a valuable account of how the mainstream historiographical discourse on Alevism, as epitomized in the work of Fuad Köprülü, is being translated into vernacular Alevi knowledges (Markussen 2012, 123–147). It exemplifies how academic concepts such as shamanism, heterodoxy, and syncretism are appropriated by Alevis. Separated from their pejorative undertones and filled instead with positive meanings (national and pluralist, centered around Anatolia as major axis of Alevi difference-understood-as-richnes s), this appropriation of academic concepts and knowledges contributes to the formation of a modern Alevi identity. As Markussen observes, the teachers of the Alevi classes that she studied "equated the syncretistic nature of Alevilik with notions of authenticity and purity—which their nationalist and academic predecessors had reserved for the Sunni-Islam of the majority population" (Markussen 2012, 146).

The Theologico-Political Work of Binary Concepts

Scholars who use the terms orthodoxy and heterodoxy in their work on Islam try to describe and explain theological, legal, as well as political matters of legitimacy, hegemony, authority, and difference. Taking a step back, we should ask what we gain when we reconstruct inner-religious relations by means of a conceptual device that directs our thinking toward binaries and dichotomies. To the extent that the orthodoxy/heterodoxy binary is defined substantively, it feeds into essentialist, ahistorical conceptions of religion. Substantive definitions, however, are ill-prepared to explain historical change and the dynamics of inner-religious pluralism. As part of his criticism of the Orientalist binary high literate/popular Islam, Karamustafa has argued that

> the methodological poverty of the two-tiered model of religion . . . not only fails to generate . . . an explanatory analysis but even obscures the obvious need for one by denying popular religion a historical dimension. The vulgar, it is understood, is timeless. Reliance on a dichotomous view of Islamic religion thus opens the way for the preponderance of externalistic explanations such as "survival of non-Islamic beliefs and practices under Islamic cover." (Karamustafa 1994, 10)

It is easy to extend Karamustafa's criticism to conceptualizations of Kızılbaş-Alevism. Defined as "heterodox," the Kızılbaş-Alevis are kept in a structural dependence to a proposed "orthodoxy." This secondary, derivative position is cemented by attributing "survivals"/"remnants" from other, that is to say, non-orthodox Islamic and non-Muslim traditions, to them. I claim that denying religiocultural formations such as Kızılbaş-Alevism originality and authenticity, depicting them instead through concepts that define them either by their supposed lack in comparison to the "orthodox high-culture" or alternatively as fusion with "unauthentic"/"secondary"/"foreign" religious or cultural elements, works toward the normalization of theologico-political hierarchies and is counterproductive to critical historical analysis. Scholarly work should not turn into an uncritical tool for the reification of vernacular patterns of hegemony, but instead be conscious and critical of the work of its concepts—especially so when these concepts are involved in discriminating politics.

　　Two-tiered models of Islam are ultimately counterproductive to an understanding of Islam as a dynamic tradition and therefore of limited use as tools for historical (or sociological) analysis. What is needed instead of the black-and-white mode evoked by binary concepts are open-ended approaches that give enough space for contingencies, convergences, as well as multilayered and multifocal perspectives that appreciate social and historical realities as an arrangement of an infinite number of grey tones. We can study Islam (and, indeed, any religion) as a historical subject only through the actions of those who associate with it, that is, through individuals and different kinds of groups and the ways they interpret and live Islam in complex and multilayered modes of incorporation, assimilation, and appropriation of practices and beliefs of whatever "origins." Those who in the context of historical analysis make ontological evaluations of the relation of practices between two or more religious traditions should at least specify the epistemological grounds on which they base their judgment and make explicit the political, theological, or philosophical convictions on which they are grounded.

Binary taxonomies such as the distinction between "major" and "minor" traditions, "high" and "popular," or "orthodox" and "heterodox" religions, and so forth lose their explanatory value the closer they approach emic perspectives. Of course, it is a sociological truism that the formation of ideal-typical categories requires a certain reductionism. Russell McCutcheon argues that the function of "binary pairs" is "to mark a discursive boundary of a structure that manages the various items that constitute actual historical existence" (McCutcheon 2007, 190). In other words, binary concepts are, beyond being heuristic tools, a means of world ordering, that is, "devices that we use and argue over while making a world that suits our differing purposes" (McCutcheon 2007, 184). McCutcheon's reflections are helpful in disentangling heuristic from political motivations behind the formation, legitimation, and maintenance of binary concepts. We have to ask to what extent binary constructs may constitute tools for the justification of particular world-ordering mechanisms that guide our perception—and to what extent they prevent us from perceiving and giving voice to those aspects that are too complex to be expressed within the constraints of binary schemes. Therefore, the more simplistic categories are (this being probably not the least reason for their popularity) the more urgent one needs to critically weigh their heuristic usefulness. As for the orthodox/heterodox binary, it fits into functionalist notions of organicity, which foster illusions of the possibility to comprehensively capture the complex socio-politico-theological dimensions of particular social contexts. I therefore follow Asad, who, within the context of his criticism

of dualist approaches to Muslim societies, suggested to rather try to com-
prehend "the social structures of Muslim societies in terms of overlapping
spaces and times, so that the Middle East becomes a focus of convergences" (Asad 1986, 11).[55]

Binary pairs have an affinity with the semantics of modern discourses
on religion, in particular the world-ordering machinery of secularism.
Drawing on Catherine Bell's work, Janet Jakobsen and Ann Pellegrini
have pointed out that the oppositions that are created as an extension of
the religious/secular binary, such as universalism/particularity and bond-
age/freedom form a circular argument, in which each binary depends on
the others: "The secularization thesis remains a site of manifold academic
and political investments precisely because of this set of associations. To
give up on the idea of secularization is to raise the specter of abandon-
ing the concepts of freedom, universalism, modernization, and progress"
(Jakobsen/Pellegrini 2008, 6). Asad similarly insinuates that binary constructs such as sacred/profane "pervade modern secular discourse" and
are in direct complicity with secularist knowledge regimes (Asad 2003,
23). Instead of reifying them, Asad's writings invite us to reflect on the
work of binary concepts within discourses of modernity and its obsession with essences, boundaries, and divergence (Asad 1986, 11–12). This
is important since that obsession has had a major impact on the field
of religious studies, and related Orientalist disciplines of secular knowledge such as Islamic studies, and provides the epistemic framework for
binary concepts as devices for the ordering of inner-religious plurality as
difference.

It is not without irony that it has been an essay by Asad himself, one
of the pioneers of the deciphering of the modern genealogy of "religion," that has contributed to a resuscitation of the concept of orthodoxy
in Islamic studies and increased confusion regarding its proper application. In *Idea of an Anthropology of Islam*, Asad defines "orthodoxy [as]
a relationship of power. Wherever Muslims have the power to regulate,
uphold, require, or adjust *correct* practices, and to condemn, exclude,
undermine, or replace *incorrect* ones, there is the domain of orthodoxy"
(Asad 1986, 15). Asad's aim in this text is to chart a new way of conceptualizing Islam anthropologically, critical of previous attempts of both
the nominalist and the substantive kind. He suggests understanding
Islam as a "discursive tradition," which he specifies as a tradition that

---

55 Cf. Boyarin's wave theory approach, discussed above.

"relates itself to the founding texts of the Qur'an and the Hadith" (Asad 1986, 14).[56]

For Asad, discursive power is not restricted to particular elite institutions, but is manifest in different levels of society: "A practice is Islamic because it is authorized by the discursive traditions of Islam, and is so taught to Muslims—whether by an *'alim*, a *khatib*, a Sufi *shaykh*, or an untutored parent" (Asad 1986, 15). However, as has been argued by Ovamir Anjum among others, Asad's relational approach ("orthodoxy" as "relationship of power") seems to be in tension with his recognition of the Koran and the Hadith as foundational texts of the Islamic tradition (Anjum 2007, 666–669). The question is whether this recognition does not privilege certain interpretations of Islam, namely those closely aligned to said foundational texts—and in this way could be understood as itself contributing to the formulation of an "orthodoxy of Islam" (Wilson 2007, 184). I do think that the critical questions raised by Anjum and Wilson regarding the system of reference for Asad's notion of orthodoxy are valid, especially with regard to the preference/privileging of textual authority (Koran and Hadith) over other sources of Islamic authority (ritual and personal charisma, for example) in *Anthropology of Islam*. In defense of Asad, it is my understanding that Asad's recognition of the Koran and the Hadith as foundational texts of Islam should not be read as a theologico-political (or normative) argument, but rather as a historical/anthropological (that is, descriptive) observation.

One should also note that Asad did not conceptualize "orthodoxy" with reference to "heterodoxy" as its binary other. Here and elsewhere Asad is very critical of binary oppositions (Asad 1986, 11–12; Asad 2003, 23). As a "relationship of power," his notion of orthodoxy contains that which is disputed within itself, rather than projecting it outside of itself as dichotomized other (i.e., as "heterodoxy"). Pursuing a genealogical approach, he is not interested in the systematics of categories, but rather in explaining their work in discourse and practice. Put differently, if I understand him correctly, orthodoxy is not a phenomenological category for him and to this extent should not be understood as tacitly fostering a particular substantive definition of Islam—which is why it cannot have a binary other. As empirical category it reflects discursive positions, but is not interested in qualifying and/or normalizing dogmatic or political/historical claims.

---

56 It should be recognized that already Marshall Hodgson, in his celebrated *The Venture of Islam* (1974), approached "orthodoxy" discursively in relation to positions of power; see Wilson (2007, 172–173).

The question remains as to whether it is meaningful to engage with the issue of Islamic normativity solely with a focus on scripture. Non-scriptural forms of normativity have always been part of Islamic cultures—be it in the form of the charismatic Sufi or Shiite saint, the authority of lineage, or the various, often regionally specific, forms of popular Islamic practices (such as meditative and ecstatic, potentially transformative rituals) themselves. I therefore think that it is ultimately wrong to conceive of scriptural and non-scriptural (charisma- or practice-based) forms of authority in Islam as being in categorical opposition to each other, even if certain Islamic polemics for sure suggest just that. In practice, however, scriptural and non-scriptural forms of authority in Islam very often complement rather than exclude each other.

Beyond Dichotomous Conceptualizations of Inner-Islamic Difference

Given the methodological and theoretical problems of binary concepts in general, and the orthodoxy/heterodoxy binary in particular, I argue against using the latter as an analytical category except for the specific heuristic purpose of subverting essentialist understandings of religion. As I have tried to show, the methodological problems that accompany such binary concepts are manifold. The very logic of the binary construct tends to reify functional perspectives, which, if brashly and uncritically read backward through history, can lead to questionable teleological *longue durée* assumptions in disregard of historical contingencies, intra- and inner-religious convergences, and the fluidity of religious boundaries in many premodern contexts. Such an approach partakes in defining religion in a static way that is likely to cement truisms about religious essences and differences.

Alternatively, I would suggest focusing on the power dynamics involved in the assertion of religious binaries and the way they relate to how inner- as well as intra-religious boundaries are established and made to appear evident in the first place. Instead of reifying particular notions of Islamic culture through binaries introduced from outside, we should scrutinize the work of such binaries both in scholarly discourses as well as within the vernacular languages into which they are translated. We should further attend to what they accomplish when they move back and forth between emic and etic discourses. This requires recognition of the imbalances of power that shape discourses on religion, to which scholars of religion/Islam themselves contribute. More principally, we should within

our analysis of things associated with religion, and Islam more specifically, strive for perspectives that increase rather than decrease complexity.
Reductionism should always be serving a clearly defined heuristic purpose and not turn into an iron cage that determines the path of a particular
investigation.[57]

If binaries such as orthodoxy/heterodoxy are used at all, than they
should be used with the goal of going beyond their confines—for example
as a subversive tool in uprooting hegemonic structures of authority and
their discourses (scholarly, political, religious). The appropriation of normalizing concepts such as the orthodoxy/heterodoxy distinction by those
generally disadvantaged by the politics of these concepts can be such a
subversive act. When Alevis, for example, turn to the term heterodoxy
in their self-signification and reinterpret it positively then they challenge
the power dynamics in the politics of theologico-political signification.
Paraphrasing Bhabha, they produce ambivalence by articulating and
re-implicating signs of cultural difference. Such re-signification can be
understood as an act of resistance against dominant discourses of cultural
hegemony (Bhabha 1994, 110–111).

To conclude these reflections on the taxonomies of inner-Islamic difference, I argue for critical awareness and reinvestigation of the conceptual
heritage of Orientalist scholarship on Islam. The concepts that I scrutinized in this chapter derive from two sources, which have some genealogical overlaps, namely (1) apologetic discourses from within the Islamic
tradition, and (2) the modern (world-)religion discourse, which developed
originally in Western Europe, but went global with the spread of Western
political, material, and intellectual hegemony over other parts of the world.
In order to understand and analyze the discussed concepts as historical
concepts we need to be aware of their genealogy. Such awareness can help
us to decipher and eradicate some of the implicit normative assumptions
inherent in parts of the conceptual toolbox of those academic disciplines
that work on religion in general and Islam in particular. This is a precondition for new and, I would argue, more interesting inquiries into the complex dynamics of Islamic history and culture. Regarding the orthodoxy/

---

57 However, Wilson is right when he argues in his critical discussion of Islamicists' usage
of "orthodoxy" that simplicity is hardly the sole or major reason for scholars sticking to such
a controversially discussed concept (Wilson 2007, 186). The continuing popularity of terms
such as orthodoxy and heterodoxy in Islamicist literature is rather to be analyzed in the
above-discussed context of the hierarchies and authorities that form the background to the
translation of concepts of religion from Christian to other religious/cultural contexts.

heterodoxy binary, for example, questions that ought to be highlighted should be—beyond functionalist and substantive approaches—of the genealogical and discursive kind, such as the following: How are notions of orthodoxy/heterodoxy established in particular discourses, and what is their theologico-political work? Who is in a position to define "orthodoxy" and "heterodoxy" in which contexts? How should the recognition of continuous cultural mimesis between scholarly and vernacular discourses impact the way in which we conceptualize the relationship between emic and etic perspectives in our work on Islam? And last but not least, what are the reasons why parts of Islamic and religious studies are still indebted to a religion discourse based on hierarchies of "doxa"?

6

Alevi and Alevilik in the Work of Fuad Köprülü and His Legacy

THE AIM OF this chapter is to describe and analyze the concept of Alevism as it appeared and developed in the writings of Mehmed Fuad Köprülü. Next to Baha Said Bey, Köprülü's writings had the most immediate and enduring effect on what the terms Alevi and Alevilik would henceforward signify in Turkey. Although the content of their writings, agendas, and methods were rather different, the two men also had important things in common. They were both, although to different degree, involved in Turkish nationalist politics and organizations in the vicinity of the CUP, even if Köprülü never became a member of the party itself. Both started to write on Alevi-related topics during the last years of the Ottoman Empire and continued this work in the Turkish Republic. A further commonality is that both were in close contact with Ziya Gökalp and influenced by his ideas.

In Köprülü's and Baha Said's texts, Alevism and the communities associated with it were conceptualized in an entirely unprecedented way. I argue that their approach amounted to the creation of a new ethno-religious category in line with the aims of the nationalist project and in direct opposition to previous speculations of Western observers, many of whom had seen in the Kızılbaş-Alevis remnants of ancient Anatolian and Christian cultures and traditions. In the following decades this new conceptualization of the Kızılbaş groups as "Alevi" slowly became part of the Turkish vernacular; gradually, it was also appropriated as a primary identity marker by those—among themselves rather heterogeneous—groups to which the new label was applied.

The Meanings of Alevi in Köprülü's Scholarship

In the following pages I will reconstruct the various connotations of the term Alevi in the writings of Fuad Köprülü. This overview helps to identify the multifaceted nature and the ambiguities of the processes through which the Kızılbaş were re-signified as Alevis at the crossroads of Islamic discourse, Turkish nationalism, and Orientalist scholarship.

Throughout the work of Köprülü we find the terms *Alevi* (both as adjective and name) and the abstract noun *Alevilik* ("Alevism") given five different meanings: (1) as Shiite in the general sense of the term, that is, in contrast to Sunnism; (2) as admirer of the *ahl al-bayt*; (3) as "extreme" Shiite; further, (4) as an adjective to signify a particular religious disposition characteristic of certain, not necessarily related, mostly Turkish, "heterodox" groups in Anatolia; and finally, (5) as name for those *ocak*-centered groups that were historically labeled Kızılbaş. At times, he appears to blend several of these meanings of the term in the same text, and occasionally, when the immediate context does not provide clarification, it is difficult to be totally sure in which way he wants the term to be understood, or whether, alternatively, the term is supposed to connote a number of the above-listed meanings simultaneously.[1] The first four significations we all find used relatively regularly in Köprülü's work since the early 1920s. Before that, including *Early Mystics*, he did not yet use the term Alevi, but rather more specific terms such as *ehl-i beyt* and Shia. The fifth signification appears in this explicit sense only in one text from 1935.

Alevis as Shiites

Köprülü appears to have used the term Alevi for the first time in his *History of Turkish Literature*. Therein he describes the poet al-Farazdaq from the early Islamic period as being known to be "a sincere Alevi" (*samimi bir "Alevî"*) (Köprülü 1980 [1920/21], 103). As far as it can be understood from the text, the notion Alevi here indicates a Shiite inclination in a general sense. Another example we find in a response Köprülü wrote to an article by Franz Babinger in *Islam in Anatolia*.[2] Both Köprülü and Babinger

---

1 Unfortunately, he never published the second volume of *Türk Halk Edebiyatı Ansiklopedisi*, for which he had announced an entry "Alevî" (Köprülü 1935b, 37–38).

2 According to Babinger's thesis, Anatolia had from the Seljuk to the early Ottoman periods been under strong Persian influence, and this influence extended over many spheres of life including art, architecture, intellectual life, language, and religion. The Seljuks were Alevi ("'Alīden ('alewī)"), that is, Shiites and Shiism would have been the official state religion (Babinger 1922, 128–130). According to Babinger, this Persian/Alevi/Shiite influence continued throughout the first centuries of Ottoman rule with prominent examples being the Sufi orders of the Mevlevis and the Bektashis (Babinger 1922, 133). In his response Köprülü defends not only the predominance of Turkish over Persian influences on the Seljuks and

qualify Shiism, in more and less explicit ways, as "heterodox," juxtaposed to an ideal of Sunnism as normative or "orthodox" Islam (Köprülü 2005 [1922], 22–24; Babinger 1922, 128–130).

Alevis as *Ahl al-Bayt* Admirers

The dominant use of the term Alevi in *Islam in Anatolia* is as an epithet for those who strongly adore Ali and the *ahl al-bayt*. It is in this more specific sense that Köprülü holds, against Babinger, that those Turks characterized by the latter as Shiite were in fact Sunni, notwithstanding "Alevi sympathies"—an example of which would be the 14th-century Mongol conqueror Timur (Köprülü 2005 [1922], 96). As Köprülü explains, Timur was, despite his Alevism (*Alevilik*), a Sunni Muslim of the Hanafi school of law. "Alevi influences had long been rather strong among even the most fanatical Sunnis, and in particular among Sufi orders such as the Yeseviye and Naqshibendiye" (Köprülü 2005 [1922], 94–95). Alevism (*Alevilik*) would indeed have been "a common characteristic among the Sunnī Şūfīs in virtually every period" (Köprülü 1993 [1922], 49). This also appears to be the earliest text in which Köprülü has used the abstract noun *Alevilik* (Alevism).

In another text of the same year he provides us with a sociologically more specific contextualization of the term Alevi. Thus he explains that "the saz poets were usually devoted to the people of the house (*muhibb-i ehl-i beyt*), that is *Alevî*, and a large number of them [were] Bektaşi" (Köprülü 1999 [1922], 266–267). This is a reference to the bards (*aşık, ozan*) of Muslim Anatolia, to whom he had already in *Origins* ascribed remnants of shamanist practices. "Alevi" is in these examples understood to be a general term for those Muslims who adore Ali and the *ahl al-bayt* (cf. Köprülü 2005 [1922], 23 fn 24). Already in *Early Mystics* Köprülü had criticized, if only in passing, the practice of categorically ascribing Shiism to currents who exalt Ali and the Twelve Imams (Köprülü 1966 [1919], 128–129 fn 41). In other words, all Shiites are Alevi in the sense of being *ahl al-bayt* devotees, but not all Alevis in that sense are Shiites.[3]

---

early Ottomans, but rigorously rejects the idea of the Seljuks' having been Shiite (Köprülü 1993 [1922], 68 fn 33).

3 We find this broader meaning of Alevi also in Babinger's text—for example, when he talks about "Ali adoration." However, unlike Köprülü, Babinger does not explicitly distinguish between Shiites and "Ali admirers" (Babinger 1922, 133). But Köprülü's use of the term Alevi in this time period was not coherent either. While both sets of meaning for Alevi (Shiite and

Alevis as Extremist Shiites

In *Islam in Anatolia* we come across a third connotation of the term Alevi, namely that of "Shiite extremist," an expression that carries both religious and political connotations, namely the profession of heretical beliefs such as the deification of Ali and a tendency to political subversion. For example, he describes Baba Ishaq, one of the leading figures of the Babai revolt in 1240, as most likely "a Turkmen baba of the extremist Alevi sect (*müfrit* Alevîyyü'l-Mezhep) and Kalender disposition" (Köprülü 2005 [1922], 41).[4] The notion reappears in *Origins of the Ottoman Empire*, where he explains that in the 13th and 14th centuries "most Turkish tribes...were under the moral influence of the extremist Alevi (*müfrit alevî*) and hetero-dox Turkmen babas, who were nothing else but the outwardly Islamized continuation of the old Turkish shamans" (Köprülü 1992 [1935], 47–48). In an encyclopedia entry of the same year he explained that the "Abdals of Anatolia" (*Rum Abdalllan*)—a 13th- to 16th-century dervish group that later merged into Bektashism—were in regard to their ceremonies and doc-trines "a heterodox (*hétérodoxe*), extremist (*mufrit*) Shiite and Alevi group" (Köprülü 1935b, 36). This text, which will be discussed in greater detail below, shows a much clearer sense of differentiation between "Shiite" and "Alevi" than *Islam in Anatolia*.

Alevis as Heterodox Anatolian Turks

The examples from the previous section, where "extreme Alevis" are related to the Babai and Turkish shamans, already point to the fourth way in which Köprülü uses "Alevi," namely as an overarching category employed to sketch a *longue durée* of a particular kind of religiosity char-acteristic of certain peripheral Muslim groups of Anatolia often identi-fied as Turkish. Where used in this way the term integrates the already discussed meanings of *ahl al-bayt* admirer and "extremist" Shiite. In Köprülü's work we find since the early 1920s examples where "Alevi" is used to indicate an organic connection between the Babai, Bektashi, and Kızılbaş. In this sense, he declares that "the Kızılbaş Turks...are Alevi"

---

ahl al-bayt supporter) are found in *Islam in Anatolia*, in other texts of the same time period the term does not—at least not explicitly—include the *ahl al-bayt* connotation (see Köprülü 1980 [1920/21]; 2005 [1925], 86).

4 Later on in the same text he also refers to the Kızılbaş as "extremist Alevis" (Köprülü 2005 [1922], 44 fn 57).

(Köprülü 1999 [1922], 266); counts the Bektashi among the "heterodox Alevi groups" (Köprülü 1935b, 30); asserts that the Babai would "resemble the various Alevi groups, whose existence in Anatolia we know from following centuries" (Köprülü 1991 [1935], 98); and refers in general terms to "Alevi Turkish currents such as the Bektaşi and Kızılbaş" (Köprülü 1935a, 1). Comparing the urban Anatolian population of the Seljuk period with the Turkmen nomads of the countryside with regard to lifestyle and religion, he already in *History of Turkish Literature* characterized the former as in principle Sunni, while describing the latter as under the influence of "Bâtınî-Alevî" Turkmen babas, who would interpret Islam in a manner fitting to their pre-Islamic customs (Köprülü 1980 [1920/21], 119–120). In all of these examples, Alevi is used as an adjective, a qualifier that is used to point to a particular trait shared by certain socioreligious groups. The term is in these examples not yet used as a proper name for a particular group, but rather as an attribute employed to sketch the *longue durée* of the evolution of Turkish religion from shamanism to the heterodox Islam of 20th-century Anatolia.[5]

Alevis as *Ocak*-Centered Kızılbaş Turks

With the exception of the first typical meaning of Alevi in the work of Köprülü, that is as Shiite as opposed to Sunni Islam, the second, third, and fourth above-discussed meanings of Alevi (as admirer of the *ahl al-bayt*, as extremist Shiite, and as a vague attribute somehow connecting these two meanings with Anatolian Turkish culture) pave the way for the fifth and most specific conceptualization of the Alevis in his work, namely as a distinct, Turkish socioreligious formation of Anatolia and Thrace centered around the *ocak* system with historical roots in the Kızılbaş movement. While this meaning of Alevi began to be popularized by other authors already in the 1920s, Köprülü used the term Alevi in this specific sense only in one text from 1935. This text is an encyclopedia entry on the Abdal and remarkable for several reasons. First, it is from a methodological viewpoint interesting that one of the sections of this long entry (33 pages) is dedicated to "Ethnography and History." This is noteworthy since the work of Köprülü in general is overwhelmingly historical.

---

5 This sense of a continuity of certain socioreligious milieus and ideas does, of course, not dependent on the term Alevi. He discussed it already in earlier publications in which he did not yet use the term Alevi, such as in *Early Mystics* (Köprülü 2006 [1919], 200).

In this ethnographic section he relies, besides secondary sources, mainly
on accounts of students of his, such as most prominently Abdülbaki
[Gölpınarlı] (1900–1982). Second, and most important for my argument,
this piece neatly shows the transition of the concept Alevi from being an
attribute, a qualifier applied to a series of different groups and currents, to
a name for a particular social formation.

Köprülü's entry on the Abdal is emblematic for the conceptual transformation that the terms Alevi and Alevilik experienced in the early decades
of the Turkish Republic. In this piece he sets out to bring together and systematize the knowledge about groups which are known as Abdal, or carry
similar names that he linguistically relates to it, covering a geography that
stretches from Turkish China to Anatolia and a time period that extends
over fifteen hundred years. Basically he distinguishes between two meanings of Abdal, although they overlap in some cases, that is, as (1) socioreligious designation and as (2) tribal designation. Of interest here are the
sections in which he discusses those groups of Turkish Abdal that he qualifies as Alevi. At first, it has to be stated that the above-discussed attribu-
tive meanings of Alevi can also be found in this entry. For example, when
he explains that the Abdal of Anatolia were Alevi, just like the Anatolian
Abdal of old and the Kızılbaş of today (Köprülü 1935b, 38). But then he
uses the term also as primary designation for a specific sociohistorical
group. Relying on information he attributes to Abdülbaki [Gölpınarlı], he
relates the following about the Alevi Abdal of Anatolia, who referred to
themselves as Abdal, but were considered Gypsies by the people: "Like
other Alevis, they have among themselves trained *dedes*; the *dede* visits
them once a year; he collects his specified annual dues; animals are sacri-
ficed. There is no difference between these rites and those of other Alevi
currents." Sometimes, those Abdal would join in the ceremonies of other
Alevis and vice versa. As a matter of fact, "in regard of their dogmas, there
are no differences between them and the other Alevi Turks" (Köprülü
1935b, 39). He continues further:

> If not all, then at least a large majority [of the Anatolian Abdal] are
> Alevis totally indistinguishable from the other heterodox groups of
> Anatolia such as the Kızılbaş and the Tahtacı; their *dedes*, like the
> *dedes* of the other groups, openly show their connections with the
> Çelebis from the center in Hacıbektaş. This means that in regard
> of rite and dogma it is impossible to separate the Abdals from the
> Alevi Turks of Anatolia, who still preserve traces of old Turkish

shamanism and about whose Turkishness there is not the smallest reason to doubt. (Köprülü 1935b, 45)

The Alevis as they are described here are not just groups that happen to be Shiite, *ehl-i beyt* admirers, or extremist Shiites, who could also be found in other parts of the Muslim world. They rather gain their specific character through particular institutions (such as the *dede*-institution, *dedelik*; and the Çelebi-family from Hacıbektaş) and practices (as those conducted during the visit of the *dede*). These institutions and practices were common to the Kızılbaş, Abdal, Tahtacı, all of whom were specific Alevi groups. In other words, in this entry the notion Alevi has become an umbrella term for culturally specific groups with a very distinctive set of practices and institutions in common.

There are instances in Köprülü's earlier publications that already foreshadow the sociologically more specific concept of Alevi unfolding in the "Abdal" entry. An example is the notion "Anatolian Kızılbashes" (*Anadolu Kızılbaşları*). In *Islam in Anatolia* he casually remarks, following a reference to the descendants of the Babai Turkmen, that the Tahtacı and the Çepni of today, indeed all "Anatolian Kızılbashes" belonged to these (descendants of the Babai) (Köprülü 2005 [1922], 43). Another example is from *Origins of Bektashism*, where he argued that the Turkmens, who could only accept a religion that allowed the continuation of their traditions of old, found this in "batınî and some Shiite currents and thus take on the form of religious sects: The heterodox groups that still live in some regions of Anatolia and Iran, which subsequently took names such as Kızılbaş, Alevi, Hurufi, and Alallahi [read Ali-Ilahi], are their offspring" (Köprülü 2002 [1925], 71).

Recognizing the Alevis as a particular socioreligious group within a primarily Turkish cultural context, Köprülü has followed in the footsteps of nationalist writers such as Besim Atalay (1882–1965), Baha Said (1882–1939), and Yusuf Ziya Yörükan (1887–1954).[6] Themselves working within the broader historical framework of Turkish religious history, to which Köprülü had contributed so enormously, these authors began already since the mid-1920s to establish what can be called the modern notion of Turkish Alevism as a generic category identifying socio-religious groups largely identical with those *ocak*-centered communities previously

---

6 The anthropologist Yörükan began to publish extensively on Alevism in the late 1920s, that is, considerably later than Baha Said and Köprülü. For a collection of his articles on Alevism see Yörükân (2006).

categorized as Kızılbaş, embedded thoroughly within a Turkish national-ist framework as carriers of a Turkish culture that reaches back to Central Asia and a shamanist Turkish past. Köprülü's article on the Abdal marks the endpoint of a re-signification that turned the Kızılbaş, generally sus-pected of being politically subversive and religiously heretical, into Alevis, who were acknowledged as Turkish; qualified as "heterodox", their harm-less syncretism was often framed more in terms of folklore and culture than in terms of religion—and could therefore be tamed within the new secularist political order.

Certainly aware of the contributions by the above mentioned authors,[7] one might ask whether there is a particular reason why it was in 1935 that Köprülü identified the *ocak*-centered Kızılbaş groups as "Alevi" in a sociological sense. Two developments might have contributed to this. First, referring to the diverse Kızılbaş groups as Alevis was by that time on the way of becoming a terminological convention among elite nationalist circles. Second, the political context of the 1930s was favorable to strong nationalist stances in political and scholarly public discourses. One might ask whether Köprülü might have found it opportune to at this point write about the Alevis more explicitly, namely as a quasi-embodiment of the thesis of Turkish continuity. The article in question does also put forward other arguments that seem to be impacted by the Turkish History Thesis.[8] What would also speak for this interpretation is the fact that he apparently did not continue or even replicate this sociological conceptualization of the Alevis in later work.

In the "Abdal" entry Köprülü also adopted a peculiar socio-geographic distinction between Bektashis and Alevis not yet that clearly identified in his earlier work. He asserts that while parts of the Abdal groups and

---

7 Interestingly, while he throughout the entry referenced as informants some of his stu-dents with field experiences on Alevi groups, especially Abdülbaki Gölpınarlı, and also some European literature with information on Alevi/Abdal, the entry contains no references at all to the publications of Baha Said Bey and Yusuf Ziya [Yörükan]—although, especially in the work of the latter, there is ample reference to the Abdal and it seems impossible that Köprülü was not aware of their publications. Yusuf Ziya graduated from the Darülfünun in 1922, where he studied philosophy in the School of Literary Studies. He might have taken classes by Köprülü. Since 1926 he taught at the Theology Department of the Darülfünun, and we know that he and Köprülü were on university committees together (Yörukan 2006, 16–19; Asılsoy 2008, 81 fn 271). Baha Said Bey was working together with Ziya Gökalp dur-ing the latter's time in Istanbul, and published, as did Köprülü, in *Türk Yurdu*. Their politi-cal interests, and to a certain extent probably also their social circles, must have overlapped considerably.

8 For the Turkish History Thesis see pp. 171–173.

their traditions and lodges had merged with the Bektashis in the 17th and 18th centuries, "it can be assumed that some Abdal groups did not merge directly with the town Bektashism (*şehir Bektaşilik*), but united with the heterodox Alevi groups of the villages, or...that they, somewhat like the other Kızılbaş groups, in the form of a sect settled and built villages in different parts of Turkey, and that a fourth group began nomadic life like the nomadic Kızılbaş tribes" (Köprülü 1935b, 36). This distinction between town-Bektashis and village-Bektashis/Alevis can be regarded as another small, but important step in the objectification of the Alevis as a specific sociohistorical formation.[9]

The Longue Durée of Heterodox Turkish Culture

Following Richard Handler, van der Veer has argued that "boundedness, continuity, and homogeneity encompassing diversity dominate nationalist discourse and social-scientific discourse to the same degree" (van der Veer 1994a, 195). In this sense, the evolution of a distinct concept of Alevism and the emergence of the Alevis as a sociohistorical group in Köprülü's opus have to be seen in relation to his broader objective of deciphering the origins and characteristic features of the Turkish national ideal (*mefkure*) and of tracing the formation of the Turkish nation as a historical subject. In pursuing this quest, one major focus of Köprülü has been, from the very beginnings of his research on the relationship between Turkish and Muslim literary and religious traditions, on indices of continuity.

The idea of ancient religious forms being fluently carried over into subsequent stages of evolution of the Turks is one of the main themes characteristic of Köprülü's work on the Islamization of the Turks and Turkish Islam. It contributes to his broader theory of the evolution of Turkish culture from ancient until modern times, characterized by religious syncretism and the dominance of national Turkish traits in their adaptation to various religious and civilizational environments. What changes in this narrative are the particulars of the religious and civilizational forms in

---

9 This distinction has, to my knowledge, been introduced by Besim Atalay, who maintained that the "Anatolian Bektashis," or "village Bektashis" (*köy Bektaşileri*) were Alevi (Atalay 1924, 7). According to Atalay the term Alevi signified the religious orientation; the group in this way designated would be Caferi (i.e., Twelver Shiite) in terms of their Islamic orientation (*mezhep*) and Bektashi and Alevi in regard to their Sufi path (*tarikat*) (Atalay 1924, 4). While Atalay's identification of the term Alevi was still relatively close to the general concept of Shiism, the way he relates it to Bektashism already foreshadows the sociologically more specific meaning that the term would soon acquire.

which the Turkish spirit manifests itself in history; what remains constant is the "national taste" and "spirit," which, though embodied over time in different forms, always stays true to its original character.[10]

In his attention to the larger historical rhythms and continuities of history and to the details of the sentiments and cultural productions of ordinary people, Köprülü's historiography reminds one of the French *Annales* school. From his student Halil İnalcık we know that after 1930 Köprülü became interested in the work of Lucien Febvre and the *Annales* (İnalcık 1978, 70). In the forward to the Turkish edition of *Origins of the Ottoman Empire*, Köprülü pays his respect to the *Annales*, in particular to Febvre, who had written an appraising review of the original French edition of the book in the journal *Annales* (Köprülü 1991 [1935], xix–xxi). Köprülü points especially to the *Annales*' appreciation of the multidimensionality of reality, which would ask for multicausal instead of monocausal explanations of historical phenomena (Köprülü 1991 [1935], xxi). But I think it would be unjust to see Köprülü as merely having imitated *Annales* methodology. Already in his earlier work he had emphasized the necessity of taking into consideration the mutual impacts of religious, political, and economic factors in studying the history of Anatolia (Köprülü 1928, vi).[11] To a certain extent Köprülü's work appears to have anticipated in particular the work of Fernand Braudel, who would later develop the concept of *longue durée* to reorient the focus of historiography from singular historical events (*histoire événementielle*) toward a perspective that highlighted underlying structures of longevity (Braudel 1987 [1958]). Köprülü continuously repeated his conviction that the religious history of Anatolia had to be researched in its continuities (*continuité*) and not as an agglomerate of singular events; nor should this history be researched by drawing too narrow geographic boundaries, but in consideration of the transregional activities and contexts of the various religious currents in question (Köprülü 1928, v; cf. 1940, xviii–xix). Even when he focused on very specific time periods, for example on the beginnings of the Ottoman Empire, Köprülü situated such focus in the larger frame of the evolution of Turkish history and a Turkish historical subject. Considering the family resemblance between Köprülü's

---

10 This grand narrative is probably spelled out most comprehensively in his *History of Turkish Literature*, hailed by Akün "as civilizational history that shows the journey of the Turkish spirit through the ages as a synthesis" (Akün 2002, 482).

11 It would be anachronistic to think that *Early Mystics* was already influenced by the *Annales*, as has been suggested by Ocak (1997, 221). The journal *Annales* was founded in 1929 by Febvre and Marc Bloch, ten years after the initial publication of *Early Mystics*.

and Braudel's appreciation for structures of historical continuity, it seems justified to apply the term *longue durée* to represent certain aspects of the former's work.

In his formulation of a *longue durée* of certain traits of Turkish national sentiment, transmitted over time in popular religious literature and culture, Köprülü needed to somehow harmonize aspects of change with aspects of continuity. To this end, Köprülü employed throughout his work, with shifting focus, three major conceptual brackets, namely shamanism, Batinism, and Alevism. All of these concepts are characterized by a certain vagueness and elasticity, which made it possible for him to connect different phases in the development of the Turkish people and their national consciousness as it emerged and developed in the journey of the Turks form Central Asia to Anatolia. In Köprülü's narrative, shamanism functions as a codeword for Turkish culture prior to Islam, geographically located in Central Asia. It was transformed as a result of Turkish migrations into Western Asia and the Turks' gradual adaptation to Islam, where it underwent a symbiosis with Batinism. This symbiosis marks the entry of the Turks into the cultural hegemony of Islam. In his entry on the Abdal, for example, he signifies the Babai as members of an Anatolian group who "belonged to *batini* currents and remind [us] in all aspects of the old *kam-ozan* [Shamans]" (Köprülü 1935b, 37; cf. Köprülü 1966 [1919], 178–179; 1980 [1920/21], 249).

While references to remainders of a shamanist past, such as the portrayal of the *aşık* as an Islamized version of the *kam-ozan*, help to link the Islamized Turks with their ancient cultural roots, Batinism reflects the symbiosis of Turkish culture with Islamic civilization, and functions as the flexible structure in which the post-shaman "heterodox" Turkish culture finds proper space to further develop and unfold itself: "The Oghuz tribes were used to *batini* currents and accepted Islam in a gradual way. But underneath the outside coat of Islam could be found the imprints of the old national customs and primitive religions" (Köprülü 2002 [1925], 70). Köprülü used the notion of Batinism to conceptualize the 13th-century Babais not only as continuation with pre-Islamic Turkish pasts, but also as Anatolian starting point of a "popular" Turkish Islamic tradition. This enabled him to integrate into one historical account groups contemporary to the Babais such as the Abdal, Kalender, and Hayderi dervishes, as well as later nonconformist and nonelite currents and dervish groups such as the Bektashis, Hurufis, and Kızılbaş, as well as the followers of Sheikh Bedreddin (Köprülü 1966 [1919], 289 and 302–304; see also Köprülü 2002 [1925]).

From the beginning of its adaptation by the Turks, Batinism reflects—in the reading of Köprülü—strong Alevi influences (in the sense of affinity to the *ehl-i beyt* and some Shiite themes). He explains, for example, that "[t]he Alevî-Bâtınî currents among the Turkmen tribes…would, under the influence of partially national and partially local customs, connect with Sufi orders like the Yeseviye and the Kalenderiye and find in 13th-century Anatolia embodiment as a religious syncretism under the name Babaism" (Köprülü 1935b, 37). According to Köprülü, such "Alevi" features became more pronounced over time, especially with Safavid influence on the Anatolian Turks since the late 15th century.

Such, in short, is the *longue durée* through which Köprülü connects Turkish shamanism, Batinism, and Alevism. This *longue durée* finds its historical embodiment in more or less clearly identifiable historical groups such as the Yeseviye-Sufi order, the Babai-movement, Bektashism and groups in its vicinity such as the Kalender, the Kızılbaş, and other "Alevi" groups such as the Tahtacı and the Abdal, and finally the Alevi themselves, who are through this narrative firmly embedded in Turkish history. The asserted connections between these religious currents and social formations create throughout Köprülü's work a complicated web of trajectories and influences, in this way marking in an allusive way the religious dimension of the continuity of "popular" Turkish culture.

Köprülü's theory of a continuity of "popular" Turkish culture is based on a kind of family resemblance that he detects between practices he related to shamanism and practices he associated with some Shiite and/or Alevi, as well as *batini* groups. It is exactly the blurry grey zone between the postulated overlap and similarity of these currents that makes Köprülü's categories in a strictly historical sense very difficult to handle and work with. The concepts shamanism, Batinism, and Alevism remain highly elusive—as do his notions of "national spirit" and "national taste." Köprülü's narrative has itself a *batini* feel to it since what changes is the "outer" form, not the "inner" quality of the historical formations under investigation in his *longue durée* of Turkish culture and religion. Ultimately, the heuristic value of these categories appears to rest on an almost Platonic epistemology.

Lastly it needs to be underlined that Köprülü's nationalism cannot be ignored when trying to make sense of his historical theories. The validity of the Turkish nation as a political project required for it to be traceable in history. Accordingly, he set out to explore the history of the national spirit in the literary artifacts of the "popular," mystical Islam of the Turks. His interpretation, based on the epistemological postulate that the national Turkish spirit existed since ancient times in primitive Turkish culture, rests on a Platonic essentialism, according to which the soul of the nation is reflected in its outward manifestations. At this juncture, Köprülü's theory of evolution of the nation stops being historical and becomes rather phenomenological. Related to this point and reminiscent of romantic idealism, Köprülü's theory appears to take for granted that societies carry some inherent aptitude to bring to consciousness the national spirit. This spirit is cast as an agent of history (an *idée-force*), embodied in culture, through which it can then be traced and studied.

Köprülü's Legacy

We frankly have to admit that the approach that [Köprülü] showed in his work to the formation of the religious and mystical life of Anatolia, his interpretations and evaluations, and hence the emerging picture, influenced, including the great expert of this subject Ir[è]ne Mélikoff, quite many young researchers like myself...And [this way] the approach that he has put forward in some of his articles and books, in particular in *Early Mystics in Turkish Literature*, has been continued. Today the Alevi Bektashi community still continues this approach. (Ocak 2010, 51–52)

Particularly in Turkey, enthusiasm about the pioneering character of Köprülü's work and belief in its lasting validity is nearly unbroken. Karpat praises "Köprülü's breadth of knowledge, objectivity, and power of analysis, as well as his predominant interest in methodology and the correct use of sources," which would provide his interpretations of Turkish/Ottoman history with credibility (Karpat 2001, 401). Ahmet Y. Ocak equally lauds Köprülü's methodology, scientific rigor, and "objective social history perspective," while simultaneously lamenting the decline of Turkish historiography in the course of the Turkish Republic (Ocak 1997, 227). While Ocak is right when he points to the dominance of ideologically driven models of historical explanation in Turkey (such as Marxist, Islamic, Turkish nationalist, and/or Kemalist ones), his idealization of Köprülü as an exemplary model of objective historiography ignores the political dimension and the methodological problems of the latter's work. It is significant that internationally recognized, influential historians such as

Karpat and Ocak, even when, as in the case of the latter, in general open and very sensitive to methodological questions,[12] have so far failed to recognize a larger problem in the study of "heterodox" Turkish Islam and the religious history of Anatolia and Balkans more generally, namely the lack of critical reflection on the basic categories and semantics through which this history is told.

The following section will provide a discussion of the approaches of some of the most important scholars working in the footsteps of Köprülü on the Islamic-Turkish traditions of Anatolia and its surroundings. My discussion will highlight what I perceive as the methodologically and theoretically problematic aspects of scholarship within the Köprülü paradigm. This said, I would like to underline that this discussion remains selective, and that my criticism does not entail a total rejection of the work of the scholars that I am here discussing.

Köprülü's Students

Continuing where Köprülü left off and filling out some of the blanks of his grand narrative, several of his students became leading authorities in major areas of his interest, with long-lasting impact on Turkish historical and social studies. Among his most important students are Fevziye Abdullah Tansel, who became a leading expert on Turkish literature;[13] the already mentioned Abdülbaki Gölpınarlı, a historian of Islam; Pertev Naili Boratav, an ethnologist and folklorist of Turkish culture and people; Osman Turan, an eminent expert on the Seljuks; Mustafa Akdağ, who dedicated his work to the socioeconomic history of Seljuk and Ottoman periods; Ömer Lütfi Barkan and Halil İnalcık, who both became internationally recognized Ottomanists, as well as Faruk Sümer, whose ethno-historic work focuses on the Seljuks and on Turkish nomadic tribes (Berktay 1983, 90; Ersanlı 2003, 224; Park 1975, 51–52). Köprülü's former

---

12 See, for example, his critical overview of publications on Alevism since the early republic (Ocak 1991), which, at a time when Alevism just started to become a subject of scholarly reflection, raised awareness concerning the politics involved in the enunciation of certain Alevi histories and identities and thus provided an important starting point for further critical investigations of 20th-century Alevi formations.

13 Tansel worked most closely together with the late Köprülü and was a source of both academic and personal support for him (Park 1975, 51). Among other things she helped in the preparation of the second edition of *Early Mystics* (see Tansel 2006 [1966], xlvi–xlix).

assistant Abdülkadir İnan (1889–1976) became the most influential advocate of the shamanism thesis in the republican period.[14]

The work of those who continued in Köprülü's footsteps shows how the normative concepts employed by Köprülü as descriptors and organizing principles for the historical manifestations of the rural, only to a limited extent literate, Turkish Islam of Anatolia and its vicinity became standard terminology. It is not difficult to identify the Köprülü school of approaching Turkish Islam in the relevant literature. Exemplary are the publications by the amateur researcher Sadettin Nüzhet Ergun (1901–1946), a man with a Sufi background, who has made important contributions to the study of popular Turkish poetry and music. In his anthology of "Bektashi Poets" he maintained that groups such as the "Bektaşi, Ahi, Abdal, Hurufi, Haydari, Kızılbaş, and Kalender" were difficult to distinguish—he therefore subsumed them all under the category "Bektashi tradition." All of these groups could be characterized as "batini" and "extreme Shiites" (Ergun 1930, 2).[15] As in Köprülü's work, the categorization of the mentioned groups in Ergun's writings reveals that "Alevi" was just beginning to be regarded as a name for a distinct socio-religious community. Thus he writes, in another text, about "'Turkish Alevi' groups, which we call Kızılbaş" (hence distinguishing between the name Kızılbaş and the attribute Alevi), while at the same time commenting on the *ayin-i cem*s of the Alevi, Bektashi, and Kızılbaş (as if these were three different groups) (Ergun 1929, 15 and 17). In some of Ergun's early writings he in fact not only follows Köprülü's arguments and repeatedly acknowledges him as *the* authority in the field, but seems also to imitate his expressions so closely that it borders on plagiarism.[16] Beyond the question of plagiarism, the

---

14 İnan published a first article explicitly on Turkish shamanism already in 1926: "Türk Şamanizme Ait," *Türk Yurdu*, no.19, 1926. Influenced by pan-Turkism, he worked since the mid-1910s on the ethnography, folklore, religion, and mythology of the Turkish people. A native from Bashkiria, where he had been involved in the nationalist struggle against Russia, he immigrated to Istanbul in 1925. There he became an assistant of Köprülü at the Institute for Turkology (Türkiyat Enstitüsü). Köprülü used the institute to support especially Tatar and Azeri Turkish intellectuals and in this way contributed to their intellectual integration in the republic (Copeaux 1997, 48; Asılsoy 2008, 79).

15 Another junior colleague of Köprülü who followed closely the latter's narrative of the continuity of Turkish "popular" religion from ancient Turkish shamanistic practices to the Anatolian Bektashi and Kızılbaş was İbrahim Kafesoğlu (1914–1984). See, for example, Kafesoğlu (1988, 122–124).

16 Compare, for example, the introductory pages to his booklet on the Kızılbaş poet Pir Sultan Abdal (Ergun 1929, 5–6), published in a book series on Turkish bards edited by Köprülü, with Köprülü (2002 [1925], 71).

close emulation of certain central topoi in Köprülü's work on "popular" Turkish Islam, such as the continuity of "national [Turkmen] traditions" among "batıni elements" in Anatolia, show how Köprülü's conceptualization of the transformation of the "primitive religions" of the Turks during their integration into Islam was already early on beginning to achieve paradigmatic status (Ergun 1929, 5).

Köprülü's student Abdülbaki Gölpınarlı made in his work similar associations between Batinism, the "extreme Shia" (*ghulūw*), Bektashism, Turkish shamanism, and the Alevis (Gölpınarlı 1969, 96–97 and 155; 2000, 130–132 and 211). He became one of the most distinguished experts on medieval Turkish Sufism in the 20th century. A devout Sufi dervish in the Mevlevi tradition, Gölpınarlı provides a good example of the conflation of theological and historical-scientific arguments about Alevism. This conflation is visible in the evolutionist model of religion that he applies in his approach to Alevism. Within a discussion of the state of Sufism as a living tradition in contemporary Turkey, he maintains that the Alevis and Bektashis, who claimed to be Caferi (i.e., Twelver Shiites) without knowing about the Caferi interpretation of the law, were now beginning to study the rules of the Caferi tradition (i.e., Twelver Shia law) and consecutively left behind their old metaphysical conceptions and "superstitious beliefs" (*hurâfeler*) (Gölpınarlı 1969, 189).[17] In the same text he remarks that "in primitive religions" (*iptidaî dinlerde*) such as Alevism the *sema* (ritual dance) was "exuberant and loud, [with] a fast rhythm," juxtaposing this to the more refined *sema* of the Mevlevi Sufis (Gölpınarlı 1969, 146).

Karamustafa has maintained that Gölpınarlı "made fresh contributions to scholarship on almost every subject his teacher had researched, departed from Köprülü's views on occasion yet did not initiate a new perspective on the Islamization of Turks and the role of Sufism in this process" (Karamustafa 2005, 72). What distinguishes Gölpınarlı from other historians of Turkish Islam in the 20th century is that he suggested an interpretation of Alevism and Bektashism that went beyond the dominant Islamic and nationalist frameworks. This is, I would add to Karamustafa, a rather significant difference from Köprülü, but has, unfortunately, not yet been explored in further detail. As for its religious character, Gölpınarlı maintained that "it is understood that Alevism is not a Sufi order (*tarikat*). But we can neither say that this path (*yol*) would be an impeccable school

---

17 Throughout his work he emphasizes that Alevis were in fact not real Shiites in the sense of following the Twelver Shia or Caferi school of law (see Gölpınarlı 2000, 193; 2003, 12).

of law (*mezhep*) since its methods [of interpretation] have never been determined. Alevism is at best a primitive school of law (*iptidâî bir mezhep*) or a primitive religion (*iptidâî bir din*)" (Gölpınarlı 1963, 4). Within the hegemonic discourse on religion in Turkey, strongly shaped by norms derived from Sunni Islam and ideals of national unity that also aimed at religious homogeneity, an interpretation that, as suggested by Gölpınarlı, regards Alevism as a religion in its own right (even if in his view a "primitive" one) has never been able to become very attractive.[18] The concept of religion that is dominant in republican Turkey derives from two sources: the Islamic tradition and Western world-religion discourse. According to traditional Islamic discourse, *din*-religion is not a universal condition. Besides Islam, only Christianity and Judaism are generally accepted as *din*. Since *din*-religion cannot, within the confines of this traditional discourse, be universalized, Alevism is generally not regarded as a religion. Seen from that angle, Gölpınarlı's characterization is significant since it illustrates the translation of the Western concept of religion, conceived of as a universal, into Turkish discourses about religion. Religion as we encounter it in this—admittedly marginal—discourse, is not entirely modeled on the Islamic *din*. As within the work of Köprülü, Gölpınarlı's work reflects a translation of the Western concept of world religion into the semantics of *din*. Accordingly, religion-*din* is here conceptualized as something that emerges in history and in that sense is secular—the Alevis as primitive religion, a notion that entails the possibility of further evolution.

Gölpınarlı also rejected a naïve nationalism as matrix for the interpretation of Bektashism. He argued for example that following the Unionist turn toward Turkish nationalism, "the Turkish Bektashis took position against the Albanian Bektashis and began to make imaginary and ridiculous claims such as that Bektashism was a national Sufi order, and even that Hacı Bektaş, not mentioning that he wrote his *Makaalat* in Arabic, was a nationalist engaged in protecting Turkish culture against Arabic and Persian culture" (Gölpınarlı 2000, 228). In this way, both with regard to his religious and his anti-nationalist approaches to the study of Alevism and Bektashism, Gölpınarlı offers alternatives to the dominant interpretations—unfortunately, however, without going into detail. Probably

---

18 As I have pointed out elsewhere, Alevis in Germany, outside the direct influence zone of the discourse on religion that dominates the public sphere in Turkey, which renders it politically difficult for Alevis to move outside an Islamic frame of reference, have been relatively more inclined to define Alevism as a religion in its own right (Dressler 2006, 285–287; see also Sökefeld 2008).

due to the incompatibility with hegemonic discourses of religious and national unity in Turkey, his views on Kızılbaş-Alevism and Bektashism never became very popular and were unfortunately not taken up by other scholars. I think that the counterfactual question as to what the dominant narratives on these traditions would look like today if scholarship had taken more seriously Gölpınarlı's alternative perspective might be worth exploring since it destabilizes the Köprülü paradigm, that is, the reading of Alevism as an essentially Turkish and heterodox Islamic entity.

Much more influential than Gölpınarlı's work were the more recent and more systematic contributions to the study of the Kızılbaş-Alevi and Bektashi traditions of Anatolia by Irène Mélikoff and her student Ahmet Yaşar Ocak. Since these two authors are widely cited, have largely remained within the Köprülü paradigm, and are considered by many the major contemporary authorities on the Alevi and Bektashi traditions, their approaches and arguments deserve to be investigated in greater detail.

Irène Mélikoff: Alevism as "Islamized Shamanism"

The French Turkologist Irène Mélikoff (1917–2009), born in St. Petersburg as the daughter of an Azeri businessman who fled with his family to France in advance of the Russian revolution, closely followed Köprülü's approach and opinions on Turkish Islam. Mélikoff was particularly interested in the shamanism thesis, the elaboration of which would become a major focus of her studies. Following Köprülü, she saw in the institutions of the Alevi *dede* and the Bektashi *baba* a continuation of the pre-Islamic Turkish shaman, that is, the *kam-ozan*, who was able to travel to the world of the spirits, could assume the forms of certain animals, and functioned as a healer and mediator (Mélikoff 1998, 9–13). Mélikoff further argued that the central Alevi ritual, the *ayin-i cem* and its particularities, such as the religious hymns (*nefes*), the *sema* dance, the ritual use of alcohol, and the participation of unveiled women, were continuations of old shaman traditions (Mélikoff 1982, 387). She also recognized remnants of shamanism in Alevi belief and mythology: thus she saw in the Alevis' concept of God the *Gök Tanrı* ("Sky God") of the shamanistic Turks; considered the mythos of the *Kırklar* ("The Forty")[19] to be a Central Asian tradition, although

---

19 The story of the *Kırklar* narrates Muhammad's ritual communion during his legendary night journey with the 39 prophets and saints, led by Ali, whose superior authority the former here recognizes.

she also acknowledged its existence in Sufi mythology; and claimed that the genealogy of the Alevi belief in *ḥulūl*, the incarnation of the divine in humans, particularly in Ali, should not be traced back to the "extreme Shia," where it admittedly also appeared, but rather to Central Asia, inspired by Manichean and Buddhist examples (Mélikoff 1998, 13–21). According to Mélikoff, the Alevi Ali imagery resembled the belief in the archaic natural forces of the not-yet-Islamized Turks, with Ali embodied in the crane bird (*turna*), who figures so prominently in Alevi poetry and ritual (Mélikoff 2001, 77–78). Therefore the Alevi veneration of Ali could be regarded as a merger of pre-Islamic Turkish cosmology with Shiite terminology (Mélikoff 2001, 75–81). Mélikoff is further able to detect shamanist themes in the *Vilayetname*, the hagiography of Hacı Bektaş Veli. Herein the saint, just like the Turkish shamans of old, fought with giants, visited the underworld, and met with spirits (Mélikoff 1962, 40–42).[20] In short, Mélikoff conceptualizes the Alevi and Bektashi traditions as a complex syncretism of Islam with Manichaean and Christian elements, which is clearly dominated, however, by Altai-Turkish, pre-Islamic shamanism.

In Köprülü's oeuvre, the notion of shamanist remnants, although figuring as a prominent topos of continuity, remained rather vague. Mélikoff embarked in her work on a much more comprehensive objectification of "shamanistic remnants"—to an extent that she qualified Alevism and Bektashism, in a manner more reminiscent of Baha Said than of Köprülü, as "Islamized Shamanism" (esp. Mélikoff 1998, chap. 1; Mélikoff 2003). Beyond the problems of historical plausibility with this approach,[21] my concern here is primarily with the concepts of shamanism, syncretism, and ultimately religion that structure her work. All of the parallels that Mélikoff draws between ancient Turkish shamanism and the Alevi and Bektashi traditions are based on the assumption of a more-or-less clearly definable and institutionalized, fairly homogeneous Turkish shamanist religion. This in itself is problematic in regard to the underlying understanding of continuity of ethnic and religious subjects and boundaries.

20 This text recounts the life and miracles of Hacı Bektaş Veli. The oldest known manuscript of it is estimated to date back to the early 16th century, but the origins of the text itself are believed to go back to the turn of the 15th century (Ocak 2000a, 31–32).

21 As for Mélikoff's work, Hamid Algar has written a sharp critique of her last major monograph, in which she attempted to bring together the main threads of her work on the origins of the Alevi and Bektashi traditions. Most importantly, he points out that "[w]hatever elements Bektashism may have inherited from an Islamized shamanism, they are fewer and less important than those derived from *Ghulāt* Shi'sm, the provenance of which the author does not adequately discuss" (Algar 2004, 688).

Here, modern conceptions of what it means to be Turkish and to be shamanist/Alevi are projected backward into premodern contexts. The deduction of Alevi practices from pre-Islamic "Turkish" practices, which she refers to as shamanism, is methodologically questionable, as is the treatment of shamanism as if it were a religion in the modern sense of the term, that is, a sphere of life that can clearly be identified and isolated from other spheres of life, and that can be analyzed neatly in regard to origins, belief, rituals, and mythology, in the sum of its parts forming a clearly distinguishable and organic system.[22] The underlying concept of religion that Mélikoff draws on is rather static, has essentialist underpinnings, and lacks sufficient conceptual differentiation between vernacular and scholarly discourses. She uses modern religion concepts, such as most prominently heterodoxy and syncretism, in a rather uncritical way, employing them as descriptors of certain modes of religiosity without any reflection on their normative and theoretical implications.

Mélikoff's student and colleague Ahmet Y. Ocak maintained in an obituary review of her life and work that "in none of her publications, in which she sympathetically studied the Alevi and Bektashi currents, did she ever stray into sentimentality, or depart from scientific impartiality into ideological and political speculations." I disagree with regard to this judgment. Mélikoff's work is part of the knowledge regime that legitimates the very religio-political power relations by means of which the Alevis and Bektashis have been simultaneously nationalized (i.e., Turkified) within the Turkish nation-state project, and religiously othered (i.e., rendered "heterodox") by the Sunni-Islamic discourse. She takes for granted and reaffirms the otherness of those groups and currents that she qualifies as "heterodox," "shamanist," "syncretistic," and so forth. The narrative that Mélikoff developed harmonizes with the Turkish nationalist project of homogenizing and streamlining Turkish origins and history. Her approach to Alevism, and even more so Bektashism, is in general sympathetic, especially where she casts Alevis and Bektashis in line with Kemalist discourse as banner holders of secularism against the threat of Sunni Muslim fundamentalism (see Mélikoff 1998, 262–277). In general terms, Mélikoff's work affirms the Turkish state's Kemalist approach to Alevism, which can be described as being geared toward assimilation of Alevism and Bektashism within the parameters of Turkishness and secular Islam.

---

22 See DeWeese's criticism (chapter 5).

It fits well with the nationalist project that Mélikoff, as Martin van Bruinessen has pointed out, minimizes the importance of Iranian, Shiite, Armenian, and Kurdish impact on the formation of modern Alevism. While

> she does acknowledge that a considerable number of Central and East Anatolian Alevis speak Kurdish... and that there are surprising similarities between the Alevi and the Yezidi and Ahl-i Haqq religions (both of which emerged among the Kurds),... she is clearly very uncomfortable with these facts. Her uneasiness is compounded by the attraction that Kurdish nationalism is increasingly exerting for at least a part of the Kurdish-speaking Alevis (and even, one may add, for some Turkish-speaking Alevis). (Bruinessen 1999, 550–551)

In other words, her deep love for the Turks and their history, lauded by Ocak, might not be consciously political, but it certainly lines up with a political project. Bruinessen insinuates that, explicitly distancing herself from previous scholarship that "had wanted to recognize Christian elements in Bektashism[,]... her emphasis on the essential Turkishness of Bektashism reflects her sympathy with Turkish self-assertion against foreign domination, political as well as academic" (Bruinessen 1999, 552).

Mélikoff's closeness to the nationalist perspective shines through not only in her focus on Alevism and Bektashism as essentially Turkish traditions, in which—strongly reminiscent of Köprülü's approach—the Turkish element always remains dominant despite acknowledged influences from non-Turkish cultures and religions. It further shows itself in her conceptualization of Alevism and Bektashism as being so closely connected that she asserts "Alevism is nothing other than a form of Bektashism" (Mélikoff 1998, xxi); indeed, the two could conveniently be represented as one "Alevi-Bektashi" tradition.[23] Such merging of Alevism and Bektashism, precursors of which can be dated back to the very beginnings of the nationalist conceptualization of Alevism as a Turkish tradition (Atalay 1924) and which is extremely popular both among Alevis as well as in the non-Alevi public sphere,[24] lines up nicely with the homogenizing quest of Turkish nationalism. The nationalist

---

23 Publications of hers bear titles such as "Exploration au coeur du Bektachisme-Alevisme," "Note de symbolique Bektachi-Alevie," and "Le problème Bektaşi-Alevi."

24 The hyphenated notion Alevi-Bektaşi is less popular among members of the Bektashi brotherhood, who are keen to stress their difference from the endogamous Alevi groups.

project conceives of religious and ethnic differences as equally dangerous. It therefore emphasizes convergences, deemphasizes discrepancies, and welcomes the rhetorical union of Kızılbaş-Alevism with Bektashism in line with a broader nationalist conception of Turkish history and the role attributed to the "Alevi-Bektashis" therein.[25]

Scholars familiar with her work will disagree on the question of how much significance to attribute to Mélikoff's underlying Turkism. It seems fair to me to characterize her work as within the semantics of what Kafadar has labeled "nationism." He used this term within a broader critique of the teleological reading of Turkish history backward through the modern lenses of nation and state, which results in an ahistorical narrative of continuity from central Asia to modern Turkey (Kafadar 2007, 8).

Ahmet Yaşar Ocak: Alevism as "Islamic Heterodoxy" and Syncretism

Ahmet Yaşar Ocak (b. 1945) is one of this generation's most prolific and influential historians of premodern Turkish Islam. Most of his work is dedicated to the textual, mostly hagiographic traditions of those Muslim currents of Turkish-dominated Seljuk and Ottoman lands that value as bases of religious authority mysticism, charisma, and lineage more than legal and scriptural knowledge. Karamustafa rightly points out that "when compared to Köprülü, Ocak has paid much more attention to the influence, on the formation of Turkish popular religion, of non-Islamic religions and religious movements such as Buddhism, Manichaeism, Paulicianism, and Bogomilism" (Karamustafa 2005, 73). In agreement with Mélikoff, Ocak does recognize the existence of shamanist remnants in the Kızılbaş-Alevi tradition. Departing from her, however, he disputes their dominance on Turkish Anatolian Islam and the Alevi and Bektashi traditions. In his monograph on Alevî ve Bektaşî İnançlarının İslâm Öncesi Temelleri ("Pre-Islamic Foundations of Alevi and Bektashi Beliefs") he specifically emphasizes his aspiration to analyze the hagiographic texts of the broader Bektashi tradition with a focus that goes beyond the more exclusive shamanism thesis supported by Mélikoff (Ocak 2000a, 10).[26] He rather tends

---

25 For a historical criticism of the notion Alevi-Bektashi see Yıldırım (2010, 25–26).

26 Written with the objective to do justice to the divergent traditions that come together in the Alevi and Bektashi traditions, this important study, of which unfortunately only a Turkish edition exists, provides insightful discussions of the impact of primarily pre-Islamic Turkish, Far Eastern, and Iranian, as well as shamanist and Christian religious motifs on Alevism and Bektashism.

to stress the historical and thematic lines that connect Kızılbaş-Alevi and Bektashi currents with what he labels "heterodox" Sufism, with particular emphasis on the Vefai Sufi order, as well as the Nizari Ismailiyya. In other words, what is characteristic for Ocak's approach is that he perceives the major roots of the Kızılbaş-Alevi and Bektashi traditions as clearly located within Islam, even if within marginal formations of it (see Ocak 1989; 1995; 2000a; 2005).

Similar to Mélikoff, Ocak's narrative and conceptual framework remains loyal to an approach that is nationist insofar as it takes national entities such as the "Turkish people" as central units of analysis. However, with his focus on the impact of traditions at the margins of Islam on the formation of Kızılbaş-Alevism and Bektashism, Ocak goes beyond the implicit Turkist paradigm in previous scholarship of the Köprülü school. This becomes especially apparent in his work on the impact of the Vefai Sufi order during the formative centuries of what he, using Köprülü's language, calls the "popular" and "heterodox" Islam of Anatolia. Ocak convincingly argues that there are considerable flaws in the storyline that connects the socioreligious milieus of the Babai movement and those currents that would eventually find a home in the Bektashi order and later on the Kızılbaş groups, with the Yesevi tradition, which has since Köprülü been regarded as a major link in the transmission of Turkish culture from Central Asia to Anatolia (Ocak 2005, 227 and 244). Instead he points out that from the 13th through the 16th century, the larger Bektashi milieu was closely connected with the Vefai order, which, originally located in Iraq and Syria, and of Sunni-Muslim faith, then in Anatolia temporarily adjusted to the "heterodox" beliefs of the local Turkish and Kurdish Muslim population (Ocak 2005, 236).[27]

Elsewhere, in a discussion of the impact of "old Turkish faiths" on the "heterodox Islamic movements" of Anatolia, Ocak remarks that the Turkish reception of the shamanism thesis paralleled the emergence of political Turkism. Thus he shows, as mentioned before, an understanding of the impact of nationalism on how religion and notions of Turkish culture have been recast in the dynamics of nation-building (Ocak 2000a, 56; see also Ocak 1991). Ocak's implicit rejection of Turkism as

---

27 More recently, however, Ocak appears to look more favorably at the possibility of a certain continuity of "heterodox" Islam from Ahmed Yesevi to Anatolian "popular" dervish movements such as the Babai and the Haydari, and then the Bektashi tradition, also insinuating that Ahmed Yesevi and his environment might not have been Sunni (Ocak 2010, 52–54).

an analytical framework for the historical contextualization of Bektashism and Alevism—which he has unfortunately never elaborated on explicitly in writing—needs to be credited with opening the doors for new possibilities of inquiry, especially a questioning of nationalist paradigms as the basis for an investigation of the Kızılbaş-Alevi and Bektashi traditions. In this way, Ocak, the most important contemporary historian in the Köprülü tradition, has contributed significantly to the creation of postnationalist spaces of exploration of the Alevi and Bektashi traditions. Nevertheless, I would hold that in regard to the central topoi and concepts that he uses in his conceptualization of inner-Islamic difference, Ocak closely follows Köprülü and justifies concepts such as heterodoxy and syncretism in a way that contributes to the objectification of normative standards of evaluation that ultimately reify problematic conventions of inner-Islamic difference and otherness. In his historiography Ocak also follows Köprülü's preference for tropes of continuity as compared to change.

A central concept in Ocak's work on the dynamics of intra-religious contact and inner-Islamic difference is that of "Islamic heterodoxy." In the introduction to a collection of articles on formations of Anatolian Turkish Sufism, Ocak credits Köprülü with having been the first to inquire into "Islamic heterodoxy," a term that the latter had used for "Islamic forms outside of Sunnism." Köprülü preferred the term heterodox, for which he sometimes also used the term Batinism, to the pejorative term *râfizî* that had been widely used in Ottoman times. However, neither he nor Gölpınarlı nor others of that scholarly tradition clearly specified what the exact content of this "heterodox" or "*batini*" Islam was. Irène Mélikoff's as well as his own work took on this important task (Ocak 1999, 16–17).

Throughout his own work on Anatolian Islam Ocak uses the term heterodoxy and its derivatives—in line with Köprülü's approach—to qualify forms of Islam that he sees as antagonistic to Sunni Islam. Parallel to the Sunni Islam/heterodoxy dichotomy he also distinguishes between "high Islam" or "Islam of the town" on the one side and "popular Islam," which he defines as "a folk Islam (*halk İslâmı*)" that produced "a popular culture, a mixture of partially mythological belief and culture" on the other side (Ocak 1999, 15–16). While "high Islam" would represent Sunnism, "popular Islam" would be of the "heterodox" kind represented today mainly by the "Alevi-Bektashis." It would, however, be wrong—and here his terminology appears to become somewhat contradictory—to associate "peripheral Islam" (*kırsal İslam*) as such with "heterodoxy" since the largest part of what constituted Turkish "folk Islam" was of the Sunni orientation; as a matter of fact, there was much overlap between Sunni and Alevi "folk Islam" (Ocak 1999, 16). Turkish "heterodox Islam," Ocak continues, could be described by means of three characteristics: politically, it displays an affinity to forms of opposition against authority; socially, it relates to nomadic culture; and theologically, it represents a patchwork that was "non-systematic, mythological, syncretistic, and oral" (Ocak 1999, 18). With regard to its religious character, "heterodox Islam" could further be defined through three dimensions: its syncretism, its mystic orientation (of Islamic as well as non-Islamic origins), and its messianistic ("mehdîci [messianique]") character, which would here be much more strongly developed than in Sunnism. The two major examples of this kind of "heterodox Islam" in Turkish history are Bektashism and Alevism (Ocak 1999, 18–19).[28]

My major claim against Ocak's conceptualization of inner-Islamic difference as epitomized in the account above is that, although his general outline of the Kızılbaş-Alevi narrative is historically more complex than Mélikoff's description and displays in general greater sensibility for methodological issues, his analysis nevertheless remains ultimately caught within the normative nets of meaning spun by notoriously ambiguous concepts and terms, such as heresy, syncretism, and heterodoxy, which he, here remaining himself within the Köprülü tradition, uses as guiding concepts in his description and evaluation of intra-religious contact and inner-religious difference. In the following, as further exemplification of the methodological criticisms developed in my earlier discussion of Köprülü's conceptualization of inner-Islamic difference (see the previous chapter) I will organize my critique of the framing of nonelite Turkish Islam as found in the work of Ocak around four interconnected methodological problems. All of them are related to the way in which he conceptualizes "syncretism" and "heterodoxy."

Methodological Problems

The first problem that I perceive in Ocak's narrative is with his approach to syncretism, which is a variety of the remnants theory discussed earlier. In his introductory chapter to *Alevî ve Bektaşî İnançlarının İslâm Öncesi Temelleri* ("Pre-Islamic Foundations of Alevi and Bektashi Beliefs") he,

---

28 Following Köprülü, Ocak generally counts as heterodox non-Sunni or non-mainstream Islamic groups or movements such as Hurufiyya, Batiniyya, Ismailiyya, and law-transgressing forms of Sufism, that is, forms of Islam that he characterizes as "having an oral and popular mystical quality" (Ocak 1998, 82).

without explicit use of the term itself, puts forward the following description of the syncretistic process and its impact on the Turks:

> It is a known sociological fact that people who for centuries pos-
> sessed and were molded within a specific culture and then, for
> whatever reasons, moved on to another culture, will during this
> transition, and even for a very long time afterwards, not totally cut
> their relations with the older culture and protect some of its ele-
> ments as they were, and some of them by fitting them into the shape
> of their new culture. With no doubt the same process has repeated
> itself in the various Turkish cultures, which began to enter Islamic
> culture at various times and locations. When they entered diverse
> religions, already prior to their acceptance of Islam, these Turkish
> societies have tried to adjust and nourish the old beliefs that were in
> conflict with the new religion, while there were also some that were
> not in conflict, with motifs taken from the new religion. The same
> thing happened in the Islamic period. (Ocak 2000a, 53)

As with the work of Fuad Köprülü, the problem with Ocak's description
is one of conceptual boundaries and continuities. His main narrative, of
which we find similar versions also in the work of many other less prominent scholars of the religious history of the pre-Muslim and Muslim Turks,
is organized around a particular relation between historical elements that
are depicted as continuous and others perceived as changing. As exemplified in the above quote, his notions of religion, particularly Islam, and
of people, particularly the Turkish people, are marked by continuity. The
mentioned religions, namely diverse (non-Islamic) religions and Islam,
do not appear to be themselves subject to change in the course of the
described syncretistic processes. Nor are the Turkish people, who, by entering and exiting a religion and by adjusting old to new elements of faith,
mold the outlook of the "new religions." Irrespective of the changes they
undergo over time, the dominant characteristic of both the Turkish people
and the source religions is continuity throughout—if not despite—history.
In contrast, what is changing in this narrative are the "Turkish cultures"
and "Turkish societies," as well as particular beliefs. Religious motifs are
adopted by the Turks and attached to new faiths. A distinction between
culture and religion—in which culture as the sphere of human activity is
where changes of particular beliefs and practices occur, while the religions
themselves, especially Islam, are static entities, which are in their essence

beyond history—appears to be implicit.[29] Ocak's narrative clearly evolves within a conceptual framework in which a mono-directional, linear history emerges as the matrix through which the Turkish people, and parallel to it a notion of "historical religion" become perceivable in contrast to historically contingent and changing cultures and minor religions.

The second methodological problem is that within Ocak's narrative, "heterodoxy" is at times objectified to an extent that it itself appears as a historical subject/agent, which in the course of time has experienced various incarnations in specific groups and movements. The following example helps to illustrate this point:

> [T]he Turkish heterodoxy that has given birth to Alevism and Bektashism has really begun with the Turkish beliefs of Central Asia. With shamanism and Buddhism it has assumed a mystical quality. It has been nourished by Zoroastrianism and Manichaeism. With the Yeseviye it has received the mark of Islam and Islamic Sufism. In this way it came to Anatolia. It has come into contact with a number of elements from neo-Platonism and from local cultures of the old pagan and Christian periods. With the motifs of Iranian Hurufism in the 15th and Safavid Shiism at the beginning of the 16th century it has acquired the shape we know [today]. This, briefly and roughly, is the real story of the roots of the beliefs of Alevism and Bektashim. (Ocak 1999, 210–211)

This quote displays an extreme case of objectification of an analytical category, namely heterodoxy, figuratively attributed the status of a historical agent that has given birth to Alevism. Even if understood as metaphorical speech, this does not undermine the work that the concept of heterodoxy here accomplishes. In what almost appears as a Platonic move, heterodoxy is essentialized to an extent that in light of its static longevity historically more easily graspable phenomena such as the Yeseviye Sufi movement or Hurufism appear in comparison as mere historical

---

29 Examples of scholarly work that offers similar conceptualizations of syncretism are legion, with variations usually only in some minor points, as for example in the preference for the specific "influences" that are highlighted. Typical is the approach of the historian of Islam Mehmet Sarıkaya, who in a chapter on "The Emergence of Anatolian Alevism" defines Alevism as a syncretistic movement that consists of elements of old Turkish tribes mixed with Islam, elements of Indian and Iranian culture, Shiism, as well as local Anatolian elements (Sarıkaya 2001, 311). For yet another similar example see the work of Yağmur Say, himself a student of Ocak (Say 2007).

contingencies. Such rhetorical transformation of concepts into historical subjects constitutes a conflation of realities of different orders, namely of the empirical and the conceptual kind, and creates epistemological problems more than it helps to answer historical questions. Such objectification of "heterodoxy" we also find elsewhere in Ocak's work, for example when he explains within a discussion of Bektashism in the context of Ottoman Sufism that "the *heterodox Islam* of the Turkmen environment…has been called *heretical* (*Râfizîlik*) by the central Ottoman administration" (Ocak 1998, 126 [emphasis added]); or maintains, again using the concept of heterodoxy on the same level of description with Islamic apologetic terms, that "[t]o understand the religious and ideological dimension of *heretical and irreligious* (*zındıklık ve mülhidlik*) *movements* especially among urban Sufi groups in the Ottoman Empire…one definitely has to investigate…the Hurufi movement, which had strongly influenced the *heterodox milieus* of the entire Middle East" (Ocak 1998, 131 [emphasis added]).

My third methodological criticism concerns the morphology of the religion concept that undergirds Ocak's description of religious change and continuity. In parts of Ocak's work the distinction between "orthodox" and "heterodox" currents within particular religions is configured within a morphological framework where the "heterodoxies" of different religions, for example Christianity and Islam, almost converge in the grey area of syncretism, described as the natural sphere of conversion: "It is thus understood that between the sheikhs and dervishes of heterodox Sufism and the rural Christian folk, priests, and monks, likewise of the heterodox kind, a rapprochement could be achieved that was much easier and more conciliatory than could have been possible between the orthodox parts of the two religions; and this, too, facilitated conversions." He continues comparing the role of the "heterodox," "syncretistic" Sufis in the conversion process of Christian Anatolians to Islam with the role that "heterodox" priests had played in the conversion of Anatolian pagans to Christianity. In this account, Christian "heterodoxy" is identified with pagan remnants parallel to the way in which Muslim "heterodoxy" is defined qua the notion of shamanistic remnants (Ocak 1980, 41–42). This approach has its merits in that it conceptualizes the boundaries between religions not as mono-directional points of exit/entry but as a space where the lines of demarcation between religions are blurred. And I would not claim that the processes of "religious change" here described as syncretism lack any historical and sociological basis. My uneasiness is with the normative charge that the terms "heterodoxy" and "syncretism" receive to

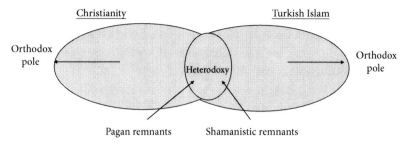

FIGURE 6.1: "Heterodoxy" in Islam and Christianity

the extent that the grey area—the state of being between clearly defined religions—that said terms refer to is implicitly defined as secondary from the perspective of rather static formations of "orthodoxy." In my understanding, the objectification of "heterodoxy" qua equation with specific beliefs and practices and specific historical groups endorses a rather static and implicitly essentialist concept of Islam and is counterproductive to historical analysis (Figure 6.1).

My fourth methodological reservation is with regard to the relation between the concepts of heterodoxy and syncretism in Ocak's work. In addition to the problem of the conflation between substantive and analytical dimensions discussed above, another issue is that the two concepts are so closely interlinked that they appear at times as mutually asserting and signifying each other, to an extent that amounts to a circular argumentation and drastically reduces their explanatory value. Ocak writes, for example, that "during the revolt of Sheikh Bedreddin, especially his deputies Torlak Kemal and Börklüce Mustafa propagated a syncretism of an Islam-Christianity-Mazdaism mixture, in other words a heterodox Islam" (Ocak 1998, 179). Elsewhere in the same work, Ocak describes Bedreddin's "ideology" as "syncretistic heterodox" (Ocak 1998, 197). The tautological nature of this argumentation is also reflected in passages where Sunni Islam (as implicit "orthodoxy") and "heterodoxy" are juxtaposed in a circular manner. Discussing the religious milieus that supported the 15th-century millenarian movement of Sheikh Bedreddin, Ocak states: "Given the fact that the Islam accepted by those people was not Sunni Islam it is apparent that it reflected an interpretation belonging to heterodoxy" (Ocak 1998, 184).[30] It is clear that heterodoxy in these examples is not a discursive concept, but is defined in relation to standards

---

30 Elsewhere he describes Bektashism as "a non-Sunni (heterodox) Sufi order" with a "syncretistic structure" (Ocak 1995, 373).

of Islamic dogma and practice reified as "orthodoxy," which is identified
with Sunni Islam. And it is for this reason that the heterodoxy/orthodoxy
distinction in the work of Ocak remains caught within the epistemic constraints of Islamic apologetics.[31]

To conclude my analysis of Ocak's conceptualization of inner-Islamic
difference, the problems that I perceive are, in continuation of my critique of Köprülü, of both a conceptual and theoretical nature. They target
the way he organizes his narrative of the formation of non-Sunni Turkish
Islam and point to conceptual problems in his underlying assumptions
about what constitutes Islam, and more broadly religion.

Beyond Köprülü

Insufficient attention to the normative connotations of the taxonomies
and terminology that Köprülü and others following him established is still
the rule rather than the exception in contemporary scholarship on Alevi
and Bektashi history. Central topoi of this scholarship are notions of religious continuity, stability of intra-religious boundaries, and an essentialist
approach to inner-Islamic difference, which is explained by problematic
(since biased) taxonomies, as for example the orthodoxy/heterodoxy binary.
In this school of scholarship it is common to associate "heterodoxy" in a
quasi-tautological manner with notions of "popular/folk Islam," "extreme
Shia" (ghulūw), Batinism, and syncretism—notions that are weighed
against a sometimes more and sometimes less explicitly formulated religious norm of Sunni "orthodoxy." Independent of whether it displays a relatively impartial (Ocak), ambivalent (Köprülü), or sympathetic (Mélikoff)
approach to its object of research, scholarship on the Alevis and Bektashis
is based on concepts that are entangled in normative notions of religion
and Islam.

My detailed criticism of the Köprülü school of rationalizing inner-Islamic
difference has two purposes. First, it intends to contribute to a critical
reconsideration of the work of our concepts in the study of religion and
Islam. Second, more specifically, it aspires to show how the dominant paradigm in the scholarship on the Alevi and Bektashi traditions is caught in

---

31 This is most obvious in an early text of his, in which he refers to 13th-century Anatolian
converts from Christianity to Islam as "ignorant" (cahil), espousing an understanding of
Islam that was "superficial and full of mistakes" (sathî ve yalan yanlış) (Ocak 1980, 33). To do
justice to Ocak, it has to be recognized that in his later work he does not use such pejorative
language.

a normative double-bind, conceptualized through notions of pejoratively configured religious otherness on the one hand, and nationist romanticizations of this very difference on the other. It cannot be emphasized enough that the resulting ambivalence is not in any way a natural reflection of the Alevi and Bektashi traditions themselves. Rather, it is a product of approaching them simultaneously through the lenses of a nationalist discourse and a religionist discourse in the tradition of both Islamic apologetics and Islamic modernism. On the one side, the nationalist discourse romanticizes the Alevis' and Bektashis' cultural and religious difference and emphasizes their role as carriers of remnants of ancient Turkish culture and religion. It situates them within a framework of national Turkish history akin to the rhetoric of national unity and sameness. On the other side, the Islamic discourse wants to annihilate or at least minimize this difference, since it perceives it as a challenge to essentialist and homogenizing notions of Islamic unity. The power of both of these discourses is still unbroken, and they continue to this day to dominate public debate on the "Alevi question" in Turkey. As a de facto minority group with a relatively weak position in the public sphere of Turkey, Alevis have still not been able to escape the constraints of these discursive formations (see Prologue).

How to Conceptualize Inner-Islamic Plurality

My critique of a conceptual apparatus that is derived from religious discourses (heterodoxy/orthodoxy) or tends to reinforce static notions of religion and culture (syncretism, center/periphery, popular/high culture) does not mean that I would dispute the legitimacy of the genuine aim to find suitable concepts with which to organize and discuss formations of inner-Islamic plurality and difference. Although the primary purpose of this study is not to offer a new conceptual apparatus as an alternative to the criticized concepts, I would like to outline, in preliminary form, some thoughts in this direction.

Implicit in my analysis and criticism are a number of criteria that concepts for the description of inner-Islamic difference and plurality should ideally fulfill. To prevent the theoretical and methodological pitfalls that I have discussed, such concepts

- should not be normative in a specific religious or political sense. They should not be intermingled in apologetic discourses and not participate in theologico-political rationalizations of power. In other words, the distinction between emic and etic discourses should be clear, and good concepts should not wander between them;

- should not cater to a concept of religion that privileges boundaries over fluidity, and static over dynamic, as well as essentializing over historicizing perspectives;
- should be formulated in an inductive rather than deductive manner; and finally
- should be guided by attention to the work that a particular concept is able to accomplish. What does a particular concept make us see, in which direction does it lead our attention? Conversely, what does it possibly prevent us from perceiving?

The challenge is to formulate concepts without contributing to sociopolitical politics of normalization. This is not an easy task. As for the description of inner-Islamic plurality, I suggest looking for non-binary concepts that are primarily descriptive and only secondarily explanatory. Exemplary is the work of Ahmet Karamustafa. He is one of the very view contemporary scholars who has not only pointed out the underlying normative politics of the traditional taxonomies employed in the study of marginalized forms of Islam, but also shown in his work on Anatolian Islam alternative ways to conceptualize inner-Islamic difference. In his study of the medieval Kalender movement he conceptualized the plurality of Islamic practices without using binaries such as popular Islam/high Islam and other problematic taxonomic devises such as "heterodoxy." Instead he proposed terms such as "deviance," "new renunciation," and "dervish piety" (Karamustafa 1994 and 2005). These terms convey a better sense of the agency of the groups under question than the classic signifiers and do not share their historical and normative baggage.[32] More recently, he has used the term "vernacular Islam" as a signifier for local appropriations of the Islamic traditions (Karamustafa 2013). The goal has to be, I fully agree with Karamustafa, to discuss the plurality of Islamic discourses and practices in a historicizing way that gives nonelite and marginalized groups and currents a proper place in the historical, sociological, and/or anthropological description. With this objective in mind I have previously

---

32 One might, however, question whether the notion of deviance as a negatively formulated indicator of inner-Islamic difference does not also share some of the normative problems discussed earlier. Karamustafa seems to have dropped this term in his more recent publications (see Karamustafa 2005, 87).

suggested differentiating between Islamic orientations with respect to the authorities that they draw on in their religious practice. Accordingly, I distinguished ideal-typically between *charisma-loyal* and *scripture-loyal* Muslim orientations (Dressler 2002, 17–18). While the former category emphasizes an Islam that is organized around the authority of charisma based on the ability to mediate between ordinary believers and the divine (such as Sufi sheikhs/Muslim saints) or on lineage (actual or figurative), the latter privileges authority derived from the scriptural tradition of Islam (in the first place the Koran and the Hadith), and the law (sharia). This differentiation between different kinds of authority models, which should not be understood as mutually exclusive, is but one suggestion for a less normative, more descriptive way of conceptualizing inner-Islamic plurality.

Conclusion

Tropes of Difference and Sameness

THE MAKING OF ALEVISM AS
A MODERNIST PROJECT

THE STUDY OF Alevism has remained astonishingly unimpressed by postcolonial and poststructuralist discourses that pose critical questions in regard to the implication of modern ideologies and issues of power and hegemony in the formation of religious identities and their relationship to secular scholarship. With particular attention on the political context of early Turkish nation-building and history-writing, this book tried to tell the story of how, through the simultaneous fermentation processes of nationalist and religionist discourses, the ethno-religious Kızılbaş communities became "Alevis," that is, "heterodox" Muslim Turks.

It has been one of the major aims of this book to show how the "Alevi question" of Turkey is historically related to the formation of secular Turkish nationalism. Since it had become a political force to reckon with in the last decade of the Ottoman Empire, religion played an important, and as I argued widely underestimated, role in Turkish nation-building. Islam has been a crucial ingredient in the mixture of knowledges and sentiments through which the ideology of Turkish nationalism gained relevance as a political and social force. In the formative years of Turkish nationalism, the ideal of Islamic unity—which hardly differentiated between national and religious ideas, sentiments, and practices—functioned as a model for the moral, social, and political community of the nation. The social bond of Islam remained an implicit component also under Kemalist politics of nationalization in the early republic. From this perspective of national-qua-religious unity, Alevi difference posed a problem that needed to be explained and controlled. Hence, the integration of the Alevis into Turkish society came along with the expectation of their assimilation into a mainstream identity discourse drawing on notions of Turkishness as well as a secular interpretation of Islam. From the perspective of this expectation, any interpretation of Kızılbaş-Alevism that questioned the thesis of its Turkishness and Islamic character appeared as a threat to the anxiously guarded ideal of national unity. Therefore, Turkish nationalists tend to be rather intolerant toward interpretations that locate the Kızılbaş-Alevis outside of Islam or rooted in non-Turkish (for example Kurdish or Persian) ethnicity and culture.

The Work of the Concept of Alevism

Within the discourse of early Turkish nationalism, the making of Alevism was directed against two polemics: first, against the standard Ottoman anti-Kızılbaş rhetoric that marked the Alevis as heretics and justified their exclusion from the centers of Ottoman life, as well as occasionally also their persecution; and second, against a Western discourse that depicted Alevism as being strongly influenced by Christianity. Against these two sets of knowledge, Turkish nationalist writers underlined the Alevis' Turkishness and Islamic orientation, which they saw as a precondition for their integration into the Turkish nation. They did that by demonstrating a continuity that stretched from pre-Islamic Turkish religious culture to the Kızılbaş-Alevis of Anatolia. This continuity was part and exemplification of the more general narrative of continuity of Turkish history and culture from ancient Central Asia to contemporary Turkey. Some of the writers who played pioneering roles in establishing this narrative of Alevi/Turkish continuity (Baha Said Bey, for example) based their argumentation on more or less explicit theories of racial pedigree; others (such as Köprülü) preferred more culturalist interpretations that cast the "Turkish spirit and taste", rather than the "Turkish people" as the historical subject and carrier of the national tradition. Either variety presented itself as scientific and nationalist in spirit. The aim was twofold: first, the theory of the Turkish and ("heterodox") Islamic character of the Kızılbaş-Alevis refuted ideas of Western/Orientalist authors, who saw in the religious and ethnic features of the former elements derived from Christian and ancient Anatolian religions, and created a discourse according to which the Kızılbaş-Alevis were at least in part descendants from Armenians and ancient Anatolian civilizations. In opposition to this narrative, the Turkish nationalist discovery of the Alevis portrayed them as heirs of an idealized Central Asian Turkish culture, religion, and nation. Depicting the Alevis as carriers of ancient Turkish traditions that over time underwent a symbiosis with Islam located them firmly within a Turkish-Islamic context. In political practice this discursive integration meant institutional (and thus material) discrimination and assimilation into the new national public. Second, the theory of the Kızılbaş-Alevis' Turkishness and Islamic "heterodoxy" functioned as an important brick in the formation of the narrative of the Turkish nation. The theory of the continuity of Turkish culture throughout the ages was proven by the argument that Alevi culture would still carry remnants of ancient Turkish culture. The Turks in this way became graspable as a historical subject.

The comparison between 19th-century missionary discourses on the Kızılbaş-Alevis and the Turkish nationalist discourses on Alevism is revealing in that it shows how the agendas behind these discourses directly shaped the representation of Kızılbaş-Alevism. While the prospect of evangelization appears as a major motivation behind the ABCFM missionaries' early engagement with the Kızılbaş-Alevis (and there was therefore a tendency among them to highlight those aspects of the Kızılbashes' "religion" that appeared to show affinities with Christianity), the main motivation behind the Turkish nationalists' interest in the Alevis was to strengthen and homogenize the national body, for the sake of which the Kızılbaş-Alevis were argued to be "pure Turks." Accordingly, the nationalist discourses on Alevism focused on the brotherhood of Turks beyond the differences of religious dogma. When it was emphasized, this difference was argued to be grounded in the continuation of ancient Turkish religious traditions and therefore it could be understood as a marker of Turkishness. The Turkish nationalist discourse on the nature of the Kızılbaş-Alevis' difference was itself not homogenous. Controversies surfaced (1) with regard to the importance attributed to Islam and (2) with regard to the nature of Turkish continuity. The writings of Baha Said reflect an approach that tries to reduce the Islamic character of the Kızılbaş-Alevis to a minimum, while at the same time displaying an ethno-racial understanding of Turkish continuity. Köprülü's approach differed on both accounts. For one, he gave more weight to the religious dimension of Kızılbaş-Alevism, the Islamic dimension of which he highlighted, even if always underlining its "heterodox" character. As for his approach to nationalism, he objectified Turkish continuity in idealist notions (such as "Turkish taste and spirit") and rejected, in accordance with Gökalp, biologist reductions of the Turkish subject.

Modern reflections on religion and nationalism in the 19th and early 20th centuries have been marked by an obsession with the dialectically related themes of alienation from and reconnection with origins, which are often essentialized in the process. The switch from the project of a multiethnic Ottomanism to an ethnically homogenizing Turkish nationalism, which began in the late Young Turk period and was continued by early Kemalist politics, demanded also a leveling of religious difference, which was inspired by implicit norms of unity in religion, and secular sameness. Still, in the early Turkish Republic the role of Islam as a key element for successful national homogenization was subdued. Kemalist secularism was deeply suspicious of not only the political, but also the social potential and public dimension of religion. The integration of the Kızılbaş-Alevis into the new national order was strongly impacted by the Kemalist prejudice against religion and, in particular, religious communalism. In contrast to the more integrative tradition of early Turkish secularist thought, as reflected in the work of Ziya Gökalp (who envisioned religion and nationalism symbiotically working together toward modernization of the society), the Kemalist order allowed religion only a secondary role in the definition of national identity. Viewed from within the nationalist framework, the Kızılbaş-Alevis were primarily Turkish, and their religious difference was—the writings of Baha Said are emblematic of this trend—played down and reframed in terms of culture. Privileging ethnic and national over religious traits, this culturalism facilitated the integration of the Kızılbaş-Alevis into the national domain.

What Did the Label Alevi Do for the Kızılbaş-Alevis?

The early 20th-century Turkish nationalist conceptualization of the Alevis established a new discursive space for not only scholarly, but also indigenous formulations of Alevism. Parallel to the narrative of Turkish continuity, a rather uncritically conceived Alevi *longue durée*—sketching the evolution of Alevism as a predominantly Turkish formation from pre-Islamic Altai Turkish traditions through its first Anatolian incarnations in the 13th century until modern Turkey—gained hegemonic status. There are no indications that "Alevism" as presented within the Turkist narrative—that is as a tradition with strong traces of pre-Islamic Turkish culture and religion, at the same time to be interpreted within the context of Islam—matched with the self-understanding of many Kızılbaş-Alevis prior to the advent of Turkish nationalism. We know that some Kızılbaş groups did at least since the second half of the 19th century self-identify as "Alevi." But there is no evidence that this identification signified more than (1) a Shiite disposition very broadly speaking, (2) rejection of the pejorative label "Kızılbaş," and (3) dissociation from outsiders—other Kızılbaş-Alevi groups included. The Kızılbaş-Alevis were culturally, ethnically, and religiously much more diverse than the nationalist discourse, homogenizing them under one label that aimed to reduce this diversity, would make one believe. I argue that it was an essential part of the work of the new concept Alevism to homogenize and discipline those to whom it was applied, thus making possible their normalization as secular Turkish subjects in line with the Kemalist ideology. For example, the new focus on the Turkishness of the Kızılbaş-Alevis worked to undermine claims of ethnic difference put forward by Kurdish Alevis. Given the imminent threat perceived by the early Kemalist state in light of Kurdish resistance against its centralization and homogenization efforts, the Turkish nationalist claims on the Alevis can be read as a move to split the loyalties of the Alevis by rallying Sunnis and Alevis under the banner of Turkish nationalism—thus preventing Alevi and Sunni Kurds from uniting in the name of Kurdish nationalism. The polarization along ethnic/national lines also made alliances between Turkish and Kurdish Kızılbaş-Alevis in the name of Alevism more difficult.

The republican state's efforts to integrate the Alevis through ethnic and religious assimilation is in continuity with late Ottoman politics. Already under Abdülhamid II in the 1890s the Kızılbaş-Alevis became objects of assimilation qua Islamization/Sunnification, clearly motivated by strategic political considerations. The beginnings of the Turkification of Alevism need to be located in the Young Turk period when the government increased its efforts to secure the loyalty of the Kızılbaş-Alevi tribes. In the Hamidian tradition, these efforts followed the logic of modernization and centralization of political authority. But Young Turk nation-building went beyond the Hamidian politics of unification in the name of Islam. In addition to Islamic solidarity and homogeneity, the ethnic composition of the population now became a major concern for the project of national unification. Henceforth, the late Ottoman and Turkish republican states put considerable effort in persuading and/or coercing Kızılbaş-Alevis to assimilate in line with the nationalist project.

It could be argued that within early republican nationalism the terms "Alevi" and "Alevilik" had an integrative aim, softening the strong connotations of political disloyalty and religious sectarianism associated with the label Kızılbaş. However, within the semantics of Kemalist nationalism the new term "Alevilik" implied entirely new sets of ethno-cultural and religious belonging. Kemalist nationalism related difference from Sunnism to difference from Turkishness. This impacted not only the Kızılbaş-Alevis, but also various other groups at the margins of Turkish society, such as the non-Muslims, the Dönme, the Nusayirs, and so forth.[1] This semantics not only marks ethno-religious boundaries and differences (through processes of othering), but is at the same time strongly interested in homogenizing those that qualify for being part of the we-group. Altan Gokalp points to this dynamic when he critically observes that the historian of Turkmen tribes Faruk Sümer would fail to distinguish between the ethnic differences among the Turkish-speaking tribes of Anatolia, and would rather focus on their commonality, uncritically identified as "Turkishness."[2]

I argue that the modern conceptualization of Alevism as a cultural-religious formation that carries roots of ancient Turkish traditions and is essentially Muslim has been rather ambivalent for them. On the one side, the new concept of Alevism was less pejoratively coined than the old term Kızılbaş, and thus provided them with a legitimate place within Turkish nationhood, hence enabling their gradual, though not easy, and still not completed integration into society. On the other hand, the term Alevi locked the conceptualization of those identified by it within a Turkish and Islamic frame of reference and hence exerts pressure to assimilate accordingly. Integration and assimilation appear here as two sides of the same coin, reflective of the work of nationalism at large.

In regard to their "religion," Alevis were from the beginning of the republic marked by those practices and beliefs that signified them as different from Sunni Islam, that is, as "heterodox". Their difference was evaluated according to the standards of Sunni Islam, which had been translated into a secular discourse. This is not a paradox, but a product of the very logic and semantics of Turkish secularism, which is obsessed with regulating religion and therefore in need of a normative standard of correct religion, in practice defined in accordance with mainstream Sunni Islamic conventions (see Dressler 2008; 2010a; 2011a; 2011b). It is undeniable that this pressure of Sunni Islamic majority discourse on the Alevi minority has borne fruit and encouraged Alevi individuals as well as Alevi

---

1 As has been pointed out by Gokalp, terms such as Yörük, Kızılbaş, Tahtacı, and even Çingene (Gypsy) were marked by this double othering according to which a true Turk is Sunni (Gokalp 1980, 32–33).

2 In his book *Oğuzlar* (1967), Sümer claimed that "there is no ethnic difference at all between the Turks, Turkmen, Yörük, Tahtacı, and Kızılbaş Alevi, who are all descendants of the Oghuz ethnicity that is Turkmen" (quoted in Gokalp 1980, 32). Pointing to the same problem, Roux points out with surprise that Köprülü did not distinguish between Yörük and Turkmen when talking about a Yörük-Turkmen dialect spoken by the tribes of Anatolia (Roux 1970, 8).

groups and organizations to move in rhetoric and practice closer to mainstream understandings of Islam.[3]

Another difficulty that the Turkish nationalist framing of Alevism
posed for the Alevis is its bias against non-Turkish ethnicities. Just
as the laicist regime denied recognition of the religious difference
of the Alevis according to the Alevis' own terms, the new focus on the
Kızılbaş-Alevis' Turkishness denied Kurmanci- and Zazaki-speaking
(Kurdish) Kızılbaş-Alevis the legitimacy of their non-Turkish ethnic identities. Whereas Turkish Alevis may regard the Turkish nationalist interpretation of Alevism as a chance for them to integrate into the Turkish
national body, Kurdish Alevis have developed their own sense of ethnic
and national difference. This made their integration from the beginning
more difficult. There are, of course, further historical reasons that made
the Kurdish Alevis tend to be more reluctant to integrate into the homogenizing fold of Turkish-Muslim unity. Since the beginning of the Turkish
nationalist state project, Kurdish Alevis witnessed closely and were themselves exposed to state violence, most drastically exemplified in the brutal "pacification" of the Dersim region in 1937–1938, the repercussions of
which can be felt still today. Kurdish Alevis were discriminated on both
religious and ethnic grounds and under double pressure to assimilate.
For mainstream Turkish nationalist discourse, keen on assimilating the
Alevis into Turkish nationhood, the existence of a considerable Kurdish
Alevi population has made this assimilation process both more complex
and more important. While suspicion is one strong Turkish nationalist
sentiment in this context, the new discourse on Alevism also developed a
powerful argument for how to solve the ethnic problem. After extending
the claim that the Alevis are Turkish to the Kurdish-speaking Alevis and
regarding them as Kurdified Turks it remained only a small step to reason
that if Alevi Kurds were original Turks than Sunni Kurds could also be
secondarily Kurdified racial Turks.

To sum up, the work of the concept Alevism provides us insights into
how Turkish nationalism and Turkish secularism jointly work toward the
creation of Turkish unity, understood as secular, but Muslim, and Turkish.
Within this context, the signification of the Alevis as "heterodox" Muslim

---

3 The same dynamic can be observed in other contexts. Yusri Hazran argues that increased
pressure to Islamize in the last three decades has contributed to a turn within the Druze
communities of Lebanon and Syria to relate more positively to Islam. The fact that the Druze
of Israel do not partake in this trend supports the argument that religious signification is
strongly responsive to particular social and political settings (Hazran 2010, 242–245).

Turks advanced their position within the discourses of both Turkish nationalism and Sunni Islam, while the subjection to these discourses at the same time undermined their freedom to independently self-identify. In other words, the designation "Turkish Alevi," marked simultaneously by notions of religious difference and ethnic sameness, located and locked their traditions within the modern and secularist discourses of nationalism and religion. Being defined and defining themselves primarily through the category Alevi, this name has in the following years become both a means and a symbol of their difference in relation to the thereby equally reified notion of Sunni Islam. On the one hand, as supposed carriers of "shamanist remnants," that is, as embodiment of the continuity of the Turkish nation, their legitimacy within nationalist discourse increased considerably. Alevis subscribing to the homogenizing dynamics of Turkish nationalism and secularism were granted a certain, though never formalized, recognition as a legitimate part of the Turkish national body and from that perspective it could be argued that their position was upgraded within the cultural hierarchy of the new state, especially in comparison to the officially recognized "minorities" of the Jewish and Christian religions, which were never really accepted within Turkish nationhood.

On the other hand, however, the same argument (carriers of ancient Turkish tradition) rendered the Alevis heretics in the view of those who subscribed to revivalist notions of Islam and aspired to a cleansing of the Islamic "religion" from un-Islamic "cultural'" additions. In other words, the price for the Alevis' integration into Turkish nationhood was nonrecognition of their religious and sociocultural difference. The simultaneous Turkification, secularization, and thus depoliticization of the Kızılbaş-Alevi tradition effectively amounted to the folklorization of Alevism, taming its otherness by de-religionizing and musealizing its culture, and declaring the social and political conflicts associated with the term Kızılbaş an overcome aspect of the (Ottoman, that is, non-Turkish) past.

National Historiography and Religiography

A major empirical focus of this book has been on the religiography of Mehmed Fuad Köprülü. The years in which he was most productive as a scholar, between the mid-1910s and the mid-1930s, were marked by the tremendous social and political changes that meant the end of a multiethnic and multireligious Islamic empire and the concomitant birth of the secular Turkish nation-state. A witness of the decline of Ottomanism,

Köprülü's political convictions were inspired by a longing for national (re-)birth. This reflected on his academic work, especially inspiring his interpretation of those groups that he subsumed under categories such as "popular Turkish Islam" or "Islamic heterodoxy."

Köprülü contributed immensely to the translation of Western scientific methodology into Turkish academic discourses. However, he was not merely an imitator of Western knowledge. Rather, Köprülü was an authoritative and respected critic of Orientalist work on Turkish, Seljuk, and Ottoman history, subjecting it to a thorough review always ready to provide a well-argued and pointed response, and in this way he impacted Western knowledge production on Ottoman and Turkish history. Within the broader Western Orientalist tradition, both in scholarship on religion and on history, he considered research on the Turks to be underrepresented, biased, and full of misconceptions. He saw his own writings and academic interventions as an important corrective to these perceived shortcomings. And he apparently was quite confident about his achievements in this regard: "[A]fter thirty years of continuous work, I am unable to refrain from saying with great satisfaction that I have succeeded in *changing* a good many of the *wrong ideas* about the role of the *Turks* in medieval history, and that many *Western scholars* finally *accept* these results" (Köprülü 1940, xxxviii).[4] Köprülü's criticism of Orientalist scholarship, however, mostly focused on empirical content and narrative framework, and only secondarily on matters of methodology. He hardly questioned the basic terminological conventions and larger theoretical contexts of Orientalist scholarship.

As a scholarly entrepreneur, Köprülü's role in the institutionalization of academic disciplines of Turkish literary and historical studies in the late Ottoman and early republican periods was enormous. Almost foreshadowing the *Annales* school of historiography, he followed a decisively interdisciplinary approach and emphasized the necessity of investigating Turkish history and culture within broader temporal and geographical contexts, employing micro as well as macro perspectives. This was politically relevant. His formulation of a Turkish subject as a historical agent is one of his most important legacies both in the context of scholarship and in the context of nation-building. Köprülü's work on the *longue durée* of national Turkish culture provided Turkish nationalism with an academically solid

---

4 Obviously, as a prolific writer, critical observer, and contributor to Turkish and international scholarship on Turkish history, he was himself not immune to criticism. See Dölen (2010, 268–270); see also Yıldız (2009, 493 fn 23).

narrative that was necessary to legitimize and make evident nationalist claims both to the outside world and to the Turkish people.

Köprülü's nationalist historiography also set the parameters for his religiography, namely the study of Alevism as a "heterodoxy" and a "syncretism" built on pre-Islamic Turkish religion cast as shamanism, and Central Asian Turkish Sufism, with incorporated elements of Shia *ghulūw*, Ismailism, as well as Batinism. He established a genealogical link connecting ancient Central Asian Turkish traditions with the Anatolian Babai and early Bektashi milieus, of which the Kızılbaş and Alevis were seen as a direct historical extension. Partially parallel to him, partially following his initiative, other early republican authors, most prominently Baha Said Bey and Yusuf Ziya [Yörükan], embarked on complementary paths of investigation. The comparison with the latter two shows that Köprülü's interest was primarily historical. Both in the texts of the amateur researcher Baha Said, as well as in the slightly later, but much more detailed, accounts of the sociologist and anthropologist Yörükan, the historical framing of Alevism remained rather coarse, functioning mainly as a frame for the ethnographic observations that took center stage in their respective contributions.

Köprülü never dedicated an entire article or book to Alevism per se. Still, his work provided the first systematic framework for the formulation of Alevism as a "heterodox Islamic" formation intimately related to Turkishness. Köprülü's account of Alevism needs to be situated in his broader narrative of the continuity of Turkishness, which he saw manifest itself historically in various aspects of culture broadly speaking, such as language, literature, and religious and social institutions. Köprülü idealized these aspects of Turkishness in the notion of the Turkish spirit. Varieties of this narrative have through the dominance of nationalist discourse become popular in public as well as in academic discourses. Not the least the Turkist framework of Turkish culture remained—the parallel, relatively marginal discourse of a Kurdish Alevism notwithstanding[5]—until today the dominant framework for the conceptualization of Alevism.

Köprülü understood that, as other people who embraced Islam, Turkish tribes had appropriated the Islamic religion gradually. Already in the first phase of this conversion process, manifest in the earliest literature

---

5 An example is Bender (1991); see also Bayrak (1997; 2009). Cf. Bruinessen (1997); White and Jongerden (2003); Ağuiçenoğlu (2010).

produced in the environment of the Turkish-Islamic symbiosis, he was able to trace a conflation of Islamic elements with traditions from previous and neighboring religions and cultures. As a sociologically (self-)educated historian, Köprülü was interested in the mechanism and cultural products of this merger of the "Turkish spirit" with the religion of Islam. In order to reconstruct and analyze this amalgamation, he needed to be able to identify its elements, categorize beliefs and practices (Islamic and non-Islamic) and further distinguish between Turkish and non-Turkish influences among the latter. Terms and concepts prominent in religious and Islamic studies of the time period, such as "heterodoxy" and "syncretism," helped Köprülü to both create clear boundaries between phenomena of different origins and legitimize their hierarchical categorization.

Despite the fact that from the establishment of the Turkish Republic onward a secularist politics, which aimed to undermine the institutional role of religion in the state organization and equally targeted the social and cultural role of religion in the public, gained strength, Köprülü continued to attribute to religion an important role in his historiography. He made religion a central focus in his analysis of the evolution of the Turks. In that regard he can be compared to other important thinkers of early Turkish nationalism, such as Ahmet Ağaoğlu and Ziya Gökalp. Despite the fact that he would in the early republic move closer to the more rigid secularism that then emerged, Köprülü amalgamated in his reflections on religion at times religious and nationalist semantics. This is not surprising. Both nationalism and normative Islam (both Islamic revivalism and Islamic modernism) rely on notions of secular time. The concept of the nation requires a linear understanding of history through which the story of its birth and evolution can be told, and its historicization demands static notions of religion, people, race, and/or culture through which the nation can be made graspable as a historical subject. Consequently, history becomes "the crucial field upon which the meaning of national symbols is defined and the life of the nation validated" (Shissler 2003, 31).

Köprülü's concept of Islam, similarly to that of Ağaoğlu, was influenced by modernist and revivalist notions of purity rationalized as "orthodox" Sunni Islam, in relation to which he would judge other forms of Islam as deviations from the Sunni model. This approach, which was widely emulated, established semantic similarities and convergences between religious and purportedly secular national/ethnic/racial notions of purity. The same mechanism also played out in the reconceptualization of Alevism as a "heterodox" Muslim community, juxtaposed against a normative model of Sunni Islam. In other words, the reconceptualization of Alevism followed the semantics of nationalism in its demand for a unitary religion (that is, Islam) deemed desirable to strengthen the moral community of the nation.

Peterson and Walhof have argued that "[b]y divesting religions of their divisive or heterodox elements, nation builders crafted templates for nationalism, unifying sets of rituals and ideals that defined new political communities" (Peterson/Walhof 2002b, 8). The example of Alevism as conceptualized by Köprülü and others reveals a more complex mechanism. Köprülü locates the evidence for the continuity of the national Turkish spirit precisely in what he labels the "heterodox" traits of Alevism, which are revealed qua comparison to the Sunni norm. It is thus not simply their Islam, but rather their "heterodoxy" that marks the Alevis as Turkish and makes their integration into the nation feasible. This means that in the case of Alevism the integration into Islamdom remains necessarily incomplete. It is through this dynamic that the Alevis' belonging to the Muslim and Turkish nation remains inevitably characterized by ambivalence. They are integrated (as Muslim Turks) into the nation, and at the same time they are marginalized with reference to their religious otherness. In a way, the nationalist conceptualization of Alevism embodies the paradox of a secular nationalism that draws on religious criteria to define itself. To the extent that Turkish nationalism implies belonging to Sunni Islam, it is inclined to other groups such as the Alevis as "heterodox".

As I have shown, the conceptualization of Alevism as a "heterodox" Turkish culture that carries traces of shamanism, which is meant to prove the continuity of Turkish national traditions from pre-Islamic Central Asia to modern Anatolia, is still widely accepted in both academic and popular Turkish discourses. A critical rereading of Köprülü and other influential early Turkish nationalist writers who contributed to the popularization of this knowledge is crucial for a demythologization and historicization of the concept of Alevism. It contributes also to our understanding of other under-researched aspects in the formation of Turkish nationalism, especially a more sophisticated look at the variety of roles that religious tropes and semantics played in the nation-building process. The gradual institutionalization of a rigid laicism as a disciplinary practice to curtail and control the role of Islam in the public sphere of the Turkish republic makes it easy to overlook the positive, affirmative role that Sunni Islam played in late Ottoman and early Turkish republican imaginations and rhetorics of national identity.

The conceptual transformation from Kızılbashim to Alevism within nationalist Turkish discourse, as exemplified in the work of Köprülü, followed the logic of secular modernity. Within this logic, both the nation and religion were depicted as historical entities that show continuity in their essential character, but may change their outer form, which is subject to the laws of secular time. The tropes of continuity and essence as formulated with regard to Islam and the nation at the same time require the formulation of their respective contingent and unauthentic others. From this point of view, mainstream Sunni Islam is elevated above secular time, a matter of providence in need of history only to fulfill its salvational role. Religious traditions at the margins of the Islamic mainstream such as Alevism, on the other hand, are seen as deviations from the true religion, the product of profane, secular history.

Outwardly purely analytical, but implicitly normative-dogmatic conceptualizations of Islam and Islamic difference are part of the legacy of an essentialist religion discourse in general and Orientalist scholarship in particular. Within Köprülü's narrative, the orthodoxy/heterodoxy dichotomy invokes a scenario in which "heterodox" Islam is by definition syncretistic, in other words, carries elements of non-Islamic origin, while Islamic "orthodoxy" represents the time-resistant religious norm (that is, implicitly, Sunni Islam). Köprülü's work offers a window in the translation and normalization of these discourses and their concepts into Turkish discourses. Different from Baha Said, Fuad Köprülü situated Kızılbaş-Alevism explicitly within the framework of Islamic heresiology. Köprülü's concept of Kızılbaş-Alevism contributed to its religious othering as "heterodox" and thereby, perhaps inadvertently, also to the normalization of the national Turkish subject as Sunni Muslim. Of course, given the homogenizing forces of modernist Islamic discourses and the universalization of Western taxonomies of (world) religion, it is not at all astonishing that a modernist scholar of Islam such as Köprülü conceptualized inner-Islamic differences with secularized taxonomies borrowed from Christianity/religion. But would it not have been possible that Köprülü, or another prominent Muslim scholar of Islam, could have rejected concepts such as heterodoxy as too much embedded in the Christian apologetic tradition to be employed by them as meaningful taxonomies for the classification of inner-Islamic difference? Could one not maintain that inner-Islamic concepts should be able to do a more adequate—in the sense of more honest—job in this work of categorization? Responding, I would suggest that it is precisely the coming together of the Islamic heresiographical discourse with the secular and universalist, modern discourse of religion rooted in

Christianity that provides the concept of heterodoxy in its application to inner-Islamic difference with evidence. Both discourses privilege scripture over oral traditions and are obsessed with creating boundaries that separate more and less "original" traditions from each other; both measure deviance from the religious norm through notions of authenticity and codified standards of belief and practice.

The convergence of (world) religionist and Islamic discourses shows itself also in the continuities between the first, Western, and the second, Turkish nationalist, "discovery" of the Kızılbaş-Alevis. As I have shown, the Kızılbaş-Alevis were already conceptualized as "unorthodox" by outside Western observers in the second half of the 19th century. For the Western observers during the late Ottoman Empire, especially the American missionaries, the main reference point for evaluating the Kızılbaş-Alevis' difference from Sunni Islam was a Christian/Protestant concept of religion. Another aspect of continuity that connects late 19th- to early 20th-century Western/Orientalist narratives with Turkish nationalist discourses on the Kızılbaş-Alevis is the very ambivalence of their representation. In the narratives of the former, this ambivalence was reflected in speculations concerning the latter's Christian and/or ancient Anatolian roots on the one hand, and their superstitious character on the other. Since the late Ottoman period, Islam and Turkish nationalism became the new parameters for the evaluation of the Kızılbaş-Alevis. From this new perspective, too, the Kızılbaş-Alevis were viewed with ambivalence: on the one side, they were attributed significance from within the nationalist framework as carriers of ancient Turkish traditions. This gave them an important place within the narrative of the Turkish nation and thus increased their cultural capital. On the other side, their religious difference from the mainstream Sunni point of view emphasized their "heterodoxy," this time configured from an entirely Sunni Islamic point of view, supported additionally by recourse to Western academic discourses on religion.[6]

I have argued that where normatively ambiguous concepts such as the orthodoxy/heterodoxy binary are used, they should be employed

---

6 Gokalp has written about this ambivalence in the representation of the Kızılbaş-Alevis in a discussion of the terminological distinctions made in Turkish nationalist discourse with regard to Turkophone nomads. If the theme is the conquest of Anatolia, Alevi groups tended to be referred to with the positively connoted term Turkmen. But when accused of incestuous practices, the same group would be qualified by terms with pejorative connotations, such as Kızılbaş, Tahtacı, and Gypsy (Gokalp 1980, 35).

in discursive manner as indicators of religio-political power relations within particular contexts—if not with the aim to subvert the hegemonic ascriptions of these terms. My criticism of Köprülü's conceptualization of inner-Islamic difference connects to the more general need for critical re-investigation of the concepts that the academic study of religion, and Islam more specifically, has inherited from classical religionist and Orientalist scholarship. The way in which his religiography conceives of the boundaries between religious discourses and practices based on clear ideas about distinctive religious traditions as rather solid is a case in point. Critique of his religiography can only be a first step in the more difficult endeavor of a comprehensive rewriting of the religious history of Anatolia and adjacent territories following the immigration of Turkish tribes and subsequent Islamization without taking recourse to religionist concepts and theories. Such rewriting needs to be more aware of the work of concepts and the ways they shape and organize our knowledge. It has to be sensitive to the theoretical, normative, and material relations of concepts to given political, religious, and academic interests and hegemonies. Only when our methodology is based on such a critical approach to our concepts can we advance more complex inquiries into the dynamics of inner-Islamic difference and plurality.

For future research on Alevism it will further be imperative to advance comparative study on the modern discourses on those groups that have been designated as "heterodox" in relation to Islam and to look into the specific epistemic contexts of these significations. One interesting comparison would be with historically related Kızılbaş-Alevi and Bektashi groups outside of Turkey (especially those of the Balkans), who were not subjected to the pressures and workings of Turkish nationalism and secularism. Another comparison would be with groups such as the Yezidi, Ismaili, and Nusayri as examples of communities that have also often been labeled "heterodox" by scholars of Islam and that in fact show various convergences with Kızılbaş-Alevi beliefs, practices, and historical experiences. What is particular about the Alevis of Turkey is that their signification as "heterodox" coincided with the formulation of a meta-narrative on Alevism that streamlined "Alevi" history and identity by putting emphasis on commonality and deemphasizing regional, ritual, and sociocultural differences. Within the complex workings of this re-signification process, the primary aim of which was to integrate them into the field of the Turkish nation, Alevis began to be understood as forming a distinct, despite regional variations in principle homogeneous, socioreligious group.

In short, the modern concept of Alevism is the product of the discourses of Turkish nationalism, Islam, and (world) religionism. The distinctiveness of the various *ocak*-centered Kızılbaş-Alevi communities has largely been lost in the mill of modernist discourses and the homogenizing machinery of the nation state. Any academic work on Alevism needs to take seriously the historically rather recent conceptual transformation of Alevism, and the methodological problems that come with it.

Bibliography

ABBREVIATIONS

ABCFM	American Board of Commissioners for Foreign Missions
AMMU	Aşair ve Muhacirin Müdüriyet-i Umumiyesi ("General Directorate for Tribes and Immigrants")
BOA	Başbakanlık Osmanlı Arşivi ("Office of The Prime Minister Ottoman Archives")
CUP	Committee of Union and Progress (İttihad ve Terakki Cemiyeti)
DRA	Directorate for Religious Affairs (Diyanet İşleri Başkanlığı)
Early Mystics	"Early Mystics in Turkish Literature" (Türk Edebiyatında İlk Mutasavvıflar, 1919)
İAMM	İskan-ı Aşair ve Muhacirin Müdüriyet-i Umumiye ("General Directorate for the Settlement of Tribes and Refugees")
JDP	Justice and Development Party (Adalet ve Kalkınma Partisi, AKP)
Origins	"The Origins of Turkish Literature" (Türk Edebiyatının Menşei, 1915)
RPP	Republican People's Party (Cumhuriyet Halk Partisi, CHP)

WORKS CITED

Açıkses, Erdal. 2003. *Amerikalıların Harput`taki Misyonerlik Faaliyetleri*. Ankara: Türk Tarih Kurumu.

Adanır, Fikret. 1994. "Turkey." In *Historical Culture—Historical Communication: International Bibliography*, edited by Karl Pellens, Siegfried Quantd, and Hans Süssmuth, 367–393. Frankfurt a. M.: Diesterweg.

Ağuiçenoğlu, Hüseyin. 2010. "Alevilik Örneğinde İnanç-Etnik Kimlik İlişkisi Üzerine Yapılan Tartışmalara Kısa bir Bakış." In *Herkesin Bildiği Sır: Dersim*, edited by Şükrü Arslan, 119–137. Istanbul: İletişim.

Ahmet Refik [Altınay]. 1932. *On Altıncı Asırda Rafizîlik ve Bektaşîlik*. Istanbul: Muallim Ahmed Halim Kütüphanesi.

Ainsworth, William F. 1842. *Travels and Researches in Asia Minor, Mesopotamia, Chaldea, and Armenia*, vol. 2. London: Hohn W. Parker.

Akçam, Tamer. 2002. "Another History on Sèvres and Lausanne." In *Der Völkermord an den Armeniern und die Shoah = The Armenian Genocide and the Shoah*, edited by Hans-Lukas Kieser and Dominik J. Schaller, 281–299. Zurich: Chronos.

Akçam, Tamer. 2006. *A Shameful Act: The Armenian Genocide and the Question of Turkish Responsibility*. New York: Metropolitan Books.

Akçura[oğlu], Yusuf. 2005 [1904]. *Üç Tarz-ı Siyaset*. Ankara: Lotus.

Akpınar, Alişan. 2004. "Bir Sahtekarlık Hikayesi ya da Kürtlerin Asimile Edilmelerine İlk Adım." *Vesta Dergisi*, no. 3–4. Accessible online. http://www.bgst.org/keab/aa20070522.asp.

Akpınar, Alişan. 2012. "II. Abdülhamid Dönemi Devlet Zihniyetinin Alevi Algısı." Unpublished paper (presented at conference "Alevi-Bektashi Communities in the Ottoman Realm: Sources, Paradigms, and Historiography," Bosphorus University, Dec. 13–15, 2011).

Akpınar, Alişan, Sezen Bilir, Serhat Bozkurt, and N. Kemal Dinç. 2010. "II. Abdülhamit Dönemi Raporlarında 'Dersim Sorunu' ve Zihinsel Devamlılık." In *Herkesin Bildiği Sır: Dersim*, edited by Şükrü Arslan, 311–334. Istanbul: İletişim.

Aktar, Ayhan. 2003. "Homogenising the Nation, Turkifying the Economy." In *Crossing the Aegean: An Appraisal of the 1923 Compulsory Population Exchange between Greece and Turkey*, edited by Renée Hirschon, 79–95. New York: Berghahn.

Aktar, Ayhan. 2009. "'Turkification' Politics in the Early Republican Era." In *Turkish Literature and Cultural Memory. "Multiculturalism" as a Literary Theme after 1980*, edited by Catharina Duft, 29–62. Wiesbaden: Harrassowitz.

Akün, Ömer Faruk. 2002. "Mehmed Fuad Köprülü." *Türkiye Diyanet Vakfı İslâm Ansiklopedisi* 26:471–486. Istanbul: Türkiye Diyanet Vakfı.

Akyol, Mustafa. 2011. *Islam without Extremes. A Muslim Case for Liberty*. New York: W.W. Norton & Company.

Algar, Hamid. 2004. Review of *Hadji Bektach: un mythe et ses avatars. Genèse et évolution du soufisme populaire en Turquie*, by Irène Mélikoff. *International Journal of Middle East Studies* 36:687–689.

Alkan, Necati. 2012. "Fighting for the Nuṣayrī Soul: State, Protestant Missionaries and the ʿAlawīs in the Late Ottoman Empire." *Die Welt des Islams* 52:23–50.

Aly, Götz, and Suzanne Heim. 2003. *Architects of Annihilation: Auschwitz and the Logic of Destruction*. Princeton, NJ: Princeton University Press.

Anderson, Rufus. 2006 [1872]. *History of the Missions of the American Board of Commissioners for Foreign Missions to the Oriental Churches*, vol. 2. Ebook. http://manybooks.net/.

Andrews, Peter Alford. 1989. *Ethnic Groups in the Republic of Turkey*. Wiesbaden: Reichert.

Anjum, Ovamir. 2007. "Islam as a Discursive Tradition: Talal Asad and His Interlocutors." *Comparative Studies of South Asia, Africa and the Middle East* 27:656–672.

Asad, Talal. 1986. *The Idea of an Anthropology of Islam.* Washington: Center for Contemporary Arab Studies, Georgetown University.

Asad, Talal. 1993. *Genealogies of Religion: Discipline and Reasons of Power in Christianity and Islam.* London: Johns Hopkins University Press.

Asad, Talal. 2003. *Formations of the Secular: Christianity, Islam, Modernity.* Stanford: Stanford University Press.

Asılsoy, Abdülkerim. 2008. "Türk Modernleşme Öncülerinden Fuat Köprülü: Hayatı, Eserleri ve *Fikirleri."* PhD diss., Marmara University.

Atalay, Besim. [1340/]1924. *Bektaşilik ve Edebiyatı.* Istanbul: Matba-i Amire.

Ayata, Bilgin, and Deniz Yükseker. 2005. "A Belated Awakening: National and International Responses to the Internal Displacement of Kurds in Turkey." *New Perspectives on Turkey* 32:5–42.

Azak, Umut. 2007. "*Myths and Memories of Secularism in Turkey. (1946–1966)."* PhD diss., Leiden University.

Azak, Umut. 2010. *Islam and Secularism in Turkey: Kemalism, Religion and the Nation State.* London: I. B. Tauris.

Baali, Fuad. 1988. *Society, State, and Urbanism: Ibn Khaldun's Sociological Thought.* New York: State University of New York Press.

Baban, Cihad. 1970. *Politika Galerisi.* Istanbul: Remzi.

Babayan, Kathryn. 2002. *Mystics, Monarchs, and Messiahs: Cultural Landscapes of Early Modern Iran.* Cambridge, MA: Harvard University Press.

Babinger, Franz. 1922. "Der Islam in Kleinasien: Neue Wege der Islamforschung." *Zeitschrift der Deutschen Morgenländischen Gesellschaft* 76:126–152.

Badger, [George Percy]. 1850. "Mission to Kurdistan in 1842." *The Colonial Church Chronicle and Missionary Journal* 4:89–95.

Baer, Marc [David]. 2004. "The Double Bind of Race and Religion. The Conversion of the Dönme to Turkish Secular Nationalism." *Comparative Studies in Society and History* 46:682–708.

Baer, Marc David. 2010. *The Dönme: Jewish Converts, Muslim Revolutionaries, and Secular Turks.* Stanford: Stanford University Press.

Baha Said. 2006 [1918]. "Anadolu'da İçtimâî Zümreler ve Anadolu İçtimâiatı," In *Baha Said Bey. Türkiye'de Alevî-Bektaşî, Ahî ve Nusayrî Zümreleri,* edited by İsmail Görkem, 111–126. Istanbul: Kitabevi.

Baha Said. 2006 [1919]a. "Memleketin İç Yüzü: Anadolu'da Gizli Mabetler I." In *Baha Said Bey. Türkiye'de Alevî-Bektaşî, Ahî ve Nusayrî Zümreleri,* edited by İsmail Görkem, 127–131. Istanbul: Kitabevi.

Baha Said. 2006 [1919]b. "Anadolu'da Gizli Mabetler III." In *Baha Said Bey. Türkiye'de Alevî-Bektaşî, Ahî ve Nusayrî Zümreleri,* edited by İsmail Görkem, 138–140. Istanbul: Kitabevi.

Baha Said. 2006 [1919]c. "Anadolu'da Gizli Mabetler V." In *Baha Said Bey. Türkiye'de Alevî-Bektaşî, Ahî ve Nusayrî Zümreleri,* edited by İsmail Görkem, 143–147. Istanbul: Kitabevi.

Baha Said. 2006 [1919]d. "Anadolu'da Gizli Mabetler VI." In *Baha Said Bey. Türkiye'de Alevî-Bektaşî, Ahî ve Nusayrî Zümreleri*, edited by İsmail Görkem, 148–152. Istanbul: Kitabevi.

Baha Said. 2006 [1919]e. "Tasavvuf ve Hür Mezhepler." In *Baha Said Bey. Türkiye'de Alevî-Bektaşî, Ahî ve Nusayrî Zümreleri*, edited by İsmail Görkem, 104–106. Istanbul: Kitabevi.

Baha Said. 2001 [1926]a. "Türkiye'de Alevî Zümreleri: Tekke Alevîliği—İçtimaî Alevîlik." *Türk Yurdu*, vol. 11, edited by Murat Şefkatlı, 105–112. Istanbul: Tutibay.

Baha Said. 2001 [1926]b. "Sûfyân Süreği. Kızılbaş Meydanı'nda Düşkünlük." *Türk Yurdu*, vol. 11, edited by Murat Şefkatlı, 201–208. Istanbul: Tutibay.

Baha Said. 2001 [1926]c. "Anadolu'da Alevî Zümreleri: Tahtacı, Çetmi, Hardal Türkmenleri yahut Yan[y]atır Zümresi." *Türk Yurdu*, vol. 11, edited by Murat Şefkatlı, 237–242. Istanbul: Tutibay.

Baha, Said. 2001 [1927]. "Bektaşîler III. Bal[ı]m Sultan Erkânı." *Türk Yurdu*, vol. 12, edited by Murat Şefkatlı, 149–165. Istanbul: Tutibay.

Bahadır, İbrahim. 2005. "Türk Milliyetçi Söyleminde Şamanizm ve Alevilik." *Kırkbudak: Journal of Anatolian Folk Beliefs* 1:5–26.

Bali, Rıfat N. 1999. *Cumhuriyet Yıllarında Türkiye Yahudileri. Bir Türkleştirme Serüveni (1923–1945)*. Istanbul: İletişim.

Balivet, Michel. 1995. *Islam mystique et révolution armée dans les Balkans Ottomans. Vie du Cheikh Bedreddîn, le "Hallâj des Turks" (1358/59–1416)*. Istanbul: İsis.

Ball, [Jasper N.]. 1857. "Letter from Mr. Ball: Kuzzel-bashes." *The Missionary Herald* 53:394–395.

Bayrak, Mehmet. 1997. *Alevilik ve Kürdler. İnceleme-Araştırma ve Belgeler*. Wuppertal: Özge.

Bayrak, Mehmet. 2009. *Alevilik-Kürdoloji-Türkoloji Yazıları (1973–2009)*. Ankara: Özge.

Bender, Çemşid. 1991. *Kürt Uygarlığında Alevilik*. Istanbul: Kaynak.

Benlisoy, Foti. 2003. "Türk Milliyetçiliğinde Katedilmemiş Bir Yol: 'Hıristiyan Türkler'." In *Modern Türkiye'de Siyasî Düşünce, vol. 4: Milliyetçilik*, edited by Tanıl Bora, 927–933. Istanbul: İletişim.

Bent, Theodore. 1891. "The Yourouks of Asia Minor." *Journal of the Anthropological Institute of Great Britain and Ireland* 20:269–276.

Berkes, Niyazi. 1959. "Translator's Introduction." In *Turkish Nationalism and Western Civilization: Selected Essays of Ziya Gökalp*, edited by Niyazi Berkes, 13–34. London: Allen & Unwin.

Berkes, Niyazi. 1964. *The Development of Secularism in Turkey*. London: Hurst & Company.

Berktay, Halil. 1983. *Cumhuriyet İdeolojisi ve Fuat Köprülü*. Istanbul: Kaynak.

Beşikçi, İsmail. 1969. *Doğu Anadolu'nun Düzeni*. Istanbul: E.

Bhabha, Homi. 1994. *The Location of Culture*. London: Routledge.

Blau, O. 1858. "Die Stämme des nordöstlichen Kurdistan." *Zeitschrift der Deutschen Morgenländischen Gesellschaft* 12:584–598.

Bloxham, David. 2005. *The Great Game of Genocide: Imperialism, Nationalism, and the Destruction of the Ottoman Armenians.* New York: Oxford University Press.

Boyar, Ebru. 2007. *Ottomans, Turks and the Balkans: Empire Lost, Relations Altered.* London: I. B. Tauris.

Boyarin, Daniel. 1999. *Dying for God.* Stanford: Stanford University Press.

Boyarin, Daniel. 2007. "Semantic Differences; or, 'Judaism' / 'Christianity'." In *The Ways that Never Parted: Jews and Christians in Late Antiquity and the Early Middle Ages,* edited by Adam Becker and Annette Yoshiko Reed, 65–85. Minneapolis: Fortress.

Bozarslan, Hamit. 2003. "Alevism and the Myths of Research: the Need for a New Research Agenda." In *Turkey's Alevi Enigma,* edited by Paul J. White and Joost Jongerden, 3–16. Leiden: Brill.

Braudel, Fernand. 1987. "Geschichte und Sozialwissenschaften. Die *longue durée*" [originally published in French in 1958]. In *Schrift und Materie der Geschichte. Vorschläge zur systematischen Aneignung historischer Prozesse,* edited by Claudia Honegger, 47–85. Frankfurt a. M.: Suhrkamp.

Bruinessen, Martin Van. 1989. *Agha, Scheich und Staat. Politik und Gesellschaft Kurdistans.* Berlin: Parabolis.

Bruinessen, Martin Van. 1997. "'Aslını İnkar Eden Haramzadedir!' The Debate on the Ethnic Identity of the Kurdish Alevis." In *Syncretistic Religious Communities in the Near East,* edited by Krisztina Kehl-Bodrogi, Barbara Kellner-Heinkele, and Anke Otter-Beaujean, 1–23. Leiden: Brill.

Bruinessen, Martin Van. 1999. Review of *Hadji Bektach: un mythe et ses avatars. Genèse et éolution du soufisme populaire en Turquie,* by Irène Mélikoff. *Turcica* 31:549–553.

Bruinessen, Martin Van. 2000. "Religion in Kurdistan." In *Mullas, Sufis and Heretics: The Role of Religion in Kurdish Society,* edited by Martin van Bruinessen, 13–36. Istanbul: İsis.

Cagaptay, Soner. 2006. *Islam, Secularism, and Nationalism in Modern Turkey: Who Is a Turk?* London: Routledge.

Cahen, Claude. 1970. "Le problème du Shî'isme dans l'Asie Mineure turque préottomane." In *Le Shî'isme imâmite,* edited by Centres d'Etudes Supérieurs Spécialisés d'Histoire des Religions de Strasbourg, 115–129. Paris: P.U.F.

Campos, Michelle U. 2010. *Ottoman Brothers: Muslims, Christians, and Jews in Early 20th Century Palestine.* Stanford: Stanford University Press.

Çınar, Alev. 2005. *Modernity, Islam, and Secularism: Bodies, Places, and Time.* Minneapolis: University of Minnesota Press.

Copeaux, Étienne. 1997. *Espaces et temps de la nation turque. Analyse d'une historiographie nationaliste 1931–1993.* Paris: CNRS Editions.

Crowfoot, J. W. 1900. "Survivals among the Kappadocian Kizilbash (Bektash)." *Journal of the Royal Anthropological Institute* 30:305–320.

Cumont, Franz. 1915. "KIZIL BASH." *Encyclopaedia of Religion and Ethics*, vol. 7, edited by James Hastings, 744–745. New York: Charles Scribner's Sons.

Davison, Andrew. 1995. "Secularization and Modernization in Turkey: The Ideas of Ziya Gökalp." *Economy and Society* 24:189–224.

De Blois, [Francois]. 2002. "Zindīḳ." *Encyclopaedia of Islam, 2nd ed.*, vol. 11, edited by P. J. Bearman, Th. Bianquis, C. E. Bosworth, E. van Donzel, and W. P. Heinrichs, 510–513. Leiden: Brill.

Deringil, Selim. 1998. *The Well-Protected Domains: Ideology and the Legitimation of Power in the Ottoman Empire, 1876–1909*. London: I. B. Tauris.

Deringil, Selim. 2000. "'There is No Compulsion in Religion.' On Conversion and Apostasy in the Late Ottoman Empire: 1839–1856." *Comparative Studies in Society and History* 42:547–575.

Derrida, Jacques. 1998. "Faith and Knowledge. The Two Sources of 'Religion' at the Limits of Reason Alone." In *Religion*, edited by Jacques Derrida and Gianni Vattimo, 1–78. Stanford: Stanford University Press.

DeWeese, Devin. 1994. *Islamization and Native Religion in the Golden Horde: Baba Tükles and Conversion to Islam in Historical and Epic Tradition*. University Park: Pennsylvania State University Press.

DeWeese, Devin. 2006. "Foreword." In *Köprülü, Mehmed Fuad, Early Mystics in Turkish Literature*. Translated with an introduction by Gary Leiser and Robert Dankoff, viii–xxvii. London: Routledge.

Dinçer, Fahriye. 2009. "Alevî Âyinlerine ilişkin 1915–1940 Döneminde Yayımlanan Metinlerde Alevi Kimliğinin Temsili." In *Kimlikler Lütfen: Türkiye Cumhuriyeti'nde Kültürel Kimlik Arayışı ve Temsili*, edited by Gönül Pultar, 134–147. Ankara: ODTÜ.

Dölen, Emin. 2010. *Türkiye Üniversite Tarihi, vol. 2: Cumhuriyet Döneminde Osmanlı Darülfünunu (1922–1933)*. Istanbul: Bilgi Üniversitesi Yay.

Dressler, Markus. 2002. *Die alevitische Religion. Traditionslinien und Neubestimmungen*. Würzburg: Ergon.

Dressler, Markus. 2005. "Inventing Orthodoxy: Competing Claims for Authority and Legitimacy in the Ottoman-Safavid Conflict." In *Legitimizing the Order: The Ottoman Rhetoric of State Power*, edited by Hakan T. Karateke and Maurus Reinkowski, 151–173. Leiden: Brill.

Dressler, Markus. 2006. "The Modern Dede: Changing Parameters for Religious Authorities in Contemporary Turkish Alevism." In *Speaking for Islam: Religious Authorities in Muslim Societies*, edited by Gudrun Krämer and Sabine Schmidtke, 269–294. Leiden: Brill.

Dressler, Markus. 2008. "Religio-Secular Metamorphoses: The Re-Making of Modern Alevism." *Journal of the American Academy of Religion* 76:280–311.

Dressler, Markus. 2009. Review of *Syncrétismes et hérésies dans l'orient Seldjoukide et Ottoman (XIVe–XVIIIe siècle)*, edited by Gilles Veinstein. *International Journal for Middle East Studies* 41:139–140.

Dressler, Markus. 2010a. "Public/Private Distinctions, the Alevi Question, and the Headscarf. Turkish Secularism Revisited." *Comparative Secularisms in a Global Age*, edited by Elizabeth Shakman Hurd and Linell Cady, 121–142. Hampshire: Palgrave Macmillan.

Dressler, Markus. 2010b. "How to Conceptualize Inner-Islamic Plurality/ Difference: 'Heterodoxy' and 'Syncretism' in the Writings of Mehmet F. Köprülü (1890–1966)." *British Journal for Middle Eastern Studies* 37:241–260.

Dressler, Markus 2011a. "Making Religion through Secularist Legal Discourse: The Case of Turkish Alevism." In *Secularism and Religion-Making*, edited by Markus Dressler and Arvind-Pal S. Mandair, 187–208. Oxford: Oxford University Press.

Dressler, Markus 2011b. "The Religio-Secular Continuum. Reflections on the Religious Dimensions of Turkish Secularism." In *After Secular Law*, edited by Winnifred Fallers Sullivan, Robert A. Yelle, and Mateo Taussig-Rubbo, 221–241. Stanford: Stanford University Press.

Dressler, Markus, and Arvind P. Mandair, eds. 2011. *Secularism and Religion-Making.* Oxford: Oxford University Press.

Driver, G. R. 1922. "The Religion of the Kurds." *Bulletin of the School of Oriental Studies* 2:197–213.

Dubuisson, Daniel. 2003. *The Western Construction of Religion: Myths, Knowledge, and Ideology.* Baltimore: Johns Hopkins University Press.

Dunmore, [George]. 1855. "Arabkir: Letter from Mr. Dunmore, October 24, 1854." *Missionary Herald* 51:54–56.

Dunmore, [George]. 1857. "Letter from Mr. Dunmore, January 22, 1857." *Missionary Herald* 53:218–220.

Durkheim, Émile. 2008 [1912]. *The Elementary Forms of the Religious Life.* New York: Oxford University Press.

Dündar, Fuat. 2008. *Modern Türkiye'nin Şifresi.* Istanbul: İletişim.

Eisenstadt, Shmuel N. 1965. *Modernisation: Protest and Change.* Englewood Cliffs: Prentice-Hall.

Eisenstadt, Shmuel N. 1999. "Multiple Modernities in an Age of Globalization." In *Grenzenlose Gesellschaft? Verhandlungen des 29. Kongresses der Deutschen Gesellschaft für Soziologie Februar 1998*, edited by Claudia Honegger, Stefan Hradil, and Franz Traxler, 37–50. Opladen: Leske+Budrich.

Eissenstat, Howard L. 2007. *"The Limits of Imagination: Debating the Nation and Constructing the State in Early Turkish Nationalism."* PhD diss., University of California, Los Angeles.

Elwert, Georg. 1997. "Switching of We-Group Identities." In *Syncretistic Religious Communities in the Near East*, edited by Krisztina Kehl-Bodrogi, Barbara Kellner-Heinkele, and Anke Otter-Beaujean, 65–85. Leiden: Brill.

Erdican, Ali Galip. 1974. *Mehmet Fuat Köprülü: A Study of His Contribution to Cultural Reform in Modern Turkey.* Istanbul: Redhouse.

Ergun, Sadettin Nüzhet. 1929. *XVIIinci Asır Sazşairlerinden Pir Sultan Abdal.* Istanbul: Evkaf.

Ergun, Sadettin Nüzhet. 1930. *Bektaşi Şairleri.* Ankara: Maarif Vekaleti.

Erhan, Çağrı. 2002. "Ottoman Official Attitudes Towards American Missionaries." In *The United States and the Middle East: Cultural Encounters,* edited by Abbas Amanat and Magnus Thorkell Bernhardsson, 315–341. New Haven, CT: Yale Center for International and Area Studies.

Erhan, Çağrı. 2004. "Main Trends in Ottoman-American Relations." In *Turkish-American Relations: Past, Present and Future,* edited by Mustafa Aydın and Çağrı Erhan, 3–25. London: Routledge.

Erickson, Edward J. 2008. "The Armenians and Ottoman Military Policy, 1915." *War in History* 15:141–167.

Ernst, Carl W. 1997. *The Shambala Guide to Sufism.* Boston: Shambala.

Ersanlı, Büşra. 2002. "The Ottoman Empire in the Historiography of the Kemalist Era: A Theory of Fatal Decline." In *The Ottomans and the Balkans: A Discussion of Historiography,* edited by Fikret Adanır and Suraiya Faroqhi, 115–154. Leiden: Brill.

Ersanlı, Büşra. 2003. *İktidar ve Tarih: Türkiye'de "Resmi Tarih" Tezinin Oluşumu (1929–1937).* Istanbul: İletişim.

Es'ad Efendi [Mehmed]. 1243[/1848]. *Üss-i zafer.* Istanbul: Matbaa-i Âmire.

European Commission. 2011. *Turkey 2011 Progress Report.* Brussels: European Commission. Accessed June 6, 2012. http://ec.europa.eu/enlargement/pdf/ key_documents/2011/package/tr_rapport_2011_en.pdf.

Firro, Kais M. 2005. "The 'Alawīs in modern Syria: From Nusarīya to Islam via 'Alawīya," *Der Islam* 82:1–31.

Fleischer, Cornell. 1986. "Mustafâ Âlî's Curious Bits of Wisdom." *Wiener Zeitschrift für die Kunde des Morgenlandes* 76:103–109.

Fouillée, Alfred. 1904. "Les fausses conséquences morales et sociales du darwinisme." *Revue des Deux Mondes.* Accessed June 6, 2012. http://fr.wikisource.org/wiki/ Les_Fausses_Cons%C3%A9quences_morales_et_sociales_du_darwinisme.

Fouillée, Alfred. 1907. *Histoire de la philosophie.* Paris: F. Alcan.

Fouillée, Alfred. 1911. *La pensée et les nouvelles écoles anti-intellectualistes.* Paris: F. Alcan.

Fraylïç, Dr., and Mühendis Ravlig [Habil Adem]. 2008 [1918]. *Türkmen Aşiretleri.* Edited by Ali Cin, Haluk Kortel, and Haldun Eroğlu. Istanbul: IQ Kültür Sanay.

Gaunt, David. 2006. *Massacres, Resistance, Protectors: Muslim-Christian Relations in Eastern Anatolia during World War I.* Piscataway: Gorgias.

Gelvin, James L. 2002. "Secularism and Religion in the Arab Middle East: Reinventing Islam in a World of Nation States." *In the Invention of Religion.* In *Rethinking Belief in Politics and History,* edited by Derek R. Peterson and Darren R. Walhof, 115–130. New Brunswick, NJ: Rutgers University Press.

Georgeon, François. 1980. *Aux origins du nationalisme Turc: Yusuf Akçura (1876–1935).* Paris: Inst. d'Études Anatoliennes.

Gilbert, T. 1997 [1873]. "Note sur les sects dans le Kurdistan." *Iran and the Caucasus* 1:203–204.

Gokalp, Altan. 1980. *Têtes rouges et bouches noires. Une confrérie tribale de l'ouest Anatolien.* Paris: Société d'Ethnographie.

Gökalp, Ziya. 1976 [1909]. "Tekkeler." In *Ziya Gökalp, Makaleler I. Diyarbekir— Peyman—Volkan Gazetelerindeki Yazılar,* edited by Şevket Beysanoğlu, 83–87. Istanbul: Milli Eğitim.

Gökalp, Ziya. 1959 [1913]a. "Cemaat Medeniyeti, Cemiyet Medeniyeti." Translated and abridged as "Community and Society" by Niyazi Berkes. In *Turkish Nationalism and Western Civilization / Selected Essays of Ziya Gökalp,* edited by Niyazi Berkes, 101–103. London: Allen & Unwin.

Gökalp, Ziya. 1959 [1913]b. "An'ane ve Kaide." Translated as "Tradition and Formalism" by Niyazi Berkes. In *Turkish Nationalism and Western Civilization / Selected Essays of Ziya Gökalp,* edited by Niyazi Berkes, 92–96. London: Allen & Unwin.

Gökalp, Ziya. 1915. "Bir Kawmin Tetkikinde Tâkip Olunacak Usül." *Milli Tetebbular Mecmuası* 1:193–205.

Gökalp, Ziya. 1959 [1915]. "Dinin İçtimaî Vazifeleri." Translated as "Social Functions of Religion" by Niyazi Berkes. In *Turkish Nationalism and Western Civilization / Selected Essays of Ziya Gökalp,* edited by Niyazi Berkes, 184–193. London: Allen & Unwin.

Gökalp, Ziya. 1959 [1917]a. "Millet Nedir?" Translated and abridged as "The Rise of the Nations" by Niyazi Berkes. In *Turkish Nationalism and Western Civilization / Selected Essays of Ziya Gökalp,* edited by Niyazi Berkes, 126–134. London: Allen & Unwin.

Gökalp, Ziya. 1982 [1922]. "Millet Nedir?" In *Ziya Gökalp: Makaleler VII (Küçük Mecmua'daki Yazılar),* edited by M. Abdülhaluk Çay, 226–231. Ankara: Kültür Bakanlığı.

Gökalp, Ziya. 1992 [1923]. "İstimlâl." In *Kürt Aşiretleri Hakkında Sosyolojik Tetkikler,* edited by Şevket Beysanoğlu, 125–130. Istanbul: Sosyal.

Gökalp, Ziya. 1959 [1923]a. "Hars ve Medeniyet" (from *'Türkçülüğünün Esasları').* Translated and abridged as "Culture and Civilization" by Niyazi Berkes. In *Turkish Nationalism and Western Civilization / Selected Essays of Ziya Gökalp,* edited by Niyazi Berkes, 104–109. London: Allen & Unwin.

Gökalp, Ziya. 1959 [1923]b. "Halka Doğru." Translated and abridged as "Towards the People" by Niyazi Berkes. In *Turkish Nationalism and Western Civilization / Selected Essays of Ziya Gökalp,* edited by Niyazi Berkes, 259–262. London: Allen & Unwin.

Gökalp, Ziya. 1959 [1923]c. "Hars ve Medeniyet" (from *Türkçülüğünün Esasları).* Translated and abridged as "The Aim of the Turkists" by Niyazi Berkes. In *Turkish Nationalism and Western Civilization / Selected Essays of Ziya Gökalp,* edited by Niyazi Berkes, 289–290. London: Allen & Unwin.

Gölpınarlı, Abdülbâki. 1953. *Şeyh Galip. Hayatı, Sanatı, Şiirleri.* Istanbul: Varlık.

Gölpınarlı, Abdülbâki. 1963. *Alevî-Bektasî Nefesleri.* Istanbul: Remzi.

Gölpınarlı, Abdülbâki. 1969. *100 Soruda Tasavvuf.* Istanbul: Gerçek.

Gölpınarlı, Abdülbâki. 2000. *Tasavvuf.* Istanbul: Milenyum.

Gölpınarlı, Abdülbâki. 2003. *Tarih Boyunca İslâm Mezhebleri ve Şiilik.* Istanbul: Der.

Görkem, İsmail. 2006. *Baha Said Bey. Türkiye'de Alevî-Bektaşî, Ahî ve Nusayrî Zümreleri,* edited and with an introduction by İsmail Görkem. Istanbul: Kitabevi.

Grenard, M. F[ernand]. 1904. "Une secte religieuse d'Asie Mineure. Les Kyzyl-bâchs." *Journal Asiatique* 3:511–522.

Grothe, Hugo. 1903. *Auf türkischer Erde. Reisebilder und Studien.* Berlin: Allgemeiner Verein für Deutsche Literatur.

Grothe, Hugo. 1912. *Meine Vorderasienexpedition 1906 und 1907,* vol. 2. Leipzig: Karl W. Hiersemann.

Halm, Heinz. 1982. *Die islamische Gnosis. Die extreme Schia und die 'Alawiten.* Zurich: Artemis.

Hamid Sadi [Selen]. 1926. "Tekke Aleviliği-İçtimai Alevilik." *Türk Yurdu* 4.21:193–210.

Hamid Zübeyr [Koşay]. 1926. "Hacı Bektaş Tekkesi." *Türkiyat Mecmuası* 2:365–382.

Hanioğlu, Şükrü. 1995. *The Young Turks in Opposition.* Oxford: Oxford University Press.

Hanioğlu, Şükrü. 2001. *Preparation for a Revolution: The Young Turks, 1902–1908.* Oxford: Oxford University Press.

Hanioğlu, Şükrü. 2008. *A Brief History of the Late Ottoman Empire.* Princeton, NJ: Princeton University Press.

Hartmann, Martin. 1918. "Die osmanische 'Zeitschrift der Nationalen Forschungen' (Milli Tetebbüler)." *Der Islam* 8:304–325.

Hasluck, Frederick William. 1921. "Heterodox Tribes of Asia Minor." *Journal of the Royal Anthropological Institute of Great Britain and Ireland* 51:310–342.

Hastings, Adrian. 1997. *The Construction of Nationhood: Ethnicity, Religion and Nationalism.* Cambridge: Cambridge University Press.

Hazran, Yusri. 2010. "Heterodox Doctrines in Contemporary Islamic Thought: The Druze as a Case Study." *Der Islam* 87:224–247.

Herrick, George F. 1866. "Letter from Mr. Herrick, November 16, 1865." *Missionary Herald* 62.3:67–69.

Heyd, Uriel. 1950. *Foundations of Turkish Nationalism: The Life and Teachings of Ziya Gökalp.* London: Luzac.

Hodgson, Marshall G. S. 1955. "How Did the Early Shi'a Become Sectarian?" *Journal of the American Oriental Society* 75:1–13.

Hodgson, Marshall G. S. 1977. *Venture of Islam,* vol. 2. Chicago: University of Chicago Press.

Hogarth, David George. 1908. "Problems in Exploration: I. Western Asia." *Geographical Journal* 32:549–563.

Hogarth, David George, and J. A. R. Munro. 1893. *Modern and Ancient Roads in Eastern Asia Minor* (*Royal Geographic Society* Supplementary Papers, vol. 3, pt. 5). London: John Murray.

Huart, Cl[ément]. 1923. "Keuprulu-Zâdè Mohammed Fu'âd. Turk Èdèbiyyâtindè Ilk Mutéçavvif-ler." *Journal Asiatique* 202:146–150.

Huart, Cl[ément]. 1927. "ḲIZIL-BĀSH." *The Encyclopaedia of Islam: A Dictionary of the Geography, Ethnography and Biography of the Mohammadan Peoples*, vol. 2, edited by M. Th. Houtsma, A. J. Wensinck, and T. W. Arnold, 1053–1054. Leiden: Brill.

Huntington, Ellsworth. 1902. "Through the Great Canon of the Euphrates River." *Geographical Journal* 20:175–200.

Ibn Khaldun. 1967. *The Muqaddimah: An Introduction to History.* Translated by Franz Rosenthal. Princeton, NJ: Princeton University Press.

Imber, Colin. 1979. "The Persecution of the Ottoman Shīʿites According to the Mühimme Defterleri, 1565–1585." *Der Islam* 56:245–273.

İnalcık, Halil. 1978. "Impact of the Annales School on Ottoman Studies and New Findings." *Review. A Journal of the Fernand Braudel Center* 1:69–96.

Irmak, Hüseyin. 2010. "Osmanlı Belgelerinde Dersim'e Dair Bazı Örnekler." In *Herkesin Bildiği Sır: Dersim*, edited by Şükrü Arslan, 245–267. Istanbul: İletişim.

Jakobsen, Janet R., and Ann Pellegrini. 2008. "Introduction." In *Secularisms; or, Times like These*, edited by Janet R. Jakobsen and Ann Pellegrini, 1–35. Durham, NC: Duke University Press.

Jongerden, Joost. 2007. *The Settlement Issue in Turkey and the Kurds: An Analysis of Spatial Policies, Modernity and War.* Leiden: Brill.

Joseph, John. 1983. *Muslim-Christian Relations and Inter-Christian Rivalries in the Middle East: The Case of the Jacobites in an Age of Transition.* Albany: State University of New York Press.

Jwaideh, Wadie. 2009. *Kürt Milliyetçiliğinin Tarihi. Kökenleri ve Gelişimi.* Istanbul: İletişim.

Kafadar, Cemal. 1995. *Between Two Worlds: The Construction of the Ottoman State.* Berkeley: University of California Press.

Kafadar, Cemal. 2007. "A Rome of One's Own: Reflections on Cultural Geography and Identity in the Lands of Rum." *Muqarnas* 24:7–25.

Kafesoğlu, İbrahim. 1980. *Eski Türk Dini.* Ankara: Kültür Bakanlığı.

Kafesoğlu, İbrahim. 1988. *A History of the Selcuks: İbrahim Kafesoğlu's Interpretation and the Resulting Controversy.* Translated, edited, and with an introduction by Gary Leiser. Carbondale: Southern Illinois University Press.

Kaplan, Doğan. 2002. "Fuat Köprülü'ye göre Anadolu Aleviliği." M.A. diss., Selçuk University, Konya.

Kara, İsmail. 2004. "İslâmci Söylemin Kaynakları ve Gerçeklik Değeri." In *Modern Türkiye'de Siyasî Düşünce, vol. 6: İslâmcılık*, edited by Tanıl Bora, Murat Gültekingil, and Yasin Aktay, 34–47. Istanbul: İletişim.

Karaca, Ali. 1993. *Anadolu Islahâtı ve Ahmet Şakir Paşa, 1838–1899.* Istanbul: Eren.

Karakaya-Stump, Ayfer. 2004. "The Emergence of the Kızılbaş in Western Thought: Missionary Accounts and Their Aftermath." In *Archaeology, Anthropology, and*

Heritage in the Balkans and Anatolia: The Life and Times of F. W. Hasluck, 1878–
1920, vol 1, edited by David Shankland, 329–353. Istanbul: Isis.

Karakaya[-]Stump, Ayfer. 2008. *"Subjects of the Sultan, Disciples of the Shah: Formation
and Transformation of the Kizilbash/Alevi Communities in Ottoman Anatolia."*
PhD. diss., Harvard University.

Karamustafa, Ahmet T. 1994. *God's Unruly Friends: Dervish Groups in the Islamic Later
Middle Period, 1200–1550.* Salt Lake City: University of Utah Press.

Karamustafa, Ahmet T. 2005. "Origins of Anatolian Sufism." In *Sufism and Sufis in
Ottoman Society: Sources, Doctrine, Rituals, Turuq, Architecture, Literature and Fine
Arts, Modernism,* edited by Ahmet Yaşar Ocak, 67–95. Ankara: Turkish Historical
Society.

Karamustafa, Ahmet T. 2010. "Hacı Bektaş Veli ve Anadolu'da Müslümanlık."
In *Hacı Bektaş Veli. Güneşte Zerresinden, Deryada Katresinden,* edited by Pınar
Ecevitoğlu, Ayhan Yalçınkaya, and Ali Murat İrat, 42–48. Ankara: Dipnot.

Karamustafa, Ahmet T. 2015. "Islamic *Dīn* as an Alternative to Western Models of
'Religion.'" In *Theory/Religion/Critique: Classic and Contemporary Approaches,*
edited by Richard King. New York: Columbia University Press [forthcoming].

Karolewski, Janina. 2008. "What is Heterodox about Alevism? The Development of
Anti-Alevi Discrimination and Resentment." In *Welt des Islams* 48:434–456.

Karpat, Kemal. 1970. "Modern Turkey." In *Cambridge History of Islam,* vol. 1, edited
by Peter M. Holt, Ann K. S. Lambton, and Bernard Lewis, 527–565. Cambridge:
Cambridge University Press.

Karpat, Kemal H. 1985. *Ottoman Population, 1830–1914: Demographic and Social
Characteristics.* Madison: University of Wisconsin Press.

Karpat, Kemal H. 2001. *The Politicization of Islam: Reconstructing Identity, State, Faith,
and Community in the Late Ottoman State.* Oxford: Oxford University Press.

Kayalı, Hasan. 1997. *Arabs and Young Turks: Ottomanism, Arabism, and Islamism in
the Ottoman Empire, 1908–1918.* Berkeley: University of California Press.

Kedourie, Elie. 1960. *Nationalism.* London: Hutchinson.

Kehl[-Bodrogi], Krisztina. 1988. *Die Tahtacı. Vorläufiger Bericht über eine
ethnisch-religiöse Gruppe traditioneller Holzarbeiter in Anatolien.* Berlin: Das
Arabische Buch.

Kehl-Bodrogi, Krisztina. 1993. "Die 'Wiederfindung' des Alevitums in der Türkei.
Geschichtsmythos und kollektive Identität." *Orient* 34:267–282.

Kehl-Bodrogi, Krisztina, Barbara Kellner-Heinkele, and Anke Otter-Beaujean, eds.
1997. *Syncretistic Religious Communities in the Near East.* Leiden: Brill.

Kieser, Hans-Lukas. 1998. "Les kurdes alévis et la question identitaire: le soulève-
ment du Koçkiri-Dersim (1919–21)." In *Islam des Kurdes* (Les annales de
l'autre Islam, no. 5), edited by Martin van Bruinessen, 279–316. Paris:
INALCO-ERISM.

Kieser, Hans-Lukas. 2000. *Der verpasste Friede. Mission, Ethnie und Staat in den
Ostprovinzen der Türkei 1839–1938.* Zurich: Chronos.

Kieser, Hans-Lukas, 2002a. "Some Remarks on Alevi Responses to the Missionaries in Eastern Anatolia (19th–20th centuries)." In *Altruism and Imperialism: Western Cultural and Religious Missions in the Middle East*, edited by Eleanor H. Tejirian and Reeva Spector Simon, 120–142. New York: Middle East Institute, Columbia University.

Kieser, Hans-Lukas. 2002b. "Dr. Mehmed Reshid (1873–1919): A Political Doctor." In *Der Völkermord an den Armeniern und die Shoah*, edited by Hans-Lukas Kieser and Dominik J. Schaller, 245–280. Zurich: Chronos.

Kieser, Hans-Lukas. 2003. "Alevis, Armenians, and Kurds in Unionist-Kemalist Turkey (1908–1938)." In *Turkey's Alevi Enigma: A Comprehensive Overview*, edited by Paul J. White and Joost Jongerden, 177–196. Leiden: Brill.

Kieser, Hans-Lukas. 2007. "Der Völkermord an den Armeniern 1915/16: neueste Publikationen." *Sehepunkte* 7. Accessed June 6, 2012. http://www.sehepunkte.de/2007/03/pdf/10400.pdf.

Kieser, Hans-Lukas. 2008. "Removal of American Indians, Destruction of Ottoman Armenians. American Missionaries and Demographic Engineering." *European Journal of Turkish Studies* 7. Accessed June 6, 2012. http://ejts.revues.org/index2873.html.

Kieser, Hans-Lukas. 2010. *Nearest East: American Millennialism and Mission to the Middle East*. Philadelphia: Temple University Press.

Kieser, Hans-Lukas, and Dominik J. Schaller. 2002. "Völkermord im historischen Raum 1895–1945." In *Der Völkermord an den Armeniern und die Shoah*, edited by Hans-Lukas Kieser and Dominik J. Schaller, 11–80. Zurich: Chronos.

King, Richard. 1999. *Orientalism and Religion: Postcolonial Theory, India and "The Mystic East"*. London: Routledge.

King, Richard. 2011. "Imagining Religions in India: Colonialism and the Mapping of South Asian History and Culture." In *Secularism and Religion-Making*, edited by Markus Dressler and Arvind-Pal S. Mandair, 37–61. Oxford: Oxford University Press.

Kippenberg, Hans G. 2002. *Discovering Religious History in the Modern Age*. Princeton, NJ: Princeton University Press.

Klein, Janet. 2011. *Margins of Empire: Kurdish Militias in the Ottoman Tribal Zone*. Palo Alto: Stanford University Press.

Köprülü, Mehmed Fuad. 1913. "Edebiyatımızda Milliyet Hissi." *Türk Yurdu* 2:667–678.

Köprülü, Mehmed Fuad. 1999 [1913]a. "Türklük, İslâmlık, Osmanlılık." In *Türk Yurdu 2*, edited by Murat Şefkatlı, 372–376. Ankara: Tutibay.

Köprülü, Mehmed Fuad. 1999 [1913]b. "Türk Edebiyatı Tarihinde Usûl." In *Edebiyat Araştırmaları*, by Mehmed Fuad Köprülü, 3–47. Ankara: Türk Tarih Kurumu.

Köprülü, Mehmed Fuad. 1999 [1915]. "Türk Edebiyatı'nın Menşe'i." In *Edebiyat Araştırmaları*, by Mehmed Fuad Köprülü, 49–130. Ankara: Türk Tarih Kurumu.

Köprülü, Mehmed Fuad. 1966 [1919]. *Türk Edebiyatı'nda İlk Mutasavvıflar*. Ankara: Ankara Üniversitesi.

Köprülü, Mehmed Fuad. 2006 [1919]. *Early Mystics in Turkish Literature*. Translated with an introduction by Gary Leiser and Robert Dankoff. London: Routledge.

Köprülü, Mehmed Fuad. 1980 [1920/21]. *Türk Edebiyatı Tarihi*. Istanbul: Ötüken.

Köprülü, Mehmed Fuad. 1999 [1922]. "Türk Edebiyatı'nın Ermeni Edebiyatı Üzerindeki Te'sirleri." In *Edebiyat Araştırmaları*, by Mehmed Fuad Köprülü, 239–269. Ankara: Türk Tarih Kurumu.

Köprülü, Mehmed Fuad. 1993 [1922]. *Islam in Anatolia after the Turkish Invasion (Prolegomena)*. Translated by Gary Leiser. Salt Lake City: University of Utah Press.

Köprülü, Mehmed Fuad. 2005 [1922]. *Anadolu'da İslâmiyet*. Ankara: Akçağ.

Köprülü, Mehmed Fuad. 1922. *Milli Tarih*. Istanbul: Kanaat.

Köprülü, Mehmed Fuad. 1923. *Türkiye Tarihi 1: Anadolu İstilasına Kadar Türkler*. Istanbul: Kanaat.

Köprülü, Mehmed Fuad. 2005 [1923]. *Türkiye Tarihi: Anadolu İstilâsına Kadar Türkler*. Istanbul: Akçağ.

Köprülü, Mehmed Fuad. 2002 [1925]. "Bektaşîliğin Menşeleri: Küçük Asya'da İslâm Batınîliğinin Tekâmül-i Tarihîsi Hakkında Bir Tecrübe." In *Türk Yurdu 9*, edited by Murat Şefkatlı, 68–76. Ankara: Tutibay.

Köprülü, Mehmed Fuad. 2005 [1925]. *Türk Tarih-i Dinisi*. Edited by Metin Ergun. Ankara: Akçağ.

Köprülü, Mehmed Fuad. 1928a. "Önsöz." In *Bektaşilik Tetkikleri*, by F. W. Hasluck. Translated by Ragıp Hulusi. Istanbul: Devlet Matbaası.

Köprülü, Mehmed Fuad. 1928b. *Milli Tarih: İlk Mekteplerin Dördüncü Sınıfına Mahsusdur*. Istanbul: Kanaat.

Köprülüzade, Mehmed Fuad. 1929. *Influence du Chamanisme Turco-Mongol sur les ordres mystiques Musulmans*. Istanbul: Zellitch frères.

Köprülü, Mehmed Fuat. 1987 [1934]. "Turks. B. (The Ottoman Turks) III. Literature." In *First Encyclopaedia of Islam, 1913–1936*, vol. 8, edited by M. Th. Houtsma, A. J. Wensinck, and T. W. Arnold, 938–959. Leiden: Brill.

Köprülü, [Mehmed] Fuad. 1991 [1935]. *Osmanlı Devleti'nin Kuruluşu*. Ankara: Türk Tarih Kurumu.

Köprülü, M. Fuad. 2009 [1935]. *Osmanlı İmparatorluğunun Kuruluşu*. Ankara: Akçağ.

Köprülü, Mehmed Fuad. 1992 [1935]. *The Origins of the Ottoman Empire*. Translated and edited by Gary Leiser. Albany: State University of New York Press.

Köprülü, Mehmed Fuad. 1935a. "Aba." In *Türk Halk Edebiyatı Ansiklopedisi: Ortaçağ ve Yeniçağ Türklerinin Halk Kültürü Üzerine Coğrafya, Etnografya, Etnoloji, Tarih ve Edebiyat Lugatı*, vol. 1, edited by M. Fuad Köprülü, 1–2. Istanbul: Türkiyat Enstitüsü.

Köprülü, Mehmed Fuad. 1935b. "Abdal." *Türk Halk Edebiyatı Ansiklopedisi: Ortaçağ ve Yeniçağ Türklerinin Halk Kültürü Üzerine Coğrafya, Etnografya, Etnoloji, Tarih ve Edebiyat Lugatı*, vol. 1, edited by M. Fuad Köprülü, 23–56. Istanbul: Türkiyat Enstitüsü.

Köprülü, Mehmed Fuad. 1940. "Başlangıç." In *İslâm Medeniyeti Tarihi*, by Wilhelm Barthold, xvii–xxxix. Istanbul: Kanaat.

Köprülü, Mehmed Fuad. 1966 [1942]. "Bahşı." In *Edebiyat Araştırmaları*, by Mehmed Fuad Köprülü, 145–156. Ankara: Türk Tarih Kurumu.

Köprülü, Mehmed Fuad. 1979 [1949]. "Bektaş." In *İslam Ansiklopedisi: İslam Alemi Tarih, Coğrafya, Etnografya ve Biyografya Lugati*, edited by İstanbul Üniversitesi Edebiyat Fakültesi, vol. 2, 461–464. Istanbul: Milli Eğitim.

Köprülü, Mehmed Fuad. 1966 [1962]. "Sazşâirleri, Dün ve Bugün." In *Edebiyat Araştırmaları*, by Mehmed Fuad Köprülü, 165–193. Ankara: Türk Tarih Kurumu.

Köprülü, Mehmed Fuad. 1989 [1965]. "Ziya Gökalp'e Ait Bâzı Hâtıralar." In *Ziya Gökalp Külliyâtı –II. Limni ve Malta Mektupları*, edited by Fevziye A. Tansel, xxiii–xxviii. Ankara: Türk Tarih Kurumu.

Köroğlu, Erol. 2007. *Ottoman Propaganda and Turkish Identity: Literature in Turkey during World War I*. London: I. B. Tauris.

Köse, Talha. 2010. *Alevi Opening and the Democratization Initiative in Turkey*. SETA Policy Report March 3. Ankara: SETA.

Kraft, Siv-Ellen. 2002. "'To Mix or Not to Mix': Syncretism/Anti-Syncretism in the History of Theosophy." *Numen* 49:142–177.

Küçük, Hülya. 2002. *The Role of the Bektashis in Turkey's National Struggle: A Historical and Critical Study*. Leiden: Brill.

Küçük, Murat. 2002. "Mezhepten Millete: Aleviler ve Türk Milliyetçiliği." In *Modern Türkiye'de Siyasi Düşünce, vol. 4: Milliyetçilik*, edited by Tanıl Bora, 901–910. Istanbul: İletişim.

Kuran, Ercüment. 1997. "Fuad Köprülü'nün Milliyetçiliği." *Türkiyat Araştırmaları Dergisi* 3:243–248.

Landen, Robert G. 2007. "Kemal Atatürk on the Abolition of the Ottoman Caliphate, 3 March 1924." In *The Modern Middle East: A Sourcebook for History*, edited by Camron M. Amin, Benjamin C. Fortna, and Elizabeth B. Frierson, 233–238. Oxford: Oxford University Press.

Langer, Robert, and Udo Simon. 2008. "The Dynamics of Orthodoxy and Heterodoxy: Dealing with Divergence in Muslim Discourses and Islamic Studies." *Die Welt des Islams* 48:273–288.

Laukötter, Anja. 2007. *Von der "Kultur" zur "Rasse"—vom Objekt zum Körper?: Völkerkundemuseen und ihre Wissenschaften zu Beginn des 20. Jahrhunderts*. Bielefeld: Transcript.

Leiser, Gary. 1992. "Preface." In *The Origins of the Ottoman Empire*, by Mehmed Fuad Köprülü, xi–xiv. Albany: State University of New York Press.

Leiser, Gary, transl. 2008. "Method in Turkish Literary History (by Mehmed Fuad Köprülü)," *Middle Eastern Literatures* 11.1:55–84.

Leiser, Gary, and Robert Dankoff. 2006. "Translators' Introduction." In *Early Mystics in Turkish Literature*, by Mehmed Fuad Köprülü, translated and edited by Gary Leiser, xxviii–xxxvi. London: Routledge.

Leonhard, Richard. 1915. *Paphlagonia. Reisen und Forschungen im nördlichen Kleinasien*. Berlin: D. Reimer.

Leopold, Anita Maria, and Jeppe Sinding Jensen, eds. 2004. *Syncretism in Religion: A Reader*. London: Routledge.

Lerch, Peter J. A. 1857. *Forschungen über die Kurden und die iranischen Nordchaldäer*. St. Petersburg: Eggers et Comp.

Lerner, Daniel. 1958. *The Passing of Traditional Society: Modernizing the Middle East*. New York: Free Press.

Levonian, Lutfy. 1932. *The Turkish Press: Selections from the Turkish Press Showing Events and Opinions 1925–1932*. Translated and arranged under direction of Lutfy Levonian. Athens: School of Religion.

Lewis, Bernard. 1961. *The Emergence of Modern Turkey*. London: Oxford University Press.

Livni, Eran. 2002. "Alevi Identity in Turkish Historiography." Paper presented at the 17th Middle East History and Theory Conference, Chicago, May 10. Accessed June 6, 2012. http://issuu.com/shia/docs/alevi-identity.

Luschan, Felix von. 1886. "Wandervoelker Kleinasiens." *Zeitschrift für Ethnologie* 18:167–171.

Luschan, Felix von. 1889. "Anthropologische Studien." In *Reisen in Lykien, Milyas und Kibyratien*, vol. 2, by Eugen Petersen and Felix von Luschan, chap. 13. Wien: Codex:198–226.

Luschan, Felix von. 1911. "The Early Inhabitants of Western Asia." *Journal of the Royal Anthropological Institute of Great Britain and Ireland* 41:221–244.

Luschan, Felix von. 1922. *Völker, Rassen, Sprachen*. Berlin: Welt-Verlag.

Madelung, W[ilferd]. 2012. "Mulḥid." *Encyclopaedia of Islam 2nd ed*. Brill Online, 2012. Istanbul Technical University. Accessed May 09, 2012. http://reference-works.brillonline.com/entries/encyclopaedia-of-islam-2/mulhid-SIM_5487.

Makdisi, Ussama. 2000. *The Culture of Sectarianism: Community, History, and Violence in Nineteenth-Century Ottoman Lebanon*. Berkeley: University of California Press.

Mandair, Arvind-Pal S. 2009. *Religion and the Specter of the West*. New York: Columbia University Press.

Mandair, Arvind-Pal S. and Markus Dressler. 2011. "Introduction: Modernity, Religion-Making, and the Postsecular." In *Secularism and Religion-Making*, edited by Markus Dressler and Arvind-Pal S. Mandair, 3–36. Oxford: Oxford University Press.

Mardin, Şerif. 1962. *The Genesis of Young Ottoman Thought*. Princeton, NJ: Princeton University Press.

Markussen, Hege Irene. 2012. *Teaching History, Learning Piety: An Alevi Foundation in Contemporary Turkey*. Lund: Sekel.

Massicard, Élise. 2005. *L'autre Turquie: Le mouvement Aléviste et ses territories*. Paris: PUF.

Massicard, Élise. 2007. *Türkiye'den Avrupa'ya Alevi Hareketinin Siyasallaşması*. Istanbul: İletişim.

Masuzawa, Tomoko. 2005. *The Invention of World Religions*. Chicago: University of Chicago Press.

McCarthy, Justin. 1995. *Death and Exile: The Ethnic Cleansing of Ottoman Muslims, 1821–1922*. Princeton, NJ: Darwin Press.

McCutcheon, Russell T. 2007. " 'They Licked the Platter Clean': On the Co-Dependency of the Religious and the Secular." *Method and Theory in the Study of Religion* 19:173–199.

Mélikoff, Irène. 1962. *Abū Muslim. Le «Porte-Hache» du Khorassan dans la tradition épique turco-iranienne*. Paris: Adrien Maisonneuve.

Mélikoff, Irène. 1982. "Recherches sur les composantes du syncrétisme Bektachi-Alevi." *Studia Turcologica Memoriae Alexii Bombaci Dicata*, 379–395. Napoli: Istituto Universitario Orientale.

Mélikoff, Irène. 1998. *Hadji Bektach. Un mythe et ses avatars. Genése et évolution du soufisme populaire en Turquie*. Leiden: Brill.

Mélikoff, Irène. 2001. *Au banquet des quarante. Exploration au coeur du Bektachisme-Alevisme*. Istanbul: Isis.

Mélikoff, Irène. 2003. "Note de symbolique Bektachi-Alevie: des douze animaux aux douze imams." *Turcica* 35:237–245.

Menzel, Th[eodore]. 1925. "Die ältesten türkischen Mystiker." *Zeitschrift der Deutschen Morgenländischen Gesellschaft* 4:269–289.

Merguerian, Barbara J. 2006. " 'Missions in Eden': Shaping an Educational and Social Program for the Armenians in Eastern Turkey 1855–1895." In *New Faith in Ancient Lands: Western Missions in the Middle East in the Nineteenth and Early Twentieth Centuries*, edited by Heleen Murre-van den Berg, 241–261. Brill: Leiden.

Mimar Hikmet [Onat]. 2001 [1928]. "Bektaşilik ve Son Bektaşiler." *Türk Yurdu*, vol. 13, edited by Murat Şefkatlı, 309–319. Istanbul: Tutibay.

Molyneux-Seel, Louis E. H. 1914. "A Journey in Dersim." *Geographical Journal* 44:49–68.

Mordtmann, J. H. 1923a. "Köprülī-zade Mehemed Fuʾād: Türk edebījātinda ilk muteṣawwiflar." *Orientlistische Literaturzeitung* 26.3:122–129.

Mordtmann, J. H. 1923b. "Türk edebiyatı Tarihi." *Orientalistische Literaturzeitung*, 26.5: 225–227.

Murre-van den Berg, Heleen. 1999. "The American Board and the Eastern Churches: the 'Nestorian Mission' (1844–1846)." *Orientalia Christiana Periodica* 65:117–138.

Murre-van den Berg, Heleen. 2006a. "Introduction." In *New Faith in Ancient Lands: Western Missions in the Middle East in the Nineteenth and Early Twentieth Centuries*, edited by Heleen Murre-van den Berg, 1–17. Leiden: Brill.

Murre-van den Berg, Heleen. 2006b. "The Middle East: Western Missions and the Eastern Churches, Islam and Judaism." In *The Cambridge History of Christianity, vol. 8: World Christianities c. 1815–c. 1914*, edited by Sheridan Gilley and Brian Stanley, 458–472. Cambridge: Cambridge University Press.

Nagel, Tilman. 1981. *Staat und Glaubensgemeinschaft im Islam. Geschichte der politischen Ordnungsvorstellungen der Muslime, vol. 2: Vom Spätmittelalter bis zur Neuzeit.* Zurich: Artemis.

Nasr, Seyyed Hossein. 1970. "Le Shî'isme et le Soufisme." In *Le Shî'isme imâmite*, edited by Centres d' Etudes Supérieurs Spécialisés d'Histoire des Religions de Strasbourg, 215–233. Paris: P.U.F.

Noyan, Bedri Dedebaba. 2006. *Bütün Yönleriyle Bektâşilik ve Alevîlik*, vol. 7: *Bektâşilik ve Bektâşilik Ahlâkı*. Ankara: Ardıç.

Nur, Rıza. 1968. *Hayat ve Hatıratım*, vol. 3. Istanbul: Altındağ.

Nutting, George. 1860. "The Kuzzelbash Koords." *Missionary Herald* 56:345–349.

Oba, Ali Engin. 1995. *Türk Milliyetçiliğinin Doğuşu.* Ankara: İmge.

Ocak, Ahmet Yaşar. 1980. "Bâzı Menâkıbnâmelere Göre XIII–XV. Yüzyıllardaki İhtidâlarda Heterodoks Şeyh ve Dervişlerin Rolü." *Osmanlı Araştırmaları* 2:31–42.

Ocak, Ahmet Yaşar. 1989. *La révolte de Baba Resul ou la formation de l'hétérodoxie musulmane en Anatolie au XIIIe siècle* (first published 1980). Ankara: Conseil Suprême d'Atatürk pour Culture, Langue et Histoire.

Ocak, Ahmet Yaşar. 1991. "Alevilik ve Bektaşilik Hakkındaki Son Yayınlar Üzerinde Genel Bir Bakış ve Bazı Gerçekler—I." *Tarih ve Toplum* 91:20–25.

Ocak, Ahmet Yaşar. 1995. "Bektaşilik." In *Türkiye Diyanet Vakfı İslam Ansiklopedisi*, vol. 5, edited by Bekir Topaloğlu, 373–379. Ankara: Türkiye Diyanet Vakfı.

Ocak, Ahmet Yaşar. 1997. "Fuad Köprülü, Sosyal Tarih Perspektifi ve Günümüz Türkiyesi'nde Din ve Tasavvuf Tarihi Araştırmalarında 'Tarihin Saptırılması' Problemi." *Türkiyat Araştırmaları Dergisi* 3:221–230.

Ocak, Ahmet Yaşar. 1998. *Osmanlı Toplumunda Zındıklar ve Mülhidler. Yahut Dairenin Dışına Çıkanlar (15.–17. Yüzyıllar).* Istanbul: Türkiye Ekonomik ve Toplumsal Tarih Vakfı.

Ocak, Ahmet Yaşar. 1999. *Türkiye'de Tarihin Saptırılması Sürecinde Türk Sufiliğine Bakışlar: Ahmed-i Yesevi, Mevlana Celaleddin-i Rumi, Yunus Emre, Hacı Bektaş-ı Veli, Ahilik, Alevilik-Bektaşilik (Yaklaşım, Yöntem ve Yorum Denemeleri).* Istanbul: İletişim.

Ocak, Ahmet Yaşar. 2000a. *Alevî ve Bektaşî İnançlarının İslâm Öncesi Temelleri. Bektaşî Menâkıbnâmelerinde İslam Öncesi İnanç Motifleri.* Istanbul: İletişim.

Ocak, Ahmet Yaşar. 2000b. "Babailer İsyanından Kızılbaşlığa: Anadolu'da İslam Heterodoksisinin Doğuş ve Gelişim Tarihine Kısa bir Bakış." In *Aleviler / Alewiten. Kimlik ve Tarih / Identität und Geschichte*, vol. 1, edited by İsmail Engin and Erhard Franz, 209–234. Hamburg: Deutsches Orient-Institut.

Ocak, Ahmet Yaşar. 2005. "The Wafā'ī Tarīqa (Wafā'īyya) during and after the Period of the Seljuks of Turkey: A New Approach to the History of Popular Mysticism in Turkey." *Mésogeios* 24–26; 209–248.

Ocak, Ahmet Yaşar. 2010. "Hacı Bektaş-ı Velî'nin Tasavvufî Kimliğine Yeniden Bakış: Yesevî, Haydarî, Vefai, Babaî, yahut 'Şeyhlikten Müridlikten Fâriğ bir Meczup'?"

In *Hacı Bektaş Veli. Güneşte Zerresinden, Deryada Katresinden*, edited by Pınar Ecevitoğlu, Ayhan Yalçınkaya, and Ali Murat İrat, 49–55. Ankara: Dipnot.

Okay, M. Orhan. 1996. "Gökalp, Ziya (1876–1924)." In *Türkiye Diyanet Vakfı İslâm Ansiklopedisi*, vol. 14, 124–128. Ankara: Türkiye Diyanet Vakfı.

Öktem, Kerem. 2008. "The Nation's Imprint: Demographic Engineering and the Change of Toponymes in Republican Turkey." *European Journal of Turkish Studies* 7. Accessed June 6, 2012. http://ejts.revues.org/index2243.html.

Oran, Baskın. 2004. *Türkiye'de Azınlıklar. Kavramlar, Teori, Lozan, İç Mevzuat, İçtihat, Uygulama*. Istanbul: İletişim.

Ortaylı, İlber. 1997. "Les groupes hétérodoxes et l'administration Ottomane." In *Syncretistic Religious Communities in the Near East*, edited by Krisztina Kehl-Bodrogi, Barbara Kellner-Heinkele, and Anke Otter-Beaujean, 205–211. Leiden: Brill.

Öz, Baki. 1995. *Aleviliğin Tarihsel Konumu*. Istanbul: Der.

Özerdim, Sami N. 1951. *Ord. Prof. Dr. M. Fuad Köprülü Bibliyografyası: 1908–1950*. Ankara: Türk Tarih Kurumu.

Öztelli, Cahit. 1996. *Pir Sultan Abdal. Bütün Şiirleri*. Istanbul: Özgür.

Park, George T. 1975. "*The Life and Writings of Mehmed Fuad Köprülü: The Intellectual and Turkish Cultural Modernization.*" PhD. diss., Johns Hopkins University.

Parla, Taha. 1985. *The Social and Political Thought of Ziya Gökalp, 1876–1924*. Leiden: Brill.

Parla, Taha, and Andrew Davison. 2004. *Corporatist Ideology in Kemalist Turkey. Progress or Order?* Syracuse: Syracuse University Press.

Pears, Edwin. 1911. *Turkey and Its People*. London: Methuen.

Percy, Henry Algernon George. 1901. *Highlands of Asiatic Turkey*. London: E. Arnold.

Peterson, Derek R., and Darren R. Walhof, eds. 2002a. *The Invention of Religion: Rethinking Belief in Politics and History*. New Brunswick, NJ: Rutgers University Press.

Peterson, Derek R., and Darren R. Walhof. 2002b. "Rethinking Religion." In *The Invention of Religion: Rethinking Belief in Politics and History*, edited by Derek R. Peterson and Darren R. Walhof, 1–16. New Brunswick: Rutgers University Press.

Planhol, Xavier de. 1958. *De la Plaine pamphylienne aux lacs pisidiens*. Paris: Dépositaire Librairie Adrien-Maisonneuve.

Poujoulat, M. Baptistin. 1840. *Voyage à Constantinople dans l'Asie mineure, en Mésopotamie, à Palmyre, en Syrie, en Palestine et en Égypte*, vol 1. Paris: Ducollet.

Privratsky, Bruce G. 2001. *Muslim Turkistan: Kazak Religion and Collective Memory*. Curzon: Richmond-Surrey.

Ramsay, William Mitchell. 1897. *Impressions of Turkey: During Twelve Years' Wanderings*. London: Hodder and Stoughton.

Reinhard, Ursula, and Tiago de Oliveira Pinto. 1989. *Sänger und Poeten mit der Laute. Türkische Aşık und Ozan*. Berlin: Dietrich Reimer.

Reynolds, Michael A. 2011. *Shattering Empires: The Clash and Collapse of the Ottoman and Russian Empires, 1908–1918*. Cambridge: Cambridge University Press.

Richardson, [Sanford]. 1856. "Arabkir. Letter from Mr. Richardson, July 14, 1856." *Missionary Herald* 52:295–298.

Richardson, [Sanford]. 1857. "Arabkir: Letter from Mr. Richardson, November 7, 1856." *Missionary Herald* 53:83–85.

Riggs, Henry H. 1911. "The Religion of the Dersim Kurds." *Missionary Review of the World* 24:734–743.

Riggs, Henry H. 1997. *Days of Tragedy in Armenia: Personal Experiences in Harpoot, 1915–1917*. Princeton, NJ: Gomidas Institute.

Rosenthal, Erwin. 1932. *Ibn Khalduns Gedanken über den Staat. Ein Beitrag zur Geschichte der mittelalterlichen Staatslehre*. Munich: Oldenbourg.

Roux, Jean Paul. 1970. *Les traditions des nomades de la Turquie méridionale*. Paris: Maisonneuve.

Ruggendorfer, Peter, and Hubert D. Szemethy. 2009. *Felix von Luschan (1854–1924). Leben und Wirken eines Universalgelehrten*. Cologne: Böhlau.

Sakal, Fahri. 1999. *Ağaoğlu Ahmed Bey*. Ankara: Türk Tarih Kurumu.

Salt, Jeremy. 1993. *Imperialism, Evangelism and the Ottoman Armenians, 1878–1896*. London: Frank Cass.

Salt, Jeremy. 2002. "Trouble Wherever They Went: American Missionaries in Anatolia and Ottoman Syria in the 19th Century." In *Altruism and Imperialism: Western Cultural and Religious Missions in the Middle East*, edited by Eleanor H. Tejirian and Reeva Spector Simon, 143–166. New York: Middle East Institute, Columbia University.

Şapolyo, Enver Behnan. 1943. *Ziya Gökalp. İttihat ve Terakki ve Meşrutiyet Tarihi*. Istanbul: İbrahim Berkalp.

Şapolyo, Enver Behnan. 1964. *Mezhepler ve Tarikatlar Tarihi*. Istanbul: Türkiye Yay.

Sarıkaya, Mehmet Saffet. 2001. "Anadolu Aleviliğinin Oluşumu." In *İslâm Düşünce Tarihinde Mezhepler*, by Mehmet Saffet Sarıkaya, 235–318. Isparta: Rağbet.

Say, Yağmur. 2007. *Alevi-Bektaşi Tarih Yazıcıları ve Anadolu Alevilerinin Tarihi*. Istanbul: Su.

Schrode, Paula. 2008. "The Dynamics of Orthodoxy and Heterodoxy in Uyghur Religious Practice." *Die Welt des Islams* 48:394–433.

Şeker, Nesim. 2006. "Türklük ve Osmanlılık Arasında: Birinci Dünya Savaşı sonrası Türkiye'de 'Milliyet' Arayışları ya da 'Anasır Meselesi'." In *İmparatorluktan Cumhuriyete Türkiye'de Etnik Çatışma*, edited by Jan Erik Zürcher, 157–174. Istanbul: İletişim.

Şeker, Nesim. 2007. "Demographic Engineering in the Late Ottoman Empire and the Armenians." *Middle Eastern Studies* 43:461–474.

Şemseddin Sāmi. 1901. *Kāmūs-i Türkī*. Istanbul: İkdam Gazetesi.

Sertel, Zekeriya. 1977. *Hatırladıklarım*. Istanbul: Remzi.

Shankland, David, ed. 2004a. *Archaeology, Anthropology, and Heritage in the Balkans and Anatolia: The Life and Times of F. W. Hasluck, 1878–1920*. Istanbul: İsis.

Shankland, David. 2004b. "The Life and Times of F. W. Hasluck (1878–1920)." In *Archaeology, Anthropology, and Heritage in the Balkans and Anatolia: The Life and Times of F. W. Hasluck, 1878–1920*, edited by David Shankland, 15–67. Istanbul: İsis.

Shaw, Rosalind, and Charles Stewart. 1994. "Introduction: Problematizing Syncretism." In *Syncretism/Anti-Syncretism: The Politics of Religious Synthesis*, edited by Charles Stewart and Rosalind Shaw, 1–26. London: Routledge.

Shaw, Stanford J., and Ezel K. Shaw. 1977. *History of the Ottoman Empire and Modern Turkey*. 2 vol. Cambridge: Cambridge University Press.

Shaw, Stanford J. 1978. "The Ottoman Census System and Population, 1831–1914." *International Journal of Middle East Studies* 9:325–338.

Shissler, A. Holly. 2003. *Between Two Empires: Ahmet Ağaoğlu and the New Turkey*. London: I. B. Tauris.

Sılan, Necmeddin Sahir. 2010. *Doğu Anadolu`da Toplumsal Mühendislik. Dersim-Sason (1934–1946)*. Istanbul: Tarih Vakfı Yurt.

Smith, Anthony D. 1998. *Nationalism and Modernism: A Critical Survey of Recent Theories of Nations and Nationalism*. London: Routledge.

Smith, Anthony D. 2004. *Chosen Peoples*. New York: Oxford University Press.

Smith, Anthony D. 2008. *The Cultural Foundations of Nations: Hierarchy, Covenant, and Republic*. Malden: Blackwell.

Smith, Anthony D. 2009. *Ethno-Symbolism and Nationalism: A Cultural Approach*. London: Routledge.

Sohrweide, Hanna. 1965. "Der Sieg der Ṣafaviden in Persien und seine Rückwirkungen auf die Schiiten Anatoliens im 16. Jahrhundert." *Der Islam* 41:95–223.

Soileau, Dilek. 2010. "Hacı Bektaş-ı Veli Dergâhı`nın Kapatılması ve Tarihsel Mirasın Paylaşımı: Babalar, Çelebiler ve Aleviler." In *Hacı Bektaş Veli. Güneşte Zerresinden, Deryada Katresinden*, edited by Pınar Ecevitoğlu, Ayhan Yalçınkaya, and Ali Murat İrat, 248–264. Ankara: Dipnot.

Sökefeld, Martin. 2008. *Struggling for Recognition: The Alevi Movement in Germany and in Transnational Space*. Oxford: Berghahn.

Soner, Ali Bayram, and Şule Toktaş. 2011. "Alevis and Alevism in the Changing Context of Turkish Politics: The Justice and Development Party's Alevi Opening," *Turkish Studies* 12:419–434.

Southgate, Horatio. 1840. *Narrative of a Tour through Armenia, Kurdistan, Persia, and Mesopotamia. With Observations on the Condition of Mohammedanism and Christianity in Those Countries*, vol. 2. London: Tilt and Bogue.

Soylu, Kerem. 2010. *Mesail-i Mühimme-i Kürdistan (Kürdistan'ın Önemli Meseleleri)*. Diyarbakır: Diyarbakır Kürt Enstitüsü.

Subaşı, Necdet. 2010. *Alevi Çalıştayları Nihai Raporu*. Ankara: T. C. Devlet Bakanlığı.

Süleyman Fikri [Erten]. 2001 [1927]. "Anadolu'nun Dinî Etnoğrafyası. Teke Vilâyetinde Tahtacılar." In *Türk Yurdu* 12, edited by Murat Şefkatlı, 229–234. Istanbul: Tutibay.

Sykes, Mark. 1908. "The Kurdish Tribes of the Ottoman Empire." *Journal of the Anthropological Institute of Great Britain and Ireland* 38:451–486.

T. C. Başbakanlık Osmanlı Arşivi Daire Başkanlığı, ed. 1982. *Atatürk ile İlgili Arşiv Belgeleri 1911–1921 Tarihleri Arasına Ait 106 Belge.* Ankara: T. C. Başbakanlık Osmanlı Arşivi Daire Başkanlığı.

Tachau, Frank. 1963. "The Search for National Identity among the Turks." *Die Welt des Islams* 8:165–176.

Tamcke, Martin. 2007. "Der Genozid an den Assyrern/Nestorianern (Ostsyrische Christen)." In *Verfolgung, Vertreibung und Vernichtung der Christen im Osmanischen Reich 1912–1922,* edited by Tessa Hofmann, 103–118. Berlin: LIT.

Tansel, Fevziye Abdullah. 2006 [1966]. "Preface to the Second Edition." In *Köprülü, Mehmed Fuad, Early Mystics in Turkish Literature,* translated with an introduction by Gary Leiser and Robert Dankoff, xlii–li. London: Routledge.

Tansel, Fevziye Abdullah. 1966a. "Memleketimizin Acı Kaybı: Prof. Dr. Fuad Köprülü." *Belleten* 30:621–636.

Tansel, Fevziye Abdullah. 1966b. "Prof. Dr. Fuad Köprülü'nün Şiirleri." *Belleten* 30:637–660.

Tansel, Fevziye Abdullah, ed. 1989. *Şiirler ve Halk Masalları: Kızılelma, Yeni Hayat, Altun Işık, Eserleri Dışında Kalan Şiirleri Tenkidli Basım. Ziya Gökalp Külliyatı I.* Ankara: Türk Tarih Kurumu.

Taylor, J. G. 1868. "Journal of a Tour in Armenia, Kurdistan and Upper Mesopotamia, with Notes of Researches in the Deyrsim Dagh, in 1866." *Journal of the Royal Geographical Society* 38:218–361.

Tayob, Abdulkader. 2009. *Religion in Modern Islamic Discourse.* New York: Columbia University Press.

Tejirian, Eleanor H., and Reeva S. Simon. 2002. "Introduction." In *Altruism and Imperialism: Western Cultural and Religious Missions in the Middle East,* edited by Eleanor H. Tejirian and Reeva Spector Simon, v–x. New York: Middle East Institute, Columbia University.

Tevetoğlu, Fethi. 1989. "Millî Mücadele Kahramanlarından: Bahâ Said Bey." *Atatürk Araştırma Merkezi Dergisi* 6:207–221.

Trowbridge, Stephen van Rensselaer. 1909. "The Alevis, or Deifiers of Ali." *Harvard Theological Review* 2:340–353.

Tulasoğlu, Gülay. 2005. *"Die Reformvorschläge eines osmanischen Staatsbeamten über die Region 'Dersim' vom Jahre 1910."* Master thesis, Heidelberg University.

Ülken, Hilmi Ziya. 2006 [1942]. "Ziya Gökalp." In *Ziya Gökalp Seçme Eserleri I,* edited by Hilmi Ziya Ülken, vii–xxxi. Istanbul: Türkiye İş Bankası.

Ülken, Hilmi Ziya. 1969. "Anadolu Örf ve Adetlerinde Eski Kültürlerin İzleri." *Ankara Üniversitesi İlahiyat Fakültesi Dergisi* 17:1–28.

Ülken, Hilmi Ziya. 1979. *Türkiye'de Çağdaş Düşünce Tarihi.* Istanbul: Ülken.

Ülker, Erol. 2007. "Assimilation of the Muslim Communities in the First Decade of the Turkish Republic (1923–1934)." *European Journal of Turkish Studies* 7. Accessed June 6, 2012. http://ejts.revues.org/index822.html.

Ülker, Erol. 2008. "Assimilation, Security and Geographical Nationalization in Interwar Turkey: The Settlement Law of 1934." *European Journal of Turkish Studies* 7. Accessed June 6, 2012. http://ejts.revues.org/index2123.html.

Uludağ, Süleyman. 1999. "*Müzakereler.*" In *Tarihi ve Kültürel Boyutlarıyla Türkiye'de Alevîler Bektaşîler Nusayrîler*, edited by İsmail Kurt and Seyid Ali Tüz, 151–177. Istanbul: Ensar Neşriyat.

Üngör, Uğur Ümit. 2005. "*CUP Rule in Diyarbekir Province, 1912–1923.*" Master's thesis, University of Amsterdam.

Üngör, Uğur Ümit. 2008a. "Geographies of Nationalism and Violence: Rethinking Young Turk 'Social Engineering'." *European Journal of Turkish Studies* 7. Accessed June 6, 2012. http://ejts.revues.org/index2583.html.

Üngör, Uğur Ümit. 2008b. "Seeing Like a Nation-State: Young Turk Social Engineering in Eastern Turkey, 1913–50." *Journal of Genocide Research* 10:15–39.

Veer, Peter van der. 1994a. *Religious Nationalism: Hindus and Muslims in India.* Berkeley: University of California Press.

Veer, Peter van der. 1994b. "Syncretism, Multiculturalism and the Discourse of Tolerance." In *Syncretism and Anti-Syncretism*, edited by Charles Stewart and Rosalind Shaw, 196–212. London: Routledge.

Veer, Peter van der. 2001. *Imperial Encounters: Religion and Modernity in India and Britain.* Princeton, NJ: Princeton University Press.

Veer, Peter van der, and Hartmut Lehmann, 1999. "Introduction." In *Nation and Religion: Perspectives on Europe and Asia*, edited by Peter van der Veer and Hartmut Lehmann, 3–14. Princeton, NJ: Princeton University Press.

Veinstein, Gilles. 2005. *Syncrétismes et hérésies dans l'orient Seldjoukide et Ottoman (XIVe–XVIIIe siècle).* Paris: Peeters.

Viswanathan, Gauri. 1995. "Beyond Orientalism: Syncretism and the Politics of Knowledge." *Stanford Humanities Review* 5:19–32.

Vorhoff, Karin. 1995. *Zwischen Glaube, Nation und neuer Gemeinschaft: Alevitische Identität in der Türkei der Gegenwart.* Berlin: Klaus Schwarz.

Wach, Joachim. 1924. *Religionswissenschaft. Prolegomena zu ihrer wissenschaftlichen Grundlegung.* Leipzig: JC Hinrichs.

Walker, Paul E. 2012. "Bāṭiniyya." *Encyclopaedia of Islam, Three*, edited by Gudrun Krämer, Denis Matringe, John Nawas, and Everett Rowson. Brill Online.

Wheeler, Crosby Howard. 1868. *Ten Years on the Euphrates; or, Primitive Missionary Policy Illustrated.* New York: A. D. F. Randolph & Co.

White, G[eorge] E. 1907. "Survivals of Primitive Religion among the People of Asia Minor." *Journal of the Transactions of the Victoria Institute* 39:144–166.

White, George E. 1908. "The Shia Turks." *Journal of the Transactions of the Victoria Institute* 40:225–239.

White, George E. 1913. "The Alevi Turks of Asia Minor." *Contemporary Review* 104:690–698.

White, George E. 1918. "Some Non-Conforming Turks." *Muslim World* 8:242–248.

White, George E. 1940. *Adventuring with Anatolia College.* Grinnell: Herald-Register.

White, Paul J. 2003. "The Debate on the Identity of 'Alevi Kurds'." In *Turkey's Alevi Enigma: A Comprehensive Overview*, edited by Paul J. White and Joost Jongerden, 17–29. Leiden: Brill.

White, Paul J., and Joost Jongerden, eds. 2003. *Turkey's Alevi Enigma: A Comprehensive Overview*. Leiden: Brill.

Wilson, M. Brett. 2007. "The Failure of Nomenclatura: The Concept of 'Orthodoxy' in the Study of Islam." *Comparative Islamic Studies* 3:169–194.

Wilson, M. Brett. 2009. "The First Translations of the Qur'an in Modern Turkey (1924–38)." *International Journal of Middle East Studies* 41:419–435.

Winter, Stefan. 2010. *The Shiites of Lebanon under Ottoman Rule, 1516–1788*. Cambridge: Cambridge University Press.

Yavuz, Hakan. 1993. "Nationalism and Islam: Yusuf Akçura and Üç Tarz-ı Siyaset." *Journal of Islamic Studies* 4:175–207.

Yeğen, Mesut. 2007. "Turkish Nationalism and the Kurdish Question." *Ethnic and Racial Studies* 30:119–151.

Yıldırım, Rıza. 2010. "Bektaşi Kime Derler?: 'Bektaşi' Kavramının Kapsamı ve Sınırları üzerine Tarihsel Bir Analiz Denemesi." *Türk Kültürü ve Hacı Bektaş Veli Araştırma Dergisi* 55:23–58.

Yıldız, Şevket. 2009. "Mehmed Fuad Köprülü (1890–1966)." In *Rewriting the Middle Ages in the Twentieth Century, vol. 2: National Traditions*, edited by J. Aurell Cardona and J. Pavon Benito, 485–514. Turnhout: Brepols.

Yörükân, Yusuf Ziya. 2006. *Anadolu'da Aleviler ve Tahtacılar*. Edited by Turhan Yörükân. Istanbul: Ötüken.

Yonan, Gabriele. 1989. *Ein vergessener Holocaust. Die Vernichtung der christlichen Assyrer in der Türkei. Eine Dokumentation*. Göttingen: Pogrom.

Zürcher, Erik J. 2004. *Turkey: A Modern History*. London: I. B. Tauris.

Zürcher, Erik J. 2008. "The Late Ottoman Empire as Laboratory of Demographic Engineering." Accessible online: http://www.sissco.it/fileadmin/user_upload/Attivita/Convegni/regionI_multilingue/zurcher.pdf.

Zürcher, Erik J. 2010. *The Young Turk Legacy and Nation Building: From the Ottoman Empire to Atatürk's Turkey*. London: I. B. Tauris.

Index

CPSIA information can be obtained at www.ICGtesting.com
Printed in the USA
BVOW04s1214260515

401616BV00001B/1/P